KU-790-802

CONTENTS

Acknowledgements

This book is the outcome of a search for the truth by bereaved families and a group of human rights activists, beginning in the autumn of 1999. Those involved include the families of the dead and the volunteers and staff of the Pat Finucane Centre (PFC) and Justice for the Forgotten (JFF). These two organisations have plundered archives, national and local newspaper libraries, and taken witness statements. This has involved hundreds of hours researching in the National Archives in London and Dublin, interviewing grieving families, and meeting agencies such as the Historical Enquiries Team (HET).

Among those involved are Alan Brecknell (son of Trevor Brecknell RIP), Paul O'Connor (PFC), Margaret Urwin (JFF), Johanna Keenan (PFC), Stephanie English (PFC), Adrian Kerr (PFC), Professor Robbie McVeigh (former chair of the PFC), Tom Griffin (Spinwatch), Cormac Ó Dúlacháin (Senior Counsel for JFF since 1996) and Greg O'Neill (JFF's solicitor). I have had the privilege of trying to put the outcome of all this work into the printed word.

I would like to thank Monsignor Denis Faul (RIP) and Monsignor Dr Réamonn Ó Muireadhaigh, whose courageous and ground-breaking work, *The Triangle of Death*, made a first (and, alas, vain) attempt to persuade the authorities to act; Roddy Hegarty, director of the Cardinal Tomás Ó Fiaich Memorial Library and Archive (Armagh); the staff of the Linen Hall Library Political Collection; and Professor Douglass Cassel of Notre Dame Law School, who, along with Susie Kemp, Piers Pigou and Stephen Sawyer, compiled the October 2006 *Report of the Independent International Panel on Alleged Collusion in Sectarian Killings in Northern Ireland*.[a]

---

a   Available at www.patfinucanecentre.org.

Those who assisted greatly during the writing of the book include: T. L. Thousand (Los Angeles), Caroline Casey (Perth, Australia – and granddaughter of Patrick Molloy, RIP), Sorcha O'Hare (Warrenpoint), Susan McKay, Seaneen White (Armagh, and another granddaughter of Patrick Molloy), Professor Paddy Hillyard (Belfast and Italy), Maura Martin (sister-in-law of Marian Bowen, Seamus and Michael McKenna), Chris McAuley (Armagh) and many others who prefer to remain anonymous.

Needless to say, I take responsibility for all errors and would ask those who notice them to alert Mercier Press for future editions.

Those most closely involved would like to thank their families for enduring their many absences from home and the neglect of domestic duties. Alan Brecknell would like thank Patricia, Paul O'Connor would like to thank Laura Pozo-Rodriguez, and Margaret Urwin would like to thank Mark. I would like to thank principally my husband, Gerry O'Hare, also my sister Jane (Madrid), her children Ana, Georgie and Teresa, and my niece Helena. Thanks also to my good friends Mary, Jude, Les, Dan, John Óg and Liz. Their support and confidence in me, however ill-founded, kept me going. In addition, thanks to Messrs Beethoven, Mozart, Sibelius and J. S. Bach for keeping me sane during the daily Armagh–Belfast commute.

Without one individual in particular, the research on which this book is based would never have begun. When Alan Brecknell first heard that RUC and UDR men may have been among those who killed his father, Trevor, he might well have been shocked but made the decision to 'move on'. That would have been a very understandable reaction. Instead, however, he embarked on a long search for the truth and has since discovered more about Trevor's death than he ever thought possible. He has gone on to extend his search on behalf of dozens of other families, who have benefited from his honesty and diligence. More than the efforts of anyone else, this book is the result of his personal courage and determination.

NOTE ON THE AUTHOR

Anne Cadwallader began her career working for the BBC after an apprenticeship with Westminster Press in Yorkshire, holding a scholarship at City University in London and completing an English degree at Exeter University, where she was Vice-President of the Guild of Students and Editor of the student newspaper.

In Ireland, she worked for the BBC in Belfast and Dublin from 1981 to 1987, before becoming a parliamentary reporter for the Irish Press Group and a producer at Raidió Teilifís Éireann (RTÉ) in 1990. She returned to Belfast in 1991 as Northern Editor of the Irish Press Group, before becoming Northern Editor for Independent Network News from 1997 to 2009.

She is the author of *Holy Cross – The Untold Story* (Brehon Press, 2004) and has worked for Reuters, *The Christian Science Monitor*, *Irish Examiner*, *The Irish Echo* (New York), *Ireland on Sunday* and others. She is now a case worker with the Pat Finucane Centre for Human Rights, based in Armagh.

Anne was born in London and now lives in Belfast. Married to a former Irish Republican prisoner, her parents, Peter and Catherine, and her sister, Susan, all served in the British Army, and her brother, Charles, is a retired police officer.

GLOSSARY

NOTE: *As used throughout the book, the terms 'Catholic' and 'nationalist' should be regarded as interchangeable. Likewise 'Protestant' and 'unionist'. The term 'loyalist' generally refers to those who supported the main paramilitary groups (the UDA and UVF) and the term 'republican' likewise to the main republican paramilitary group (the Provisional IRA).*

B Specials: Members of the Ulster Special Constabulary (USC) – a part-time force disbanded in 1970.

CID: Criminal Investigations Department of the RUC.

CIÉ: Córas Iompair Éireann – public transport company in the Republic.

Dáil/Dáil Éireann: The main house of the parliament of the Republic of Ireland (Oireachtas).

DUP: Democratic Unionist Party – the more radical of the two main unionist parties.

ECHR: European Court of Human Rights.

Fianna Fáil: Irish political party originally formed from those who opposed the Treaty with Britain signed in December 1921.

Fine Gael: Irish political party originally formed from those who supported the Treaty of 1921.

GAA: Gaelic Athletic Association (in Irish, Cumann Lúthchleas Gael), an influential amateur sporting and cultural organisation with over one million members, sometimes accused by unionists of being political as it supports the Irish language, music and dancing. Until 2001 it banned members of the RUC or British Army from membership.

Garda Síochána: The police force of the Republic of Ireland.

Glenanne: The name of a townland (see below) in South Armagh, where a farmhouse belonging to RUC Reservist James Mitchell was situated. 'The Glenanne Gang' was the name used to describe the group of UVF men, RUC officers and UDR soldiers who colluded in murders across Counties Armagh, Tyrone, Down and across the border in the mid-1970s.

GOC: General Officer Commanding the British Army in Northern Ireland.

HET: Historical Enquiries Team – a police unit established to review all conflict-related deaths, answerable to the chief constable of the PSNI.

INLA: Irish National Liberation Army – a republican paramilitary group formed in 1975 from Official IRA members and left-wing republicans.

Internment: Incarceration without trial, used in Northern Ireland from 9 August 1971 for (mainly republican) suspects.

IRA: Irish Republican Army – a republican paramilitary group, also known as the 'Provos', formed in 1970 following a split with the Official IRA.

IRSP: Irish Republican Socialist Party – considered to be the political wing of the INLA.

JFF: Campaign group 'Justice for the Forgotten'.

MI5: British security service responsible for domestic counter-intelligence.

MI6: British security service responsible for foreign counter-intelligence.

NAI: National Archives of Ireland.

NAUK: National Archives of the United Kingdom.

NIO: Northern Ireland Office.

Orange Order: Formed in 1876 (named after King William of Orange) to defend Protestant interests, including the reformed faith and the union with Britain, and to oppose Irish independence. Catholics are barred from membership.

PFC: Pat Finucane Centre – investigates abuses by state forces and advocates on behalf of families bereaved in the conflict. Named after Pat Finucane, in whose murder the British state and loyalists colluded, the centre believes, like him, in using the rule of law to vindicate human rights.

PIRA: Provisional Irish Republican Army (see IRA above).

PRONI: Public Record Office of Northern Ireland.

PSNI: Police Service of Northern Ireland (changed from RUC in 2001).

RHC: Red Hand Commando – a section of the UVF.

RTÉ: Raidió Teilifís Éireann – Ireland's national television and radio broadcaster.

RUC: Royal Ulster Constabulary – the police force in Northern Ireland from 1 June 1922 to 4 November 2001.

SAS: Special Air Service – an elite regiment of the British Army specially trained for covert operations.

SCRT: Serious Crime Review Team – set up to re-examine conflict-related deaths.

SDLP: Social Democratic and Labour Party – a nationalist political party supporting a united Ireland achieved through non-violence.

SEPs: Surrendered enemy personnel.

Sinn Féin: Republican political party, considered to be the political wing of the Irish Republican Army (IRA).

SMG: Sub-machine gun.

SOCO: Scenes of Crime Officer, who logs forensic and ballistic information.

Special Branch: Specialist intelligence-gathering unit of the RUC.

SPG: Special Patrol Group of the RUC – an elite anti-terrorist unit.

Taoiseach: The prime minister of the Republic of Ireland. Translates into English as 'chief'.

TAVR: Territorial Army Volunteer Reserve.

TD/Teachta Dála: Member of Dáil Éireann, the Irish parliament.

Townland: A term used in Ireland to describe a small geographical division of land.

UDA: Ulster Defence Association, formed in 1970 and not declared illegal until 1992; the organisation used the cover-name of Ulster Freedom Fighters (UFF) to claim sectarian killings.

UDR: Ulster Defence Regiment – a mainly Protestant, locally recruited regiment of the British Army formed in 1970 and regarded as the successor to the B Specials (see above).

UFF: Ulster Freedom Fighters (see UDA, above).

ULCCC: Ulster Loyalist Combined Co-ordinating Committee. This replaced the Ulster Army Council and comprised representatives of the UDA, UVF, Red Hand Commando, Vanguard Service Corps/Ulster Volunteer Service Corps, Down Orange Welfare, Loyalist Association of Workers and Orange Volunteers.

UTV: Ulster Television – Northern Ireland TV channel.

UUP: Ulster Unionist Party. Until recently, the larger of the two main unionist parties.

UUUC: United Ulster Unionist Council.

UVF: Ulster Volunteer Force, formed on 1 January 1913 and reorganised as the Ulster Special Constabulary before being reformed in 1966 as the UVF. Declared illegal on 28 June 1966,[1] it was de-proscribed on 14 May 1974 (the order came into effect on 23 May) in a failed attempt by the British government to wean the organisation off violence and into politics, and then re-proscribed on 3 October 1975. It sometimes used 'Protestant Action Force' as a flag of convenience.

UWC: Ulster Workers' Council – an ad-hoc group of loyalist paramilitaries and unionist politicians which organised strikes and roadblocks to defeat (successfully) the 1974 Sunningdale Agreement on power-sharing and the Council of Ireland.

VCP: Vehicle checkpoint.

Vanguard: Vanguard Unionist Progressive Party (VUPP), known as Ulster Vanguard. Militant unionist party of the 1970s under the leadership of William Craig. Its paramilitary wing was the Vanguard Services Corps.

LIST OF MAIN OFFICIAL FIGURES IN THE BOOK

Northern Ireland politicians

Brian Faulkner: Ulster Unionist leader and Prime Minister of Northern Ireland (March 1971–March 1972). Chief Executive of the short-lived power-sharing Executive.

Gerry Fitt: Founder and first leader of the Social Democratic and Labour Party (SDLP).

Ian Paisley: Founder and first leader of the Democratic Unionist Party (DUP).

William Craig: Founder of Vanguard in February 1972.

John Taylor: Ulster Unionist Party MP for South Tyrone.

John Hume: A founder member of the SDLP and its second leader.

Seamus Mallon: SDLP politician, appointed its deputy leader in 1979.

British politicians

Edward Heath: Conservative Party Prime Minister, 1970–4.

Harold Wilson: Labour Party Prime Minister 1964–70 and 1974–6.

William Whitelaw: Secretary of State for Northern Ireland, March 1972–November 1973.

Merlyn Rees: Secretary of State for Northern Ireland, March 1974–September 1976.

Roy Mason: Secretary of State for Defence, 1974–6, who ordered the deployment of the SAS in County Armagh. Secretary of State for Northern Ireland, September 1976–May 1979.

Margaret Thatcher: Leader of the Conservative Party and Opposition from February 1975; elected Prime Minister in May 1979.

Irish politicians

Jack Lynch: Fianna Fáil Taoiseach, November 1966–February 1973.

Liam Cosgrave: Fine Gael Taoiseach, March 1973–July 1977.

Paddy Cooney: Fine Gael Minister for Justice, 1973–7.

Garret FitzGerald: Fine Gael Minister for Foreign Affairs, 1973–7.

Royal Ulster Constabulary – Chief Constables

Sir Graham Shillington: November 1970–3.

Sir James Flanagan: November 1973–April 1976.

Sir Kenneth Newman: May 1976–January 1980.

Sir John (Jack) Hermon: January 1980–June 1989.

British Army General Officers Commanding (GOC) Northern Ireland

Sir Harry Tuzo: 1971–3.

Sir Frank King: 1973–5.

Sir David George House: 1975–7.

Others

Justice Henry Barron: Retired Supreme Court judge who led the enquiry into the Dublin and Monaghan bombings (and other bombings in the Republic of Ireland).

Commander Dave Cox: Former London police officer, and Director of the HET (2005 to present).

Father Denis Faul and *Father Raymond Murray:* Catholic priests and civil rights campaigners.

Fred Holroyd: NI Special Military Intelligence Unit (whistle-blower).

Robert Nairac: British Army captain, member of Four Field Survey Troop (an undercover surveillance unit of the Special Reconnaissance Unit), abducted in South Armagh and presumed killed by the IRA in May 1977.

Colin Wallace: UDR captain, senior information officer (psychological operations) (whistle-blower).

John Weir: Armagh Special Patrol Group 1973–5 (whistle-blower).

Timeline of Attacks

1972

12 July: Paul Beattie shot dead by the IRA in Portadown; Jack McCabe and William Cochrane killed in McCabe's Bar, Portadown

15 July: Felix Hughes, Portadown, killed by loyalist gunmen

21 July: Bloody Friday – twenty-two bombs detonated by the IRA in Belfast

31 July: Three republican bombs in Claudy kill nine

22 Aug: Nine killed by an IRA bomb in Newry

27 Aug: Éamonn McMahon disappears – his body is found four days later

4 Oct: An attack on the Connolly house, Portadown, leaves Patrick dead and Mary and Christopher injured

23 Oct: UDR/TAVR King's Park base in Lurgan raided for arms by the UVF

1 Dec: Two killed and 127 injured in two loyalist car bombs in Dublin

20 Dec: Alphonsus McGeown shot and killed

28 Dec: The UVF bombs Belturbet, Clones and Pettigo

1973

18 Jan: Joseph Weir killed in Portadown

20 Jan: A bomb blast in Dublin kills Thomas Douglas

9 March: Patrick Turley shot in Portadown, but survives

5 August: Bernadette and Francis Mullan shot dead and their two-year-old son wounded near Moy; former UDR man Isaac Scott shot dead at Belleeks

22 Aug: Seán McDonnell shot dead in Newry

28 Aug: Two loyalist bombs explode in Armagh injuring twenty

23 Oct: The UVF raids Fort Seagoe, Portadown, for arms

28 Oct: Pat Campbell shot dead at his home in Banbridge; Francis McCaughey seriously injured by a loyalist bomb planted on his family's farm and dies on 8 November

12 Nov: Three bombs detonated in Armagh and one in Quinn's Bar, Dungannon, by loyalists

1974

6 Jan: Tommy Toland shot and injured in Lurgan

17 Jan: Daniel Hughes killed in an attack on Boyle's Bar, Cappagh

11 Feb: Attempted murder of Marian Rafferty and Thomas Mitchell

19 Feb: Attack on Traynor's Bar leaves Patrick Molloy and Jack Wylie dead

5 March: A UVF bomb attack on a house in Mourne Crescent, Coalisland, injures nine

7 May: James and Gertrude Devlin shot dead, Coalisland

17 May: Three bombs detonated in Dublin and one in Monaghan killing thirty-four in total

16 Sept: The UVF bombs a factory in Pomeroy, killing Michael McCourt

27 Oct: Anthony Duffy abducted and shot dead by the UVF in Portadown

7 Nov: The IRA bombs the King's Arms pub in Woolwich, killing two

20 Nov: Patrick Falls killed in Aughamullan

21 Nov: The IRA bombs the Mulberry Bush and Tavern in the Town pubs, Birmingham, killing twenty-one

29 Nov: Bombs detonated in Hughes' Bar, Newry, fatally injuring John Mallon, and McArdle's Bar, Crossmaglen, wounding Thomas McNamee, who died a year later

1975

10 Jan: Republican John Francis Green shot dead

10 Feb: Attack on Hayden's Bar, Gortavale, leaves Arthur Mulholland and Eugene Doyle dead

19 Feb: James Breen shot and killed

6 March: Edward Clayton killed by a car bomb

1 April: Dorothy Trainor shot dead and her husband Malachy wounded

3 April: Martin McVeigh shot dead in Portadown

11 April: Owen Boyle shot – he subsequently dies on 22 April

21 April: Marian Bowen and her brothers Seamus and Michael McKenna killed in a bomb blast, Killyliss

27 April: Bleary Dart's Club attacked – Joe Toman, Brendan O'Hara and John Feeney killed

18 May: Francis Rice stabbed to death

24 May: Bomb attack on the Grew family in Moy, no one killed

31 July: Miami Showband massacre

15 Aug: RUC Reservist William Meaklin abducted and killed; Norman (Mooch) Kerr shot dead by the IRA in Armagh

22 Aug: Attack on McGleenan's Bar, Armagh, leaves John McGleenan, Patrick Hughes and Thomas Morris dead

24 Aug: Colm McCartney and Seán Farmer shot dead at a fake UDR checkpoint, Altnamackin

1 Sept: Denis Mullen killed at home in Moy; the IRA attacks Tullyvallen Orange Hall, Newtownhamilton, killing five

4 Sept: The UVF attacks McCann's Bar near Ballyhagan, fatally injuring Margaret Hale

2 Oct: The UVF kills twelve in attacks across Northern Ireland

23 Oct: Peter and Jenny McKearney shot dead on their farm outside Moy

29 Oct: The UVF shoots dead James Griffin in Lurgan

15 Dec: Ronald Trainor killed by a bomb in Portadown

19 Dec: Kay's Tavern, Dundalk, attacked and Hugh Watters and Jack Rooney killed; Donnelly's Bar, Newry, attacked leaving Patsy Donnelly, Michael Donnelly and Trevor Brecknell dead

26 Dec: Vallely's Bar near Loughgall attacked and Seamus Mallon fatally injured

31 Dec: An INLA bomb at Central Bar, Gilford, kills William Scott, Richard Beattie and fatally injures Sylvia McCullough, who dies two days later

1976

4 Jan: An attack on their home in Whitecross leaves John-Martin and Brian Reavey dead and their brother Anthony fatally injured; Joe, Declan and Barry O'Dowd are shot dead on the family farm at Ballydougan

5 Jan: Ten Protestant workers shot dead by the IRA at Kingsmill

7 March: Packie Mone killed in a car bomb in Castleblaynie

17 March: A car bomb left outside the Hillcrest Bar, Dungannon, kills Andrew Small, Patrick Barnard, Joseph Kelly and James McCaughey

7 May: Tully's Bar, Belleeks, bombed, but there are no fatalities

15 May: Almost simultaneous attacks on the Eagle and Clancy's Bars in Charlemont leave Fred McLoughlin, Felix (Vincy) Clancy, Seán O'Hagan and Robert McCullough dead

17 May: The IRA kills Robert and Thomas Dobson, apparently in retaliation for 15 May attacks

5 June: Michael McGrath injured in an attack on the Rock Bar, Granemore

25 July: Patrick (Patsy) McNeice shot dead at his home

16 Aug: Step Inn, Keady, is bombed, killing Betty McDonald and Gerard McGleenan

11 Oct: Peter Woolsey shot on his farm in Cornascreibe near Portadown

1977

19 April: William Strathearn shot dead in Ahoghill

1980

28 Feb: Brendan McLaughlin shot dead in Belfast

INTRODUCTION

Truth exists; only falsehood has to be invented.

Georges Braque, French artist, 1882–1963

Driving through Armagh's 'Orchard County' today, it would be easy to imagine that it has always been this tranquil. Thousands of apple trees stretch over the rolling hills around neat little villages with quaint names such as Charlemont and Tandragee. It is particularly lovely in the spring, when pink and white apple blossom covers the trees like rosy snow. But look more closely.

In the grey, stone-walled churchyards, there are a disproportionate number of graves dating from the 1970s. Ragged union flags hang from lampposts in some of the villages. There are other, less obvious signs of trouble: the ruined farmhouse where an elderly couple were shot at close range as they sat at their kitchen table; the derelict cottage, once the home of a young family but abandoned after the father was shot dead answering a knock at the door; and the new bricks in one corner of a country bar, where a father of nine was blown to pieces in a no-warning pub bombing.

A gang rampaged through this peaceful-looking countryside in the mid-1970s, and their actions were tolerated, even encouraged, by some whose duty it was to enforce the law. The countryside was blighted. Congregations plodded wearily, year after year, to grim funerals in the churned-up mud. Two local priests, Fr Raymond Murray and Fr Denis Faul, called the area the 'Triangle of Death' and the name stuck.

This book tells the story of these events, beginning in July 1972 and ending around 1978. The range of the 'Triangle' stretches beyond Counties Tyrone and Armagh, to Dundalk and Monaghan in the south and down to Dublin. The most northerly attack was in Ahoghill,

County Antrim, and the most southerly (within Northern Ireland) in Crossmaglen, County Armagh. To give a sense of the impact of the murders on a terrified community, the first half of this book outlines the events in a strict narrative sequence. The second half then examines the implications from the legal, security and political perspectives.

Over 120 people were killed by this loyalist gang, and permutations of it, with tacit assistance from members of government forces – more than eight times as many people as were killed on Bloody Sunday. Thousands of family members and neighbours were deeply affected. But not for one moment should anyone suggest that the agony was restricted to one community. One has to look no further than the Kingsmill massacre of January 1976, when ten Protestants were slaughtered, to see how both communities suffered. Dozens of RUC officers and UDR soldiers also lost their lives in the years recalled by this book, and many more were to die in the years following.

Collusion does not resolve conflict – it fuels it. The Historical Enquiries Team (HET) says that a belief among the nationalist community that collusion was taking place 'contributed to the spiralling violence in the area' and 'UDR soldiers, whether on or off-duty, were considered prime targets for republican paramilitaries'.[1] I do not pretend to focus here, however, on anything other than loyalist violence and the members of one particular, and vicious, gang. Numerous books have already been written about the IRA, but very few have dealt with the relationship between loyalists and the state.

I do not claim that every RUC officer or UDR soldier was collusive, or every loyalist was manipulated, or every judge or British cabinet minister mendacious. I do, however, contend that enough was known, or should have been known, by sufficient people in places of authority, to prevent many of the murders described. I also contend that Britain, like other colonial powers in dozens of conflicts, used what amounted to 'surrogates' to prosecute its battle against insurgents.

This work should act as a catalyst for an overarching examination of what happened. It could prevent the poison of the past seeping into the present and future. For those who suffered the most – the dead and their families – the victims cry out not for vengeance but for the truth. As the Chinese proverb says, 'If you seek revenge, dig two graves.' This book is an attempt to reach out towards the truth and belatedly, but hopefully, provide a context for everyone now arguing for an agreed mechanism – a truth or legacy commission – to begin to heal Northern Ireland's wounds.

There have been many books written about collusion since the 1990s. Some of them three-quarters true, some less so. Their worth is limited because readers are unable to tell whether their claims are founded on hard evidence or merely on conjecture. Throughout this book, every effort has been made to provide sources for the claims.

The facts gathered here are the result of hard work, starting in autumn 1999 and carried out by a group of dedicated researchers (see the Acknowledgements). Official documents, first-hand interviews, forensic evidence and police enquiries are, wherever possible, cited – though, for legal reasons, we cannot tell everything we know, or name all the perpetrators.

Many facts come from private reports written for the bereaved families by the HET. Set up by Sir Hugh Orde, a previous Chief Constable of the PSNI, to review (not reinvestigate) conflict-related murders, the HET relies on existing documentary, forensic and other police evidence. This very imperfect process for the recovery of the truth is, to date, often the only mechanism available to the bereaved to gain access to official police records. Many families have been bitterly disappointed by HET Reports. In some cases, while collusive actions appear to be evident, HET Reports fail to draw the obvious conclusions. In July 2013, Her Majesty's Inspectorate of Constabulary (a British police oversight agency) found the HET had acted unfairly, illegally and with undue leniency in investigating deaths where members of the British armed forces (on official duty) were responsible. The HET's future is uncertain, but the political class has failed, so far, to come up with an alternative. The Consultative Group on the Past's considered proposals for a Legacy Commission were dumped following an orchestrated commotion over a relatively minor recommendation (a £12,000 recognition payment for all bereaved families).

For the doubting reader, I have provided copious notes to counter claims of speculative conclusions. For most readers these should not interfere with what is, essentially, an honest account of how people were slaughtered, families devastated, a community intimidated, justice denied and a society dragged further into bloody conflict. Occasional repetition of key facts is intentional, to guide the reader through a complex story with multiple personalities and interlocking events.

I make no claim for 100 per cent accuracy. More information emerges every year from the darkness of the past. Mistakes and misunderstandings will be corrected in future editions.

I have erred on the side of caution when citing claims by whistle-blowers (such as former RUC officer John Weir and former British military intelligence officers Fred Holroyd and Colin Wallace) as they sometimes rely on third-hand information. I have referenced the rare occasions when I rely on their uncorroborated statements, so readers can decide for themselves. Some readers will undoubtedly accuse me of being partisan, but I have done my best to speak the truth. Facts sometimes need comment and interpretation to reach that truth.

This is an ugly story dealing with sectarian murder and the abject and inexcusable failure of the British and Irish states to abide by their own democratic principles and to vindicate the rights of their citizens, thereby prolonging the conflict.

Two words that do not crop up often in the book are 'love' and 'respect' – but they do belong here. The bereaved families still mourn their relatives. They love their murdered mothers, fathers, sons, daughters, wives and husbands. Those who work with them, and understand their great loss, respect that as something beautiful, despite everything.

1

BLOODING-IN (1972)

What answer from the North?
One Law, one Land, one Throne.
If England drive us forth
We shall not fall alone!

Rudyard Kipling, 'Ulster 1912'[1]

If you like a quiet life, Portadown on 12 July is generally not an ideal place. The 'Orange Citadel' is usually tense as the annual 'Twelfth' parades get under way to the sounds of flutes and thumping drums floating over the town centre and the surrounding housing estates.[2] July 1972, however, was particularly tense, even for Portadown. In Northern Ireland the Troubles were just over halfway through their bloodiest year; there were a further twenty-two years to go.

Bloody Sunday, six months earlier, had been a watershed – ending the hopes of many that the civil rights movement could move peacefully towards political and constitutional reform. Young Catholic men were queuing up to join the IRA. By the end of 1972, over 400 people (more than one a day) would be dead.

To set the political scene: on 24 March 1972, Brian Faulkner, the unionist prime minister of Northern Ireland, was informed by London that unionist rule was over.[3] Westminster then assumed 'full and direct responsibility' for the governing of Northern Ireland.[4] Faulkner and the entire unionist community felt 'betrayed'.[5] The prorogation of Stormont was a huge blow to Protestant confidence. The loyalist response was bloody and indiscriminate, but for the first half of 1972, focused almost totally on Belfast. Of the thirty-one loyalist killings in the first half of 1972, thirty were in Belfast, with the remaining one just outside

5 37/65

Between 1969 (around the time the conflict began) and July 1972, loyalists killed fifty-six people, but no one had been killed in Portadown for sectarian or political reasons for over forty years.[7] The town, however, would not remain free of blood for much longer. A nucleus of UVF killers was forming, who soon began spreading death and destruction as far south as Dublin. By the end of 1972, seven people in the town had been killed, some in the most brutal circumstances. Over the next five years, in various permutations, and with the collaboration of others from Dungannon (to the north-west) and villages such as Markethill (to the south), a loyalist gang was to kill more than eighty men, women and children in Mid-Ulster alone – far out of proportion to similar rural communities in Northern Ireland.

So what had changed? Bearing in mind the horrors to come, the question is worth addressing in some detail. For centuries, Portadown had seethed with sectarian tensions, but until July 1972 no one had been killed for decades. One answer lies in the fast-moving political circumstances. On 20 June 1972, British government representatives (and at least one MI6 man) met IRA leaders for secret talks near the border in County Derry. That meeting laid the groundwork for an IRA ceasefire starting on 26 June, contingent on a 'reciprocal response'. Four days later, a spooked UDA began to organise 'no-go' areas, amid fears that London was on the brink of making historic concessions to republicans.

On Friday 7 July, republican leaders met British ministers again, for talks in London at the Chelsea home of the then Minister of State for Northern Ireland, Paul Channon. The talks failed as both sides hopelessly over-estimated each other's ability to manoeuvre. The fragile IRA ceasefire broke down on 9 July, in a dispute between local republicans and the British Army over the allocation of homes to refugee Catholic families in Lenadoon, Belfast.

In Portadown, community relations – always fragile – were on the slide. The catalyst for the first murder in forty years was the

1972 Orange parade in the town, traditionally held every year on the Sunday before 12 July to commemorate a generation of young men who died in the First World War. Many unionists believed their community's blood sacrifice at the Somme guaranteed the union. Portadown's nationalist residents, based in one enclave of the town centred on Obins Street, formed a 'Resistance Council', calling on the police to re-route the parade away from their homes. The IRA warned it would 'take action' if this was not done, and the UDA threatened counter-action if it was. The scene was set.

On Saturday 1 July, eight days before the parade, nationalists built barricades around their enclave. On 9 July, with just hours to go before the Orangemen marched, the British Army moved in and cleared the barricades, using tear gas and rubber bullets. Once the streets were cleared, the soldiers stood by and watched the parade. It was escorted by at least fifty UDA men dressed in full paramilitary regalia,[8] who saluted the Orangemen as they marched through the disputed area[9] without any intervention from police or soldiers.[a]

Three days later, in the early hours of the Twelfth itself, Portadown was rife with rumours of planned attacks and counter-attacks. In one of dozens of localised incursions, a group of Protestants[b] was spotted in an alleyway in a Catholic area of the Churchill Park estate.[10] Local republicans who can still remember that time say they believed the group was intent on burning Catholic homes.[11] Shouts went up and the IRA opened fire. A young Protestant, Paul Beattie, aged nineteen, fell dead. Loyalist fury was intense.

A pathologist's report to the inquest states that Beattie, an apprentice butcher, was hit by two bullets, one penetrating both his lungs and

a   In 1972, London viewed some UDA actions as 'comparatively harmless vigilante activity' (NAUK DEFE 24/824).
b   In a later trial of Denis Allen Jackson, a 'vigilante' accused of possessing three bullets, he 'admitted carrying masked and armed UDA men to and from Churchill Park housing estate in Portadown where a Protestant teenager, Paul Beattie, had been shot dead on the night of July 11', *Irish News*, 7 April 1973.

heart, the second his lower back.[12] The report goes on to say that Beattie had been on 'vigilante patrol' with his father in a housing estate adjacent to his own and that, at about 2.50 a.m., they had seen 'two men acting suspiciously' and had gone to investigate. The two men had disappeared and Beattie and his father had 'started to look around the houses'.

As they turned a corner, they heard a bottle break and 'immediately there was a shot'. Beattie said, 'Daddy, I have been hit. Run,' then turned himself and ran. There was another shot 'and he fell face forwards to the ground. His father went to his assistance. A crowd gathered and an ambulance took him to hospital, where he was found to be dead.' The last line of the pathologist's report reads: 'He had a stocking mask over his face at the time.'

At his funeral, a Methodist minister, Rev. R. S. F. Cleland, described the killing as a 'bestial crime against the law of God'. He appealed to those who thought of vengeance to instead 'exercise loving kindness, justice and righteousness'.[13] Among the 110 wreaths at the funeral were ones from 'The Officers and Volunteers, Lurgan Battalion UDA', 'Edgarstown Loyalists', 'Commander and Battalion Portadown UDA' and various other paramilitary units. An evil genie was released from its bottle.

In an almost immediate retaliation, fifteen shots were fired at a house where a wake was being held for a Catholic woman killed in a car crash. But worse, far worse, was to come.

Within hours, a hooded loyalist gunman attacked McCabe's Bar in the town, killing both its Catholic owner, Jack McCabe, and a Protestant customer, William Cochrane. Both were shot at close range, the killer getting in close enough to inflict terrible wounds. Jack was shot in the back of the head; William directly in the face. Cochrane, a fifty-three-year-old ex-serviceman and council worker, was particularly unlucky. He was shot simply because he was drinking in what was perceived to be a 'Catholic bar'.[14] McCabe had attended Blackrock College in Dublin, the *alma mater* of the prosperous southern middle class, before returning to Portadown to run the family business. He was vice-chairman of the local hospital, a school governor and involved in numerous charities.[15] Jack's wife, Eilagh, and their seven children were away on holiday.

The killer was Ralph (Roy) Henry, a thirty-three-year-old former RUC officer from Craigavon.[16] At his trial, two juries failed to agree on a verdict, but a third in 1974, held in Downpatrick, found Henry guilty.[17] On at least one occasion the public gallery had to be cleared after intimidating gestures were made to witnesses.[18] The trial judge ordered a policeman to stand on duty in the public benches to prevent further abuse.[c] On virtually every appearance in court, Henry shouted, 'No surrender.' About a dozen supporters shouted, 'Keep up the fight,' as he was taken down to begin his sentence.

In the three days after the McCabe's Bar killings, thirteen people were killed in separate incidents in Belfast. Then loyalists struck again in Portadown. Felix Hughes, a forty-seven-year-old married man with six children, was abducted on 15 July. After fruitless public appeals, three weeks later British Army frogmen searching a UDA 'no-go' area found his body in stagnant water in a ditch off the River Bann. The corpse had been tied to a mattress and weighted down with stones.[19]

Felix Hughes

At the inquest, evidence was given that at least seven men (and probably around twelve) were involved. Forensic evidence had been found in three different vacant houses. Hughes, whose only affiliation was to his local accordion band, had been abducted, tortured, beaten and finally dispatched with a single shot to the head. A sixteen-year-old defendant, 'on the run' from a training school, who seemed 'relaxed', smoking and smiling in court, pleaded guilty to manslaughter.[20] He

---

c   This was one of the last politically linked murder trials held in Northern Ireland before a jury. Soon afterwards, so-called 'Diplock', no jury, courts were introduced, purportedly to prevent the intimidation of jurors.

was sentenced to eight years detention.[21] Charges against another
youth were dropped.

On 21 July, the IRA detonated a co-ordinated series of twenty-
two bombs in Belfast, in what became known as 'Bloody Friday'. Nine
people, Catholic and Protestant, including two British soldiers, were
killed and 130 people were injured. In the little County Derry village
of Claudy, on 31 July, nine people were killed when three republican
bombs exploded on the main street. Again the victims were both
Protestant and Catholic, and aged between eight and sixty-five. Two
people, aged fifteen and nineteen, were killed during 'Operation
Motorman', when the British Army removed the 'No Go' barricades
from the streets of Derry.[22]

On 22 August, in Newry, nine people lost their lives in an IRA
bombing and, a few days later, six people lost their lives in separate
incidents, including, in Portadown, Éamonn McMahon, a Catho-

Éamonn McMahon

lic. Éamonn (aged nineteen) was last seen on 27
August after visiting his girlfriend in Lurgan. Four
days later his body was found in the River Bann
with a rope around his neck. He had also been tortured. A pathologist told his inquest that Éamonn's
body had been bruised by fists or blows from a blunt
instrument. He had died from 'fresh water drown-
ing'. In December 1973, two men, originally charged with murder,
were convicted of Éamonn's manslaughter.[d] They were a seventeen-
year-old 'junior soldier', Alan George Dowey, and a twenty-year-old
man, Kenneth Best, who both admitted abducting Éamonn, along
with two other men with whom they had been drinking.[23]

On 4 October, Patrick Connolly (aged twenty-three) was the next
person murdered in Portadown. His family was living in the mainly

---

d   Prosecuting lawyers withdrew the murder charge, with the approval of the trial
judge, who said there was not the required evidence of intent to constitute a murder
charge.

Protestant Brownstown estate. Later, this was to become almost 100 per cent Protestant, but in 1972 there were still Catholics living there. The family was subjected to increasingly intimidating threats. They were verbally abused. Missiles were thrown at them on their way home from work or socialising and, three months before the fatal attack, a bottle was thrown through a window of their home.

Paddy Connolly, the father of five boys, including Patrick, was a former sailor in the Royal Navy, who had seen action in the Far East and witnessed the horrific results of the nuclear bombings on Hiroshima and Nagasaki. He was confident he could handle a gun safely to protect his family and asked local police repeatedly for a character reference to allow him to obtain a firearms certificate. The police continually insisted, however, that an attack on the family was very unlikely as, they said, loyalists would not attack a terraced property squeezed between the homes of two Protestant families.

Paddy, Mary (his wife) and their sons Patrick and Christopher (aged twenty) were in their living room on 4 October when a grenade smashed through the window. All four were seriously injured. Mary and Christopher suffered shrapnel wounds. Patrick lay where he fell, between two chairs, and was unconscious and moaning when his father reached his side. Cause of death was given as intra-abdominal bleeding due to blast injuries.

'I can remember my mother at his graveside, crying her eyes out and clawing at the soil. Even his dogs seemed to know something terrible had happened. One of them whined miserably and kept circling Patrick's grave.'

Tony Connolly, Patrick's brother

Patrick Connolly

Mary's injuries included multiple cuts, with the severing of nerves to her arm and puncture wounds to her chest. Christopher's lung was punctured and he had serious wounds to the chest and neck.

He describes finding himself on his hands and knees in the scullery, bleeding from wounds in his face. He never worked again.[24]

None of the Connollys had any political connections. Rumours spread though that the family had been making bombs and had been killed in a premature explosion – a suggestion disproved by the forensic evidence. (The grenade's 'fly-off lever' was found outside, proving it was thrown from outside into the house.) No one was ever charged or convicted, so who was responsible and where did the murder weapon come from?

The 1958 Model 36 Mills hand grenade was used exclusively by British and Commonwealth forces. The HET states, 'it is widely acknowledged that throughout the Troubles, paramilitary groups had access to British army ammunition'.[25] A 'large number' of grenades, it says, had found their way into Northern Ireland as 'souvenirs' from conflicts in which the British Army was involved in the 1960s and 1970s such as Aden, Borneo and Oman. Police discovered that, eighteen months before the attack on the Connollys, 'a number' of hand grenades had been stolen from HMS *Ark Royal*. Intelligence reached the RUC Criminal Investigation Department (CID) that an ex-serviceman in Portadown was the most likely source. He was neither arrested nor interviewed.[26]

Underscoring the dangers of British Army weapons becoming available for loyalist use, ten days after Patrick's murder, loyalists stole fourteen self-loading rifles (SLRs) and ammunition from a British Army base in Belfast. This was dwarfed by a massive raid staged in Lurgan by the UVF on 23 October 1972. At 4.20 a.m. on that morning, at the joint UDR/TAVR base at King's Park, armed men overpowered the sentry. Eighty-five SLRs, twenty-one SMGs, 1,300 rounds of ammunition, flares and flak jackets were taken.[27] Clearly, loyalists were tooling-up for a long campaign. As they left, one of the raiders told one of the 'sleeping guards' that they were the UVF, saying, 'Don't worry. We won't harm you. All we want are the weapons which we'll put to better use than you before December.'[28]

According to an August 1973 British Army internal briefing paper on 'Subversion in the UDR', prepared for the office of the British prime minister, those responsible took so much away with them that they were forced to dump a proportion of their newly acquired arsenal close to the camp.[29] More significantly, however, an internal investigation (quoted in the same British Army document) concludes:

> It is quite apparent that the offenders knew exactly what time to carry out the raid. Had they arrived earlier, they may have been surprised by returning patrols and, had they arrived later, they may have been intercepted by the Tandragee Power Station guard returning from duty. The very fact that all the guard weapons had been centralised and there was only one man on the main gate, a contravention of unit guard orders, was conducive to the whole operation. The possibility of collusion is therefore highly probable.

No one has ever been held responsible for the raid. There is no evidence that those responsible for the breach of duty were disciplined. According to an Irish government briefing paper, the UVF claimed responsibility and 'stressed that the captured weapons would never be used against the security forces'.[30] The document gives examples of the damage caused by just one of the eighty-one guns taken in this raid, including an indiscriminate attack on a bar in Belfast docks, when an English ship's captain, Thomas Curry, aged fifty and from Lancashire, was shot dead. The same gun was also used in a kidnapping and at least ten attempted UDA killings in Belfast (clearly the UDA and UVF were sharing weapons). A second gun was used to kill a sixteen-year-old County Donegal Protestant, Henry Cunningham.[e]

---

e   On 10 August 1973, driving home with his brothers from a building site, he was shot dead by loyalists standing on a bridge over the M2 motorway, because the vehicle was registered in County Donegal and they assumed that all those inside were Catholic. The RUC investigation into his death lasted a mere three weeks. For

Within two days of the 23 October raid in Lurgan, Brigadier Denis Ormerod, commanding officer of the UDR, told Belfast Rotary Club that UDA membership would not disbar a man from joining his regiment.[31] The fact that loyalists were routinely taking guns from British armouries was already established in Belfast, London and Dublin. A letter from the head of the Garda Síochána's security unit, C3, dated November 1972, sent to a colonel in the Irish Defence Forces intelligence section, noted that the *RUC Gazette* admitted that 262 weapons had been stolen that year: 'I think it could be assumed that many, perhaps the majority, were stolen by the UDA, probably with the connivance of the UDR.'[32]

On 24 November, in preparation for a meeting between the British Prime Minister, Harold Wilson, and the Irish Taoiseach, Jack Lynch, British officials drew up a briefing paper on the UDA. It informed Wilson that British soldiers and RUC officers were instructed to direct operations 'against their criminal extremist elements whilst making every endeavour to maintain good relations with law-abiding citizens in the organisation. Unarmed, locally-resident vigilante type patrols should be tolerated.'[33] The British government knew that the UDA was involved in murder and the wholesale theft of its weapons, for obvious purposes, yet it was still intent on maintaining 'good relations' with at least some of its members.

Loyalists then hit again – this time south of the border. On 1 December, two people were killed and 127 injured when two car bombs exploded in the centre of Dublin.[f] At the time, the Dáil was debating an amendment to the Offences Against the State Act which would give the courts much greater powers against the IRA, including a provision for jailing anyone on the word of a senior officer. Mary Robinson, a lawyer who went on to become President of Ireland,

---

years, the Cunningham family was told that the IRA was responsible. (*Source*: family interview with PFC.)

f   For more on these bombings, see Chapter 7: Bombs Know No Borders.

called it 'a form of internment by judicial process'.[34] These explosions influenced the outcome. After a one-hour adjournment, Fine Gael abstained and the amendment was passed.

Just before Christmas, there was another killing in Mid-Ulster. Alphonsus McGeown (aged nineteen) was shot and killed when he got off the Portadown bus near his home at Loughgall. A friend with him, Malachy Hamill (also nineteen), was shot and wounded. In their booklet *The Triangle of Death*, Fathers Raymond Murray and Denis Faul make the point that a 'Sterling sub-machine gun [military weapon] was used. A number of these had been "stolen" in the area without a shot being fired in their defence.'[35] No one was ever charged or convicted.

By the end of 1972, loyalists had killed 121 people, including two in Dublin, two teenagers in County Cavan and at least five in the immediate Portadown area. They were stealing or otherwise purloining UDR weapons at such a rate that the British Army drew up monthly lists. Yet at the end of the year, at a time when hundreds of IRA suspects were being interned without trial, the British Army's 'Arrest Policy for Protestants' recommended no action at all against the UDA.[36] Far from it. The policy document says, 'Ministers have judged that the time is not at the moment ripe for an extension of the arrest policy in respect of Protestants.' Moreover, it went on, people holding 'certain defined positions' in Protestant groups should not be regarded as 'dangerous terrorists, as we regard officers in the Provisional IRA'. In response, the deputy under-secretary of state (army) said he agreed with RUC objections to the term 'Protestant terrorists'. The same public servant benignly categorised the activities of UDA members as ranging from 'UVF-type thuggery' to 'comparatively harmless vigilante activity and political activism'.[37]

2

'My God, Not This' (1973)[a]

> At the hospital, when she realised Daddy was really dead, Mum was so grief-stricken the staff strapped her down on a mattress.
>
> *Donna Barry on her parents, Patrick and Margaret Campbell*

In 1973, both Ireland and Britain joined the EU. Nationalists boycotted a border poll in Northern Ireland and the British government published constitutional proposals for a devolved power-sharing assembly at Stormont and a Council of Ireland.[b] By then loyalist violence had spread from Portadown to its hinterland.

On 18 January 1973, a Catholic, Joseph Weir, was shot and killed in West Street, Portadown. A married man, he had a family of four daughters and three sons. During the trial of William Sloan, convicted of his murder, Joseph was described as a 'quiet man, devoted to his family and who liked nothing better than a spot of weekend fishing'.

On 20 January, another bomb exploded in central Dublin. This one killed Thomas (Tommy) Douglas, an engaged twenty-one-year-old bus conductor from Stirling in Scotland.

On 7 February, the United Loyalist Council, led by William Craig, staged a one-day general strike to 're-establish some kind of Protestant or loyalist control over affairs in the Province, especially

---

a Patrick Campbell's last words, author interview with family.
b Power-sharing proposals providing for Catholics and Protestants to govern Northern Ireland together were agreed at talks held at the British Civil Service Training College at Sunningdale, Berkshire, on 9 December 1973.

over security policy'.[c] Loyalists also attacked RUC stations in protest at the internment of the first Protestants.

On 9 March, Patrick Turley (aged thirty-two), a Catholic lorry-driver who lived with his sister in Craigavon, was beaten by a number of men as he left a bar to go home.[1] He was kicked and punched before being forced into a nearby house, where he was robbed and beaten again. The gang then produced a gun and said they were going to kill him, before forcing him into his own car and driving out of Portadown. He was shot in the back and head before being left for dead in the countryside. Turley survived, but he was confined to a wheelchair for the rest of his life. Later, the gun used in the attempted murder of Patrick Turley – a Spanish-made 'Star' pistol – was used to kill Dorothy Trainor, in the attempted murder of Malachy Trainor (her husband), in another non-fatal shooting[2] and was one of the two weapons used to shoot John Francis (Francie) Green in County Monaghan.

The Star, a 9 mm small-calibre weapon, serial number 344164, had originally been the legal personal-protection firearm issued to a UDR Private, Robert Winters, a founding member of the modern UVF.[3] Winters was robbed by three men in Portadown late at night in March 1973. He says he was 'struck on the head with a blunt instrument' and knocked out, requiring admission to hospital.[4] Clearly, his assailants knew who Winters was and had targeted him to obtain the weapon.

In May 1974, Portadown UDA man John Warke Moore was convicted of attempted murder and possession of a firearm, and sentenced to twelve years in jail for the attack on Patrick Turley. A second UDA man, Gordon Liggett, was convicted in March 1974 of grievous bodily harm and possession of a firearm and sentenced to eight years in jail. Before his trial began, a third defendant, George Hyde (nineteen),

---

c   The United Loyalist Council comprised the UDA, the Loyalist Association of Workers and other loyalist paramilitary groups.

was battered to death on 27 December 1973 inside Long Kesh camp.[d] There were allegations that he had given information to the RUC.

An RUC intelligence report claims that the pistol was passed by the UDA to the UVF in a weapons exchange after Turley's attempted murder.[5] It was also used in March 1973, in Loughgall, when loyalists fired four shots through the windows of a house at the Catholic owner sitting at his fireside, and was later found, along with twenty-eight other weapons, on land belonging to Norman Greenlee near Armagh in August 1979.[e] UDR man David George Teggart, who was later sentenced to seven years for possessing weapons, had taken the firearms to Greenlee's land.

On 3 April 1973, the home of a Catholic family at Orpheus Drive, Dungannon, was bombed. Though there were no injuries, the bombing is significant as it led to a man who later rose (or sank) to notoriety first coming to public notice. The bomb was left on the window sill of the house. Thankfully, it caused no injury to Patrick Devlin or his three children inside. John James Somerville was arrested in September 1980 and admitted that he and others had planted the bomb (he would not name his accomplices). He claimed the Devlin family had refused to serve members of the security forces in their grocery shop. Convicted in 1981, he was sentenced to fourteen years for this attack.[f]

On 26 June, the UDA murdered Stormont SDLP Senator Paddy Wilson and his secretary, Irene Andrews.[6] Both were stabbed repeatedly and their bodies left on a mountain-side overlooking North Belfast.

The equally inhuman and cowardly way that Francis and Bernadette

---

d   Though officially renamed 'Her Majesty's Prison, Maze' in late 1972, it was still colloquially called Long Kesh.

e   Greenlee was arrested in follow-up searches after a £200,000 post office robbery in Portadown.

f   John Somerville was also convicted of the murders of three members of the Miami Showband on 31 August 1975 and of the murder of Patrick Falls on 20 November 1974. See Chapter 12: Her Majesty's Murderers.

Mullan, the next to die in Mid-Ulster, were killed on Sunday 5 August almost defies description. They were at home in their farmhouse outside Dungannon near the village of Moy when the killers struck. Thomas, their seventeen-year-old son, told the inquest that when he arrived home to find what the killers had left behind, he could not believe his eyes. He had run in and out of the house 'a few times trying to figure out what had happened'. Inside, his mother lay dead – shot at least twenty times. She had been in the kitchen with her husband, Francis (aged fifty-nine). Their two-year-old son, Michael, had been standing between them.[7] The killers had opened fire from just inside the door. Bernadette had taken the brunt of the attack. Francis, who appeared to be getting ready for bed and was only partially clothed, had six bullet wounds. The toddler was shot four times in the legs.

Bernadette Mullan   *Francis Mullan*

The inquest was told at least twenty-nine bullets had been fired in total. An entire magazine had been emptied from a sub-machine gun used in the attack.[g] The other weapon used was a .455 revolver.[h] So it was hardly surprising that Thomas could not comprehend what he saw when he arrived home. He was treated for severe shock in hospital.

When the police arrived, they washed the blood off Michael. A constable told the inquest that when he arrived, Francis was lying dead inside the door, shot in the face, while Bernadette was lying

g   According to the Barron Report, 2003, 'Information Received Concerning Certain Weapons', the SMG was also used to attack the home of Thomas McAliskey at Coalisland, County Tyrone, the day before the Mullan killings.

h   The .455 Smith & Wesson revolver was also used in two non-fatal attacks and in the killings of Daniel Hughes on 14 January 1974, James and Gertrude Devlin on 7 May 1974, Patrick Falls on 20 November 1974 and Owen Boyle on 11 April 1975 (five killings in six attacks).

crouched, presumably trying to make herself a smaller target. Two-year-old Michael was lying across her head and crying, his pyjamas covered in his own and his mother's blood.

Fr Denis Faul and Fr Raymond Murray wrote in *The Triangle of Death*: 'Local people were able to give the names of suspicious characters and their cars which were seen in the vicinity of the Mullan house and the roads leading to it, but nothing was done. This double assassination, and the failure to arrest or intern a single suspect, made the Catholic people realise that the RUC and British Army had no interest in stopping the sectarian assassinations, which were serving a useful purpose.'[i]

It is telling that, even at this early stage, nationalist suspicions locally turned almost immediately to whether the SMG had been 'stolen' from the UDR. A spokesman for the local branch of the Republican Clubs (the political wing of the Official IRA) demanded in vain that the ballistics of all UDR weapons be tested to see if they had been used. 'The UDR in Moy, Dungannon and Coalisland area are allowed to take their guns home when they are off duty. I demand that all of these are seized and ballistic tests carried out on them by an independent expert,' the spokesperson said.[8] Many lives may have been saved if this request had been heeded.

Moy, from then on, became the centre of a six-year-long series of sectarian killings. Twenty-six people were killed within a ten-mile radius of the village. The gang, and permutations of it, responsible for these killings are believed to have operated out of three centres: Moygashel (Dungannon); Ted Sinclair's farm in the townland of Canary,[j] and what used to be known as 'Bond's Plantation' – a large estate later acquired by the National Trust and now known as The

---

i   Clearly, even at this very early stage, the two priests believed loyalist violence had a political purpose.

j   Sinclair was a farmer, loyalist, leading Orangeman and former B Special. See Chapter 12: Her Majesty's Murderers.

Argory.[9] The nascent loyalist grouping was beginning to get into its stride.

In August 1973, the British were concerned enough about what was going on inside the UDR to commission a study, 'Subversion in the UDR'.[10] The findings were hair-raising – or they should have been, given that the UDR was increasingly being deployed in Catholic areas. Among the twenty-page document's more dramatic conclusions was that between 5 and 15 per cent of all UDR men 'have paramilitary links with widespread joint membership of the UDA' (which remained legal until 1992, despite patently being involved in multiple paramilitary shootings and bombings). The report also concluded 'that some soldiers are undoubtedly leading double lives' and that 'the UDR is the single best source of loyalist weapons and their only significant source of modern weapons'. Joint membership of the UDA and UDR was positively encouraged, as the 'Civil Adviser' to the General Officer Commanding (GOC) the British Army in Northern Ireland wrote in July 1972: 'One important (but unspoken) function of the UDR is to channel into a constructive and disciplined direction Protestant energies which might otherwise become disruptive.'[11]

'Subversion in the UDR' also noted that 'the primary loyalty of many of its [UDR] members was to Ulster rather than the British government' and there was a 'self-confessed dearth of British and RUC intelligence on UDR–loyalist links', while in 'many areas, UDR commanders consider dual membership normal'. There was no discussion in the report on measures that might be taken to counter these grim conclusions. On the contrary, the only debate appeared to centre on the loss of morale should any action be taken. It claimed that if all the subversives were rooted out, it could have resulted in a very small regiment indeed. Commenting on the report, A. W. Stephens, a civil servant heading an intelligence unit at the Ministry of Defence in London, said, 'I wish I could say that its contents come as a surprise, but I am afraid they do not.'[12]

A confidential letter sent in June 1972 to the Ministry of Defence in London from the British military HQ in Northern Ireland had argued against limiting recruitment to the UDR, as:

> This could lead to men joining a paramilitary organisation such as the UDA as an alternative to the UDR. For these reasons it is felt that it would be counter-productive to discharge a UDR member solely on the grounds that he was a member of the UDA. I am sure this moderate line towards UDA supporters is the right one in light of the role of the UDA as a safety valve. In my opinion it would be politically unwise to dismiss a member of the UDA from the UDR unless he had committed a military offence.[13]

Loyalist sectarian murders, meanwhile, continued. In County Down on 22 August, just seventeen days after the Mullans were slaughtered, Seán McDonnell, a twenty-one-year-old Catholic, was shot dead, devastating his family and his fiancée, Agnes O'Hare, who witnessed his abduction. Seán had left school at fifteen to work on the family farm, but at the time he was killed he was a heavy-plant driver. He had met Agnes two years before and they planned to marry in 1974.

To give a full account of this murder, however, it is necessary to backtrack to 9 July. That day, Isaac Scott, a former member of the UDR from Mayobridge in County Down, was shot dead at Belleeks, near Newtownhamilton, South Armagh. He was starting his car as he left Tully's Bar with a female friend, when several shots were fired through his windscreen, killing him almost instantly. It was in an apparent retaliation for this IRA attack that the UVF targeted Seán McDonnell – though he was a totally innocent victim with no connection to either the IRA or Isaac Scott.

Seán and Agnes were talking over their wedding plans in his Hillman Hunter car outside her home after a night out playing bingo. At about 11.30 p.m. two masked gunmen ordered him out of his car and forced him into the back of one of the gang's two vehicles. Agnes heard the driver of one of the cars say, 'This is for Isaac Scott.'

Agnes' mother, Rose, heard her daughter screaming hysterically outside their front door and, as she saw the lights of one of the gang's cars disappearing, heard six gunshots. Agnes' father, Patrick, and her brother Patsy quickly drove in the direction of the shots, but found nothing. Patsy drove to Newry police station to report the events. The police then discovered Seán's body near the smouldering remains of a car – about three to four fields from Isaac Scott's family home, two-and-a-half hours after Agnes had last seen Seán alive. The family was haunted for decades by reports that he had been tortured. In fact, he died very soon after his abduction. He had been shot eleven times.[14] It was a cold, clinical slaying.

The gun used to kill Seán was a standard British Army-issue Sterling SMG used in four other attacks in which three people were killed.[k] John Somerville was convicted for murdering one of those killed by the same weapon (Patrick Falls). Both he and his brother Wesley were also involved later in the Miami Showband killings (in July 1975), in which three members of the band were murdered and two UVF men were killed by their own bomb.

Because so much weight is given here to ballistic links between killings, it is important to state that, while they cannot prove the same person pulled the trigger, they are an indication that the perpetrators at least knew one another. In report after report, the HET states that, where they have discovered significant ballistic links, while such evidence is 'extremely important for investigators' it does not 'necessarily implicate individuals'. Paramilitary groups often held weapons in pools or armouries under the control of a central figure

---

k   An attempted murder in Coalisland in May 1973, a gun-and-bomb attack on the Maghery Hotel in June the same year, the shooting of Patrick Falls outside Coalisland in November 1974, and the killing of Eugene Doyle and Arthur Mulholland at Hayden's Bar, Pomeroy, in February 1975.

or 'quartermaster', and shared them out. The multiple use of a specific weapon by various individuals at different locations and different time periods occurred frequently, but when a weapon was used in a similar type of attack, in a similar area and at around the same time, it is impossible to avoid the conclusion that the attackers were linked.

Reliable, modern weapons were a valuable asset. Experienced killers often preferred to use their 'favourite' weapon – one on which they could rely and whose provenance they knew. Ballistic links are a key factor in the series of murders examined here and used as a reliable guide to link different murders.

The McDonnell family believes that one of the gunmen who killed Seán was Robin Jackson (whose home village was just the other side of Newry from the murder scene).[1] John Weir also claims that Jackson was involved.[15] RUC intelligence received at the time stated that the gun had been 'stolen' from a member of the Ulster Special Constabulary (the B Specials). Seán's inquest was held at Banbridge Orange Hall, the local courthouse being closed for redecoration. It seems an insensitive decision in the circumstances.

The violence continued to escalate. In Armagh, two loyalist car bombs exploded in Catholic areas of the city on Monday 28 August. Although no one was killed, twenty people were injured, four seriously (two soldiers, a seven-year-old boy suffering from head wounds and a sixty-six-year-old woman who had a heart attack).

On 23 October – exactly a year after the raid on Lurgan TAVR base and not far away – the UVF staged a second raid on a British armoury. This time they hit Fort Seagoe, the armoury of E Company, 11 UDR Portadown. During this raid, twelve armed men stole four rifles, two SMGs, five pistols, flak jackets, pocket radios, five Bardic lamps[m] and ammunition.[16] In this case there is strong evidence of

---

1   Jackson was a leading loyalist and multiple murderer. There will be more about Jackson in later chapters, including in Chapter 12: Her Majesty's Murderers.

m   Bardic lamps emit a strong light and were used at checkpoints by British soldiers, inside assistance. Connecting doors that should have been locked were left open, a supposedly alarmed fence was cut through, and the raiders even apparently knew the lock combination on a cabinet containing the armoury keys. A document discovered in the British National Archives, Kew, quotes an interim report into the raid, citing 'grounds to suggest that the raiders had assistance from members of H or B Coy 11 UDR'.[17]

Searches were carried out for the missing weapons and, among others, the home of Winston Buchanan outside Portadown was searched. Nothing from the Fort Seagoe raid was found, but police did find 140 pounds (64 kg) of explosives, two grenades, bomb-making equipment, two radios and 5,000 rounds of assorted ammunition. Buchanan told police he had been forced to store the contraband by Robin Jackson, Roy Metcalfe[n] and an RUC man.[o] This did him no harm when it came to sentencing. For this massive haul, Buchanan received just one year in jail.

The HET Report into the killing of Banbridge trade unionist Patrick (Pat) Campbell notes that, on 7 November 1973, fourteen days after Buchanan named Robin Jackson to the RUC, police raided Jackson's home. 'Although the reason for the search of Jackson's house was not recorded,' says the report, 'it is most likely that it was carried out as a direct result of Jackson being named during the earlier Portadown armoury theft search and arrest operations'.[18] The gap is critical because during that time (four days after he had been named by a man caught in possession of a substantial quantity of arms and explosives) Jackson was still at liberty and shot Pat Campbell dead.[p]

At the time of his death, Campbell was thirty-four and the father

---

including the UDR.

n   Robert (Roy) Metcalfe was killed by the IRA on 18 October 1989.

o   The IRA shot the RUC man dead in 1975.

p   The HET Report into Patrick Campbell's killing does not mention any other suspect. Wesley Somerville is named in *Lost Lives* as Jackson's accomplice.

of three children. An outspoken opponent of sectarianism, he was involved in a cross-community amateur boxing club in Banbridge and

Patrick Campbell

was president of the Northern Ireland branch of the National Union of Footwear, Leather and Allied Trades. Pat had objected at work both to a minute's silence for the dead of Bloody Sunday and to the British Army using the factory canteen. The man who shot him dead, Robin Jackson, was a self-confessed member of the UDA and the UDR.[19]

On 28 October 1973, Pat was at home with his wife, Margaret, and three children when, shortly after ten o'clock, a knock came at the door, which Margaret answered. The two men outside said they wanted to speak to her husband. When Pat came to the door, they immediately tried to overpower him, shouting, 'You had better come with us', and dragged him outside. Margaret, who had returned to the living room, heard her husband tell the men that anything they had to discuss, they could say where they were. Margaret then heard a scuffle as Pat was dragged down the pathway. He somehow managed to break free and ran back into what he believed was the safety of his own hallway. It was then that one man produced a gun and fired a shot. Margaret, who had run back into the hallway, saw flashes. She heard Pat's last words, 'My God, not this.' She saw the second man lifting a longer gun and pulling the trigger. Pat fell face downwards in the hallway directly in front of her. The men fled. Pat was still alive and semi-conscious when a neighbour rushed to his aid and lifted his head. The dying man took one last look at his wife.

When the police arrived, they found Margaret kneeling at her stricken husband's side as he lay covered in a blanket. A doctor arrived and found Pat to be unconscious. When his clothing was cut away, the doctor saw bullet wounds and quickly intubated him before the ambulance took him to hospital. Pat was declared dead on arrival at the hospital. He had been hit by at least nine bullets, 'causing his rapid death'.[20] The two attackers had long before escaped in a car, which was found about half an hour later just outside Banbridge.

The UDA, using its cover name, the UFF, admitted responsibility, claiming that Pat was in the IRA. The statement also claimed responsibility for an attack on a Lurgan bar owned by an SDLP member earlier on the same evening. (The gang had thrown a hand grenade at the front of the bar, injuring a barman in the legs. As they drove away, they fired shots indiscriminately, hitting a passing teenager in the chest and arm, causing him serious injury. Both men recovered.) Police later confirmed through ballistic tests that the same gun had been used in both attacks.

Margaret Campbell told police she had seen neither of the gunmen before that night, but that she had got a good look at them as she answered the door and when she saw them grappling with her husband.[21] She described both men quite clearly to the police on the day after the killing. Man number one, armed with the handgun, who had fired the first shot, she described as having a moustache and round, slightly bulging eyes. That man, she firmly maintains to this day, was Robin Jackson.

Aside from its personal impact on his family, for whom it was an untold tragedy, Pat Campbell's murder is also historically significant: Jackson went on to become a mass murderer.[22] Dozens of families have been left in grief, dozens of women widowed and scores of children left fatherless because Jackson was not stopped in his tracks. If Seán McDonnell was not his first victim, then Pat was.

The RUC's failure to put Jackson behind bars at this early stage is worth examining in some detail. At first sight, it seems incomprehensible. The gunmen were not masked and Margaret was a potentially convincing eyewitness, ready and willing to give evidence.

Jackson, then twenty-five, was officially an unemployed lorry driver living with his wife in Lurgan, County Armagh.[q] He had previously been employed for five years from November 1965 at Down Shoes Ltd in Banbridge, where Pat Campbell worked. Three years after leaving the shoe factory, and two months before Pat's murder, Jackson had joined a UDR unit also based in Banbridge.

Four days before Patrick Campbell's murder, Jackson was named by Winston Buchanan, but it was not until over a week after the murder that RUC Special Patrol Group (SPG) members searched Jackson's home (a modern terraced house on a Protestant housing estate). There they found seventy-nine rounds of 7.62mm ammunition, a .22 revolver and a notebook containing handwritten names, addresses and car registration numbers. As a member of the UDR, he was entitled to keep a standard self-loading rifle and thirty rounds of ammunition at home. He was thus in breach of the Firearms Act.

During questioning, Jackson admitted he had worked alongside Pat. He denied police suggestions that he and Pat had argued, but admitted having a fight with Pat's brother over 'a trivial matter'.[23] Jackson claimed he didn't even know where Pat lived until two days after the murder when, he said, a friend's wife had pointed out the dead man's house to him.

He was unable to account for his movements on the night of the murder, guessing that he was at home watching TV. When the RUC asked why Jackson thought Pat had been killed, he offered an explanation that Pat had opposed the stopping of machinery at Down Shoes in sympathy with three young Scottish soldiers murdered by the IRA.[24] The questioning RUC officer pointed out that Pat had also opposed the stopping of machinery in sympathy after Bloody Sunday. Jackson said he was unaware of that.

During questioning the following day, Jackson claimed he was in

q   *The Sunday Times* (London), 7 March 1999. Jackson was at that time already 'Brigadier' of the Mid-Ulster UVF, arming his unit from a raid he carried out in 1973 on the UDR armoury at Queen Street, Lurgan.

the UDA – then a legal organisation. He continued to deny knowledge of Pat Campbell's murder. He then agreed to take part in an ID parade, declining the offer of having a solicitor or a friend present.

At home in Banbridge, two police officers came to Margaret Campbell's door and brusquely told the traumatised woman to get a coat as she was being brought for an ID parade.[25] She said she was brought abruptly into the same room as Jackson, unprepared and without warning.[26] The first face she saw when she began viewing the line was Jackson's (in the number nine position). She recognised him immediately as her husband's murderer.[27] She paused momentarily but – she said – she could not bring herself to touch him on the shoulder, as the RUC had asked, before continuing down the line towards the number one position.[28] She said she then walked back to position nine, stopping in front of Jackson but again without touching him. Police asked if she had identified anyone. She replied that she was not sure, before bursting into tears and leaving the room.[29] Police told her she would have to try again to positively identify Jackson.

Margaret's account differs, in one slight but vital detail, from the police account of the time. She remembers being brought back into the parade room and again stopping in front of Jackson before continuing to the number four position. She then remembers turning back towards Jackson and declaring, 'That's him.' An officer then asked her to indicate with her hand which man she was identifying. Margaret's memory is that she was so horrified at being confronted with her husband's killer that she could not bring herself to touch him. She became distraught and had to leave the room.[30]

The police account resembles Margaret's in that she was brought back into the room and again commenced to view the parade from position nine towards position one. Like her account, the police say she stopped at the four position before turning back towards the number nine position. There, the account written by Inspector Quinn reads:

She stopped about two feet from that position, turned her head towards me and stated, 'That's him'.

I asked Mrs Campbell to place her hand on the person she was referring to. She then stepped forward and placed her hand on Robert Robin Jackson. On touching Jackson, Mrs Campbell again became emotionally upset and burst into tears and I had to assist her from the room.[31]

Whether or not Margaret touched Jackson, she had by this stage given several clear indications that Jackson was the gunman, either by stopping, touching, verbally identifying him or by bursting into tears in front of him. When Jackson was told he had been identified, he replied that he was innocent and said, 'In my heart, I know nothing about it.'[32]

Margaret gave a witness statement to police saying the man she had identified had been the gunman with the moustache and the 'big, bright' eyes who had 'done the talking' on her front doorstep. She said she was sure within reason that she had identified the right man. He had been the only man in the ID parade, she said, who 'even remotely resembled the man who came to my door on 28 October. The moustache seemed somewhat different but the other facial expressions were quite similar.'

Jackson, meanwhile, was being taken back to Banbridge for further interrogation. During the journey, he broke down crying. From the back of the car, he remarked to two police officers, 'I am in trouble now because Mrs Campbell would remember the colour of every hair on the man's head who had been at her door and shot her husband.'[33] The RUC now had a positive ID and an admission, of sorts, from the same man – Jackson.

Back in Banbridge RUC station, Jackson changed his story and began to claim, for the first time, that he already knew Margaret personally, after meeting her with Pat at a social club three weeks previously. Margaret said at the time, and is adamant now, that she had never seen Jackson before he shot her husband. If she had known him, she says, she would have told Pat who had been at the door asking for him.

Jackson had a visit from his wife the following day. After she left, he told police that, come to think of it, he knew Mrs Campbell well: 'My wife told me that. She [Margaret] spoke to me on several occasions and called me Robin.' On further questioning, he changed his story yet again and said he wasn't sure.

Questioned about the notebook found at his home with the names, addresses and vehicle details, Jackson stated that every one of them was an IRA man. He had taken the names from court reports in the local papers, he said. He feared that, as a UDR man, any one of them might have shot him in the back. There is no evidence that the RUC checked the local papers to see if Jackson was lying. Thirty-five years later, the HET did check. Although five of the names were linked to the IRA, only one of the more than thirty remaining names had convictions at the time the notebook was found. Jackson claimed that the vehicle details were from suspect cars and taken from UDR files, but the details related to people as far away as Derry and County Meath. Jackson's explanations did not add up. The HET comments that, had this elementary piece of detective work been done, it would have thrown doubt on Jackson's veracity and the questioning of Jackson on this point and others is 'disappointing'. The RUC did, however, charge him and he was remanded in custody.

Police, concerned that the case against Jackson was still weak, spoke to his employer and discovered yet another discrepancy. Jackson had told them his employer had broken the news to him about Pat's death. The police discovered it was the other way round. Another witness claimed that he had seen Pat and Jackson talking two days before the murder. Both this account and the testimony of his employer could have allowed police to challenge Jackson's honesty.

The police knew Jackson could not explain where he was at the time of the murder. He had also been identified by Margaret. He had broken down and made an admission to police about her recognising the 'colour of every hair on the man's head' who had killed Pat. He had lied about how he found out about the shooting and had changed his story about knowing Margaret. Two officers, more senior in rank than the detective who prepared the file for the DPP, agreed he should be prosecuted and the papers were sent to RUC headquarters for final vetting. A detective inspector there concluded, against all the recommendations of the local police, that a *prima facie* case had not been built, as the ID evidence was 'tenuous'. The inspector said he was 'extremely doubtful' whether the murder charge could be sustained beyond a preliminary examination in court.[34]

On 3 January 1974, the DPP wrote to the chief constable, saying 'this case was discussed in conference this afternoon'.[35] Those at the discussion included, the letter said, an RUC inspector, a super-intendent and an official from the DPP's office. They had decided the evidence was insufficient to support a charge of murder, which should be withdrawn. Margaret's identification of Jackson at the parade had been too vague, they concluded. She had halted in front of him, moved on and then returned to him. She had burst out crying and left the room. The prosecution case was fatally flawed. A defence lawyer, it was argued, could have claimed that (while she was out of the room recovering from her flood of tears) police had coaxed her back to identify Jackson correctly. Jackson appeared before Belfast magistrates to allow the courts to strike out the murder charge. The charge of possessing ammunition at his home on 7 November (over and above his UDR allowance) was also dropped.

The DPP's decision is open to question. The courts could have been allowed to decide. Instead, on 4 January 1974, Jackson walked free – the first of many occasions. Margaret Campbell continues to blame herself for the 'mistakes' she made at the ID parade. Despite the HET and many others reassuring her that she is not to blame, she holds herself culpable for the DPP's failure to prosecute. 'I feel I have failed my husband, my children and all those people Jackson killed after he murdered Pat,' she says. She remains inconsolable and seems likely to carry a sense of guilt to her grave.[36] No one else was ever arrested, let alone convicted, for Pat Campbell's murder.

The HET Report concluded that the gunmen probably intended to kidnap Pat first before killing him, and that his actions in resisting were courageous. The report said that the UVF was responsible (despite the UFF/UDA claim) and the supposed motive, that Pat was an IRA man, is nonsense. Pat had no connection whatsoever to any paramilitary group. 'This allegation was nothing more than a self-serving justification for those who perpetrated a sectarian murder,' the HET Report states. A more likely motive was his prominence as a trade union leader and his standing within the local community. 'Pat's murder has all the hallmarks of a sectarian murder of a prominent Catholic community figure by loyalist terrorists.'[37]

The HET concluded that Margaret showed 'exemplary courage and integrity throughout the harrowing experience of taking part in the identification process. Her conduct ... cannot be faulted and she should never question herself around the ultimate outcome.' On Jackson, the HET accepted that 'His later notoriety, with the benefit of hindsight, raises suspicions about his involvement and gives rise to the concerns expressed by the family.'[38]

Pat's murder set a pattern that was repeated in the string of other killings carried out by Mid-Ulster loyalists in the 1970s. The UVF would routinely claim that its latest victim was a 'republican' when, in reality, he or she was a soft target – a Catholic living in a rural area with no means of self-defence.

The Sterling SMG used in Pat's murder was later used in a series of shootings, including an attempted double murder, for which Derek McFarland, at various times a member of three branches of the security forces, was convicted.[r] Jointly charged with McFarland in that attempted murder was Stuart Ashton, who was also convicted of a string of loyalist attacks,[s] one being an aborted pipe bombing of a house near Moy. UDR man Samuel McCartney was also charged in connection with that bombing.[39] And so another deadly pattern emerges – an inextricable knot linking loyalists, their weapons and the UDR.

Margaret Campbell has kept faith with her husband. She has never given up trying to establish that Jackson was responsible for Pat's murder. Despite her grief, she engaged with the HET. Her daughter, Donna, says she will pursue every avenue to prove Jackson was the killer and that the RUC was protecting him. Others speculate that it may have been at this early point in his career as a loyalist assassin that Jackson was 'turned' and became an RUC agent.

* * *

On an autumn morning near Aughnacloy, Francis McCaughey (aged thirty-three) was on his way to milk the family's herd of cows.

He drove to the milking shed daily to meet his brother Michael, who lived close by, to relieve their ageing parents, Sarah Ann and Edward, of this task. On this particular morning, 28 October 1973, Francis happened to get to the byre door before Michael. As he entered the shed, a bomb went off, knocking him to the ground and

Francis McCaughey

---

r   The attempted murder of Marian Rafferty and Thomas Mitchell in February 1974. McFarland was an RUC Constable between May 1969 and October 1970, a Ministry of Defence police constable from July 1972 to October 1975 (when he was based at Castledillon, a base for British Army covert operations between Armagh and Portadown), and a UDR private from November 1975 to 1977, when he was dismissed for reasons unknown.
s   Including the double murder of Patrick Molloy and Jack Wylie in a no-warning pub bomb explosion at Traynor's Bar between Armagh and Moy on 19 February 1974.

lacerating his legs. Michael was nearby and heard the blast. He saw smoke and sheets of corrugated iron from the shed flying through the air. He ran to help his brother. When he saw what the bomb had done, he went to call an ambulance and a priest.

Sarah Ann McCaughey had also heard the explosion and seen the smoke. She rushed to her son's side. He was still conscious and said he felt cold. When Michael returned to his brother, Francis was being tended by his parents and neighbours, one of whom had put a pillow under his head to try to make him more comfortable. Another neighbour put his sweater over the stricken young man's legs, while his wife, a nurse, gave first aid. Francis was taken to hospital in Dungannon, from where he was rushed to Belfast. His left leg was amputated, but on 8 November he died from his injuries and associated bronchopneumonia, having clung on to life for eleven days after the explosion.[40]

His autopsy concluded that he had bruising of his brain from the blast as well as shattered legs, a dislocated elbow and other injuries. Initial RUC reports speculated that it could have been an IRA booby-trap bomb intended to kill patrolling soldiers. That was the version of events later given by a barrister acting for the Northern Ireland Office at the inquest. However, a letter sent to the PFC in April 2003 from a PSNI chief inspector states that the UFF/UDA was responsible. The bomb, made with sodium-chlorate-improvised explosives, had been placed just inside the door to kill or injure whoever opened it.

Shortly after the bombing, three suspects were arrested. One said Francis had bought a bit of land behind the local police station for use by the local GAA club and he had 'heard' this was the motive for the bombing. The suspect clearly disapproved of this, as the police notes show he remarked that the land was 'in a loyalist area'. Newspapers speculated that the attack was an attempt to clear the few remaining Catholics out of a mixed-religion area.

A few weeks after the bombing that killed Francis, Secretary of State William Whitelaw banned the 'Ulster Freedom Fighters' (UFF), a flag of convenience for the UDA, but the UDA per se remained legal. Both the SDLP and the Catholic Church had been bringing pressure on Whitelaw to ban the UDA, but he refused, saying it 'would drive the organisation underground, with a consequent decrease in intelligence about its activities. It would also involve the Army in possible confrontations with large sections of the Protestant population in areas where the UDA is strong, such as the Shankill and east Belfast, confrontation which the Army apparently wishes to avoid.'[41]

On 12 November, three car bombs exploded at Catholic-owned bars in Armagh city, and that evening loyalists also bombed Quinn's Pub in Dungannon, injuring three people. A former UDR soldier, Arthur Roger Lockhard of Richhill, was convicted of planning routes and targets for the Armagh bombs. UDR man William Thomas Leonard admitted involvement in the bombing of Quinn's Pub, Dungannon, but was never prosecuted.[t]

Outside Mid-Ulster, political developments were progressing. In mid-November, the UVF called a ceasefire. It said it wanted to pursue a political path. The ceasefire lasted forty-three days. On 21 November, the power-sharing Executive was declared, in the teeth of loyalist opposition (there was as yet no agreement on a Council of Ireland). Five days later, loyalists disrupted assembly proceedings at Stormont. The DUP and Vanguard, along with Harry West (a leading opposition UUP member) formed the United Ulster Unionist Council (UUUC), pledged to bring down power-sharing.

On 6 December 1973, at the British civil service staff college at Sunningdale in Berkshire, a deal was struck on the Irish dimension

---

t   At the time of his admissions of involvement, Leonard was already in jail serving two life sentences for the shooting of James and Gertrude Devlin.

(the Council of Ireland) to accompany power-sharing. Four days later, the UDA and UVF – along with other loyalists – founded the Ulster Army Council to resist the Sunningdale proposals. But the Executive met on the last day of the year, calling for 1974 to be 'The Year of Reconciliation'. These aspirations were to be dashed. 'The Year of Blood' would have been a more accurate title.

3

'KILLING THE NEIGHBOURS'
(1974)[a]

I will remember forever
The soft plump of the bomb
Exploding in the distant pocket of the night.

'The Cavern' by Réamonn Ó Muireadhaigh (Fr Raymond Murray)

The first attempted murder in Mid-Ulster in 1974 came when Tommy Toland (aged forty-one) was shot on the evening of Sunday 6 January in Lurgan. A man fired at random from a passing car, hitting him in the hand and both legs. In the days that followed, the still-legal UDA issued a statement claiming responsibility.[b]

Concerned about a Dublin High Court ruling that the reunification of Ireland did not require the consent of a majority in Northern Ireland, the UUP leader, Brian Faulkner, travelled south to meet the Taoiseach, Liam Cosgrave. The following day, an SDLP assembly member, Hugh Logue, called the Council of Ireland 'the vehicle that would trundle unionists into a united Ireland'. That day (17 January) at 7.40 p.m., loyalists went to Boyle's Bar, a small country pub in the village of Cappagh, County Tyrone, and opened fire at random, killing Daniel Hughes, a seventy-two-year-old retired farmer. At the time of the shooting, there were five people in the building (one a Protestant). Two men were chatting to landlord Francis Boyle in the kitchen while watching a fourth man, a sixteen-year-old local youth,

---

a   Quote from the author's interview with relative of a victim shot dead in 1976.
b   Robin Jackson was arrested and questioned about this attack but let go without charge.

carry out repairs to a settee. Daniel Hughes had then arrived on the scene and was leaning against the kitchen door-frame with his back to the bar entrance when two masked men stepped into the hallway behind him.

Francis saw the machine-guns. Daniel took a step backwards into the hallway and turned to face the men. He didn't stand a chance. He was hit eleven times and died instantly. Bullets, fragments of glass and splintered wood showered three of the four men in the kitchen. One was hit in the chest and body. Francis was hit in the arm. Then came a slower, second burst of gunfire. The survivors remained inside the kitchen until three minutes later when local people, alerted by the sustained noise of shooting, arrived. One, a nurse, began trying to revive Daniel before realising it was hopeless and turning to help the two other injured men.

Daniel had recently retired from his part-time job, driving a van to deliver groceries for a local shopkeeper, and from working his small,

ten-acre patch of land. He was described by a friend as 'a harmless soul' who spent most evenings in the bar talking with old friends.[1] Nine of the eleven bullets that hit him had gone straight through his body, perforating every one of his major internal organs. One was later found lodged in the small of his back and another in his left hip. He died very quickly.[2]

Daniel Hughes

The whole village heard the shooting, with an eyewitness describing the bar as being covered in blood and riddled with bullets.[3] The description Francis gave of one of the assailants noted his large, prominent eyes (a description also given by Margaret Campbell of the man who shot her husband – Robin Jackson).

A claim of responsibility came from a group calling itself the 'Donaghmore-Pomeroy Battalion of the UVF' – but what local people felt then, and still believe, is that a gang operating out of Moygashel was responsible. The gunmen fired at least thirty-five times. They used a Sterling SMG[c] and a Smith & Wesson-type revolver.[d] The ballistic evidence told the police that the attack, despite being outside their usual geographical range, was the work of the same gang responsible for a string of other killings and attempted killings.

Daniel was a widower, with one daughter who had moved to the USA long before the shooting. Desmond Mullan of Cappagh, the sixteen-year-old who had been fixing the settee, has never forgotten his old friend and inspired a recent decision to install a permanent memorial plaque to Daniel in Boyle's Bar.

Two days after the Cappagh shooting, on 19 January, the UVF tried to wipe out the entire SDLP leadership. They were attending a meeting at the Dunowen restaurant in Dungannon and were evacuated minutes before a bomb exploded. Those who escaped included Gerry Fitt, Austin Currie, John Hume, Paddy Devlin, Ivan Cooper and Paddy O'Hanlon.

Two weeks later, loyalists tried to kill Marian Rafferty (aged nineteen) and her boyfriend Thomas Mitchell (aged twenty) near Moy. They were parked about 100 yards from her home when a car drew up and raked their car with gunfire. The top of one of Thomas' fingers was blown off and twelve bullets hit Marian. Her parents heard the shooting and, coming out to investigate, met Thomas carrying Marian in his arms. They were rushed to the South Tyrone hospital,

---

c   The Sterling, whose serial number had been removed to disguise its origin, was later used to kill Gertrude and James Devlin, Eugene Doyle and Arthur Mulholland at Hayden's Bar, and in the Miami Showband massacre, for which two UDR men were convicted, along with John Somerville. The same weapon was used to shoot dead three members of the O'Dowd family.

d   The Smith & Wesson, before Daniel's shooting, had been used in the abduction of two men in County Armagh, a non-fatal gun-and-bomb attack on the Maghery Hotel; the killings of Bernadette and Francis Mullan and the attempted killing of their son, Michael. Subsequent to Daniel's killing, the same Smith & Wesson was used in the attack on James and Gertrude Devlin (for which a UDR man was convicted), the murder of Patrick Falls (for which John Somerville was convicted), and the murder of Owen Boyle.

where Marian underwent five hours of surgery to remove the bullets. She survived.

A man who worked in a local quarry, Stuart Ashton, was arrested on 28 April 1980 and admitted involvement in a list of crimes, including the attack on Marian and Thomas. On 4 May 1980, Derek McFarland was arrested and also admitted attempting to murder the two young people.[e]

Just two weeks after the shooting at Boyle's Bar, and about twenty miles (32 km) to the south, the UVF attacked a similar target, Traynor's Bar, on the road between Armagh city and the village of Moy. Traynor's served a cross-community clientele in a rural part of County Armagh and among its customers that evening were Patrick Molloy, a Catholic, and his Protestant friend Jack Wylie. They had been friends for years and often met in the bar for a social pint or two and a chat.

Pat had ten children with his wife, Nora, who was originally from County Galway. They met when she was working as a 'clippie' on the buses in Birmingham, England. The large family lived in a cottage on a piece of land Pat had inherited from a maiden aunt. They supplemented the modest income Pat earned as a tractor driver for the local council by growing potatoes and other vegetables and fruit, and by 'apple turning' (peeling) for local orchard owners.

Traynor's Bar was a simple, single-storey extension built onto a substantial double-storey home. On the evening of 19 February 1974, nothing seemed amiss until customers smelled a slight burning. Pat and Jack were together as usual, sitting on a bench close to the front of the bar. Pat rose from his seat to ask the barman if something had been thrown on the fire to cause the bad smell.

The barman went to check the fire. Pat returned to his seat next

---

e   Ashton and McFarland both appeared before Lord Chief Justice Lowry in May 1981. Both men admitted attempting to murder the couple and were sentenced to fifteen years in jail. McFarland was sentenced to a further twelve years for possession of a firearm.

to Jack. A massive blast rang around the countryside. The front of the bar was demolished in the explosion. The seat of the blast was close to both men. Pat was found under rubble, lying on his back, unconscious, with no pulse and not breathing. A doctor who arrived within thirty minutes pronounced him dead.[4]

Pat Molloy

'Daddy liked game-shooting and darts and he supported the GAA. He was always smartly dressed, his shirt always ironed and his shoes shining. He loved watching cowboy movies and wrestling on TV. He was witty and funny and very much man of the house.

'I was only fourteen years old when Dad died. I guess I went off the rails a bit later. Losing him turned me into a bit of a loner. I would have done anything to please him. I was angry with him too – after all, if he had been at home and not in Traynor's, he would not have been killed.'

Michael Molloy, Pat's youngest child

Jack Wylie was also found in the rubble, lifeless. Fr Raymond Murray anointed both men. It affected him badly. He later wrote a poem, 'The Cavern', which tells how he discovered the two men's bodies lying at angles in the dark of the shattered bar:

Resting in peace,
Dressed in grey dusty shrouds,
Over the dryness of death.

The bar was in the process of collapsing in on itself, but people who had heard the bomb still braved the crumbling ruins in a vain bid to help those caught inside.

Two hours later, the BBC in Belfast took an anonymous call claiming responsibility for the UFF/UDA. The caller claimed that IRA men drank in the bar. The claim was inaccurate in both respects. The UVF, not the UDA, had carried out the bombing, and IRA men did not drink in the bar.

British Army explosives experts concluded that the bomb had been left on the front porch. It created a crater two feet (60 cm) across and four inches (10 cm) deep. The device had contained between twenty and fifty pounds of explosives.[5]

The post-mortem examination found that Pat had died after his skull had been fractured. Death was virtually instantaneous. The family was devastated. When the inquest was called, Nora Molloy had barely half-an-hour's notice from the police. She managed to get a lift, just in time, to travel into Armagh city, and was forced to sit at the back of the courtroom, unable to hear the proceedings.[6]

There were no immediate charges brought and by October the investigation had ended. Six years later, however, there was a breakthrough. At the time that Traynor's Bar was blown up, Stuart Ashton was living in Annaghmore and working at a quarry at Loughgall, County Armagh, owned by UDR man George (Geordie) Elliott.[f] Ashton was arrested in April 1980 (for reasons unknown; there is no record in police notes) and taken to Gough Barracks in Armagh city.[7] He had known one of the victims of the bombing in Traynor's, Jack Wylie. They were neighbours and attended the same church.

Ashton was interviewed on fourteen occasions over five days. The most significant interview was the fifth, on Tuesday 29 April, during which he admitted, among a string of other crimes, his involvement in the Traynor's Bar explosion. He said he had made the bomb at the home of Orangeman and former B Special Edward Tate Sinclair. He also named Derek McFarland and two other men: 'Suspect 3' (a former UDR man, named in court in a separate case for receiving stolen British Army ammunition and later killed by the IRA) and another man.[8] Ashton said the bomb had been made in either a gas

---

f   Elliott was a leading Ulster Unionist and UDR man. He was shot dead by the IRA at a cattle mart in Ballybay, County Monaghan in June 1980, aged forty-seven.

cylinder or a beer keg, and that he had driven it the 2.5 miles (4 km) south from Sinclair's farm to Traynor's Bar in his own car and placed it outside the main door before lighting the fuse and running away.

He admitted he knew there were customers inside, as he had heard the sound of people talking. During his twelfth interview, Ashton gave the police more information – that Sinclair had driven a second car involved in the bombing and that former RUC Constable Derek Mc-Farland had been a passenger. Ashton said he had been sworn into the UVF on Sinclair's farm in 1973, a year before the bombing, and that the man who had sworn him in was Wesley Somerville.[9] Twenty-seven other charges were levelled against Ashton – mainly for attempted murders and bombings. He pleaded guilty to the vast majority (with the notable exception of the murder of Pat and Jack, for which the judge convicted him) and was sentenced to life with concurrent sentences of between five and eighteen years for twenty-three other offences.

Those with whom he conspired at various stages in his bombing career included two UDR men and, of course, former B Special Edward (Ted) Sinclair.[g] Ashton served fifteen years in jail for the double murder at Traynor's and the other offences. He was released in March 1993 and is said to have become an evangelical Christian.

One of the crimes of which Sinclair was convicted in January 1977 (before Ashton implicated him in 1980 in the Traynor's Bar explosion) was possession of two guns: one used to murder Peter and Jane McKearney and the other used in the Miami Showband massacre. For these and other explosives and weapons offences, Sinclair served barely three years. He was released in May 1979. The following year, Ashton's evidence led police to him again for the

---

g   They were David Dalziel Kane (expelled from the UDR in 1973 for a 'negligent discharge' and later convicted for murdering Fred McLoughlin in a UVF gun attack on the Eagle Bar in May 1976) and Samuel McCartney. Kane was in the UDR from November 1971 to February 1973. McCartney was in the UDR from 1977 until his arrest on 5 May 1980.

earlier attack at Traynor's in 1974. Sinclair denied involvement and was released without charge, despite Ashton's information that he was directly involved in the double murder. Eighteen months later he was picked up again by police and questioned about Traynor's and other offences. Again he denied these and was released without charge. He led a charmed life, it seems. Sinclair died in 1985 of natural causes.

Derek McFarland, at the time a married man aged thirty-four from Loughgall, who had been employed by three separate branches of the security forces, was arrested on Ashton's information and questioned about the murder of Pat and Jack, along with other offences. He denied involvement in the attack on Traynor's Bar, but made other admissions and was sentenced in May 1981 to terms of between eight and fifteen years in jail. Five months later, he requested the royal prerogative on health grounds and died the following month.[10]

For nineteen-year-old Patricia Molloy, her father's sudden death had a particularly terrible impact. Her wedding day was fixed for the following week. With the family focused on the funeral, people were too shattered to think about a wedding. Just twenty-four hours after her father was buried, Patricia was married to Arthur Casey. Only close family attended. The reception was cancelled. Patricia still remembers, with a grimace, how the wedding photographer quipped that he 'understood' about the tragic circumstances, but 'couldn't she just smile a bit?'[11]

Nine days later, in the British general election (which in Northern Ireland was turned into a virtual referendum within unionism on power-sharing), UUUC anti-power-sharing candidates swept the board. The pro-power-sharing parties had no electoral pact. The SDLP held on to West Belfast, but otherwise eleven of the twelve seats went to anti-Sunningdale candidates. Labour won in Britain, narrowly, with Harold Wilson appointing Merlyn Rees as Secretary of State for Northern Ireland.

On 5 March 1974, the UVF bombed a house in Mourne Crescent,

Coalisland, County Tyrone. It was one of hundreds of bombings that year, and is mentioned here only because of those involved. The gang kidnapped two men in a bread van and loaded a bomb into it before driving into the middle of a Catholic housing estate. The explosion damaged several houses and injured nine people, four seriously, including a five-week-old baby girl, whose head was lacerated.

On 13 March, Trevor Barnard of Jackson Villas, Moygashel, was charged that he, and others unknown, had unlawfully imprisoned the two men in the bread van, and with possession of 124 rounds of ammunition. Two days later, brothers John and Wesley Somerville appeared at Belfast magistrates' court, also on charges of assaulting and kidnapping the two men. They were granted bail of £600 each.

When Barnard appeared in court, a prosecuting lawyer said he and the Somervilles had been involved in the kidnapping but not the bombing. On 24 October 1974, Barnard was sentenced to one year's imprisonment for possession of the ammunition, and the following month to a further two years for the kidnapping.

No explanation can be found for the mysterious evaporation of the charges against the Somerville brothers – both notorious loyalists. It was reported in *The Irish Times* (after his subsequent death at the scene of the Miami Showband attack in 1975) that Wesley had been acquitted in 1974 in connection with the loyalist attack on the housing estate.[12] Had the Somerville brothers been convicted on this charge, many lives might have been saved.[h]

UDR man William Thomas Leonard (later convicted for the double killing of James and Gertrude Devlin) admitted involvement in the same attack. A prosecution file was sent to the DPP but a decision was made not to prosecute him, with no reason given.

The political and security temperature was rising. On 19 March, *The*

---

h   Barnard published a sympathy note for Wesley, his 'friend and comrade', from jail after the Miami Showband attack.

Times (London) published an article by its correspondent in Ireland, Robert Fisk, claiming that SAS members had been sent secretly to Northern Ireland 'to serve as military undercover intelligence agents in Belfast and Londonderry'.[13] In response to anticipated concerns from Dublin (the British Prime Minister and the Taoiseach were due to meet on 25 April), Secretary of State Merlyn Rees sent a memorandum to the Secretary of State for Defence, defending the use of plainclothes patrols and, while accepting that SAS men had been deployed, denying that an entire unit had been sent to Northern Ireland.[14]

On 23 March, a new group – the Ulster Workers' Council – was announced, demanding new elections to the power-sharing assembly and threatening civil disobedience. On 4 April, Rees announced he would lift the proscription on both the UVF and Sinn Féin (to take effect on 23 May) and phase out internment.[15] Four days later, he met the UWC leadership – which was not (as yet) considered a serious threat to power-sharing.

By then, however, the loyalists in Mid-Ulster were really beginning to hit their stride. They were combining membership between different areas and sharing weapons, obtaining intelligence from UDR sources and maliciously injecting 'intelligence' back into the UDR when it suited their purposes. At this already dangerous time, the British Army decided to expand the UDR's role into intelligence-gathering. The reason given in an April 1974 memorandum by the vice-chair of the general staff was to gather 'intelligence on terrorist activities'.[16] There was no conceivable excuse for this. Loyalist infiltration of the UDR was already well established.

The loyalist gang's next murder, three months after the Traynor's Bar bomb, was the shooting of a Catholic couple five miles (8 km) away, just across the county border in County Tyrone. James Desmond Devlin, aged forty-five, and his wife, Gertrude, aged forty-four, lived with their four children, aged between twelve and seventeen, in a substantial home, Congo House, in the countryside outside

Dungannon. Both were members of the SDLP. James was a former GAA county footballer and managed his brother's bar in the village of Coalisland. Gertrude was a librarian in the same town.

Late in the evening of Tuesday 7 May 1974, Gertrude had driven as usual into Coalisland to pick up her husband from work (James had no driving licence). Her daughter, Patricia, aged seventeen, was with her, because Gertie liked the company. They stopped on the way home to pick up fish and chips for James' supper. Between midnight and one in the morning, Gertrude was driving with Patricia beside her in the front of the car while James sat in the back with his supper. They had reached the single-track, unpaved lane connecting the roadway with their home when the killers struck.

A man stepped out of a gap in the hedge on Patricia's side of the road, dressed in combat gear. He raised his hand as if signalling the car to stop.[i] He was carrying a long-barrelled gun. Gertrude probably thought it was a British Army patrol. Patricia also thought he was a soldier and said so to her mother, but when he was six feet (1.8 m) from the front of the car, the 'soldier' opened fire. Patricia felt the windscreen coming in on top of her as the burst of gunfire continued. She heard her mother saying that she'd been hit and screaming, 'I'm dead.' From behind her on the back seat, she could hear her father, too, saying he had been hit.

Patricia was wounded in the right thigh and forearm, and was covered in blood. The shooting stopped and she heard her father opening the back door and saying he was going to run for help. Then the shooting started again. Patricia lay still, with remarkable courage and presence of mind, pretending to be dead. A second gunman then opened fire with a .455 handgun from a vantage point inside a field of barley. After the shooting stopped, Patricia got out of the car,

---

i   See also the killings of Seán Farmer and Colm McCartney and the Miami Showband killings, which involved bogus military checkpoints.

and believing her parents were still alive, ran for help to the nearest neighbour's house, about a third of a mile away. Unknown to Patricia, however, both her parents were already beyond any help.

The neighbour called the police and a local doctor treated Patricia's injuries – five bullet wounds – before rushing to her parents' side, but nothing could be done for them. Gertrude was still strapped into the driver's seat, her head lying back over the headrest; and James was lying face down on the rear seat with his head towards the open door. James had been hit three times in the chest – any one of the wounds would have been fatal, and four times in his left arm. Gertrude had four wounds in her chest and abdomen, any one of which could have killed her. She also had three wounds in her upper right arm and one in her upper left arm. Her face, neck, body, both arms and left leg were also lacerated. Both had died rapidly.

James and Gertrude Devlin

'I remember my childhood as a golden time. We had a dog, cats and hens. We grew gooseberries and we had an apple orchard. There was a large chestnut tree close to the house. It was, in short, an idyllic country upbringing which ended forever that day in May.'

Eamon Devlin

'I was so proud of Mother. She was gorgeous-looking, lively, talkative. She was committed to better opportunities for everyone. She believed in a new way of doing things, in people being able to live as they wanted.'

Patricia Hourigan-Devlin

The Coalisland branch of the SDLP immediately issued a statement, viewing 'with grave concern the apparent lack of a follow-up operation by the security forces. It would appear from recent events that a well-organised assassination squad is in operation in this area.'[17] Cardinal William Conway told mourners at the funeral mass, 'In the past three days I have looked upon the coffins of seven utterly innocent people who have been ruthlessly cut down. During the past week eleven people have been murdered, one a woman member of the security forces, the other ten all Catholics.'[18] Patricia was too ill to attend the funeral. From her hospital bed, she watched her parents' cortège pass. She 'celebrated' her eighteenth birthday in the same place.

The police went through the usual motions, but, apart from Patricia, there were no eyewitnesses. A near-permanent UDR checkpoint at a nearby electricity sub-station did not seem to be on duty that night.[j] Fifteen months later, however, there was a breakthrough. In August 1975, a man was arrested after a bombing in Dungannon. William Thomas Leonard, a single, twenty-one-year-old phone engineer living in the loyalist stronghold of Moygashel was also a member of the UDR. Detective Inspector Harold Colgan interviewed Leonard about the murder of the Devlins. On 21 August, two days after his arrest, he made a comprehensive statement admitting his guilt. He said he had joined the UVF fifteen months before the murders and was informed of plans to kill the Devlins a few days in advance. He was told when they usually arrived home and took part in a dummy run at their home the night before the shooting.

On the night of the murder, Leonard had picked up the two gunmen from Moygashel, one of whom was wearing what he described as a British Army uniform, the other carrying a plastic bag containing the guns.[k] He then dropped them off near Congo House and waited while they shot the Devlins. Leonard had even seen the headlamps of the couple's car as it turned into the lane, before hearing the sound of gunfire. He then waited for the gunmen to return and drove them back to Moygashel. Leonard told police the names of the two gunmen

---

j   In *The Triangle of Death* Fathers Faul and Murray say the removal of UDR patrols just before loyalist killings was a common experience.

k   Neither can be named here to avoid prejudicing future legal action. One was a UDR man.

but, because he had not actually witnessed the shooting with his own eyes, the two men he identified were never charged. The police did not look for anyone else in relation to the killings.

While Leonard was charged with murdering James and Gertrude, he escaped being charged with the attempted murder of Patricia because, the DPP ruled, he 'did not know' that she was in the car.[19] Leonard also admitted a string of other offences, including acting as a lookout at the Dungannon pub bombing in 1973, hijacking a CIÉ bus at Aughnacloy in June that year and placing a bomb at a second public house in Dungannon in August which injured five people.[20] He also admitted hijacking a car and placing a bomb in it which damaged a third bar in Dungannon (injuring one person), and abducting two bread-deliverymen and using their van to carry out the bombing at Mourne Crescent, Coalisland.[1]

What is truly extraordinary about Leonard's court appearances, however, is that his membership of the UDR features nowhere in his prosecution file. Nor was it included in the file prepared for the judge when deciding the length of his tariff (as a convicted murderer, Leonard would have been sentenced automatically to life, with the judge deciding the tariff – that is, how long he must spend in jail before becoming eligible for parole). Who suppressed this information from the public and the courts? And why?

Leonard's role as a supposed public servant, sworn to uphold the law and protect life through his membership of the UDR would surely have had implications for his sentencing. The HET Report concludes that this absence is 'inexplicable', especially given the public, political and media focus on UDR links to loyalist paramilitaries.[21] The trial judge, on being told that Leonard was attending evangelical meetings in Dungannon, said it was a pity he had not become

---

1   The two Somerville brothers were also charged with this offence, though not convicted. Trevor Barnard was convicted in connection with the abduction. Leonard was not charged despite his admission.

a Christian before murdering the Devlins. Sentenced in December 1975, Leonard was released in August 1985.

Two other men were interviewed about the Devlin shootings (the two that Leonard named). The officer in charge of the inquiry, Detective Inspector Harold Colgan, was certain they were the gunmen.[22] 'Suspect 1' was a twenty-five-year-old man from Moygashel,[m] who denied involvement. He was, however, charged and convicted of two explosives-related offences and sentenced to twelve and ten years, to run concurrently.

'Suspect 2' was a twenty-seven-year-old farmer, part-time UDR man and the second man Leonard picked up.[n] His home was raided by police, who found three handguns, a quantity of ammunition and two home-made bombs. There is no documentation relating to the charges he faced – other than the bald fact of an alleged conviction recorded on an unspecified 'note'. The HET discovered during their investigation of the Devlin murders that the paperwork had 'been weeded' – that is, removed – 'from the system'.[23] The HET Report adds, 'The reason for the removal of his conviction and sentencing details cannot be established. HET enquiries in regards to this issue are on-going.'

William Leonard spoke to the HET during its review of the Devlin murders in July 2009. He told them he had joined the UVF through a mixture of 'immaturity and coercion' and had 'adopted a Christian way of life' soon after the murders. The HET notes that eleven months after the Devlin shootings, Leonard – by his own admission – had bombed a house in Dungannon, an apparent contradiction to his claim of living a Christian life.

Over thirty years after the Devlins were killed, when the HET began examining the ballistic history of the Sterling SMG used to murder them, they hit a rich seam of evidence, despite its serial number

---

m   He cannot be named here to avoid prejudicing future legal action.
n   He cannot be named here to avoid prejudicing future legal action.

being removed. Before it was used to kill the Devlins, it had already been used to murder Daniel Hughes at Boyle's Bar. It was later used in a series of nine UVF murders including the Miami Showband massacre, in which at least another two UDR men were directly involved.

Were there concerns in London that UDR men were slaughtering civilians? Two letters from July 1974 shine a light on the British civil service's attitude to loyalist infiltration of the UDR. In one, dated 15 May 1974, a lieutenant colonel tells a civil servant in the Ministry of Defence that 'the RUC may have attempted on some occasions deliberately to conceal criminal records' (to facilitate recruitment into the regiment), a fact he finds 'very disturbing'. In another, a different civil servant admits 'some relaxation of security screening for UDR' recruits and that 'If news of this … were to leak out … it could be distinctly awkward.'[24]

Were there concerns regarding the use to which UDR weapons were put? On 1 October 1974, a Northern Ireland Office security paper reported that UDR soldiers were keeping 950 rifles, 434 SMGs and 1,866 pistols for personal protection at their homes. Since 1970, the paper said, 213 of these weapons had been 'lost' – mostly in 'planned raids on armouries', though only eleven had been 'lost' from the homes of UDR members. 'Some people,' the paper said, 'joined the RUC Reserve only in order to have legal access to a weapon.'[25]

The .455 Smith & Wesson revolver used during the Devlin shootings was also used to shoot dead Francis and Bernadette Mullan (and in the later murders of Patrick Falls° and Owen Boyle).

The four orphaned Devlin children were split up and sent to various boarding schools and to live with relatives. They no longer live in Northern Ireland. All are taking a case to the police ombudsman demanding to know why Leonard's membership of the UDR was suppressed and querying whether 'Suspect 2' was an RUC informer.

---

o   For which John Somerville was convicted.

Two days after James and Gertrude were killed, the UDA joined the anti-power-sharing UUUC and the UWC.

On 10 May, the RUC raided a house on Myrtlefield Park in middle-class South Belfast. Inside an apartment under surveillance, they found a top IRA man, Brendan 'The Dark' Hughes. Among his papers they discovered what has since become known as the IRA's 'Doomsday Plan' in the event of all-out civil war.[26] The papers were essentially a defensive plan in the event of loyalist pogroms against the nationalist population in Belfast. The RUC described them as 'the most important seizure ever in Ulster'. The British Army 'PsyOps' department was told that the papers included proposals to 'burn to the ground' loyalist areas of Belfast,[p] and they were portrayed to British Prime Minister Harold Wilson as IRA plans for a scorched earth policy. At least that is how he described the documents when he spoke in the House of Commons on Monday 13 May: 'a specific and calculated plan on the part of the I.R.A., by means of ruthless and indiscriminate violence, to ferment inter-sectarian hatred and a degree of chaos, with the object of enabling the I.R.A. to achieve a position in which they could proceed to occupy and control certain predesignated and densely populated areas in the City of Belfast and its suburbs'.[27]

Brendan Hughes himself said he was never questioned about the documents during interrogation in Castlereagh. In contrast to other experiences after arrests, he said, that time the detectives gave him a relatively easy ride.[28]

The 'Doomsday' dossier was dramatically presented to Taoiseach Liam Cosgrave by the British Ambassador to Ireland at a hastily organised meeting in Dublin on 13 May. On the same day, less than a

---

p   'Psychological operations, or "PsyOps", are planned operations to convey selected information to audiences to influence their emotions, motives, objective reasoning, and ultimately the behavior of governments, organisations, groups, and individuals. The British were one of the first major military powers to use psychological warfare in World War II, especially against the Japanese.' Source: *Dictionary of Military and Associated Terms*, US Department of Defense.

week after the Devlins died, three men sat around a table in the Victorian Gothic grandeur of Stormont Castle for their regular Monday-morning meeting. Over their tea and biscuits, the General Officer Commanding the British Army in Northern Ireland, Sir Harry Tuzo, the Chief Constable of the RUC, Sir Graham Shillington, and the Northern Ireland Secretary, Merlyn Rees, were surveying the political landscape. An all-out strike by the UWC against the power-sharing Executive seemed inevitable,[q] but despite all the blood and savagery taking place around them,[r] from the minutes of the meeting it seems there was no particular sense of urgency.[29] Shillington said it had been a 'very good week' and there had been 'good co-operation between the UDR, the Army and the Police'.[30] Tuzo agreed, saying that the UDR had made 'some good captures'. Though there had been fifty (illegal) UDA roadblocks over two hours in Belfast the day before, Sunday, these were described in the minutes as a 'well-disciplined operation'.[31]

The following day, 14 May, the UWC finally declared the anticipated strike that would bring down power-sharing. It began on 15 May, with loyalists sealing off the port of Larne, blocking roads and hijacking buses. Rotating four-hourly power cuts began. On 16 May, milk began to be dumped, the UWC ordered pubs and bars to close, questions were asked in the House of Commons and increasing numbers of people failed to make their way into work. The next day was the single bloodiest in the entire conflict.

On Friday 17 May 1974, at 5.30 p.m., three no-warning car bombs detonated in Dublin city centre.[s] Twenty-seven people (including a French woman whose family had survived the Holocaust, an Italian

---

q   Two weeks later, having disrupted normal life, the UWC got its way by forcing the resignation of the Executive, thus paving the way for twenty more years of conflict.

r   There were no fewer than nine shooting incidents every day that week, including the murders of two RUC men and of five Catholics – three in Belfast and two, Gertrude and James Devlin, in Dungannon.

s   For a full account of the Dublin and Monaghan bombings, see Chapter 7: Bombs Know No Borders.

citizen and a full-term unborn baby) lost their lives. Ninety minutes later, a fourth car bomb exploded outside a bar in Monaghan town, where a further seven people died. The Dublin car bombs exploded during the rush hour – at the busiest time on the busiest day of the week – ensuring maximum casualties. As well as the thirty-four dead, whose ages ranged from the unborn to eighty, over 300 people were injured.[t] Many of the dead were horribly mutilated. One was decapitated. The carnage was indescribable.

Two days after the Dublin and Monaghan bombings, Merlyn Rees announced a 'State of Emergency' as the UUUC agreed to support the UWC strike. Shops in Northern Ireland reported panic buying. People were asked to use the telephone only in emergencies. Five hundred more soldiers arrived from Britain.

On 25 May, Harold Wilson gave his now-famous 'spongers' statement on British TV: 'British taxpayers have seen the taxes they have poured out … going into Northern Ireland. Yet people who benefit from this now viciously defy Westminster, purporting to act as though they were an elected government; people who spend their lives sponging on Westminster and British democracy and then systematically assault democratic methods. Who do these people think they are?'[32]

The speech was predictably counter-productive. Ordinary Protestants interpreted the jibe as aimed at them, not the UWC leadership. Some even defiantly took to wearing small bits of sponge on their lapels. Three days later, Brian Faulkner and the unionists on the Executive resigned and power-sharing collapsed. The UWC strike, after just fourteen days, had succeeded.

After the Dublin and Monaghan bombings, in which they had been centrally involved, the Mid-Ulster UVF for some reason known only to themselves began to claim murders using the name 'Protestant

---

t   A total of thirty-three adults and children died that day. The thirty-fourth victim was the unborn child of one victim who was nine months pregnant.

Action Force'. They were soon back in action on their home turf. On 16 September, the UVF placed a bomb at a factory in Pomeroy, County Tyrone. When it detonated, inside a radio, it killed the company's managing director, Michael McCourt (aged thirty-one), who was engaged to be married.[u]

In the early hours of 5 October 1974, a shop run by Catholic Paul McNeice at Ardress was badly damaged in a bombing. Less than ten days later, he re-opened his business in a hut – but two men got out of a car and shot him four times. He survived.[v]

Stuart Ashton was convicted of both the bombing and the shooting, along with a string of other offences including murder, attempted murder and bombings in the east Tyrone area. He admitted making the bomb, along with Ted Sinclair, and said Sinclair had driven him to McNeice's shop.[w] Ashton also admitted driving the car on the day that Paul McNeice was shot, and that a former UDR man, David Henry Dalziel Kane, and another man were in the car with him, and that these two men had shot Paul. Ashton told police that they had left from Sinclair's house and that Sinclair had collected him (Ashton) after he burned the car. Because Ashton refused to repeat these claims in a sworn statement, they were inadmissible as evidence and Sinclair was not charged.

On 27 October 1974, the UVF in Portadown once more showed its claws. Anthony Duffy, aged eighteen, and a friend were hitching a ride

---

u   A suspect for the bombing at Hayden's Bar (10 February 1975) was also a suspect in this bombing, but it is unclear which unit of the UVF was responsible.

v   One of the guns used to shoot Paul was also used in the murders of Joe Toman, John Feeney and Brendan O'Hara at Bleary Darts Club on 27 April 1975.

w   Sinclair was a major loyalist figure during the mid-1970s. He is believed to have been involved in numerous attacks in the Mid-Ulster area at the time, including the bombing of Traynor's Bar on 19 February 1974 (in which Patrick Molloy and Jack Wylie were killed) and the non-fatal bombings of Brannigan's Bar (Charlemont, 9 April 1974), the Cosy Corner Bar (Annaghmore, 18 May 1974) and Clancy's Bar (3 January 1975). He was involved in the bombing of the Grew family home in Moy on 24 May 1975. The Luger used in the Miami Showband killings was also found on his property.

Anthony Duffy

home from Lurgan when they were abducted. The friend managed to run off, but Anthony was beaten and shot dead. According to reports from the trial of the two Portadown men accused of the murder, the teenager was badly beaten in a house in the predominantly Protestant Edgarstown estate before being strangled and shot, and his body was dumped in a country lane on the southern outskirts of the town.[33] The accused men both got life sentences for the murder. Two girls gave evidence of seeing both in the back room of the house where Duffy was murdered. One witness testified she had heard 'kicking and struggling'. Fred Holroyd claimed that both men were convenient pawns to protect the real culprits, who were covert RUC/British agents.[34]

Between Anthony Duffy's death in Portadown and the next victim in Mid-Ulster, there was a mass escape from Long Kesh and an announcement that the names of soldiers killed in Northern Ireland would not be added to war memorials, because the conflict was not classified as a war.[35] It was also at this time that the IRA took its campaign to Britain. On 7 November, its members threw a bomb through a window of the King's Arms pub in Woolwich, killing an off-duty soldier and a civilian. Much worse was to come before long in Birmingham, a city where, coincidentally, the next victim, Patrick (Pat) Falls from County Tyrone, had just spent three happy years.

Pat had been born in the townland of Aughamullan, just outside Coalisland on the shores of Lough Neagh, and had studied hard to become a pharmacist. In 1957 he met his future wife, Maureen, who was from Galbally, also in County Tyrone. They married in 1960 and had six children. But Patrick's business in the mainly Protestant Braniel estate in East Belfast did not flourish (locals would not patronise his pharmacy for sectarian reasons) and Pat moved his young family to Handsworth, Birmingham, in 1971. Maureen loved it there, but Pat always longed to return home to Aughamullan. When his brother Joe asked him to take over the family business – a combined post office, village store and local bar – it seemed to Pat a dream come true. He flew home to complete the paperwork.

Two weeks later, however, Maureen got the worst news possible. Pat had been working behind the bar on the night of 20 November when at least two gunmen came to the door. One gunman, wearing a slit-eyed hood, walked to where Pat was standing before calmly firing several shots at his head. He then turned to walk out and, noticing a customer sitting near the doorway, shot him too, in the shoulder. Pat's body was found at the end of the bar with two bullet wounds to his head and further injuries to his left arm and right hand. The guns used were a Sterling SMG and a .455 Smith & Wesson revolver, both with long and bloody histories involving ten other killings.[x] Joseph Falls identified his younger brother's body in the morgue.

'He was full of fun and laughter. He was great at the fox-trot and quick-step. You would hear him singing around the house. His favourites were "Where Do You Go To My Lovely?" and "White Christmas". I think about him all the time. I talk about him all the time. I cry on my own about him all the time. The grief doesn't get better. In fact, it gets worse. I know I will never get over it.'

Patrick Falls   Maureen Falls, Pat's widow

The following morning, Thursday 21 November, three masked men claiming to speak for the 'Protestant Task Force' (PTF; a name used by the local UVF unit, which also claimed all its members were former British military personnel) gave an interview to a Belfast

---

x   An attempted killing in Coalisland in May 1973; a non-fatal gun-and-bomb attack at the Maghery Hotel, Birches, in June 1973; the killing of Seán McDonnell; and, after the killing of Pat Falls, the killings of Arthur Mulholland and Eugene Doyle. The Smith & Wesson had been used in an attempted double murder in June 1973 linked to the Maghery Hotel attack; the killings of Francis and Bernadette Mullan; the killing of Daniel Hughes; the killings of James and Gertrude Devlin; and the killing of Owen Boyle. Neither weapon was ever recovered.

paper, the *Sunday News*, claiming to have killed a man twelve hours previously.[y] While these further claims were not printed by the *Sunday News*, the PTF had also told the paper's journalist that the victim was a 'Provo officer' and had been 'making bombs in Birmingham'.[36] Clearly, then, the killers knew within hours of the shooting that Pat Falls had been living in Birmingham.

There is no evidence at all that Pat was either a 'Provo' or had been involved in bomb-making of any kind. He left Birmingham weeks before the pub bombings there. Nearly six years after Pat was killed, police investigating UVF activities in Dungannon, Portadown and Newry, arrested John Somerville.[z] At the time of Pat's murder, Somerville was aged twenty-nine and lived in Moygashel, eight miles (13 km) from the scene. His brother, Wesley, died eight months after Pat, when a bomb he was planting inside the Miami Showband's van exploded prematurely.

When John Somerville was questioned after the Miami Showband attack, he made no admissions and was released without charge. There is no evidence that he was interviewed then about the shooting of Pat Falls, though the two attacks were linked ballistically. When arrested six years later, however, he made admissions about Pat's killing and other serious crimes, making a self-serving statement that the target had been an IRA meeting in Falls' Bar.[37] He admitted carrying the .455 revolver, limiting his role to 'firing three or four shots' at Pat and one at a man he claimed to have mistakenly thought was armed as he left the bar. Somerville also admitted his roles in the Miami Showband attack, a bombing in Dungannon and the hijacking and burning of the CIÉ bus at Aughnacloy in March 1973. He was given four life sentences for the murders and twenty years for attempted murder, serving seventeen years in jail before his release

---

y   The journalist was interviewed by police but gave no further details and is now too infirm to be questioned.

z   John Somerville's involvement is dealt with at greater length in Chapter 12: Her Majesty's Murderers.

in November 1998. He has since become an evangelical Christian.

The only item of intelligence the HET has recovered relating to Pat's death was received in the first half of 1975. It named three men coming out of a Portadown bar on the night of the killing – one of them was John Somerville; the others were his brother Wesley and 'Suspect 1' (one of the two men Detective Inspector Harold Colgan was convinced killed Gertrude and James Devlin).

A day after Pat was shot, the IRA bombed the Mulberry Bush and the Tavern in the Town pubs in Birmingham. Twenty-one people died. Six Irishmen were arrested (and served sixteen years in jail) and the British government began drafting a 'Prevention of Terrorism Act' (PTA), described by its author, Home Secretary Roy Jenkins, as 'draconian measures unprecedented in peacetime'.[38]

Nine days after Pat had been shot dead, two bombs exploded just twelve miles (19 km) apart. One, at Hughes' Bar in Newry, led to the death of John Oliver Mallon (he died on 15 December). The second, at a tiny bar called McArdle's in Crossmaglen, led to the wounding of Thomas McNamee, who died a year later.

John Mallon was twenty-one years old, a cheery joker, a canny backer of horses and a shrewd poker-player. He lived with his parents and

fourteen brothers and sisters in Newry and dreamed of emigrating to Canada with his girlfriend, Brea. He had contracted meningitis at the age of fifteen and his brother Michael remembers how, at the crisis of his illness, John had spoken of travelling through a dark tunnel before seeing a bright light.[39] Ever afterwards, John had believed he would die young. 'I'm going to die when I'm twenty-one,' John

John Mallon

had told Michael. 'But I'm not afraid because I know there's something there afterwards.' On 29 November 1974, as he played darts in Hughes' Bar, his local pub, the blast from a loyalist bomb left outside blew him off his feet.[40] The HET Report says that the blast surged down a corridor and hit John full-on, blowing some of his clothes off. He clung on to life for two weeks, but the injuries he had suffered finally proved fatal. The undertaker discouraged the family from viewing his body, saying the image would never leave them.

The family then began asking questions. Was there any connection with a bombing on the same night at McArdle's Bar, Crossmaglen? Why was the nearby security barrier, usually closed, open on the night of the bombing? Why, despite there being fifty-two people injured, did only four people give witness statements? As for McArdle's Bar, the two main mysteries about that attack are why that bar was selected and how the bombers got into, and out of, a predominantly republican village like Crossmaglen – possibly the village most heavily patrolled by the British Army – without detection? Why choose to bomb a bar in Crossmaglen when there were so many other potential targets? Why pick a bar in a village where soldiers patrolled day and night?

It might have appeared impossible, but get in and out the bombers did, after leaving their device at the front of McArdle's Bar, where it exploded at about 11.30 p.m. Rubble and shards of glass were strewn about. Several of the twenty people inside the bar were thrown to the floor, and six of them were injured.[41] Thomas McNamee was sitting close to the door and bore the brunt of the explosion. He was the most severely injured and was rushed to hospital, where his spleen was removed. Eight holes in his bowel were stitched up and he was released from hospital in time for Christmas 1974. The good recovery he appeared to have made, however, was temporary. By June 1975, he was ill again and, six months later, had a serious relapse. Thomas' internal organs had been torn apart: he suffered obstructions, adhesions and infections and died of peritonitis aged fifty-five in November 1975.

Because it had taken Thomas so long to die, the police did not begin a murder enquiry until a year after the explosion. On the night of the bombing, a burnt-out car was discovered half a mile from a major cross-roads in South Armagh known as Ford's Cross. It had been stolen in Portadown days before the bombing. Some wondered if the intended target had been Paddy Short's Bar just around the corner. Paddy was a local character and his bar was a mandatory watering-hole for visiting journalists.

Aside from the link to Portadown (the stolen car) and the divisional commander's view that the UVF was responsible, the only link between the Hughes' and McArdle's bombings and the Mid-Ulster series of killings is a claim from former Armagh SPG member (and convicted murderer), John Weir.[aa] An affidavit sworn by Weir on 3 January 1999,[42] and quoted by the HET in its report, claims that UDR man Robert McConnell carried out the McArdle's attack using a getaway car provided by RUC Reservist James Mitchell and his housekeeper, Lily Shields. No hard evidence has yet been produced to back up his statement – none of the three named was questioned about the attack.[ab]

As the bombs that night at Hughes' and McArdle's Bars took place so close together, were similar in target, without warning and were of roughly the same size and lit with a fuse, the HET considers it likely that they were linked. There was no other loyalist gang operating in the greater Portadown/Armagh area capable of such bombings.

In 1974, loyalists had killed 131 people on both sides of the border, yet the UDR (between 5 and 15 per cent of whose members were in the UDA, UVF and other loyalist groups, according to the British Army's own internal assessment) was playing an increasingly vital role in counter-insurgency with its intelligence-gathering operations strengthened.[43]

The bloodshed continued into 1975.

---

aa Weir was later convicted of murder and claimed in his 1999 affidavit that senior RUC officers knew of collusion between loyalists and police/UDR. See Chapter 9: The 'Short Arm' of the Law.

ab McConnell was also allegedly involved in the Dublin/Monaghan bombings, the shooting of John Francis Green and the killing of Seán Farmer and Colm McCartney. He was shot dead by the IRA in April 1976. For more about Mitchell and Shields, see later chapters.

4

TURNING TO MURDER (1975)

*... since 1972 Catholics have borne the brunt of sectarian murders ...
even this year, for every two Protestant victims there have been about
three Catholic victims.*

*Letter from senior NIO official to the General Officer Commanding
British troops in Northern Ireland, Sir David House, 12 December 1975*

*Sectarian assassination has a loyalist spring. When the loyalists feel
threatened they turn to murder.*

Internal memo from senior British civil servant to colleague, 9 May 1975[1]

The first murder of 1975 took place on the southern side of the
border. On 10 January, republican John Francis (Francie) Green, who
had escaped from Long Kesh internment camp, was shot dead in
disputed circumstances in County Monaghan. His family, and others,
believe that British forces illegally crossed the border to kill him.[a]

On the northern side of the border, exactly a month later and
within three months of their killing of Patrick Falls, the Moygashel
unit of the UVF struck again. This time, the targets were customers
in Hayden's Bar, a quiet country pub with a mixed clientele in the
small village of Gortavale, near Pomeroy, County Tyrone. At around
9 p.m. on 10 February, the door opened and, according to the barman,
machine-gun shots rang out. Witnesses describe a masked gunman
in a blue nylon boiler-suit, and another wearing a khaki coat and a
peaked-cap, who both fired continuously for around two minutes.[2]

When they left, two men lay dead or dying. Arthur Mulholland

---

a   A full account of Green's killing can be found in Chapter 7: Bombs Know No
Borders.

Arthur Mulholland   *Eugene Doyle*

(aged sixty-five) died instantly at the scene, while Eugene Doyle (aged eighteen) died in hospital five hours after the attack. Each had been shot seven times. Four others were wounded. The bar's porch was littered with 9 mm bullet cases. The furniture, spirit bottles and walls were riddled with bullet holes. There were four large pools of blood on the floor, and bar chairs and tables had been upturned as people dived for cover.[3] It was, as one local newspaper described it, a 'holocaust of horror at a lonely roadside bar'.[4]

Eugene had given Arthur a lift to the bar earlier that evening. Both were Catholics, lived in the area and had no political or paramilitary connections. They became the tenth and eleventh victims of loyalist attacks in the Pomeroy area. Even at the time there was a general belief that the attacks were being co-ordinated. The SDLP's Austin Currie said that evidence of the same guns being used showed that the killings were centrally organised.[b]

Although the RUC launched what they called a 'massive man-hunt',[5] the HET review showed glaring omissions and errors in what it calls a 'poor' RUC investigation.[6] Record-keeping was not well managed, intelligence was not followed through, alibi evidence was not checked and 'opportunities to conduct arrest and search operations seem to have been missed'.

More specifically, when suspicion fell on the notorious Moygashel-based brothers Wesley and John Somerville, their alibis were risible –

---

b   One SMG used at Hayden's was also used to kill Daniel Hughes, James and Gertrude Devlin, three members of the Miami Showband, the O'Dowd family and Brendan McLaughlin. The other SMG has been linked to an attempted killing in Coalisland (May 1973), an attack on the Maghery Hotel (June 1973) and the killing of Seán McDonnell and Patrick Falls. The car used was sold by William Nimmons, who was convicted of involvement in the Derrymeen bombing on 31 May 1975.

yet they were never checked.[7] Wesley said he was at a UVF prisoners' meeting at the Golden Hind (a known loyalist haunt) in Portadown. He declined to back this up with the names of anyone else who had been there. John said he was at a 'political meeting' in Moygashel Orange Hall and also declined to offer any back-up evidence. Neither man was arrested. Police may have assumed that both would have simply rustled up witnesses at short notice, but their stories could still have been checked for contradictions. The HET Report calls this a 'missed opportunity' – a judgement some might consider an understatement. In addition, a named source told the RUC that Wesley Somerville was seen in the company of William John Nimmons, who sold the car used on the night of the attack.[c] The name 'Somerville' was also included in two further intelligence items.

According to intelligence reports discovered by the HET within RUC files relating to the Hayden's Bar attack, two of the men had strong security force links and one of them employed a third suspect. 'Man A' in the HET Report is understood to have been a thirty-nine-year-old farm worker, employed by a man identified in the report only as 'Man B' – who is understood to have been a thirty-five-year-old member of the RUC Reserve.[d] 'Suspect 2' (a part-time UDR man and one of two prime suspects in the killings of the Devlins nine months earlier) was named in one source and one anonymous RUC intelligence report as being involved in the Hayden's Bar shooting. As reported earlier, he was arrested in mid-1975 after police searching his home found three guns, ammunition and two bombs. While he was later charged with unlawful possession of firearms and ammunition, the explosives appear to have been overlooked. He was never questioned about the attack at Hayden's. Even more bizarrely, after appealing unsuccessfully for bail on 9 September 1975, he simply disappeared

---

c   Six months after the Hayden's Bar attack, the Miami Showband killings forced an RUC clamp-down on loyalist activity and Nimmons was arrested.

d   Neither man can be named here to avoid prejudicing future legal action.

off the radar. The HET was unable to find any court papers indicating whether he was convicted or acquitted – though it did find 'a note' of some indeterminate kind that he had been convicted.

Questions also arise from the Hayden's attack about a mysterious twenty-five-year-old 'Man from Sandholes' (a townland nearby) named in an anonymous letter to the RUC as behaving suspiciously near the bar just before the attack. The letter-writer claimed that this man had tried to book a flight to New York on the day of the killing. On checking, the RUC discovered this was true but, because he had no passport or visa, he had been unable to travel. When he was arrested, the HET says, he had an explanation for this mysterious behaviour and provided witnesses for his movements on the night of the attack. The HET does not say, however, what these explanations are, and the families are left wondering what could have made anyone attempt to book a flight to New York without a passport.

'Man B', the RUC Reservist named in intelligence as being involved in the shooting, also provided an alibi of sorts to investigating police. He claimed to have been in Liverpool with his wife on the night and the following morning (11 February 1975). The RUC attempted to verify his account. They discovered he had left the hotel not, as he had claimed, on Tuesday 11 February, but at 11.21 p.m. on the previous Sunday, giving him just enough time to return home and take part in the attack. Unaccountably, however, his fellow officers failed to question him about this discrepancy. The HET Report says: 'There is nothing within the case papers that indicates whether this possibility was considered or what further enquiries were carried out.' It appears that 'Man B's' wife was not approached or interviewed either. Summing up its view on the RUC enquiry, the HET says this 'obviously raises questions about possible collusion that cannot be satisfactorily addressed'.

Less than two weeks after the attack on Hayden's Bar, James Breen, a popular forty-five-year-old part-time press photographer and father of two young sons, was having dinner with Kathleen, his wife, after getting home from work in a Lurgan optical factory. There was a knock at the door. James (and his eight-year-old son) went to see who it was and a gunman shot him. With four bullet wounds to his stomach and chest, he died on his way to hospital.

The only connection the family had to anything political was that Kathleen, who ran a home-decorating shop, had a brother, Hugh News, who was a local SDLP spokesman. Loyalists had launched a grenade-and-gun attack on his Lurgan bar on the same night that Patrick Campbell was shot dead, 28 October 1973 (and using the same gun). Kathleen told the inquest that her husband had political views and was not afraid to express them. She thought this might have had something to do with his killing.

Two weeks after James' death, on 6 March, Protestant Edward Clayton was killed when a bomb exploded under his Ford Cortina car. Edward's car had been used in the attack on James Breen, and police had examined but later returned it.[8] Edward was described as a part-time community worker who regularly played guitar at functions for old people in the area. The RUC said Edward was an innocent man and was not connected to any paramilitary organisation. His death remains a mystery.

Even at that time, despite regular sectarian attacks, loyalist leaders still had access to senior government officials. A note of a meeting between UDA leaders and a senior British government representative held on 21 February shows that, as the meeting concluded, the UDA men were advised to go and discuss their concerns about policing at RUC headquarters.[9] Despite having the ear, it seems, of civil servants and senior police officers, loyalists continued to attack and kill Catholics.

Their next victim in Mid-Ulster was Dorothy Trainor, aged fifty-one, who had bridged the great divide. In the bitterly polarised community of Portadown, Dorothy, a Protestant had married a Catholic, Malachy, and they had ten children. On the night of 1 April 1975, she decided to join Malachy at a dance at Portadown's British Legion club, partly to show off a new coat. Between 1 and 2 a.m., as they walked home through the 'People's Park', two gunmen struck. One yelled at Malachy that he was 'going to put a stop to you'.[e] He then grabbed him from behind. The couple tried to make a run for it. Shots rang out and Dorothy fell. As Malachy shouted out that they were 'dirty bastards' and tried to go to her aid, another gunman shot him.[10] He could see his assailant grinning as bullets hit him in the chest and finger. One more shot rang out, hitting him in the neck and knocking him to the ground. He tried to crawl towards Dorothy, who was lying not far away, but then lapsed into unconsciousness. At least six shots had been fired at point blank range, killing Dorothy almost instantly. Malachy was hit three times. The couple lay there in the darkness of the park, bleeding from their wounds, for an hour before they were found.

Malachy was still in intensive care when he discovered Dorothy had died. He was too ill to attend the funeral. Dorothy was buried at the Protestant church at Drumcree (it later became the focus for protests over the re-routing of the annual Orange parade in the town).

'She always had time for a hug, no matter how busy she was. She was a quiet wee woman. Mum was always telling us she loved us, no matter how busy she was cleaning and cooking. Life was brilliant – and then it all went mad.'

Desmond Trainor, Dorothy's son

Dorothy Trainor

The police began their investigations and, for a time, they seemed hopeful. After all, Malachy thought he had recognised one of the gunmen as living in the nearby Edenderry estate. However, despite the RUC making photofit pictures of the two suspects, there is no evidence that these were circulated through the media.[11] There is no

---

e   The Trainor family say Malachy was not involved in political activity of any kind.

evidence either that they were circulated internally to see whether any officer recognised the killers. The enquiry seems to have been superficial, to say the least. The HET states, 'There is nothing ... that records the duration of the investigation, any links made with other enquiries, the result of specific lines of enquiry, why some obvious lines of investigation were not adopted or any comment on progress achieved or reasons for the lack of developments.' No one was ever arrested, interviewed, charged or convicted in relation to the shootings.

No exhibits were recovered other than the bullets, though they told a bloody tale of their own. All had been fired from the same Spanish-made Star 9 mm small-calibre weapon, serial number 344164, originally the personal-issue firearm allocated to UDR Private Robert Winters and stolen from him in March 1973. The Star was eventually recovered in August 1979, over four years after Dorothy's killing. Police arrested serving UDR man David George Teggart, and on land belonging to Norman Greenlee in Richhill, County Armagh, they discovered the Star pistol. The pistol was destroyed in 1982, but the HET is unable to tell the family why Malachy's photofits were never used. 'Available records do not show an effective police investigation,' it says. 'Realistic evidential opportunities seem to have been missed or disregarded.'[12]

A mere two days after the UVF killed Dorothy Trainor, it launched another attack in Portadown. This time, its victim was a young man who had just moved into a new home with his wife, who was four months pregnant with their first child. Martin McVeigh had no paramilitary or political connections and was cycling home from work when he was singled out and shot down in cold blood, less than a mile from where Dorothy had been killed.

The night her husband was killed, Deirdre McVeigh was at home waiting for him, having prepared a light supper. At the end of his shift, Martin fetched his bicycle and set off for the short ride home when a gunman stepped in front of him and shot him once in the chest. Two children who witnessed the shooting said they had the impression of a confrontation before the shots rang out. They saw sparks, two men beside Martin, and then his falling body. The two men bent over Martin before running off.

Isobel, Martin's sister, passed by in a friend's car within seconds of the shooting. She saw Martin standing beside his fallen bicycle, one arm over his chest and the other up in the air as if to say 'Stop'. As the car drove past, Isobel looked around but could no longer see Martin. She shouted to the driver to stop. Leaping out, she saw her brother lying on the ground. She rushed to his side and tried to lift him up. He did not appear to be bleeding, but Isobel instinctively knew something was badly wrong. She feared he had had a convulsion or heart attack and whispered in his ear, 'You'll be all right, son, you'll be all right.' But unknown to her, a bullet had been fired straight through Martin's chest. Someone in the crowd said there had been shots, but Isobel didn't think her brother had been shot as there was no blood. An ambulance was called, but Martin was dead by the time it reached Craigavon Hospital.

'Martin was the youngest of seven children, the baby of the family. He was mad into hurling. He loved going out and wearing the latest fashions.'

Eddie McVeigh, Martin's brother,

'He loved music: The Beatles, The Stones, Led Zeppelin. He loved Irish traditional music as well.'

Deirdre McKee, Martin's widow

Martin McVeigh

The gunmen had fled in a blue Vauxhall Viva car with an Armagh registration number beginning AIB. There were only 157 such cars in Northern Ireland at the time. Nine detectives traced all of them within four months. It was good police work. However, none of the owners admitted to being in the area. Police suspicions about the vehicle increased. It became their main line of enquiry. But the trail went cold. Although the police were 'convinced' that a blue Vauxhall Viva car had been used by the gunmen, this, inexplicably, was never followed up beyond identifying the owners. 'Clearly,' says the HET Report, 'this should have been done. The vehicle owners should have been further researched and a structured elimination process created ... These lines of enquiry should have been more robustly pursued, and, as later events would show, a significant investigative opportunity was missed.'[13] One of the 157 car owners, as it turned out, was the father of Garfield Gerald Beattie, a member of the TAVR,[f] who was later convicted of three other killings.[g] Beattie is also strongly suspected of involvement in killing another three people in the near-simultaneous attacks on the Eagle Bar and Clancy's Bar in Charlemont on 15 May 1975.[h] Had the RUC followed through on its main line of enquiry – the Vauxhall Viva car used by the killers to escape after shooting Martin – it would have led to Beattie. It is clearly very possible that the lives of these six people (and possibly others, as Beattie was a prolific murderer) would have been spared.

The gun used to kill Martin was an Enfield .38 revolver (one of the weapons stolen in the UVF raid on 23 October 1973 from E Company 11 UDR depot at Fort Seagoe, Portadown).[i] It was in a follow-up search after this raid that the cache of arms and explosives was found on Winston Buchanan's land and he told police that Robin Jackson was one of three people who had forced him to keep the cache. This, however, is far from being the only link between Jackson and the killing of Martin McVeigh. Four years after Martin was killed, police stopped a car near Portadown and arrested the three men inside. They were Robin Jackson and two other notorious loyalists, Philip

---

f   Beattie joined the TAVR on 24 September 1974, and was still a member at the time of the attack on Clancy's Bar and the Eagle Bar on 15 May 1976 (HET Report – Fred McLoughlin).

g   Denis Mullen, 1 September 1975; Fred McLoughlin, shot 15 May 1976, died 31 May 1976; and Patsy McNeice, 25 July 1976.

h   Vincy Clancy, Seán O'Hagan and Robert McCullough.

i   A raid, described by the HET as likely to have been collusive, on the armoury used by Robin Jackson's UDR unit.

'Shilly' Silcock and John Thompson.[j] Police retrieved a weapon from inside the car. It was the Enfield .38 pistol used to kill Martin McVeigh. Despite the fact that Jackson (and the two others) had been caught red-handed in possession of a murder weapon, police did not interview them about Martin's killing. The HET says this is 'inexplicable'. (The McVeigh family is currently taking a complaint to the NI police ombudsman seeking an explanation.)

Meanwhile, Jackson's charmed life continued and the UVF and UDA remained legal.

* * *

Killyliss is the name of a townland, little more than a crossroads, among green fields in the Tyrone countryside south-west of Dungannon. Over a hill to the north of the crossroads is the nearest village, the mainly Protestant Castlecaulfield. At Drumhirk, between Castlecaulfield and Killyliss, lived Marian Bowen (aged twenty-one), who was due to give birth around 7 May. She had been working as a hairdresser in Manchester, but had come home to Ireland to marry Thomas Bowen (aged twenty-three). The couple were living with his mother, Eileen. Eileen had really taken to her son's young wife and everyone was looking forward to the baby's imminent arrival.

The Bowens had lived for generations in a small cottage at Killyliss, but it had fallen into disrepair. Thomas had plans to move his new wife and baby into this old family homestead, and he and Marian were spending every available moment renovating it in preparation for the baby's arrival.[14] Thomas, who was working in a butcher's shop in nearby Ballygawley, travelled to the bungalow in Killyliss after

---

j   Five months after Martin McVeigh's murder, according to Special Branch daily record sheets, cited in ECHR Brecknell v the United Kingdom judgment (2008, pp. 4, 12), Silcock was involved the bombing at Donnelly's Bar that killed Trevor Brecknell, Patsy Donnelly and Michael Donnelly. He is identified as 'Suspect T' who was also cited in the Barron Report (2006, p. 115) as a suspect in the deaths of Colm McCartney and Seán Farmer.

work every evening, as well as on his Wednesday half-day, and after lunch every Sunday. The renovations were coming on well. Marian was painting the walls and picking out curtains. A neighbour was working on the pipes to the hot-water cylinder.

On Sunday 20 April, Marian and Thomas would normally have been at the cottage, but instead they decided to visit her mother at Altedavin, a few miles south towards County Monaghan, staying up late playing cards with her two brothers, Michael (aged twenty-nine) and Seamus (aged twenty-three). Michael knew a bit about plumbing and offered to take a look at the new hot-water cylinder the following morning before going with Seamus (who worked on the family farm) to buy agricultural machinery.

On Monday morning, Thomas went into work in Ballygawley as usual. Michael and Seamus left the family home at Altedavin and drove north to the cottage at Killyliss.[15] Marian drove south from her mother-in-law's home at Drumhirk to meet them there. No one saw Michael, Seamus or Marian alive again. By 12.50 p.m. the three of them were blown, quite literally, to pieces. Marian's baby girl was dead too. Nothing was left of the new curtains or freshly painted walls. The cottage was reduced to splintered planks of wood, corrugated iron, and lumps of concrete. Pieces of the copper immersion tank had been turned into lethal shrapnel and littered the fields and lanes.

Thomas arrived on the scene about ten minutes later and had to be restrained from rushing into the ruins. A priest told him there were no survivors. A doctor at the scene sedated him before pronouncing the brothers and sister dead at 1.30 p.m.[16]

Arrangements were made to have the three bodies taken to the nearest morgue in Dungannon. During a post-mortem examination, a pathologist quickly noticed that Marian had been heavily pregnant. But where was the baby? The hospital contacted police back at the cottage and asked them to look for another body: the body of a baby. That afternoon, they found the infant girl, lying under heavy rubble in the ruins of what had once been a bedroom. She had been blown clear out of her mother's body. She had a beautiful head of dark hair just like her mother. She would have died instantly. An unspeakable grief descended on the entire McKenna and Bowen families that has never faded.

| Marian Bowen | Michael McKenna | Seamus McKenna |

'Seamus was very quiet, a serious man. Michael loved laughing and impersonating people. When Marian was a prefect, she wouldn't stand for any nonsense on the school bus. She was determined, she was sporty and she loved a laugh. Our Mother never, ever recovered from the shock of losing all three – and her granddaughter.'

Bridget Carr, sister of Marian, Seamus and Michael

Deeply upsetting for the grieving family was an incident on the evening of the explosion. As the local undertaker, Massie McAleer, was loading the baby's coffin into a hearse to be taken to the morgue, British soldiers, standing around, laughed. Some even kicked the wheels of the hearse. Questioned by the HET in 2011, Mr McAleer still remembered the incident. With its customary understatement, the HET Report says his testimony 'makes uncomfortable reading'. What happened to the family 'whilst trying to come to terms with the loss of their loved ones cannot be excused,' it says.

As the family mourned, the RUC began investigating the triple killing. The hot-water cylinder had been installed the previous Wednesday behind cupboard doors in a corner. Forensic tests showed it had been the seat of the explosion. The police conducted house-to-house enquiries. Nobody had seen anything suspicious. A number of

British Army checkpoints had been in place in the hours before the bombing. None reported anything unusual.

The day after the explosion, a local constable reported that he had seen a lorry on a country road on Saturday 19 April. The driver, aged about twenty, and his 'mate', aged about seventeen, had asked for directions to the Bowens' cottage. Thomas said it was not a genuine delivery as none was due that weekend. In any case, everything was being ordered from a local firm that already knew the roads. The HET considers this to be of 'significant importance', but there is nothing to suggest the constable was questioned and it is not known whether the driver and his companion were treated as suspects or if any further enquiries were made about them.

The British Army technical officer estimated the bomb contained between fifteen and twenty-five pounds (6.8–11 kg) of explosives and was placed two feet (61 cm) above the ground inside the cupboard near the hot-water cylinder. It had been detonated electronically by the opening of the cupboard door.

Four days after the bombing, Fr Denis Faul accused the authorities of 'wilful neglect'. Despite seventeen recent assassinations, he said, there had been no arrests. This amounted to a 'one hundred per cent failure rate' by the police to protect Catholic lives. Former British soldiers and those expelled from the UDR should be checked out, he said. It was extraordinary that 'people whose names were raised time and time again were not given a brisk interrogation without any of the twenty-eight methods of brutality that had made the RUC infamous throughout Europe'.[17]

Then two developments threw a great deal more light on the terrible tragedy at Killyliss. First, on 30 April, the Banbridge unit of the Protestant Action Force (PAF)[k] admitted responsibility for three

---

k   Regarded as a cover name for the UVF to distance itself from murders that caused unusually high levels of public condemnation.

attacks in which eight people had died: Killyliss, the Bleary Darts Club killings (see below) and the killing of Owen Boyle (also below).

Another, and even more significant, development came when a very similar (though non-fatal) attack was mounted six weeks later, just seven miles (11 km) from Killyliss, at another townland near Dungannon, called Derrymeen. On 31 May 1975, at 5.15 a.m., a bomb exploded at a bungalow under construction belonging to a local Catholic man about to be married. It contained between five and ten pounds (2.3–4.5 kg) of commercial explosives and was detonated using an alarm clock mechanism. The detonation of two bombs at two Catholic-owned homes, both under renovation for young couples, so close together in both time and place, was highly unusual. It could hardly be a coincidence.

There was to be no breakthrough on the Derrymeen bombing, however, until the Miami Showband massacre on 31 July 1975. Between 1 and 5 August, investigating police in the hunt for the Miami Showband killers arrested, among others, three loyalists from the Moygashel/Dungannon area: Laurence Tate (aged twenty-five), a full-time UDR man (who conveniently pre-dated his resignation to the day of the Derrymeen bombing),[1] Howard Henry McKay (aged twenty-five) and William John Nimmons (aged forty-five). The three were all eliminated from the Miami Showband investigation but admitted involvement in the Derrymeen bombing, leading to convictions for causing an explosion and the possession of explosives, and to twelve- and ten-year concurrent prison sentences.

With three men in custody for the Derrymeen explosion, with its striking similarities to the Killyliss blast, it seems obvious that they

---

1   Tate joined the UDR on 10 August 1971 and was still a member when he was arrested in August 1975. In custody and having made admissions, he requested a discharge and was allowed to give his date of resignation as 31 May 1975, two months earlier, the date of the Derrymeen bombing in which he admitted involvement, a date the HET says is 'hardly likely to be coincidental'.

should have been questioned about the bombing that killed Marian, her baby, Seamus and Michael. Yet they seem not to have been. The only record the HET could find linking the three men to Killyliss is a short police statement saying that the three 'made no comment about the Bowens'. The HET, in unusually strong language, concludes that, given the proximity of the bombings, the 'denomination of the victims and the type of explosion, it is incomprehensible that the officer in charge of the case did not consider the connection'.

When Tate came to court, he was described as a 'former' UDR man. He had resigned on the day of his arrest. The HET says this is far from being unique. In other cases, it says, it has also come across incidents when 'an individual facing prosecution has had their security force service records altered … to remove the link between security force members and illegal activities, or to protect the name of the security force organisation'.[18]

The McKenna and Bowen families are left with many unanswered questions and a grief that passes from one generation to the next.

The next person to die was Owen Boyle. He had been shot before the bombing that killed the four at Killyliss, but survived until 22 April. Owen and his wife, Winnie (sister of Francis McCaughey, who was killed in the cow-byre bombing eighteen months previously), lived near the village of Aughnacloy. He had started off in life with very little. One of eleven children, brought up in South Tyrone, he had by the age of forty, through sheer hard work and ingenuity, started his own small business. He was a welder by trade, but that description does not do him justice. He was known, far and wide, for his ability to fix, or replace, just about anything needing repair on a farm. A lifelong Pioneer (a member of an Irish organisation for Catholic teetotallers), he and Winnie were raising eight children in a brand new home on a scrap of land he had bought from a Protestant neighbour outside the town. The only organisation in which he was involved was the GAA.

On 11 April 1975, Winnie was washing the dishes and talking

Owen Boyle

to Owen about a new camera she had bought so they could take photos of their youngest daughter, Noreen. Owen was standing directly opposite the kitchen window. The house was so new it had no curtains. Winnie said, 'Seven of the children were in the front room. Owen and I were talking in the kitchen at the back. I heard a rattle and thought at first it was a fault in the radiators … Then Owen staggered past me and more bullets kept on coming through the window. I guided him to the sitting room, made him as comfortable as possible, and ran for help.'[19]

The parish priest arrived, then a doctor. Owen was still conscious and asking why this had happened to him. He 'wasn't involved in anything'. The sergeant who called to the scene remembers his words: 'Ah sergeant, why should they do this to me? I never did anything to no man.'[20]

Owen had obvious multiple wounds to his abdomen, chest, left shoulder and chin. But internally it was worse than that. He had taken two bullets in his left lung and had serious internal injuries. He and Winnie travelled to hospital by ambulance, where Owen had emergency surgery and then began to show signs of improvement. Over the next few days, though, his condition worsened and he died on 22 April.

A police investigation began, but the HET can find no evidence that any scenes-of-crime examination was made at the back of the house, from where the gunmen had fired at Owen. House-to-house enquiries drew a blank; vehicle checkpoints before and after the murder did not provide any new leads, nor did public appeals. No one was questioned, arrested, charged or convicted in relation to Owen's murder, but the six bullets recovered told a story that links Owen's case to many others. Three had been cruelly doctored with a cross sawn into the nose to give them a 'dum-dum' effect (to cause maximum damage on impact).[m] The killers had used two guns: a .38 Webley-type revolver and a .455 Smith & Wesson. The second was linked to five other killings and attempted killings between June 1973 and November 1974 – all attributed to the UVF.[n]

Neither weapon has been recovered and there is no ballistic information to suggest they were used again after Owen's murder. No motive was ever established other than naked sectarianism. There are pointers, however, as to why he, rather than any other local Catholic, was singled out, which relate to his relative business success and his purchase of land to build his house (which had previously been part of a Protestant-owned farm and whose owner had suffered some local criticism for daring to sell it to a Catholic). Winnie never spent another night in that house. She lived for the next three months with Owen's family before the parish raised enough money to put a deposit on a small house opposite the church in Aughnacloy. Since the murder, the Boyle family has searched repeatedly for reasons. Was it just that local loyalists had been jealous of Owen's business success?

One man, in particular, was openly resentful. One day, two of the younger Boyle children were walking with the family dog when he drove his car straight at them, forcing them to jump off the road and killing the dog outright. Another local businessman, an officer in the UDR, was also openly hostile to Winnie.[21]

Not long after Owen finally lost his fight for life, the UVF struck again, about thirty miles (48 km) away. At that time, if you knew where to look in the countryside just south of Lurgan, you could drive down a muddy lane to an unprepossessing building. It was, despite its humble appearance, the rather grandly named 'Bleary Darts Club' – a popular

---

m   Dum-dum bullets (first manufactured at the British arsenal at Dum Dum near Calcutta and banned under international conventions) expand or fragment after hitting the target.

n   The attempted murder of two men at The Argory, County Armagh, in June 1973; and the murders of Francis and Bernadette Mullan, Daniel Hughes, Gertrude and James Devlin and Patrick Falls.

haunt of a group of friends and neighbours who ran it themselves. The people who lived around were of mixed religions, and the darts club was the same. Religion and politics as subjects of conversation were banned by the management, such as it was. Joe Toman was in charge and he did not take kindly to anyone breaking this rule. Joe was a joiner, aged forty-seven and a non-drinker. Three years previously, he had come upon the aftermath of an IRA bombing and had gone to the assistance of the injured British soldiers. He was also the father of six children aged between thirteen and twenty-one. They, and his wife, Betty, idolised him.

Though few outside its immediate neighbourhood had ever heard of the Bleary Darts Club, its happy anonymity was about to end. At about 10.40 p.m. on 27 April, the door of the club was kicked open and, with no warning, three gunmen fired into the groups of customers. There were about thirty men inside enjoying a late Sunday-night drink.

Michael Green, who had been at the club for about two hours, saw the perforated black muzzle of a Sterling SMG poking its nose inside the door. He threw himself to the floor. The firing stopped. Someone had the presence of mind, and the bravery, to turn off the lights. Then there was a second burst of gunfire followed by several single shots, then someone else had the courage to kick the door shut. Michael Green lifted his head and, even in the limited light, could see three of his friends lying beside the fireplace and the door.

From where he had been standing outside, Jim Feeney saw the flashes of gunfire. He thought there were around forty. He heard the getaway car leaving the scene before he ran inside the club to find his father, John, and two others lying dead or dying.° Three men (Joe Toman, Brendan O'Hara and John Feeney) had been fatally wounded, while another customer, a Protestant, was seriously wounded.

---

o   Jim Feeney never recovered from the experience of witnessing his father's killing and, some time later, took his own life.

Joe Toman

'I can still remember the smell of him – wood and putty – his work smell. He was always spick-and-span. You could have seen your face in his polished shoes. He was great with his hands. He once built a boat. Dad missed out on so much. Life was never the same again.'

Eileen McCann, Joe Toman's daughter

Joe Toman was rushed to hospital but had been shot through the head and had died almost instantly. Coming to the scene five minutes after the shooting, Joe's son-in-law, Eugene McCann, saw what he swears to this day was an SMG, propped up on what looked like a tripod, silhouetted in the headlamps of police vehicles in the yard outside the club. He also remembers seeing at least one box of Eley No. 4 shotgun cartridges. The police apparently did not notice either the gun or the box of ammunition. There has never been any explanation as to where they came from or subsequently disappeared to. The clubhouse walls were pitted with thirty-one bullet holes. The gunmen had sprayed the inside of the room, moving their fire in a clockwise direction. Forensic tests showed a 9 mm Sterling SMG, a Webley .455 calibre revolver and a twelve-bore shotgun had been used.

RUC enquiries focused on five weapons thefts, including three from British Army armouries. Nothing useful was discovered. But they had more luck with the Webley. It was spotted by a member of the public on farmland near Donaghcloney, County Down.[p] They had even more luck with the Sterling – it was found three months later at the scene of the Miami Showband massacre.[q]

p One month before the Bleary attack, the Webley had been used in the attempted murder of Paul McNeice at Ardress, County Armagh (14 March 1975), for which Stuart Ashton was convicted. He was also convicted of a large number of other offences including the bombing of Traynor's Bar on 19 February 1974.

q The Sterling was originally held at RUC Central Stores before it was transferred to the Ulster Special Constabulary at Donaghcloney, County Down, from where it was reported stolen in 1970.

The RUC say they carried out house-to-house searches that night (though this is hotly disputed by local people, who insist there were none). The following morning they raided Eugene McCann's house with a summons accusing him of transporting illegal alcohol. Joe's body had not even been brought home at that time.

Eugene himself was never interviewed. The RUC do not appear to have carried out any fingerprinting at the club either.[22] There was scant intelligence about the attack. Eugene, if the police had interviewed him, could have told them he had seen Robin Jackson, exactly a week before the attack, in a car with another man scouting the area. The car's side windows had been misted up when Eugene first saw it. It had driven past him, done a U-turn and driven back towards him. This time a front window had been wound down and Eugene had an umimpeded view of the passenger. He recognised him instantly. It was Robin Jackson. It had scared Eugene. He knew Jackson to be a loyalist with a reputation for yelling abuse at young Catholics passing his front door.[23] Jackson's driver, said Eugene, was a UDR man he recognised. (He is understood to be a man named in one of the police intelligence reports relating to the darts club shooting, and was later shot dead by the IRA close to the border.)

The RUC closed down the investigation just two weeks after the triple killing.[24] It could hardly be dignified with the title 'investigation' – more a 'box-ticking' exercise. The bereaved families, of course, never forgot the three dead or the horror of the night when gunmen burst into the club and opened fire on the defenceless people inside. Even now, every single Sunday evening of her life, at the precise time of the attack, Joe Toman's daughter, Eileen, gets up from her seat and meticulously goes around her home, closing curtains and locking doors as if she could lock out the memories and the death of her father.[25]

Geography might not, at first sight, appear to link the death of Castlewellan man Francis Rice, a seventeen-year-old Catholic killed in Rathfriland, County Down, to this series of murders. On 18 May 1975, he was abducted as he walked home late at night, was viciously stabbed to death and his body left on the roadside. In claiming his murder, the Protestant Action Force (a UVF cover name) said they had killed him because he was linked to the Official IRA. Three years later, *An Phoblacht/Republican News* (the Provisional Sinn Féin newspaper) named him as a member of the Provisional IRA. Someone with information that Francis was a republican (albeit they named the wrong group) had clearly passed information to the killers. The link to the Bleary Darts Club killing comes with John Weir's claim that Robin Jackson was involved (though Jackson's favoured *modus operandi* was more usually an SMG).[26]

On 24 May 1975, the UVF tried to kill the entire Grew family of eight by bombing their home in the village of Moy. Six children were inside when the bombers struck. Though most of the house was destroyed and the children were taken to hospital, none was badly wounded. In 1981 a serving UDR soldier, Derek McFarland, and Stuart Ashton were convicted of involvement in this and many other offences.[r] During interviews, Ashton told the police that Ted Sinclair drove a scout car, and that Sinclair and two others had made the bomb at his farm.

On 27 July 1975, leading Portadown loyalist Billy Hanna, a former UDR man, was shot dead by UVF associates including Robin Jackson,[27] possibly because they believed he had become a British agent – or simply in one of many internal UVF power-struggles.[s] Among those

---

r   McFarland served from May 1969 to October 1970 as an RUC constable; from 9 July 1972 to 24 October 1975 as a Ministry of Defence constable based at Castledillon, County Armagh; and from November 1975 to 1977 as a private in the UDR (dismissed from the UDR in 1977). McFarland was therefore a member of the UDR at the time of the bombing of the Grew family home.

s   In 1951, Hanna won a Military Medal in Korea. He was dismissed from the UDR in 1973 when he was found to be in possession of illegal ammunition. The Webley used to kill him was used in two other attempted murders and a post office robbery at Scarva, for which loyalist Sammy McCoo was convicted. The gun was allegedly involved in murdering Billy Hanna was Harris Boyle, who, just four days later, died in a premature explosion as he tried to kill members of the Miami Showband.

At that time, one of the very few places in Northern Ireland at which young Protestants and Catholics could meet was a showband dance. Most towns had a dance hall and they were also dotted around the countryside on both sides of the border. In July 1975, Francis (Fran) O'Toole, a handsome young man with a ready smile, was the lead singer fronting the Miami Showband. The group was mixed – two of its regular members were Protestant. Religion and politics didn't matter to them. But for at least two people watching carefully in the audience in Banbridge on the last day of July 1975, religion did matter.

The UVF wanted to give the impression that these 'Irish' show-bands were involved in something sinister. The plan was to set up a bogus UDR checkpoint as the band left Banbridge, stop them on the main road, hide a bomb inside the vehicle under cover of 'searching' it and then wave them on down the road to Dublin. When the bomb exploded, it would kill the eyewitnesses to the bogus checkpoint. The gang wanted people to assume that the band was carrying explosives and weapons across the border, and every showband in Ireland would then become suspect.

Whoever dreamed this up must have congratulated himself on a cunning plan. What could possibly go wrong? Two men, seen by a doorman to be behaving suspiciously (they were both older than the young audience members, and one swore at him), are believed to have attended the dance to make sure the band left as planned. The scouts then alerted their associates waiting on the main road to Newry. Everything was in place. All the gang had to do was wait until

---

recovered in a hedge near Portadown on 11 November 1976 alongside a Sauer automatic pistol used in the Miami Showband attack.

The Miami Showband

they saw the minibus leaving Banbridge for Dublin. In Banbridge, the band's drummer, Raymond Millar, left to drive home to Antrim. The band's road manager, Brian Maguire, had agreed to give two girls a lift to Newry. As he drove there, he noticed a Triumph car driving first behind him, then overtaking him at speed, and then slowing down again, but he drove on without further incident.[t]

Brian McCoy, the band's trumpet player, was driving a second minibus carrying everyone else home. Des McAlea, the band's saxophonist, remembers seeing men dressed in what appeared to be UDR uniforms, one of whom stepped out into the road, waving the usual red lamp. The minibus halted at the junction of the main Belfast–Newry road and Buskhill Road – a minor country lane that led to Robin Jackson's home village of Donaghmore.

Brian explained to the UDR men who they were. Fran suggested Brian pull closer into the kerb to avoid a collision with traffic coming up behind them. Stephen Travers (bass guitarist) remembers Brian being quite relaxed. The band members were ordered out of the minibus and told to stand in line with their backs to the main road. A gang

---

t   A Triumph car was later discovered to belong to an associate of Jackson, Portadown loyalist Samuel Fulton Neill, himself later murdered in an internal dispute.

member, in full UDR uniform, began collecting names and dates of birth. Two UVF men, Wesley Somerville and Harris Boyle, began 'searching' the vehicle. Stephen was worried they might damage the instruments and had a few words with them. Somerville and Boyle lifted their bomb into the rear of the minibus. It consisted of ten pounds (4.5 kg) of explosives, a wrist-watch timing device and an electric detonator. Almost immediately, the device exploded, killing instantly both Somerville (who was blown into a field) and Boyle (who was blown the opposite direction, into the roadway). The minibus was destroyed.

The shockwave hurled the band's five members through a hedge which was set on fire. Des McAlea, in the light of the flames from the burning vehicle, saw Brian McCoy lying beside him and Stephen Travers badly injured. Quickly telling Stephen he was going to get help, Des ran back into the road, past the burning minibus and towards a car that stopped and took him to Newry. Stephen can remember being in pain and everything seeming to happen in slow-motion – his friends Fran O'Toole and Tony Geraghty (lead guitar) fell on top of him through the hedge.

Fran and Tony, however, were not seriously injured. Recovering quickly, rather than running away and saving themselves, they began dragging Stephen further away from the burning minibus. The surviving UVF men then opened fire, killing Fran, Tony and Brian. Stephen was also injured further, though it had not yet sunk in that he had been shot. He managed to crawl to the edge of the field.

At least one of the killers had paid particular attention to Fran. He was shot between eighteen and twenty-one times in the face, head, neck, right shoulder and chest. Other bullet wounds to his right forearm indicated he had been shot at close range. Police found a Sterling SMG in the hedge and a .38 Enfield (Albion Mk II) Smith & Wesson-type revolver lying in the roadway.

Within twelve hours of the killings, the UVF issued a self-serving press statement:

A UVF patrol led by Major Boyle was suspicious of two vehicles, a minibus and a car parked near the border. Major Boyle ordered his patrol to apprehend the occupants for questioning. As they were being questioned, Major Boyle and Lieutenant Somerville began to search the minibus. As they began to enter the vehicle, a bomb was detonated and both men were killed outright.

At the precise moment of the explosion, the patrol came under fire from the occupants of the other vehicle. The patrol Sergeant immediately ordered fire to be returned. Using self-loading rifles and sub-machine guns, the patrol returned fire, killing three of their attackers and wounding another.

This entire statement was not only untrue – it was demonstrably so. The UVF 'patrol' never came under fire. There was no car. The 'occupants of the other vehicle', far from firing, were themselves savagely mown down. *Combat*, the UVF newsletter, blatantly carried a UDR sympathy note: 'The Portadown, Lurgan and Dungannon UDR Centres deeply regret the tragic death of their colleagues-in-arms, Major Harris Boyle and Lieutenant Wesley Sommerville [*sic*]'. This UDR reference was spotted in Dublin. The Irish Ambassador in London raised it with an official at the Foreign and Commonwealth Office, who told him that, 'naturally', enquiries had already been made.[28] In the margin of the note, however, the same official had written, 'We must look into this.' So, it appears London was spinning Dublin a line.

The police went about their work, photographing the scene, cataloguing exhibits and interviewing witnesses.[u] Within three weeks they had arrested sixteen men. Among them was UDR man Thomas Raymond Crozier, taken from his home in early August. The RUC, this time, appeared to be acting with commendable zeal.

---

u   An unexplained line of enquiry was one detective's theological conversation with John Somerville before writing his statement of admission of guilt on 23 September 1980.

Searches and arrests continued apace and with some sense of urgency. The two governments, for the first time, issued a joint statement. Not that London and Dublin were entirely singing from the same hymn sheet. London was irritated by claims from Dublin of 'security force involvement', which, it said, were 'totally without foundation and were rightly repudiated'.[29]

Five days later the British were forced to backtrack. A Northern Ireland Office civil servant noted to a colleague in the Foreign Office that he had officially informed the Irish Ambassador to London that a serving UDR man had been charged with murder.[30] While this was 'unfortunate', he said, there was 'always the risk of the bad hat [*sic*] in any large organisation'. The RUC, he said, were 'pretty certain' that they knew the identities of all involved, but 'there seemed no prospect of charging any others with murder – evidence was not available'. Either the civil servants or the RUC were wrong. In the end, three men were convicted of the murders: UDR man James Roderick Shane McDowell (arrested at Robin Jackson's home in Lurgan[v]), UDR man Thomas Raymond Crozier and loyalist John Somerville.[w]

The Miami Showband massacre had taken place close to Jackson's home turf of Donaghmore. He was by then well known (to the police) as a loyalist killer. It must have been as plain as day that Jackson was involved. Arrested on 5 August, he was questioned about the deaths but claimed police had mistreated him and he was released without charge two days later.[x] That was it as far as Jackson was

---

v   McDowell was found in Jackson's home by police searching for the killers of Peter and Jane McKearney on 23 October 1975. Released almost immediately, McDowell was, however, discharged from the UDR because of his association with Jackson. He was rearrested in January 1976 after evidence from the Miami Showband scene implicated him.

w   Somerville was arrested first, soon after the attack (18 August), and was re-arrested in September 1980, five years later, when he made admissions of guilt (along with confessing to the murder of Patrick Falls in November 1974).

x   The two CID officers Jackson accused of punching him were found guilty and fined £10 each, but were acquitted on appeal.

concerned, until 18 May 1976, when, in an unrelated police enquiry, the proverbial smoking gun emerged through the miasma.

For reasons still unknown, on that date farmer and former B Special Ted Sinclair was arrested and a weapons cache (guns, explosives and bomb-making equipment) was found on his substantial farm at Canary in County Armagh. It would appear that Sinclair made admissions to police about at least one other weapon on his property because, in highly unusual circumstances, he was allowed to return to his farm, ostensibly to milk his cows, in the company of Detective Chief Inspector Frank Murray, no less.[y] While in the milking shed, Murray discovered a Luger pistol behind a wall fan. The Luger was intact, its magazine containing four bullets. Alongside the gun, though not attached, was a home-made silencer – a long, metal tube wrapped in black insulating tape. The muzzle end of the gun had been drilled to accept a fixing grub-screw on the silencer. The two clearly belonged together. The HET reported that when Murray questioned Sinclair about the Luger, Sinclair replied that 'a boy' had left the gun with him five weeks earlier.[31]

The Luger, silencer and magazine were then separated and put into three exhibit bags for fast-track forensic examination. Sergeant Hillis of the RUC fingerprint laboratory carefully removed the sticky tape from the silencer and discovered two of Jackson's fingerprints on the metal barrel. The police then made a significant discovery. The Luger had been used at the Miami Showband massacre. They now had a link between it and Jackson. But the story gets even more interesting. Someone within the RUC's fingerprint department had made a minor error. They noted, wrongly, that Jackson's prints had been found on both the tape and the barrel. For ten days after 20 May (when the police had discovered Jackson's prints on the Luger linked

---

y   The HET Report on the Miami Showband calls this a 'ruse' to prevent other loyalists discovering Sinclair's co-operation with police.

to the Miami Showband killings) they made attempts to find and arrest him, without result (but were later successful). By that time, then Detective Superintendent Ernest Drew had been given the correct information, that Jackson's fingerprints had been found only on the metal silencer, but not on the tape. For whatever reason, Drew kept this information to himself and went to interview his suspect. Did he imagine that other officers were protecting Jackson?

Drew placed the Luger, the metal silencer and the magazine – but not the tape – on an interview table between himself and Jackson. Jackson denied handling any of them. Drew asked him if he would have an explanation, should his fingerprints be found on the pistol, the silencer or both? Jackson again denied handling any of the items, but suddenly, and unprompted, began to volunteer information. Though there was no insulating tape on the table in front of him, he began to explain why his fingerprints might be found on such a piece of tape – should it exist. Jackson went on to say that he had been helping out at the Portadown Loyalist Club one night. Sinclair was also there. Sinclair had asked Jackson for some tape. Jackson then told Drew he had provided Sinclair with part of a roll of tape he was using behind the bar.

Drew may have asked Jackson at this point where this talk of tape had come from? Whether he did or not, Jackson made a written and sworn statement. It said that on 24 May (a week before his arrest) a detective superintendent and a detective sergeant, neither of whom he named, had told him that his fingerprints had been found on tape wrapped around a metal silencer. Further, he said, the same officers had told him that he 'should clear [sic] as there was a wee job up the country that I would be done for and there was no way out of it for me' (verbatim quote taken from RUC notes quoted in the HET Report on the Miami Showband attack). Drew now had a statement from Jackson explaining why his prints might have been found on the sticky tape. His prints, however, had never been found there.

Only police officers could have seen the note, produced by their own fingerprint department, wrongly stating that Jackson's prints had been found on the tape. Only police officers could have given Jackson the incorrect information. For reasons that remain unexplained, it appears Jackson was never re-interviewed about his involvement in the Miami Showband killings.

'There is nothing within the case papers,' says the HET Report, 'that established whether or not Jackson was re-interviewed about the murders of Fran and the other members ... whilst in custody at Armagh, or even whether the investigation team was informed of these developments'. The HET says it 'would have expected to find some record that he had been interviewed about the murders, and that the murder enquiry team had been updated about his arrest and the recovery of one of the weapons used in the murders'. [32]

It is worth repeating here what had just happened. The RUC had ballistic evidence (the Luger) linking Jackson to the Miami massacre, they had Jackson's claim that fellow officers had tipped him off, and they had evidence arising from Drew's decision to conceal the mistake over the location of the fingerprints. Drew reported what had happened to his Divisional Commander at Armagh, Chief Superintendent William Harrison, stating that Jackson appeared to have been informed (wrongly) as to where his fingerprints had been found and that he had been tipped off about this a week before his arrest. Drew's confidential internal RUC report stated that, if the allegation was true, it constituted a 'grave breach of discipline and police confidentiality on the part of the officers concerned'. [33] Drew also told Harrison that he had referred this aspect of the case to the RUC Complaints and Discipline Department for investigation.

It is unclear what happened to Drew's complaint from that stage onwards (this is subject to further investigation by the NI police ombudsman). The HET says, however, that on 29 July 1976, Drew's full report – along with Harrison's recommendations – went to RUC

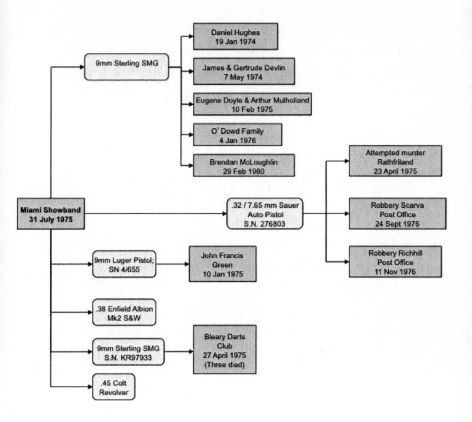

Ballistic links between the Miami Showband and other attacks

headquarters. It was then allocated to a superintendent for assessment and recommendations – which was the requirement before any further decision by the DPP. So far, so good.

The superintendent, however, while sending Drew's report to the DPP (it is unclear what happened to Harrison's input) attached a one-page note confined to legal issues over Jackson's alleged possession of the Luger and ammunition. The note to the DPP remarked: 'in his opinion there was no evidence that Jackson ever had the items in his possession and it could not be proven that Jackson was the "boy" Sinclair referred to' when Murray first asked him about the Luger found in his cowshed. The upshot is that, when Jackson stood trial in November 1976, the only charge he faced was possession of the silencer. He was acquitted, with the trial judge saying the evidence: 'did not prove that Jackson knew he was in possession of a Luger silencer, nor did it show that he had assented to such possession'. Incredibly Jackson walked free.[z]

The Douglass Cassel International Panel of Enquiry, commissioned by the PFC to investigate all the 'Glenanne'-related murders, concluded there was 'credible evidence that the principal perpetrator [of the Miami Showband attack] was a man who was not prosecuted – alleged RUC Special Branch agent Robin Jackson'.

In the very month that the Miami Showband killings took place, July 1975, the British government was analysing the problem of sectarian assassinations. Faced with incontrovertible proof that the UDA and UVF were heavily involved, London sent out a memo to all its embassies.[34] 'The murders,' says the document, '[are undertaken] by groups of, or individuals more or less loosely organised and connected with the well known terrorist groups, the UVF and the UDA.' The document goes on to say 'it is fair to say that their leaders do not make great efforts to restrain their members', but it has not been 'our practice to apportion blame publicly. Our line is that murders are perpetrated by criminally minded elements on both sides of the sectarian divide.'[35] The British government then clearly knew, and admitted to itself that it knew, that both the UDA and UVF were engaged in 'terrorism' and sectarian murders – yet both groups were still legal. Meanwhile, the line went out from London – blame both sides.

Two weeks after the Miami Showband massacre, on 15 August, the IRA abducted a twenty-nine-year-old married former RUC

---

z   Another link between Jackson and the Miami Showband attack is that he, another Portadown loyalist, Samuel Fulton Neill, and one of the two UDR men convicted, Crozier, had been arrested together, illegally carrying shotguns, in a field outside Banbridge not long before the attack.

Reservist from his mobile shop near Crossmaglen in South Armagh. William Meaklin's body was found two miles (3 km) from his home in Newtownhamilton. The IRA accused him of intelligence-gathering in the strongly republican area. Despite lurid rumours, a post-mortem report showed there was no evidence that he was tortured. He had died, brutally, from laceration of his spinal cord and lungs caused by a dozen or more .357 bullets to the head, neck and chest.[36]

The same day that Meaklin was shot dead, the IRA also shot dead a Protestant DJ in Armagh city. Norman (Mooch) Kerr (aged twenty-eight) was a friend of Harris Boyle (blown up by his own bomb during the Miami Showband ambush). Kerr's mother said he had been murdered because of this friendship.

About 200 yards from where Mooch Kerr was shot dead, stood McGleenan's Bar, in English Street in the centre of Armagh. John McGleenan (aged forty-five) had bought it three years previously. He lived overlooking the ancient city with his wife, Maura, and five children – three daughters (Mary, Róisín and Fiona) and two sons (Seán and Michael). On the night of Friday 22 August, John was in his bar serving customers alongside his daughter Mary. Her grandfather, Dominic Newbanks, was sitting at the bar enjoying a drink.[37]

John McGleenan

John must have been a bit taken aback as, for the first time ever, local police had inspected his bar for underage drinkers. An inspector, accompanied by one female and two male constables, then set off for other inspections in Armagh, ending up at ten o'clock in the town of Richhill, five miles (8 km) away.

Just as the police were arriving at Richhill, two masked men ran into McGleenan's. One shot John in the chest. He fell to his knees and died almost instantly. The other left a bomb on the bar before both ran out. The bomb exploded and the bar was all but demolished. Two more people died in the blast – Patrick Hughes (aged thirty, who was found dead in the rubble) and Thomas Morris (twenty-two, who died in hospital five days later). Ten more people were injured.

Young Mary had thrown herself to the floor behind the bar when the shooting started. Her grandfather came behind the bar, lifted her and took her out a side door into the garden. From there they heard the bomb exploding.

Mary's sister Róisín was crossing the street when she saw a car approaching. She heard the shooting, turned back towards the bar and saw the two masked gunmen emerging from it, walking backwards and firing before making off. She then saw the bomb exploding.[38]

Inside the bar, there were horrific scenes. One man had been shot in the back but still managed to run away from the bomb. Another man, a male nurse, tried to help John but he came into contact with a live electric cable, which stunned him temporarily. Francis Duffy, who saw John being shot, ran to phone an ambulance. After the explosion, he lost the use of his legs but urged helpers to leave him and rescue John instead. People who heard the explosion rushed to the scene and tore through the rubble with their bare hands, despite reports of a second device. They continued their search until after dawn. The explosion created a crater a foot (30 cm) deep and twenty-one inches (53 cm) wide.

The getaway car, which had been stolen from Portadown two days previously, was found outside the town, in a private lane leading to a group of large houses. The enterprise had been professionally carried out. John had been killed by a single .45 bullet to his chest. His body had suffered minor injuries in the explosion, but it was the bullet that killed him. Existing police papers only say an unnamed 'suspect' was questioned. No one was ever charged or convicted.[39]

A 2004 review of the case carried out by the PSNI Serious Crime Review Team (SCRT) concluded that the UVF in Portadown was to blame.[40] There were not two gangs operating in Mid-Ulster with the same *modus operandi*. The PFC believes it was the work of the same gang, or permutations of it, that was behind the bombs in Dublin and Monaghan, and other attacks north of the border.

The RUC found no under-age drinkers during its trawl of eight bars in Armagh and one in Richhill that night.[41] The McGleenan family wonders why four police officers were deployed checking bars for under-age drinkers when the entire city feared a retaliatory attack for the killing of Mooch Kerr. Why are there such detailed reports about the under-age trawl, and virtually nothing about a gun-and-bomb attack on a bar in which three people died? The McGleenans are seeking answers from the NI police ombudsman.

Dublin was concerned enough about the pattern of events for the Irish Ambassador to Britain to ask, at a meeting held in London on 20 August, about security force collusion in Mid-Ulster.[42] The ambassador told a junior British minister that the garda commissioner had received a well-sourced report about collusion stating that 'four RUC officers were also members of the UVF and one of them had been actively engaged in recent terrorist operations in the Murder Triangle'. The British civil servant was scandalised at the Irish ambassador's suggestion. London demanded to be told the source's identity. The Irish side refused, citing concerns about the source's safety. As they squabbled over the source of the claim, nothing was done about the claim itself.

And still the UVF and UDA remained legal organisations.

On 24 August 1975, two workmates were travelling back home from that year's All-Ireland football championship semi-final matches between Tyrone and Kerry minors, and Derry and Dublin seniors. Colm McCartney had left his mother's house in Castledawson, County Derry, to drive his new Ford Cortina to Moy to pick up Seán Farmer for their jaunt to Croke Park, Dublin. Seán had waved goodbye to his wife, Margaret, and four sons as Colm arrived for their day 'up for the match'. They both worked at the

Colm McCartney

same engineering works in Newry, Colm as a fitter and Seán as a digger driver. Both were young, fit and full of life.

The match ended at five and by six they were on their way home. There were the usual diversions because of bomb threats, but nothing out of the ordinary. Until, that is, they reached a remote rural spot called Altnamackin. As Seán and Colm travelled home, unknown to them, an RUC patrol had stumbled on a fake UDR checkpoint, probably set up to ambush GAA supporters – just like them – returning home from Croke Park. The RUC patrol had been immediately suspicious of the checkpoint. It did not seem quite right. The lead RUC man, Frederick Bartholomew, did not recognise any of the 'soldiers'; he knew there were no planned checkpoints in the area and there were no military jeeps about.[43] The three police officers in their car, wearing civilian jackets over their uniforms, watched the approaching UDR men with caution. One 'soldier' asked to see a driving licence. He had an odd accent and long hair. The policemen's suspicions grew. The 'soldier' shone a light into their car. Spotting their police-issue weapons, he jumped back, saying, 'It's you! Police!'

The patrol car sped away from danger. Confirming with their base by radio that there were no scheduled patrols in the area, they chose not to investigate further, instead merely returning to Newtownhamilton where they told their story to the lieutenant in charge of the British Army duty platoon and warned gardaí across the border that an apparent fake checkpoint was in place just inside Northern Ireland.[44]

The HET has spoken at length to Frederick Bartholomew. He says he was patrolling with two constables of only a few weeks' service. He is sure that the 'soldiers' they came upon were wearing standard British Army-issue uniforms. The torch and 7.62 self-loading rifle they were holding, he said, were regulation issue. Bartholomew stated to the HET that he knew the men were not from Newtownhamilton UDR. He had then been faced with two possibilities: either it was an IRA ambush (highly unlikely, as that part of South Armagh is predominantly Protestant) or the soldiers had 'strayed' from the Keady direction. But, he said, he was not sure how many armed people had surrounded the police car. Driving away, he said, had seemed safer than challenging them. Although Bartholomew had known there were no scheduled checkpoints in the area, neither his patrol, nor the British soldiers in Newtownhamilton, raised the alarm or left their base to search out those manning the fake checkpoint. The only alarm raised was with gardaí.[aa]

While all this was going on, Seán Farmer and Colm McCartney had arrived at the fake checkpoint and been shot dead. Colm's cousin, the poet Seamus Heaney, wonders in 'The Strand at Lough Beg' how events might have unfolded:

> What blazed ahead of you? A faked road block?
> The red lamp swung, the sudden brakes and stalling
> Engine, voices, heads hooded and the cold-nosed gun?

'He left home laughing, joking and full of life. We never saw him alive again. My mother lost two earlier children and had waited five years for his arrival. He was her "blue-eye". He was smart, well-educated, someone you could always go to for advice and help. Whatever he did, he did well.'

Ignatius (Nishi) Farmer, Seán's brother

Seán Farmer

Within minutes of Bartholomew's armed patrol speeding off, a man was walking his dog along the same road. He saw a parked car facing towards him. Assuming it was a courting couple, he crossed the road to avoid it. As he did so, the car door opened and he heard three or four shots. Retreating from the noise into a gateway, he recalls

---

aa Bartholomew told the HET that the RUC had not asked him to try to pick out the 'soldiers' from suspects' photos because he was doubtful he could – though any civilian eyewitness to a double murder would normally have been asked to at least try. A policeman should similarly have been asked to do so.

seeing a battery-powered lamp in the roadway. He quickly took cover behind a tree. He then heard footsteps and a man shouting repeatedly, 'Stop, stop.' Another bang followed and then a scream. The silence was broken again by more shots, as many as ten. Then more silence before a car engine started and the vehicle slowly moved off.[45] It slowed down near him, its lights off, before moving on again.

The frightened man ran to a friend's house. The two of them set off in his car. They saw the outlines of two bodies in the road. Seán was lying on the grass verge, his face covered in blood. Colm was lying face down in the road, dead. The men rang for the police.

Other GAA supporters arrived on the scene. One driver had to swerve to avoid the bodies in the road. The newcomers also established that Colm and Seán were dead.[ab] One went to a nearby house and asked to use the phone. The woman who answered the door said she had no phone. Inexplicably she declined to give the name of the area.

The newly arrived witnesses then heard an explosion nearby and saw the silhouette of a burning car off the roadside. It was Colm's new car, the one in which he had taken such pride and in which he and Seán had set off in such high spirits that morning. The killers had driven it off, doused it in petrol and set it on fire to destroy any forensic evidence. The two shocked drivers and their five passengers, all of whom had come from the same match as Seán and Colm, then drove together to Keady to raise the alarm.

None of these eyewitnesses was ever contacted again by police until the HET sought them out over thirty years later. The witnesses had even offered at the time to return to the location of the bodies, but that was declined by police in Keady, who said the scene might be booby-trapped. The eyewitnesses pointed out that they had already moved one of the bodies, to see if there was any point in trying to revive Seán and Colm, and they had come to no harm – but the police still declined

---

ab One was Colm's first cousin, but he didn't recognise him in the dark.

their offer. As for the subsequent police inquiry, the HET says there is 'nothing within the case file to suggest a co-ordinated investigation strategy or response from the RUC'.[46]

Seán and Colm's bodies were taken by helicopter to Bessbrook British Army base, and from there to the morgue in Newry. Seán had been hit six times in the head, back and body, and Colm four times in the back and chest.

Three weapons were used in the killings: a .455 Webley Mark VI revolver, a 9 mm Luger pistol and a .45 Colt automatic pistol. Both the Webley and the Luger were used four months later to kill the three Reavey brothers (4 January 1976). The Luger was also used in the later attack in June 1976 on the Rock Bar (in which all the assailants were serving RUC officers).[ac]

Three years later, in December 1978, police questioned the RUC officers directly involved in the attack on the Rock Bar and the murder of William Strathearn.[ad] They made three admissions: first, that among those involved in murdering Seán and Colm was a serving RUC officer (and loyalist bomber) Laurence McClure; second, that two serving UDR men had also been involved in the shooting;[ae] and third, that a man named in an intelligence report (received immediately after Seán and Colm were killed) as Philip Silcock was one of the gunmen.[47]

By this time, McClure was already in custody. He denied involvement and was never charged with the murders of Seán and Colm. Though RUC intelligence reports (both in 1975 and, again, after the arrests of the police officers in 1978) suggested that Silcock was involved,

---

ac The Webley and Luger were also both linked to two non-fatal attacks.

ad After RUC man William McCaughey was arrested in December 1978.

ae One soldier, a member of 2 UDR, was shot dead soon after by the IRA. Two years later, police began to treat him as a suspect for the killing of Seán and Colm. The IRA also shot dead the second soldier, Corporal Robert McConnell, in 1976. After the first UDR man was shot dead, an IRA caller rang the *News Letter* offices in Newry citing retaliation for the killings of the 'two men returning from the Gaelic football match'.

the police made no effort to question him – or another UVF man (who cannot be named here for legal reasons, but who was named in earlier RUC intelligence) – and he was never charged with involvement in these murders. The HET Report on Colm's and Seán's killing says it can offer 'no satisfactory explanation for this' and can find no record of any decision-making process to justify the RUC's failure to act.

There are yet further unanswered questions. The inquest file was sent from Bessbrook to the sub-divisional commander at Newry for 'certain amendments' before it was sent to the coroner.[48] As a result, it appears that the only independent eyewitness statement taken was removed from the file 'on the instructions of the Sub-Divisional Commander'. The HET comments: 'There are no records that explain the reason or rationale that supports that action.' At that time, police could redact or remove eyewitness statements from inquest files to avoid the identity of the witness being made public. In this case, the eyewitness (the man walking his dog, who had seen the attack) was contacted by the HET. He said he had not asked for his statement to be removed. So who removed it, and why? Was someone trying to cover something up? Another mystery.[49]

The HET's conclusions at the end of its lengthy report are damning. First, Colm and Seán were random targets singled out merely because they were travelling home from the GAA match and were therefore presumed to be Catholic. The original police investigation, it says, barely existed: 'In the absence of records or documented policy, it is difficult to ascertain that any investigation took place at all, after the initial scene examination: Witnesses were not interviewed and de-briefed thoroughly; no appeals were made for other sightings of the VCP or information.' Even taking into account the huge pressures of work at the time, it says, there was intelligence naming two people in the Mid-Ulster UVF as being responsible, and yet 'No action was taken … and there is no record that it was made available to investigators' (that is, Special Branch intelligence was not passed to CID investigators).

The HET says it can find no explanation: 'The use of UDR uniforms (mentioned in intelligence, described by Sergeant Bartholomew and his police colleagues) would surely have caused immense concern if this were an isolated incident. However it was not.' Three weeks earlier, the HET continues, the Miami Showband massacre had taken place. Two bogus UDR checkpoints within a month – both of them, as it turns out, involving serving UDR officers, yet almost incredibly, there is no evidence of a scrupulous RUC investigation.[af]

In its conclusion on the killing of Seán and Colm, the HET says the two men were innocent victims caught in a 'murderous ambush' of sectarian violence, and while intelligence named two of the culprits, nothing was done. Coming so soon after the Miami Showband incident, it should have triggered a major response. The HET concludes:

> Members of the Nationalist community and relatives of the victims in cases such as these, are convinced that investigations were not rigorously conducted, in a deliberate effort to conceal security forces' involvement and perpetuate a campaign of terror by loyalist paramilitaries against Catholic citizens. The HET is unable to rebut or allay these suspicions.
>
> The HET review has uncovered disturbing omissions and the lack of any structured investigative strategy. Junior officers seem to have been left unsupported and uninformed; indisputable evidence of security forces' involvement with loyalist paramilitaries in one case, followed by significant evidence of further co-operation just weeks later, should have rung alarm bells all the way to the top of Government; nothing was done; the murderous cycle continued.[50]

Long before the new information was received in 1978, there was already widespread belief in the nationalist community of UDR

---

af   Patricia Devlin also said that the man who stepped out to halt her parents' car (in May 1974) was in a military-style uniform.

involvement in the murder of Colm and Seán. The HET says this belief 'contributed to the spiralling violence in the area' and, as a direct result, 'British Army personnel, UDR soldiers, whether on or off-duty, were considered prime targets for republican paramilitaries'.[51] The HET also highlights 'high level concerns regarding elements of the security forces considered "too close to the UVF" and "too ready to hand over information"', and 'worries that loyalist extremists had heavily infiltrated the UDR'. Yet nothing was done. As a result, not only did Catholic civilians continue to die, but members of the security forces did so too, as confidence in law and order broke down.

And London? What questions were being asked there? On 28 August 1975, four days after Seán and Colm were killed, Secretary of State Merlyn Rees sent a memo to British Prime Minister Harold Wilson, in which he said, 'Assassination squads masquerading as VCPs create new problems and also make necessary some reappraisal of the activities of the UDR.'[52] But Rees' focus wanders immediately from the recent killings of five civilians by armed soldiers to blaming the SDLP, accusing the party of 'concentrating on the two incidents of unofficial VCPs with possible UDR involvement, in order to mount an attack on the reliability of the UDR and indeed of the RUC Reserve'.

Meanwhile, the republican retaliation (to which the HET refers in its report) was already taking place. At the end of August, the IRA killed UDR man Robert Frazer outside Whitecross as he backed his car out of a farmyard.[53] A witness says he heard gunfire and saw two hooded gunmen, one of whom pointed a gun at him while the other dragged Robert's body from the car. The men made their escape when the farmer raised the alarm. Willie Frazer, Robert's son, has claimed that many of the UDR men killed in the area by the IRA were 'those who were helping the SAS and special forces ... Other members of the UDR weren't assassinated'.[54] Another UDR man shot dead by the IRA, Robert McConnell, was – according to his nephew, Brian – gathering intelligence for British 'special forces'.[55]

The day after Frazer's murder, and ten miles (16 km) away, Joseph Reid, a part-time lance-corporal in the UDR, was shot dead at the front door of his home by a male caller.[56] As well as being in the UDR, he was also an Ulster Unionist councillor. The party's local MP, Harold McCusker, had called on 'all able-bodied men to defend their districts through the framework of the Ulster Defence Regiment and the RUC Reserve'.[57] Reid was the fourth person to be killed in South Armagh in the space of a week. The British government's response was to send in more troops.[58]

Further north, the village of Moy, north of Armagh city, was home to the family of Denis Mullen, a man who stood up both for himself and his community.[59] Denis and Olive, his wife, were both active in the SDLP. They had two young children (Denise, aged three, and Edward, aged one). Denis was the first Catholic employed as an ambulance man at the South Tyrone Hospital, Dungannon, and in 1973 won promotion to the position of controller.[60] For a time, he was frozen-out at work, as not everyone approved of a Catholic being given such a senior job. Denis was also chairman of the newly formed SDLP branch in Moy and was travelling widely to recruit members.

On 1 September 1975, renovations were under way at Denis and Olive's new bungalow, and friends and family were helping out. That evening, he drove home a friend and his son who had been painting a ceiling. Some windows in the house were still without curtains. Denis came home and went through the usual routine of locking the garden gate, then locking and barring the front door. He then had about a ten-minute chat with Olive before they both heard a loud thud at the front of the house. Olive ran to check that the children were sleeping safely, while Denis went to the front door to investigate the 'thud'.[ag]

---

ag The killers had thrown a sod of grass and mud at a window, causing the 'thud'. As the gang had predicted, it caused Denis to come to the front door.

'It was a time of great excitement, there was a great buzz in the air, a feeling of hope that we were moving forward. The atmosphere was electric. Sure, we thought, just now and again, that maybe our lives might be at risk but we never seriously thought that anyone might try and kill us.'

Olive Mullen, Denis' widow

Denis Mullen

There was a loud burst of gunfire. Olive, in the children's bedroom, heard Denis cry out and ran back towards the door. When she saw his bleeding body and realised what had happened, she turned towards the kitchen, hearing bullets smashing through the windows as the gunman outside fired at her as she ran. Once in the kitchen, where she thought she would be safer, she lay on the floor to avoid further bullets until the gunfire stopped. It was ten long minutes before she felt it was safe enough to climb through the kitchen window and run to a neighbour's house to call an ambulance and the police. Denis was by then beyond help. Denise had left her bed and was at her dead father's side, and the toddler's white nightgown was covered in his blood.

When the police arrived, they told neighbours there might be a bomb in the house and prevented them removing Denise and Edward (who was still in his cot). For about thirty minutes, the two children were alone in the house with their dead father. Olive was nearby under sedation.[61]

The gunmen were not seen fleeing the house, but a police dog picked up a scent and trailed it to the Callan River behind the bungalow. Grass and weeds there had been trampled down on both banks. This was how the gunmen had made both their approach and escape.

Police found no fewer than twenty-six bullet strike-marks on the front of the Mullen's house, mainly around the front door. Denis had been hit by seventeen bullets in the front of his body, legs and right arm, and had died very quickly.

At Denis' funeral, Denis Haughey of the SDLP described him as 'a kindly and gentle Christian, a man of peace. He served the community in innumerable ways.'[62] His funeral was attended by 2,000 mourners, including ambulance staff from across Northern Ireland.

Police made the usual appeals and house-to-house enquiries. Four months after the murder, the senior investigating officer wrote in the files that 'no persons had been brought to justice'. Case closed, it would appear. But, ten months later, a former part-time member of the TAVR, Garfield Gerald Beattie, was arrested and interviewed by a team of nine officers in Armagh over six days, led by then Detective Inspector Maurice Neilly.[63]

At first, the detectives' main focus was on the murder of Patrick McNeice eighteen days earlier. Beattie admitted his role in that murder and that of Fred McLoughlin in the Eagle Bar at Charlemont on 15 May 1976 (see the account of this in Chapter 5). Beattie also then confessed to his role in Denis' murder, claiming he had been told in a bar in Portadown that to be accepted into the UVF he would have to take part in 'a hit job'.[64] Beattie had then been told that 'Mullen, an IRA man' was to be murdered and he had been introduced to two other UVF men at the same bar with whom he carried out the attack.[ah]

Beattie told police that he and a second gunman had walked along the side of an orchard to the Mullens' home. To attract the attention of those inside, Beattie had thrown a lump of clay at a window, breaking it. That was the thud that Denis and Olive had heard. Denis had opened the front door and Beattie had opened fire. He 'did not stop firing at Denis until he had fallen to the ground'.[65] Beattie and

---

ah Far from having any IRA links, the HET says Denis Mullen was 'clearly a hard-working family man respected by those who knew him'. This was one of many murders planned in loyalist bars. In some cases (Denis Mullen, the McKearneys, Patrick McNeice and Brendan McLaughlin) the killers were drinking before they set out. In others they 'celebrated' with a drink after a killing (for example, at Harry's Bar, Banbridge, according to the Barron Report, after the attack on Kay's Tavern/Donnelly's Bar in December 1975).

the other gunman had then run away (the second gunman firing one shot at the house as he fled). They re-crossed the river and were picked up by the third man before dropping the guns off.

On 12 August 1976, Beattie took police officers to a bog in Annaghmore from where, in a drain, he recovered the machine gun and magazine that had been used to murder Denis Mullen.[ai] On 17 August, he was charged with the murder and those of Fred McLoughlin and Patrick McNeice.[66] During police interviews, Beattie said he had been a UDA member for the first half of 1975 but had shot Denis as part of an initiation rite into the UVF. In September 1977, Beattie was convicted of three murders and the possession of a firearm. He received three life sentences and fourteen years (for the firearm offence), to run concurrently. He served sixteen years in jail before being released in March 1993.

Nine months after Beattie was sentenced, on 16 May 1978, police arrested William John Parr at his home in Annaghmore. Parr was aged eighteen at the time of Denis' murder. He was interviewed by a team of nine police officers, again led by Detective Inspector Neilly, over a period of four days. He said he had been friends with Beattie since school and had regularly played darts and cards with him. He was also friendly with another man, whom the HET calls 'Suspect A', former UDR man William Corrigan.[aj] Parr said Beattie had asked him to meet Corrigan for a drink on the night of Denis' murder. They drove to collect the guns, with Parr at the wheel. Beattie spoke about 'shooting a Provo'. Parr heard the shooting. Beattie and Corrigan then emerged and got into the car. Beattie had said 'that was a good

---

ai   In separate trips, Beattie led the RUC to three arms caches.

aj   Corrigan, named as a former UDR man in an *Irish Times* report of 18 January 1979, was convicted in 1976 of handling ammunition stolen from the UDR by soldier Joseph Denis McConville. There were claims at the time that Ministry of Defence-issue ammunition was used in Denis' killing and in others in the Moy area. Corrigan was shot dead by the IRA on 14 October 1976. His son, Leslie, was also shot, and died on 25 October.

shot'. Parr, who claimed in court to have acted under duress, was convicted of Denis' murder and given a life sentence. He was released after eleven years. The HET can find no evidence that Corrigan was ever questioned about Denis' murder.

Another key suspect in the murder was Edward Tate Sinclair, who was, at the time, a thirty-nine-year-old man farming fifty acres, a leading Orangeman and former B Special. The HET says that the RUC 'considered Sinclair to be potentially responsible for the planning and co-ordination of a number of sectarian killings, including that of Denis and other attacks during the period 1973–6 in Moy, Dungannon and the surrounding area'. When Sinclair was questioned by the RUC in 1980 about Denis' murder, he denied involvement, but admitted he had seen a 'loyalist terrorist walking across his [Sinclair's] land on the night of the murder'. Sinclair said he was tending to his cattle when he heard shooting and 'had seen a man he knew, carrying an SMG across his land'. He had spoken to the man but claimed he did not question him about the gun he was carrying or the earlier sound of gunfire.[67]

Aside from the fact that Sinclair's account stretches credulity beyond breaking point, the armed man he saw, we now know, was Joseph (Joey) Lutton, who at the time Sinclair named him to police was already in jail serving life for the murder of Fred McLoughlin (killed in an attack on the Eagle Bar on 15 May 1976 with the same weapon used to kill Denis). At the time of Fred's murder, Lutton was a serving RUC Reserve constable (though his occupation was given in court as a 'cheese processor'). The HET has been unable to establish whether Lutton was ever questioned by the RUC about Denis' murder, despite being identified by Sinclair and, as he was already in jail, being amenable. Sinclair was not charged with any offence relating to Denis' murder, despite his admissions.

Nor did the RUC ever check out Olive Mullen's evidence, given to them in the days after Denis' murder, that former UDR man Corrigan had come to the house in disguise (clearly scouting it out in advance of the murder). Olive had recognised Corrigan because he had once lived next to her parents. When he came to her home dressed as a nun pretending to be collecting money, Olive had noted his large boots and hands. She had even challenged him before chasing him off. Olive was working at the time as a dentist's assistant and was alert to the shape of people's faces. Corrigan, she remembers, had a 'Class 3' malocclusion of the teeth, where the lower jaw juts forward. The police never followed up her evidence.[68]

On the day that Denis was shot dead, an internal British government memorandum noted in relation to the UDR that 'there are well-established doubts about the Regiment's reliability', but again the writer's focus is less on the problem and more on the complainants.[69] The SDLP (bemoans the memo's author) 'makes much play of minority fears about the UDR', though he concedes that the British Army needs to be 'awakened' to the 'need to exercise adequate operational control of the UDR'. Within hours of this memo being written, no doubt in the safety of a London office, Denis was dead. Denise and Olive Mullen are taking their many concerns over the RUC investigation to the NI police ombudsman.

Eight days after Denis' death, on 9 September, a senior Northern Ireland Office official sent a memo to a colleague headed 'The UDR and the Catholic Community'.[70] In it, reference is made to SDLP complaints, acknowledging two areas of concern, one being UDR connections to the UVF and the second being the 'availability of arms and ammunition'.

On the same day that Denis was killed, 1 September, the IRA launched a gun attack on Tullyvallen Orange Hall in Newtownhamilton. Members of the lodge were meeting inside, as they did on the first Friday of every month. The meeting had just moved on from prayers when two gunmen, entering from a kitchen at the back, sprayed the hall with bullets. Another gunman fired through a window. Five people were killed and seven more injured. A two-pound (0.9 kg) bomb placed inside failed to explode or there would have been even more casualties. It was an indiscriminate, sectarian attack.

Three days after the IRA attack on Tullyvallen Orange Hall, the UVF launched a gun-and-bomb attack on a bar in the countryside between Armagh city and Loughgall. McCann's Bar sat on a hillside overlooking the area's apple orchards and the mainly Catholic village of Ballyhagan. It was frequented generally, but not exclusively, by Catholic older men and, on the night of the bombing, was busy, as it was payday and a football team was socialising after a training session. An extended family of sisters and their husbands had also gathered at McCann's to say *au revoir* to Margaret (Peggy) Hale, who was due to return to England the next day with her husband, Walter, also originally from County Armagh.

Nine years earlier, in 1964, Peggy and Walter had moved to Scunthorpe, England, where they were raising their five children, aged between twelve and four. As usual, they had returned home to Armagh for their summer holidays. As the family chatted over their drinks, at 10.10 p.m. the door burst open and two masked men carrying handguns opened fire. They then threw a bomb into the bar. A witness heard one of the gang shouting, 'We have got you now, you bastards.' Another witness heard a man shout, 'Start shooting, boys.' People scattered in all directions, and it was Peggy's terrible ill-fortune to run in the wrong direction. When the bomb exploded, she sustained appalling internal injuries. Twelve other people in the bar were injured non-fatally, either by gunfire or the explosion.[71]

Margaret 'Peggy' Hale

One of the injured, Aiden McGeough, already shot three times, had seen the gunmen reloading and then noted a smoking green bag lying beside him. With amazing courage, he dragged the smouldering bag as far as he could into a kitchen, crawling, as he couldn't walk. Another customer, Seamus Hughes, threw a bar table at the gunman as he was being fired upon, forcing the man to move from the doorway. Despite being trapped in the rubble after the explosion, Seamus managed to make his way outside.

Peggy's husband, Walter, was with her as she was dragged from the rubble, and went to hospital with her in an ambulance. She was severely injured and was ventilated in intensive care. As she deteriorated, doctors discovered her small bowel had been perforated, causing peritonitis. Peggy never regained consciousness and died after a cardiac arrest on 22 September 1975, eighteen days after the bombing. Intelligence information provided to police at the time named a known twenty-two-year-old UVF man from Portadown whose name featured in court reports relating to an earlier murder.[ak] He was questioned the month after the bombing, but made no admission of guilt and was released without charge. The following year, the same man is believed to have been one of four men who placed a bomb at the Step Inn in Keady, which killed two people. Ten years after the murder at McCann's, a man approached Kathy O'Hare, Peggy's sister, and apologised. Another sister, May, said the attitude of detectives towards the family at the time was hostile and unsympathetic.

As the bombs continued to explode in Northern Ireland, the new leader of the British Conservative Party, Margaret Thatcher, had regular meetings with Prime Minister Harold Wilson and Secretary of State Merlyn Rees. At their meeting on 10 September, Rees expressed to both leaders that 'Unfortunately, there were certain elements in the police who were very close to the UVF and who were prepared to hand over information, for example, to Mr Paisley.' One

---

ak The man's name is known but cannot be used here for reasons of confidentiality.

official at the meeting reported, 'The Army's judgment [was that] the UDR were heavily infiltrated by extremist Protestants and that in a crisis situation they could not be relied on to be loyal.'[72]

Nine days later, Gerry Fitt, the SDLP MP, told Harold Wilson he feared a loyalist pogrom against Catholics and that, two days previously, the bar at Stormont had been full of UDA and UVF members chatting to William Craig, the Vanguard leader.[73]

On 2 October, twelve people died in a series of UVF attacks across Northern Ireland: four Catholics were killed in a gun attack on a bottling plant in central Belfast; two others in separate bombings; while two Protestants were killed and four UVF men died in a premature explosion near Coleraine.[al] The following day, the UVF was once again proscribed.

* * *

Peter and Jenny McKearney

Peter (aged sixty-three) and Jane (aged fifty-eight and always known as Jenny) McKearney both suffered from chronic heart complaints. Peter, a former textile worker in the Moygashel linen works, was particularly ill: a stroke had paralysed one side of his body. The couple lived on a small farm just outside the village of Moy with their five children: Seán (aged twenty-four), Frank (twenty-three), Marian (twenty-one), James (twenty) and Paul (seventeen). None had any paramilitary or political connections.[74]

The evening of Thursday 23 October 1975 started off very much

---

al   One of the four dead UVF men's fingerprints were found on a dagger near the scene of the murder of Christy Phelan in County Kildare in June 1975. Phelan had come upon a gang of UVF men near his home who were setting a bomb on railway lines. They had intended blowing up republicans attending the annual Wolfe Tone commemorations. Fortunately, the bomb detonated late, avoiding a large-scale loss of life. Christy Phelan was stabbed through the heart.

as usual for the McKearney family. Peter and Jenny were sitting in their kitchen at the back of the house having their evening meal while two of their sons, Frank and James, were out on the farm loading pigs into a trailer. Within minutes of leaving the farmhouse, however, the brothers heard a car driving towards their home. It changed gear, then the two men heard a short burst of automatic gunfire, followed by two longer bursts, followed by the sound of a car driving away. Rushing back to the house they found the front door open. They were met by a scene of carnage.[75]

Jenny was not moving. James fetched a cup of water for his mother before realising she was beyond help. She was lying on her back in the tiled hallway, bleeding from eleven bullet wounds in her chest, body and legs. Following her initial wounding, the pattern of injuries showed that she had been shot again after she had fallen. Peter was in the smoke-filled kitchen, lying near the back door, hit by between fourteen and eighteen bullets in his chest and body.

Frank and James came to the awful realisation that they had just heard the sound of the car used by their parents' killers driving to the house to carry out the foul deed – and the sound of the same car driving away. Frank ran to his uncle's house nearby to phone for help. The shooting had begun at 7.40 p.m. By 8 p.m. a detective sergeant was on the scene. James then had the terrible task of identifying his dead parents. One can only imagine the grief and shock felt by the five orphaned McKearney children.

The car had been stolen about five hours earlier and was recovered, intact, in the rural townland of Bovean about two miles from the McKearneys' farmhouse. Who could have carried out such a truly awful deed, killing this defenceless couple sitting quietly in their home in the County Armagh countryside?

The police began their investigation. They found twenty-nine spent cartridge cases and sixteen bullet heads in the house. They ordered road checks. They interviewed potential witnesses. They visited loyalist haunts. They carried out house-to-house enquiries.[am] They made appeals for information through the press. Meanwhile they had some luck. Half an hour after the shooting, a regular British Army foot patrol in Portadown stopped a car containing four men whom they recognised as UVF members – one of whom was also in the UDR.[76] The soldiers were not aware of the shooting at that time, so this was just a lucky chance. Having 'satisfied themselves' about the men's identities and movements, the patrol allowed two of the four men to continue on their way.[77] However, they detained the other two, one of whom was the UDR man.

Both men were taken to the local police station and interviewed. By then, news of the McKearney killings was out. The two men's hands were swabbed and were found to have traces of firearms residue. Thus the RUC had two men in custody, whom they knew to be UVF members, shortly after a loyalist double murder and with potentially incriminating forensic evidence on their hands. The presence of firearms residue, without corroborating evidence, however, was not considered sufficient to press criminal charges against the UDR man (as he was legally entitled to carry weapons).[an] The second man was also released, as his explanation was that he had shaken the hand of the UDR man and thus contaminated his own hands. (One might be forgiven for seeing this as something of a 'get-out-of-jail-free' card for UDR men and their associates.)

The HET has, through examining the movements of a blue Vauxhall Viva car seen close to the murder scene (and close to where the getaway car was abandoned), concluded that it was carrying a four-man unit of the RUC Special Patrol Group at the time of the

---

am Houses searched that night included those of Robin Jackson, where UDR man James Roderick Shane McDowell was arrested. He was later charged with involvement in the Miami Showband murders.

an The HET Report into the McKearney killings points out: 'It would need to be proved that the arrested people had no legitimate reasons for the presence of such residue. The residue cannot be evidentially linked to a specific firearm or ammunition.'

shootings. SPGs were deployed at that time and place, says the HET, specifically because of the high incidence of loyalist killings in the area. But, it goes on: 'The reason for the SPG vehicle's presence during these specific times and at those locations cannot be established. There is nothing within the investigation papers to establish if the police officers were spoken to during the course of the investigation.'

The SPG was there to prevent loyalist killings. Two such killings took place close by. The getaway car was abandoned close by. Yet there are no records of the unit members being questioned or even that they attended the murder scene, as might have been expected from a specialist anti-terrorist unit.

Five months after Peter and Jenny's murder, the police were getting nowhere, and in March 1976, an RUC report said no one had been brought to justice and no group had claimed responsibility. Two months later, however, the situation changed. On Tuesday 18 May, for reasons that remain to be established (as there are no police records), a detachment of military police and Royal Engineers searched the farm of Edward Tate Sinclair – farmer, Orangeman and B Special. There they found firearms, firearm components, assorted ammunition, commercial explosives and bomb-making materials. The HET notes that 'Sinclair was present during the search operation and co-operated by pointing out some of the hiding-places from where firearms, ammunition and explosives were recovered.'[78] One of the guns was a .38 Colt automatic pistol, serial number 36330. It was found in Sinclair's bedroom, examined and test-fired. It was one of the guns used to murder Peter and Jenny McKearney.

Sinclair was questioned over two days in Portadown. The HET cannot find the records of those interviews, despite intensive searches – but their tenor, it says, can be established from the prosecution file. Sinclair said he had bought the gun for £10 in a pub in Moy, three to four years before, for his own protection. He refused to say who had sold it to him. He then said he had loaned the weapon to 'a boy', who kept it for five months. He would not name the 'boy' and could not say why the 'boy' wanted the gun.

Told at this stage by an interviewing officer that this same gun might have been used in a shooting incident, Sinclair replied, 'Well, I'm on a sticky wicket.'[79] As for the other guns and ammunition, Sinclair said he was holding them for others, whom he would not name. The HET Report comments: 'The natural course of the questioning should then have continued in regards to Peter and Jane's killings but, according to the statements, it appears it did not.' Reading between the lines, then, there are very significant but unanswered questions about the way the police conducted the interview with Sinclair. Possibly, the HET suggests, the results of the test-firing of the gun, linking it to the McKearney killings, had not yet reached the interrogating officers.

Police questioned Sinclair for a further four days about other serious crimes in Mid-Ulster (no records of these interviews can be found either). By then, the test-firing results must have been available, although it is not known if they were passed to interviewing officers, or if indeed Sinclair was ever questioned about the McKearney killings.

On 24 May 1976, Sinclair was charged with having illegal firearms. The following January he appeared in court, pleading guilty to various charges of possession of firearms and explosive substances, for which he received concurrent sentences, the longest of which was for six years. He left jail two years and four months later – on 24 May 1979 – three years to the day since he was first charged. Almost exactly a year later, on 5 May 1980, he was arrested again and questioned about another gun found on his farm, a .45 revolver, but there is nothing in the police papers to suggest he was questioned about the McKearney killings at that time either.

The man who was questioned about, and convicted of, the McKearney murders was Garnet James Busby, though he was not detained until two days after Sinclair's second arrest. Busby, who had been rejected by the UDR and RUC for employment, as well as by the Prison Service, was initially interviewed for six days and released without charge. The HET could find no records regarding these interviews, but an ex-detective sergeant remembers that Busby was questioned about the McKearney killings and denied any involvement.

Six months later, in December 1980, Busby was arrested again, on suspicion of involvement in the bombing of the Hillcrest Bar in Dungannon on St Patrick's Day 1976, in which four people lost their lives. During seven days of interviews he was also questioned about two other, non-fatal, pub bombings and, on 11 December, admitted involvement in the McKearney killings. Busby told of how, three or four days before the attack, he had gone to a loyalist club in Portadown where the murders were planned.[ao] He told police he had been armed with 'a small pistol' and had fired one shot at the McKearneys' front door before the gun jammed. He said the gun found at Sinclair's farm was the one he had used, and that a second man, who he would not name, fired the Sterling SMG at the defenceless couple.

Busby gave two different accounts of the 'one shot' he admitted firing: (a) into the ground; and (b) at the front door. The bullet was actually discovered in Jenny's clothing. The second gunman, he said, had then run into the house towards the kitchen. Busby said his gun had remained obstinately jammed. The two gunmen, Busby said, had been driven back to the loyalist club in Portadown.

Busby was charged with murdering the McKearneys, and with other fatal and non-fatal offences. He pleaded guilty and was sentenced to life imprisonment; to twelve years for possession of the Colt pistol; and to four further life sentences for his role in the Hillcrest Bar bombing and other offences including UVF membership.[ap] On the

---

ao Peter and Jenny had no links to the IRA, but another family of the same name, who lived close by, were regarded as republicans. Clearly, Busby and his associates did not bother to make even the most basic checks.

ap The Hillcrest Bar bombing was carried out in Dungannon on 17 March 1976,

day of his conviction, a police intelligence report was created stating
that Sinclair had organised the murder and that Busby was one of
two gunmen. Two other men were also named in the intelligence
report, one of whom has strong, distinct and varied security force
connections.[aq] Busby served sixteen years and was released in February
1997.

Sinclair was arrested again in December 1981. He was, this time,
questioned about the murder of Peter and Jenny, and said he 'drove
the car used in the murders', but 'could not admit to it'. For some
reason, again, this potentially productive line of police questioning
did not continue. The following day, he was questioned again. He
said: 'I am not denying I wasn't involved.' As this statement was open
to interpretation, the interviewing police officer then asked whether
he was 'therefore agreeing to being involved in the murders'. Sinclair
replied: 'I'm not saying anything, I can't afford to.' Four days later,
he was charged with the McKearney killings, but six months after
that, the DPP directed that the charges be dropped as he 'did not
consider that his [Sinclair's] admissions were sufficient to support a
case'.[80]

The SMG used to kill the McKearneys was discovered to be a
weapon 'stolen' from the UDR base at Glenanne on 20 or 21 May
1971. It was used in a string of attacks both before and after the
McKearney killings. There remains further tantalising evidence from
the shootings. Two high-quality fingerprints found at the farmhouse
remain to be identified. They did not match Busby, Sinclair or forty-
two other loyalist paramilitaries against whose prints they were
compared. The HET found ten other people whose fingerprints they
considered worth checking, but these were also negative. So, there is

---

and four people died, including two teenage boys. He was also convicted of bombing
O'Neill's Bar in Dungannon on 16 August 1973 and Quinn's public house in
Dungannon on 12 November 1973.

aq The name is known but cannot be used for reasons of confidentiality.

another assailant who has yet to come under suspicion, who is still unidentified, for the grotesque crimes committed at Peter and Jenny McKearneys' farmhouse.

On 29 October 1975, the UVF in Lurgan shot dead a former Catholic member of the Royal Irish Rangers, James Griffin (aged twenty-one). He was one of eight children and had left the regiment after being bullied. Despite his past membership of the British Army, he was still targeted because of his religion. A masked gunman fired through the front window of his home, witnessed by his young brother, who was playing outside. Two weeks later, police found the murder weapon after a post office robbery and arrested two youths. In May 1976, four local men were convicted of involvement in the shooting: Alistair Little, George Charles Conlon, William Paul Jenkinson and George Gates, a work colleague of Jim Griffin. Alistair Little admitted he was the gunman.

In the House of Commons on 4 November, defending his decision to ban the UVF, Secretary of State Merlyn Rees gave what might be called the understatement of the decade. The UVF, he said, had 'departed from the path of political argument'.

On 15 December, Ronald Trainor (aged seventeen) – son of Dorothy, who had been shot dead in April of that year – was killed in a bomb explosion at the family home in Portadown. Six people were injured in the blast, including five family members. Ronald was a member of the IRSP. In March 1978, Ronald's brother, Thomas, was also killed – again in Portadown by the UVF.

On 19 December, the UVF went into overdrive, launching a double gun-and-bomb attack in Counties Louth and Armagh, killing five people in one evening. In Dundalk it bombed Kay's Tavern, killing two men, Hugh Watters and Jack Rooney.[ar] As pandemonium broke out, and the Watters and Rooney families were searching in the

ar   More on the bombings can be found in Chapter 7: Bombs Know No Borders.

burning ruins for Hugh and Jack, there was more tragedy to come north of the border.

Ann Brecknell was in Daisy Hill Hospital in Newry, recovering from giving birth two days earlier to her first daughter, Róisín. At Donnelly's Bar, not far away in the village of Silverbridge, her husband, Trevor, aged thirty-two, was planning to 'wet the child's head' in celebration.[81] Friends and work colleagues from a small engineering plant nearby had joined him in the small bar, attached to a filling station and a house owned by a local couple, Gerard and Marie Donnelly. The atmosphere was typical of any Friday night in thousands of bars up and down the country. People were looking forward to the weekend ahead, and to Christmas, which was less than a week away.

Patsy Donnelly

Patsy Donnelly (no relation to the bar owner), aged twenty-four, was filling his car up with petrol on his way to see his girlfriend.[82] Michael Donnelly, Gerard and Marie's son, still just fourteen, was helping out at the petrol pumps. People were just beginning to hear news of the carnage in Kay's Tavern across the border when a car drew up to the pumps and a man opened fire with an SMG, hitting Patsy Donnelly in the head. He fell dead, face-down, near the pumps. Another man, John Taylor (Ann Brecknell's brother-in-law) was hit in the shoulder and jaw and collapsed. From where he lay on the ground, he could see the blurred figure of a gunman, laughing.

Young Michael Donnelly ran into his dad's bar, where about twenty-six people were enjoying their evening. The gunman followed him. Inside, Margaret Taylor (Ann Brecknell's sister and John Taylor's wife) was talking to Trevor, who was about to raise his glass. Margaret saw Michael running into the bar, immediately followed by a gunman who opened fire, hitting her in the head. Another man, Brendan McConville, was also hit, taking cover under a pool table. He later described the gunman as having a 'Mexican-style moustache'. Another customer, Jimmy McCreesh, remembers standing near Trevor and seeing the gunman push his weapon through a small glass pane in the inner door. As he turned away, Jimmy was hit twice in the back.

Other customers had already dived for cover. Five people were immediately hit with bullets, including Trevor Brecknell.[83] Jimmy says Trevor was dead before he hit the ground.[84]

'He had a lovely nature. I would be quick-tempered but not him. If we fought and went to bed without speaking, he would come home the next day at lunchtime to make it up … He was easy-going. He could cook anything. He loved Irish music and dancing. He supported Aston Villa and I used to hear him yelling at the television if he disagreed with the ref.'

Trevor Brecknell

Ann Brecknell, Trevor's wife

A second man then ran into the bar, throwing in a bomb. It exploded with a blue flash as the gunmen ran out and the bar was plunged into darkness.[85] Customers were buried under rubble. Fourteen-year-old Michael Donnelly was hit on the head by fragments of rubble and killed. His father, Gerard, heard the shots and was caught in the rush of his fleeing customers when the bomb went off. He returned in the darkness and, using a flash lamp, found the body of his son in the debris.

Michael Donnelly

Ambulances began taking the dead and injured to the nearest hospital, Daisy Hill, in Newry. Ann Brecknell saw them arriving, little realising how her life was about to change. Pathology reports show that all three of the dead had died instantaneously from head wounds.

The RUC did not move in to examine the scene until the following day (the Royal Scots Dragoon Guards, who had been on the scene just after the bombing, had withdrawn after heavy stoning from an angry crowd). As the HET puts it, 'There was significant hostility towards the security forces (particularly the Army) in the area, with considerable suspicion locally that the security forces were colluding with loyalist paramilitaries.'[86] The Red Hand Commando group admitted responsibility for both the Kay's Tavern bombing and the killings at Donnelly's Bar.

Detective Sergeant Gerry McCann, one of relatively few Catholic detectives at the time, headed the RUC investigation.[87] From eyewitness accounts, the gunman armed with the SMG appeared to be a known loyalist from Portadown.[as] Hoping for an early arrest, McCann circulated a photofit picture to Special Branch in Portadown and waited to hear back. And waited. But with no response. Finally, knowing his suspect would be at the unemployment benefit office in Portadown at a specific time, McCann went there himself and brought along an eyewitness. The suspect duly put in an appearance – but to McCann's surprise had substantially changed his appearance. McCann found this highly suspicious. Had the suspect been tipped-off about the photofit circulating within Special Branch in Portadown? Since then, however, the HET has established that the suspect was named within Special Branch databases as having been involved in the Donnelly's Bar attack. McCann was never told this, but his hunch had been correct all along. The individual was never arrested for questioning about the Donnelly's Bar attack.

There is more evidence of collusion. The bar's owner, Gerard Donnelly, told McCann about a rare police raid on his premises six days before the attack. The officers had insisted on visiting his own residential quarters, and opening all its doors.[88] It had seemed like a genuine raid at the time. The RUC had warned him against serving drink after hours and to under-age customers. Now he wondered if they had been scouting the premises. McCann searched the police attendance record at Forkhill police station, but there was no record of the raid. The HET also comments on the 'highly unusual' absence of

---

as The suspect's name is known but cannot be cited for legal reasons.

this record. South Armagh was at that time a dangerous environment for police, so such a check would routinely have required pre-planned British Army back-up. The HET concludes that the police 'check' was in fact 'pre-attack reconnaissance', in which case it was carried out entirely by RUC members.[89]

There are other unanswered questions. In the garda 'Jobs Book' kept about the Kay's Tavern explosion are details of two cars: a grey Volkswagen Golf and a blue Ford Cortina, along with their registration numbers. Where did these crucial details come from? There is nothing within RUC files to indicate they knew about the cars or passed the details to the gardaí. The Ford was being used by a twenty-six-year-old man, linked to the UVF, living in the town of Tandragee.[90] He was seen drinking in Harry's Bar in Banbridge an hour after the Donnelly's Bar attack (in a group also including a man named in RUC intelligence as having been involved). This was clearly a potential line of enquiry, but the HET says, 'There is nothing in the case papers to indicate that enquiries were carried out, or that the investigation team knew about it.' There is nothing either in RUC files to show if any known loyalists owned a Golf (a new model on the market at the time).

According to Judge Barron's report into the Dundalk bombing and related attacks, the garda 'Jobs Book' note, arising from the Kay's Tavern explosion, says that three hours after the blast, 'the following members of the UVF were seen drinking in "Harry's Bar" in Banbridge, County Down, apparently celebrating something, it is thought the Dundalk job ...'. The Barron Report goes on to name nine people in the group – six of whom were notorious loyalists.[91]

The same Barron Report says that the gang arrived at Harry's Bar between 9 p.m. and 9.30 p.m. They seemed to be celebrating 'some recent happening'.[92] Information recently provided by the HET was that only two (Robin Jackson and a UDR man[at]) had arrived between

---

at   Identity known but cannot be cited for reasons of confidentiality.

9 p.m. and 9.30 p.m. The remaining seven did not arrive until about 10.30 p.m. That arrival time means those seven could have been involved in the attacks on both Kay's and Donnelly's bars that night. The RUC never provided this critical information on timings to the Garda Síochána. Nor was this vital nugget of information, which could have broken the case wide open, passed to Detective Sergeant Gerry McCann, who was the lead detective into the triple murder. This failure, says the HET, was 'extraordinary'. McCann himself, in an interview with the HET, says the information he did get was 'muddled and conflicting'. He seems, says the HET, to have been left with 'little support'.[93] Yet again, Special Branch officers were failing to assist their colleagues investigating a crime.

As for the explosives, the RUC files give no details of what, if any, lines of enquiry were followed. An unattributable reference says the amount was estimated at ten pounds (4.5 kg) of commercial explosives (the blast created a crater 1 foot 9 inches (53 cm) in diameter, 7 inches (18 cm) from the front door of the bar). A police photographer attended the scene, pointlessly, sixteen days after the event: 'There is nothing ... that establishes why this was not carried out earlier. By then the scene had been significantly cleared of debris.'[94]

As so often before, the HET had to rely on ballistic evidence to make some sense of who was responsible for this attack. And it yielded telling answers. The gun used was the Sterling SMG, serial number UF57A30490, 'stolen' from Glenanne UDR base and used in attacks where eleven people died.[au] Among those convicted of involvement in these eleven killings were a British Territorial Army private, a former UDR man and a serving RUC man.[av] Various others

---

au There is no evidence that this theft was ever investigated by the RUC. The weapon was destroyed on 27 April 1978 and could not be used as evidence in three subsequent trials. Its other victims, as well as those who died at Donnelly's, were Denis Mullen, Peter and Jenny McKearney, the Reavey brothers, Fred McLoughlin, and Patsy McNeice.

av Garfield Beattie, David Kane and Joseph Lutton respectively.

(ten in total) are suspected of handling this weapon.

No one was arrested in the months after the Donnelly's Bar killings. It was only three years later, after the kidnapping of Fr Hugh Murphy and the arrest of RUC man William McCaughey for the murder of William Strathearn, that more information emerged.[aw] A team of forty RUC detectives then carried out over 100 interviews. The outcome of the RUC investigation was that Laurence McClure and Sarah Elizabeth (Lily) Shields admitted their limited involvement in the Donnelly's Bar attack.[ax] They 'claimed to be unaware of the exact target and its purpose, but realised [it was] an illegal act.'[95]

McClure admitted that, on the night of the attack, he had been at James Mitchell's Glenanne farm along with others including UDR man Robert McConnell. McClure (who drove the killers to the target, and who lived close to Mitchell's farm) and Shields had then waited, posing as a courting couple, at an Orange Hall, about eight miles (13 km) from Donnelly's Bar. After half an hour, McConnell and two other attackers got into the car and McClure dropped them off close to Mitchell's farm. McClure claimed it was not until the next day that he realised what the three men had done. Shields admitted her involvement and gave a similar story to McClure's, without naming the men they had picked up.

Both were charged with failing to give information. Three years later, however, all the charges were dropped because of a lack of 'admissible evidence'.[96] There was not enough to convict Shields and McClure, according to the prosecuting authorities, because of insufficient corroborating evidence that those they had picked up had actually carried out the attack, or that they (McClure and Shields) had known where

---

aw William McCaughey was a former member of the Armagh SPG, who joined the UVF. See Chapter 11: Ridding the Land of Pestilence and Chapter 12: Her Majesty's Murderers.

ax McClure was a serving RUC constable and former member of the Armagh SPG. Shields was housekeeper to ex-RUC Reservist James Mitchell, owner of the farm at Glenanne. She refused to co-operate with the HET. She died in March 2011.

it was to take place. Because the case against them was entirely on their own admissions, more serious charges were not considered for the same reasons. Former Armagh SPG officer John Weir has named both McClure and Shields and three UVF men who, he said, had gathered at Mitchell's farm after the attack. He confirmed that the attack was co-ordinated with the Kay's Tavern bombing in Dundalk.[97]

In his 1978 interviews with police, however, McClure contradicted himself. In one interview he said those involved in the 1975 Donnelly's Bar attack and the 1976 Rock Bar attack were not the same gang.[ay] In a second interview, however, he said both attacks were carried out by himself and 'a crowd of ordinary fellows', adding, 'Silverbridge and Rock Bar was just arranged amongst ourselves'.[98] This contradictory slip is precisely the kind of gift that any self-respecting detective should jump on in a bid to force admissions from a suspect. The HET says detectives did not push home the contradictions to McClure, or ask what he meant by 'ourselves'. This 'oversight' precluded more serious charges being made against him.[99]

Shields is also exposed as a liar. In her 15 December 1978 interview with the RUC, she admitted she had been the girlfriend of McClure's UDR co-conspirator, Robert McConnell, since 1971 – while maintaining that she did not know who he was when she and McClure collected him after the Donnelly's Bar killings. The HET, by implication again, criticises the RUC men who questioned her, adding: 'Her failure to name him as one of the three suspects was not challenged during the interview process.'[100]

There are more statements damning the RUC in the HET Report on Donnelly's Bar. During their interviewing of McClure, RUC detectives referred to admissions made by Mitchell after his farmhouse was raided and bomb-making equipment was discovered in 1978, but the HET says it 'can offer no reasonable explanation why

---

ay   For details of the Rock Bar attack, see Chapter 6: 'A Policeman's Boots'.

the interviews did not explore the obvious evidential opportunities that were emerging'. Another suspect for the attack was named by John Weir. In the Barron Reports he is referred to several times as 'Suspect T', and on one occasion is identified as 'Shilly'.[101] The European Court of Human Rights report on the case of Brecknell v. the United Kingdom goes further and identifies 'Suspect T' as Portadown loyalist Philip 'Shilly' Silcock, although it also points out that the PSNI believed 'much of what John Weir alleged is based on hearsay allegedly having been told to him by other police officers'.[102] Others, including Barron, the Gardaí and the HET, consider Weir to be a largely credible witness.[103]

The Brecknell family is taking a case to the NI police ombudsman, and the HET is referring its concerns to the same office.

After the double bombing in Silverbridge and Dundalk, the newly arrived GOC, Lieutenant General Sir David House, ordered a call-up of UDR in the area. The authorities knew the UDR was heavily infiltrated by loyalists, yet it was this very force of men that was to be deployed. Allegations were already being made that British Army-issue bullets, if not guns, had been used in many shootings in 1974 and 1975, including the killings of both the McKearneys and Denis Mullen. Seamus Mallon, then SDLP security spokesman and later the party's deputy leader, lived in Markethill, South Armagh. He regarded sending the UDR into the area as:

> … utter and dangerous madness in view of the cloud hanging over the force as a result of at least circumstantial evidence of their connection with loyalist paramilitary activists. Until it has been proved conclusively that this force has not been infiltrated by loyalist murder gangs, it should not even be contemplated using them in a full-time capacity in South Armagh or any other area.
>
> [It is] the surest way of swinging support back to the Provisional IRA … because local people will look at the UDR presence as blatant

harassment and intimidation carried out to placate extreme loyalist politicians.[104]

On 29 December, ten days after the Donnelly's Bar gun-and-bomb attack, a Northern Ireland Office civil servant wrote to a colleague in the Foreign and Commonwealth Office about concerns raised by the Irish chargé d'affaires on proposals to step up deployment of the UDR. The chargé d'affaires had raised concerns about what he called UDR 'bias'. The letter's British author blustered that he had 'bridled' at this criticism and had accused Seamus Mallon of 'spreading malicious and irresponsible stories about the UDR'. He had, he said, reassured the Irish chargé d'affaires about the 'careful screening process' UDR recruits had to go through, while conceding that 'inevitably there would be the odd individual whose loyalties lay elsewhere'.[105]

On 26 December, the UVF attacked Vallely's Bar, a modest country pub between Portadown and Loughgall. A married father of two, Seamus Mallon (no relation to the SDLP politician), was seriously injured and died four days later. Survivors speak of the lights going out and panic, with people shouting for help. Dominic Vallely, the bar's owner, helped to drag out some of the injured and discovered pieces of the burning bomb-van scattered across a wide area.[106] More than 2,000 people attended Seamus Mallon's funeral.

On the last night of the year, a five-pound (2.3 kg) INLA bomb in the Central Bar, Gilford, Co. Down, presaged a bloody new year to come.[107] Three people died in the attack, which was widely regarded as the INLA's revenge for the bomb attack two weeks previously that killed seventeen-year-old Ronald Trainor, a member of its youth wing.[az] William Scott, a twenty-eight-year-old civil servant, lost

---

az   Ronald Trainor's mother, Dorothy, was shot dead by loyalists in April 1975 and at the time of Ronald's death his father, Malachy, was still recovering from injuries sustained in the same attack.

both legs and died two hours after the bombing. Richard Beattie, a married man with five children, also died in the no-warning blast – clearly aimed at a bar used almost exclusively by the local Protestant population, a purely sectarian target.

During the 'festive' month of December 1975, nine people had been killed between Portadown and Dundalk. People thought it couldn't get any worse, but they were wrong – within two weeks, seventeen more local people would be dead. In his 1975 end-of-year summary, the British Army's Commander Land Forces had pointed to Belfast and Mid-Ulster as hotbeds of sectarian violence where, he conceded, the 'majority of attacks were probably carried out by Protestant extremists'.[108] (Rarely are the words 'loyalist terrorists' or even 'loyalist paramilitaries' used in British official documents.)

A neat summary of the year's events is provided by two senior civil servants contemplating the wreckage (during a debate between themselves about the relative merits of the reintroduction of internment): 'A large proportion if not the majority of the mayhem in 1975 has been loyalist perpetrated; this is certainly so in relation to sectarian killings.'[109]

5

'THE MURDEROUS CYCLE CONTINUED' (JAN–MAY 1976)[a]

> Certainly the Catholic population (and indeed some Protestants) believe that there must be a 'Mr. Big' directing Protestant murder gangs, particularly just before elections.
>
> *Internal memo from senior MI6 official to senior British civil servant, 14 May 1975*[1]

Just as 1975 had ended, 1976 began in horror and blood. Its first victim was Sylvia McCullough, a married thirty-one-year-old Protestant woman who had been injured in the INLA Central Bar bombing in Gilford two days previously.[2] Three days later, two events occurred that, even by County Armagh's standards at the time, were truly shocking and triggered an equally savage revenge attack.

The first shooting took place at Whitecross – about four miles (6 km) from Mitchell's farm at Glenanne on Sunday 4 January. The Reavey family – a quiet, close-knit, modest and hard-working group of people – were at home. Sadie and James Reavey had eleven children, most of whom still lived at home. The family were all in work. Nothing terribly well paid: one was a joiner, another a nurse, another a bricklayer, another a plasterer. Sadie baked bread and James grew vegetables. Plain country people without pretensions. There was no tradition of politics in the family, though James knew the SDLP's Seamus Mallon socially. Both were avid GAA men.[3]

That Sunday evening, Sadie, James and three of their children

---

a   From the HET Report on Colm McCartney and Seán Farmer.

went to visit her sister nearby while brothers John-Martin, Brian and Anthony stayed at home. Just before six o'clock in the evening, the three brothers were sitting in armchairs at the fireside watching *Celebrity Squares* on TV.[4]

It was Anthony who first noticed the barrel of a gun poking through the front door. At first he thought it was soldiers. Moving forward to look more closely, he saw he was wrong. There were no soldiers. What he saw was the outline of three men in the hallway, two behind the one in front, who was nearly six feet tall and wearing a pointed hood with eyeholes.[5]

The sound of gunfire almost immediately drowned out the voices on the TV programme. John-Martin, sitting to the left of the fireplace, collapsed to the ground. Brian and Anthony ran into a bedroom, with the gunmen following them, shooting repeatedly. Anthony dived under the bed furthest from the door as the sound of gunfire went on and on. Sheltering there, he could hear the sound of Brian groaning and the gunmen kicking in doors and running around the house, looking for more victims. When the gunmen left, despite multiple bullet wounds to his legs, Anthony got up, checked his brothers, both of whom he realised were already dead, and stumbled next door for help.

Fr Peter Hughes, the parish priest, who knew the Reavey family well, gave Brian and John-Martin the last rites. Then, concerned because Anthony could not stand upright, they took care of him in a neighbour's house. The priest then set off with a heavy heart to tell the brothers' parents what had happened.[6]

Another brother, Oliver, who had given his parents a lift to Camlough, had returned home as Fr Hughes was saying prayers over his brothers' bodies. He had touched John-Martin, lying in a pool of blood, and realised he was beyond help. Anthony, lying on their neighbour's floor, explained to Oliver that Brian had also been hit and was in the bedroom. Oliver returned home and found Brian's body. Eugene, another brother, was at his own home about three miles (5 km) away when another priest, Fr Con Malone, broke the terrible news.

John-Martin Reavey

Brian Reavey

John-Martin just wanted to get out into the world and work. He loved his days as an apprentice "brickie" – particularly the banter of his work-mates. His favourite record at the time was "A Whiter Shade of Pale".[7] He was nick-named "Joe Fandango" at work – after "We skipped the light fandango, turned cartwheels 'cross the floor".[8]

'Brian was very athletic, a marathon runner and footballer. He played for St Killian's and for the County Armagh minor team. He trained as a joiner and was always making something lovely for the house. He could have become an artist, an engineer, or even a PE teacher, if he had had the chance.'

Eugene Reavey, brother of John-Martin, Brian and Anthony

The police moved into the Reavey home and began to examine it forensically. They discovered forty-three spent 9 mm bullet cases, one live 9 mm round and fifteen bullet heads. Thirty-five strike marks were listed in the lounge, passageway and bedroom. Unaccountably, however, they failed to locate two spent bullet cases which the family found three days later on the bedroom floor.

A getaway car was found on fire. It had been stolen in Armagh the day before the shooting. Police doused the burning vehicle and took it to a garage in Camlough – but they failed to take the basic minimum precautions required to preserve footprints or tyre marks.[b]

Ten minutes before the Reavey brothers were shot, an eyewitness

---

b   The Reavey family continues to be deeply concerned both at police forensic failures and the search of the house, which was conducted as though the police were searching for evidence to implicate the bereaved family.

(never questioned by the RUC) said he was stopped at an apparent official 'military or police checkpoint'. The HET has found no record of such a checkpoint. The fact that it had no deterrent effect, says the HET, may indicate that it was a fake and manned by 'persons acting in concert with the attackers'.[9]

No fewer than four guns had been used to attack the three brothers: a 9 mm Parabellum-calibre Sterling SMG whose breach block had been doctored,[c] a standard Sterling SMG,[d] a 9 mm Luger-type pistol[e] and a .455 Webley revolver.[f] John-Martin had been hit at least fourteen times and died from injuries to his neck and body. Brian had been hit four times in the chest and body.

'Anthony was tall with red hair. Even before he left school, he was raising turkeys to make some extra shillings. He was a mixture of the athlete and the artist. He played for various county under-age teams and the St Killian's senior team, but he also wrote poetry.'

Eugene Reavey, Anthony's brother

Anthony Reavey

Anthony died twenty-six days after the shootings. He was still on crutches from his injuries but apparently making a good recovery and was staying with his girlfriend in the village of Belleeks, County

---

c   The Parabellum-calibre Sterling was also used in the attempted murder of Mick McGrath and others at the Rock Bar on 5 June 1976.

d   The Sterling SMG was stolen from Glenanne UDR base and also used to murder Denis Mullen, Peter and Jenny McKearney, Trevor Brecknell, Michael Donnelly, Patsy Donnelly and Fred McLoughlin, and in a non-fatal attack at Tully's Bar, Belleeks. It was surrendered by Garfield Beattie (TAVR) in August 1976 after its use in the murder of Patsy McNeice on 25 July 1976.

e   The Luger was used in two non-fatal shootings in South Armagh, in September and December 1974, to kill Seán Farmer and Colm McCartney at Altnamackin, and in the attempted murder of Mick McGrath at the Rock Bar.

f   The Webley's serial number had been removed. It was also used to shoot Colm McCartney and Seán Farmer and in two non-fatal incidents in South Armagh. Recovered at Camlough in June 1978.

Armagh, when he was suddenly taken ill. His inquest stated that he died from a brain haemorrhage. The cause of death was initially given as 'natural causes', as he allegedly had a congenital weakness in a cranial blood vessel. This verdict, however, which appeared to ignore Anthony's physical and mental ordeal, was later overturned and the words 'open verdict' were inserted.[10]

When the HET began examining the available intelligence, many of the names that came up were already familiar from other cases. Despite a plethora of suspects, the HET has been unable to find any evidence of arrests, or whether Special Branch intelligence was ever passed to those who could make the best use of it – detectives investigating the killings. The HET says it can find 'no satisfactory explanation for this', but the obvious explanation is the usual one: Special Branch was keeping intelligence to itself rather than passing it on to colleagues in the CID.[11]

Former RUC Armagh SPG member John Weir claims in his 1999 affidavit that UDR man Robert McConnell was one of the gunmen who attacked the Reavey brothers.[12] In June 2006, members of the HET Command Team spoke to Weir in Dublin. He further asserted that the Reavey family's perceived links to the SDLP may have been a motive for the killings, intended to 'destabilise or influence political situations'.[13]

The RUC never questioned Phelim McGuinness, a farmer who lived opposite the Reaveys, about anything he saw or heard, but the HET points to a significant incident before the shooting which remains unexplained. On 2 January, Phelim and Brian were alone in the Reavey home when up to six men opened the front door and ordered them to lie face-down in the front garden.[14] The men, dressed in military-style uniforms, did not act like soldiers but one spoke with an English accent. They held a whispered discussion among themselves before leaving with no explanation. Neither Phelim nor Brian had mentioned this to anyone else to avoid causing anxiety. The

HET says the incident was 'hugely significant' and may have been either a scouting run or an aborted attack.[g]

Kevin Reavey, a cousin of the three dead men, also told the HET how, in the immediate aftermath of the shooting, an investigating officer in the family home appeared to be searching in cupboards. The officer stated he was looking for 'bullets and ammunition'. Kevin took this to infer that the officer had been instructed to search for such items in the possession of the victim's family. Incensed at the implication, Kevin forcibly pushed the RUC man out of the door, after which 'a brief scuffle' ensued.[15]

In the days and weeks after the shootings, far from being treated with sensitivity and respect, the Reavey family was abused and harassed by police and British soldiers. In particular, British soldiers insulted and abused the victims' grief-stricken mother, Sadie, as she travelled home from visiting Anthony in hospital.[16] The HET calls these actions 'appalling treatment' and also notes the 'efforts made by employers, clergy and politicians to stop the harassment, criminal damage to property, abuse and assaults to members of the Reavey family'. In the years since, Eugene Reavey has also been subjected to unsubstantiated claims made by former DUP leader Ian Paisley under the cloak of parliamentary privilege. Despite repeated requests, Paisley has to date refused to apologise.[17]

In its conclusion, the HET Report says the family was innocent and unconnected to any paramilitary activity. The murders were brutal and inhumane, and an instance of senseless sectarian violence. As for motive, the report suggests that because the family was well respected and prominent, with influence in the local community, murdering them would 'frighten their friends, other Catholics and supporters of the nationalist agenda'. It also says: 'Post-incident intelligence

---

g   According to the HET Report into the Reavey killings, this also showed 'a degree of planning and victim selection'. The killers possibly decided to wait until there were more potential targets in the family home.

indicates that a loyalist paramilitary gang (which included members of the security forces) was responsible for the murders and that the murders were linked to others in the area.'[18] It claims the paramilitary organisation most likely to have been responsible was the Mid-Ulster UVF, and, as members of the RUC and UDR were involved with this group, it follows that 'similar collusion could have taken place in these murders' (a reference to other murders where the HET believes it has also established collusion). The HET's use of the word 'could' here, however, is a serious understatement. One of the weapons used to slaughter the three Reavey brothers is linked through ballistics to the Rock Bar – a gun-and-bomb attack later in the year, on 5 June 1976, carried out entirely by police officers.

Dave Cox, director of the HET, has apologised (in person and in writing) to Eugene Reavey and his family for the 'disgraceful' harassment they suffered. The way they were treated by some members of the security forces, the HET says, is inexcusable. The HET also wrote to Sadie Reavey (who died in July 2013) informing her in writing that there is no trace of anything linking her sons to any paramilitary organisation or any criminal activity.[19]

When Anthony Reavey, who was just seventeen years old, gave his formal statement to police, it ended very poignantly. He stated quite simply that he had no idea why anyone would wish to harm him or his family.

Sixteen miles (26 km) away from the Reavey home on the same day as their shootings – 4 January – over the deceptively peaceful-looking fields and villages of Counties Armagh and Down, events were also developing in the townland of Ballydougan, the home of the O'Dowd family. Barney O'Dowd ran a farm and a successful coal- and milk-delivery business. Sixteen members of his extended family, six of them children, had gathered for an informal New Year party in Barney's L-shaped farm bungalow, 110 yards (100 m) up a lane leading from a minor road.[20]

It was a Sunday evening, and the following day it would be time for everyone to pick up the reins of everyday life and go back to work. Among the party were Barney's sons Barry (aged twenty-four), an oil-rig worker home from the Orkney Islands for the holidays, and Declan (aged nineteen), a quarry-man.[21] Also visiting the house was Joe O'Dowd, Barney's sixty-year-old brother.

Mingling among these were other family members, including Barney's wife, Kathleen, and their children Mary (aged twenty-three), Eleanor (thirteen) and Cathal (eleven). Also there were Joe's daughters, Una McCorry (aged thirty-two), Bernadette (twenty-three) and Deirdre (twenty-one), Una's husband, Joe McCorry, and their children, Aine (aged seven), Michael (five) and Philip (three), and a neighbour's child, Aine Gaffney (aged twelve).[22]

The kitchen and living room were full of laughter and chatter as the three generations enjoyed their evening. Barry was playing the piano. Kathleen was in the kitchen with her son Declan, her niece Una, Una's husband, Joe, and their children. She heard a knock at the front door and went to open it, assuming it was another guest arriving.

Instead of a greeting, however, three men with stocking masks over their faces pushed their way in, telling her they had come 'for money'. One stood with a gun held in both hands. Kathleen tried to close the door but the men pushed past her. She fled back to the kitchen. The first masked man, carrying an SMG, ran into the living room where Barney, Barry, Joe, Deirdre, Bernadette and Aine McCorry were sitting. Barney stood up and was shot in the wrist. The force spun him around and he fell towards the fireplace. The gunmen then began shooting at everyone in the room as they tried to take cover and protect the children. Bernadette and Deirdre pushed Aine behind the piano and covered her with their bodies.[23] Barney looked on in horror as his son Declan, by then in the hallway, was shot, dying instantly.

The same gunman then turned back to Barney and shot him four more times in the thigh and stomach. Thirty shots had been fired before the gunman stopped. The masked men turned and left.[24] Surviving family members emerged from under cover to find Joe dead in the living-room doorway, Barry dead beside the piano and Declan dead in the hallway. Barney was still alive but bleeding from his many injuries and was lying across his dead son Declan's knees. Joe McCorry called for an ambulance, the police and a priest. Twenty-two-year-old Noel O'Dowd, Barry and Declan's brother, arrived back from mass at 6.45 p.m. to find this scene of grief, confusion and blood. He drove to his uncle's house nearby for help and returned with his cousin Gregory.[25]

The first ambulance arrived to find two men lying in the hallway, one dead and the other wounded. It rushed Barney away for treatment and carried Declan's body away as well. The second ambulance found two more bodies lying lifeless and took them to the morgue. There, Seamus O'Dowd, Joe's son, identified his father's body and that of his two cousins, Barry and Declan.

Joe O'Dowd   *Declan O'Dowd*   *Barry O'Dowd*

The pathologist's reports found that Joe had been hit with three bullets, causing nine separate entry/exit wounds (one bullet fragmented while another grazed his head before hitting his arm). Massive internal injuries to his lungs and aorta had caused his rapid death. A line of three bullets had hit Declan, the first two of which had wounded him in the heart and lungs and would have caused his instant death. The first bullet which hit Barry was in the head and would have caused immediate death. The second two caused only superficial injuries. The three men had each been shot with three bullets.

The getaway car was stolen from Lurgan on the afternoon of the shootings. It was found burned out, and thus forensically useless, near Gilford, County Down, three miles (5 km) from the O'Dowd home.

Police scenes-of-crime officers arrived to begin their grim task, but the HET comments that nobody appears to have taken direct and effective control of the scene. 'Crime scenes should be preserved and access to them strictly controlled and recorded,' it says, to avoid cross-contamination and the loss or destruction of forensic opportunities. The HET concludes, however, that this was probably just 'incompetence' rather than anything more sinister.[26]

The HET also lists where the bullet heads were found – showing how wildly the gunmen fired in their determination to kill as many people as possible. Seventeen bullet heads and nineteen bullet casings were found. The obvious question arises: where were the two missing bullet heads?

That discrepancy was resolved in 2006 – thirty years after the attack – when HET investigators met Ronan O'Dowd. He had discovered the two bullet heads a month after the shooting when moving a settee. The fact that they were not noticed by investigating officers, says the HET, 'cannot be explained'.

Questions remain on the lack of urgency and determination shown by the RUC. Were any checkpoints set up? Was everyone in the house questioned? Why was a neighbour, held by police for twenty minutes that evening, not asked if he had seen anything suspicious? Despite all these apparent policing failures, three suspects were arrested in Lurgan the day after the shootings. (The RUC papers give no hint as to why or by whom.) Though the three were interviewed, all were released without charge – again, there are no records of the interviews.

Barney O'Dowd, despite being shot five times, was able to tell police two weeks after the shooting that he believed he recognised one of his assailants – a local loyalist with a distinctive jawline whom he had known for twenty years. The loyalist Barney named had bulging eyes – similar to another, far better-known, loyalist gunman, Robin Jackson. The detective sergeant in charge believed Barney might be mistaken and questioned him closely to try to ascertain which, if either, of these two men had been the gunman Barney recognised.

Despite the detective's reservations, seventeen days after the shooting he arrested the loyalist Barney had named and questioned him over three days.[h] The man denied involvement and gave the names of four men who, he said, would provide him with an alibi. The four men had all been drinking heavily on the day of the shooting. They had gone to the wake of one of the victims of the INLA's Central Bar bombing and had visited some of those injured.

The HET examined their alibis. The statements for the time of the shooting (6.30 p.m. on 4 January) were, it says, more vague than is normally acceptable for clearing a serious suspect. Tests were carried out on an anorak owned by the man Barney named. Traces of lead and antimony (firearms residue) were found on the left cuff, right front shoulder and inside both lower pockets. The loyalist said he had neither owned nor fired a shotgun since 1964 – twelve years earlier. The HET, having reviewed all this, concludes there was nothing to explain the firearms residue on the clothing of the man Barney named as a gunman. Nor is there any record of police following this up.

The same man was also named by a caller to the RUC on Portadown's confidential telephone recording service. The caller, who rang at 9 a.m. on 14 January (ten days after the murders) and again at 9 a.m. the following day, said, 'The man who murdered the O'Dowds, Ballydougan, is [name and partial address provided].' The named man was questioned and released without charge. The anorak and all other forensic evidence have been destroyed. No one was ever charged with the murders of Barry, Declan and Joe, but, yet again, the ballistic evidence stands a silent witness. A single firearm was used – a

h   The man has never been convicted and cannot be named for legal reasons.

standard British Army-issue, Sterling SMG with its serial number carefully removed – used to kill thirteen people in total.[i]

Robin Jackson's name crops up as a suspect for the O'Dowd killings twice in RUC intelligence files – once the following year and again eight years later, in 1984, when he was named by an informant as 'the headman/shooter'.[27] In some detail, the same informant said that the killers had hidden their weapons behind a telegraph pole in Waringstown, having escaped across the fields.

Seven men were named in police intelligence files between mid-1977 and 1984 as being responsible for the carnage. Six were known members of the Mid-Ulster UVF, but there is nothing in the RUC files to say whether these names were passed to the investigation team, or if any further enquiries were made. Yet again, it seems, RUC Special Branch treated intelligence as if it was their personal property.

In July 1976, seven months after the murders, some of the O'Dowd family reluctantly decided they should move away from Ballydougan. Before they left, Barney asked for a meeting with the RUC to be updated on the inquiry. Two officers arrived at his home but were dismissive and hostile, refusing to answer questions.[28] No member of the family has since been contacted by the police. One of Joe's sons, Gabriel, went to Lurgan RUC station in the mid-1980s and asked about allegations of Jackson's involvement. He was told Jackson's name was on the file but that 'nothing could be done to bring him to justice'.[29] The inquest into the three deaths lasted just one day.

Ronan O'Dowd, Joe's nephew, has now given what the HET terms 'highly significant' evidence. A day before the murders, he saw what may have been a 'dummy run'.[30] Ronan described seeing a red Austin or Morris car close to the family home between noon and

---

i   Daniel Hughes; James and Gertrude Devlin (William Leonard, UDR, convicted); Eugene Doyle and Arthur Mulholland (RUC man and UDR man suspected); the Miami Showband killings (two UDR men convicted); members of the O'Dowd family and Brendan McLaughlin (28 February 1980).

2 p.m. on Saturday 3 January, while he was out walking. He saw two men standing at the front of the car holding bulky radios with long aerials. Their faces were covered with masks and, because of that and the radios, he had assumed they were police or the British Army, and paid them no further heed. His last view was of the men looking towards his home and walking into a field. The lane where he had seen the car was used the following day as the getaway route. Ronan had spoken of this to the senior investigating detective within a couple of days of the murders, but there are no records on what lines of enquiry the detective pursued, if any, or whether a link was made between the sighting and the getaway car.

In addition to this evidence, a friend of Declan's told the HET he had the impression of being followed all day on 3 January. While he and Declan were at a local garage, a 'blue Mini' with four men inside, and a Ford carrying two men, had pulled up behind them. Both vehicles then drove off, but the same Mini overtook them later.[31]

When Noel O'Dowd returned to work after compassionate leave, a woman colleague told him that a co-worker had spoken of hearing talk of a planned attack on the family. Noel immediately told the police. There is nothing in the RUC papers to say if this was ever checked. The overheard conversation allegedly took place in Harry's Bar, Banbridge – the same bar where the gang who bombed Kay's Tavern and Donnelly's Bar in December 1975 had met to 'celebrate' their attacks.[32]

The HET Report concludes that the O'Dowd family was subjected to a 'callous', 'brutal', 'pre-meditated', 'orchestrated' and 'horrifying' attack for motives unknown other than 'bigoted, sectarian violence'. It said the attack had been co-ordinated to take place at the same time as the shootings at the Reavey home, and that the same gang was responsible. The Reaveys and the O'Dowds were becoming prosperous through hard work and enterprise. Perhaps that was enough to make them loyalist targets. Both families were also broadly sympathetic to the SDLP (Barney O'Dowd had acted as a party electoral observer at polling stations in Lurgan, where previously Catholics had not dared to show their faces).

So who did carry out the Reavey and O'Dowd killings? John Weir said in his written affidavit that Jackson was not only involved in murdering the O'Dowds, but had also planned the co-ordinated attacks on the Reaveys with RUC Reservist James Mitchell at the Glenanne farmhouse.[33] Weir further stated that fellow RUC Armagh SPG member William McCaughey was directly involved (this was corroborated by McCaughey himself, in a private message to a member of the Reavey family via a loyalist intermediary).[34] McCaughey denied being the gunman who shot the Reaveys and claimed that James Mitchell and his housekeeper, Lily Shields, had ferried the gang to and from the attack.[35] At a meeting with the RUC Serious Crime Review Team looking at the O'Dowd case, a detective chief inspector named one suspect as Roy Metcalfe.[j]

IRA retaliation for the killings of the Reaveys and O'Dowds was immediate, terrible and inexcusable.[36] The day after the six shootings, in the townland of Kingsmill, republican gunmen ambushed a minibus carrying sixteen men home to Bessbrook from work in Glenanne – a regular, routine journey.

At the start of the journey, there were five Catholic passengers, and eleven Protestants – but four Catholics got out at Whitecross, as usual, leaving only one Catholic worker in the van. As it cleared a rise, a man stepped out, flashing a torch. Up to a dozen armed men then emerged from the hedges along the lane. The driver assumed it was a security checkpoint and stopped. The sole Catholic left on the bus, Richard Hughes, was told to step forward. His workmates, fearing he was

---

j   After the major arms find on his land in October 1973, Winston Buchanan said Metcalfe, Jackson and an RUC man had forced him to store the weapons. Metcalfe, Robin Jackson's brother-in-law, was killed by the IRA on 18 October 1989. The RUC man (who cannot be named for reasons of confidentiality) was also later killed by the IRA.

going to be killed by loyalists, tried to prevent him identifying himself as Catholic. Hughes was ordered to 'get down the road and don't look back'. Gunmen then opened fire on the eleven remaining defenceless workers. More than 100 bullets were fired in less than a minute. Ten were killed outright while the remaining man, Alan Black, survived, despite sustaining eighteen gunshot wounds.

After the initial screams, Alan Black recalled years later, 'There was silence. I was semi-conscious and passed out several times with the deadly pain and cold. I must have been lying at the roadside waiting on the ambulance for up to 30 minutes. It was like an eternity. When help arrived I could not get the words out quick enough. I was afraid I'd die and nobody would ever know what happened. I was hysterical and wanted to tell everyone – the ambulance men, nurses, doctors, police.'[37]

The IRA has never admitted responsibility. The claim came using the name 'South Armagh Republican Action Force'. The weapons used, however, were employed in 110 other attacks, many of them claimed by the IRA, including the five killings at Tullyvallen Orange Hall on 1 September 1975 and the killings of an RUC chief superintendent and a superintendent on 20 March 1989.[38] In its report on Kingsmill, the HET says the attack was planned before the twin attacks on the Reaveys and the O'Dowds – but also accepts it was carried out in direct response to those six murders.

Eugene Reavey remembers the Royal Marines stopping him on his way to work every morning for five days after the Kingsmill massacre. The routine was the same every day. The soldiers would order him, at gunpoint, into a tributary of the River Blackwater and force him to kneel in the cold water so it flowed just under his nose and he could barely breathe. Each day, an officer stood beside him in the river, pointing a gun at his head and demanding to know the names of the gunmen responsible for Kingsmill. The soldier would then pull the trigger. Eugene would clench his teeth and wait for the bullet which, thankfully, never came. It was a battle of wills. Eugene stubbornly refused to change his route to work and eventually the Marines gave up. He did not think there was any point making a complaint to the RUC.[39]

London had a real crisis on its hands. Fifteen people had been killed in two days (a sixteenth, Anthony Reavey, died later). Northern Ireland, yet again, teetered on the edge. The authorities knew they had to do something or civil war was a possibility.

More than thirty years on, by examining declassified 'top secret' documents now publicly available, it is possible to reflect on the authorities' thinking – and their actions. At Stormont, civil servants were considering their options. Internment, such a disaster in 1971, was theoretically back on the agenda. On 7 January 1976, the military top brass and their political counterparts decided it would be a good idea to draft two battalions of the UDR into South Armagh, along with 420 regular British Army soldiers.[40]

Meanwhile, loyalists were sabre-rattling. At a meeting with Secretary of State Merlyn Rees that same morning, the ULCCC[k] had spoken of further murders and 'unrestrained retaliation' if the IRA continued attacks on Protestant targets.[41] The British Secretary of State for Defence, Roy Mason, proposed that County Armagh be categorised, in his words, a 'Special Emergency Area', with the reintroduction of internment, deployment of the SAS and control of all cross-border traffic. Prime Minister Harold Wilson said a decision had already been taken to deploy the SAS in Armagh.[42]

To reassure the Irish government about such a drastic move, a senior civil servant was ordered to send an explanatory telegram to the British Ambassador in Ireland. The SAS, the telegram would say,

---

k   The Ulster Loyalist Combined Co-ordinating Committee, which replaced the Ulster Army Council and comprised the UDA, UVF, Red Hand Commando, Vanguard Service Corps/Ulster Volunteer Service Corps, Down Orange Welfare, Loyalist Association of Workers and Orange Volunteers (most of these groups were illegal). The ULCCC aimed to prepare a unified 'Ulster Army' in the event of a British withdrawal from Northern Ireland.

was being deployed because 'sectarian killings could be countered only with a highly-professional surveillance capability'.[43] The crisis was so serious that, also on 7 January, senior politicians from both the Labour and Conservative parties were called to Downing Street, where the prime minister explained that the British Army's high-readiness 'Spearhead' battalion had already been deployed in Armagh and he had invited the Taoiseach to London to explain why.[44]

Rees confirmed that other steps such as curfews, ID cards and even the laying of small minefields along the border were not being ruled out.[45] He also told the meeting that he had met with the UDA the previous day, where the loyalist delegation had complained about the Irish tricolour being flown in Crossmaglen. The following day, a White Paper dated 8 January 1976 was prepared, detailing the SAS unit that had been selected for deployment in County Armagh.[l] It was to be the eighty-five-strong unit at that time on duty in Dhofar, training groups of local tribesmen (firqats) for what are euphemistically called 'irregular operations'.[m] Their knowledge of counter-insurgency operations in a mountainous desert apparently made them an ideal choice for deployment in South Armagh.

On the same day, when Irish Justice Minister Paddy Cooney met Rees in Dublin, he raised concerns about the dangers posed by the SAS. Not, that is, the deployment of such a unit of trained killers in South Armagh, but of the propaganda value the IRA might extract from the news.[46] Cooney asked Rees to be sure to stress that the SAS would also be used against loyalists. No mention is made in the minutes of a meeting the following day of either the Reavey or O'Dowd murders; the focus was entirely on the IRA.

---

l   Individual members or (officially) former members of the SAS were already active in Northern Ireland in a unit called the 'Special Reconnaissance Unit'. A White Paper is a government proposal.

m   Firqats were groups of Dhofaris turned against their former comrades-in-arms to fight alongside the SAS in quelling the rebellion against the sultan of Oman. See Chapter 13: From Dhofar to Armagh for further details of SAS activities in Dhofar.

On 10 January, Harold Wilson contemplated a nightmare vision of a possible future for Northern Ireland. In a note (described by the Prime Minister himself as 'apocalyptic'), Wilson said he was preparing for the worst – civil war.[47] He examined the possibility of a British withdrawal and considered the policy option of giving Northern Ireland a 'high degree' of self-government. Britain's role would be reduced to merely representing Northern Ireland diplomatically on the international stage. If Northern Ireland overthrew all established conceptions of British law and order, wrote Wilson, Her Majesty's government could not undertake a law and order responsibility.[48]

The following Sunday, 11 January, the top brass met again – at the British prime minister's official country residence, Chequers. They included not only Wilson, Rees and Roy Mason, but also the British Army's Commander of General Staff, its Commander in Northern Ireland and the usual top civil servants.[49] The focus was, again, almost entirely on the IRA (as though the loyalist threat did not exist). Sir David House, British Army GOC Northern Ireland, said their 'main enemy' was the IRA, though he conceded that there had been considerable violence from what he called 'Protestant paramilitaries'. But, he added, 'this had usually been in response to action from the Provos'.[50]

The 'dirty men' in South Armagh, said House, were the IRA, and he hoped the Garda Síochána would follow through on its promise to 'harass' them. House then went on to express a view that no 'pressure' should be put on 'people north of the Border' (i.e. loyalists) as this would be the 'wrong response'. It would 'disillusion' them, he said.[51] Wilson, responding, said he feared another UWC strike or even a Rhodesian-style unilateral declaration of independence.[52]

Despite a nonchalant attitude towards loyalists, figures provided by Wilson in the House of Commons on 12 January speak volumes. Of the thirty-nine civilians killed in County Armagh in 1975,[n]

---

n   There had been a mistake in the calculations. The accurate figure is thirty-eight:

twenty were killed by the UVF, seventeen by republicans and one by the British Army.[53] Yet in all these high-level crisis discussions, virtually no actions against loyalists or any debate on the dangers posed by UVF infiltration of the UDR or RUC were considered. Quite the contrary, in fact, as Wilson praised the 'volunteer soldiers of the UDR' whose job was 'to protect their fellow citizens'.[54]

As crisis meetings were convened in London, despite the on-going UDA campaign of sectarian murder, UDA leaders, including 'Supreme Commander' Andy Tyrie, were secretly meeting Northern Ireland Office officials in North Down. Tyrie congratulated British officials on the mobilisation of the UDR into South Armagh and the introduction of the SAS, adding that he hoped the security forces would 'now be given a free rein to demolish the Provisional IRA'.[55]

It is worth re-stating that by the beginning of 1976, the British government and its army were well aware that the UDR was heavily infiltrated by, among others, Tyrie's own paramilitaries. Three years earlier, British Army research concluded that between 5 and 15 per cent of UDR members were in various loyalist armed groups.[56] Yet at a time of such a crisis, London chose to deploy this very force into the seething sectarian cauldron that was South Armagh. No wonder Tyrie was gleeful.

On 10 February, Cardinal William Conway, the head of the Catholic Church in Ireland, and nine other bishops met Harold Wilson at Downing Street. Where, inquired the cardinal, did the UVF get its guns? Merlyn Rees replied, 'Canada.'[57] This is in direct contradiction to the British Army's internal analysis, which was that the main source of all loyalist weapons was the UDR, and the regiment was the 'only source' of modern weaponry.

Another document shows that, very soon after the Reavey and O'Dowd killings, the RUC – and by extension London – had a good

calculated from McKittrick (1999) *Lost Lives* (1st edn).

idea of who had killed the O'Dowds and the ten Kingsmill workers. On 13 January, at a meeting in Stormont Castle, the RUC Chief Constable, Sir James Flanagan, told Rees that forensic tests had established that the IRA weapons used at Kingsmill had all been used in previous attacks.[58] He also said that 'links with past Protestant extremist atrocities had similarly been established in the case of the weapons used in the murder of the O'Dowds' (there is no mention of the Reaveys).°

Meanwhile, a training cadre of the SAS was deployed in South Armagh on 9 January, according to a paper prepared the previous day for the prime minister. Fifteen men were due to join them two days later, until an intended total of around sixty men were deployed.[59] This was confirmed in mid-February (in a Ministry of Defence briefing prepared for Roy Mason before his visit to SAS headquarters in Hereford).[60] In fact, an advance party of eight SAS men arrived first, followed by eighty-five more who had recently returned from Dhofar. SAS duties were primarily 'prolonged covert observation of suspected terrorists' houses, their pubs and bars … with a view to capturing or killing the terrorists'.[61] But SAS men also patrolled alongside the UDR and the regular British Army, and were based at their joint barracks at Bessbrook.

While the great and the good met in London and Belfast, discussing their official response to the bloodshed, others were doing the same. The UVF was determined to retaliate for Kingsmill. Various plans were hatched, chief among them being to attack either a convent in Newry or a Catholic primary school. Weir claims the target was to be Belleeks primary school, five miles (8 km) from Kingsmill.

---

o   The gun used to kill the O'Dowds was also used to kill Daniel Hughes, James and Gertrude Devlin, Eugene Doyle and Arthur Mulholland, Francis O'Toole, Anthony Geraghty and Brian McCoy (Miami Showband), and Brendan McLaughlin in February 1980. In total, three UDR members were convicted in relation to these killings.

William McCaughey has confirmed that this was a target, along with an alternative – Our Lady's Grammar School in Newry (which also housed the Sisters of Mercy Order). Speaking to the BBC, McCaughey said:

> The intention would have been to kill the occupants of the building, quite simply, and it would have been nuns and anyone else who happened to be there. It would have been a case of meeting republican terror with greater loyalist terror. That would have been the rationale behind it. Pretty sectarian, pretty extreme stuff but the murders of ten innocent, working-class Protestants was pretty sectarian, pretty horrific.[62]

In February 2001, during a meeting between PFC researchers and John Weir in Paris, Weir said (UDR man) Robert McConnell had devised the plan to attack the primary school in Belleeks, aiming to kill the thirty children who attended the school, along with their teachers: 'Massive retaliation was expected after Kingsmill. A big, big job was planned which would make Kingsmill small by comparison.'[63] Weir also claimed that what he termed 'McConnell's handlers' (i.e. British military intelligence) had considered and approved the anticipated outcome. If the Belleeks school had been attacked, it would have meant outright civil war.

'McConnell's handlers would have wanted provocation in order to cause civil war,' Weir told the PFC in Paris. 'A rural school was the target – the small school by Belleeks. McConnell was the driving force. He was not a criminal or a madman. He was willing to do it because the end would have justified the means.' Weir claimed, however, that, when the plan went to Belfast, the UVF leadership there vetoed the attack because they, too, feared civil war would be the outcome. The UVF leadership, said Weir, already suspected that McConnell was being manipulated by British military intelligence. Blunders made by UVF commanders suggest they might not have been the sharpest tools in the box – but even they began to wonder if they were being used.

The planned attack and events leading up to it, i.e. the murders at Donnelly's and Kay's bars, the killings of the Reaveys and O'Dowds (in all of which there is clear evidence of security force involvement) and the IRA's bloody response at Kingsmill, were a potential tipping point in the conflict. At the time, according to Colin Wallace, MI5 was dominated by hardline officers who deeply distrusted Harold Wilson's Labour government.[64] Elements in the British military and security establishment had long been suspicious of Wilson's allegiances, believing him to be 'a red in the bed', drifting dangerously towards an all-Ireland solution. They were bitterly opposed to Sunningdale, which gave the Irish government a role in Northern Ireland, and, Wallace says, had been covertly encouraging the 1974 UWC strike to bring down power-sharing. If the planned Belleeks school attack had gone ahead, prompting potential outright conflict, it would have provided those spoiling for an all-out fight with the IRA plenty of justification for a 'gloves-off' policy. With violence spiralling out of control, as McConnell and his handlers had planned, the hawks in the Ministry of Defence and MI5 would have swept the board. Given what is now known about successive British colonial strategies in Kenya, Malaya and elsewhere, it is reasonable to assume there were those in London itching to use similar tactics in Northern Ireland – albeit covertly.[p]

McCaughey insisted in his interview with the BBC that the plan was abandoned because there was not sufficient support 'on the ground' after so many recent killings. Either way, neither the school nor the convent was attacked.

Robert McConnell was shot dead by the IRA three months after

---

p   See Chapter 13: From Dhofar to Armagh for an account of these previous counter-insurgency campaigns.

the slaughter at the Reavey and O'Dowd homes. Like so many others, he took what he knew about the Mid-Ulster series of murders and the people behind them to the grave. He was thirty-two. His mother had died six weeks earlier. His cousin's wife witnessed his murder. Two or three men opened fire, hitting him five times in the head.

If the suspicions of some of his associates at the time were correct (and McConnell was a military intelligence agent) then one question arises: was anyone co-ordinating the attacks that culminated in the Kingsmill massacre and the 15 January 'civil war' summit at Downing Street? The three weeks leading up to Kingsmill included the attacks on Donnelly's Bar in South Armagh and Kay's Tavern in Dundalk, leaving five dead. Then there were the attacks on the Reavey and O'Dowd families, leaving a further six dead. All these attacks were linked to the same group of people, focused on James Mitchell's Glenanne farmhouse. The group included serving members of the RUC and UDR. Were they simply running amok? Or was someone, or some organisation, pulling their strings?

At a meeting with Chief Constable Hugh Orde and Assistant Chief Constable (ACC) Sam Kincaid in 2004, PFC staff asked if there were any plans to question McCaughey, a former police officer, about his plan to attack a convent or a primary school. Orde turned to Kincaid, who paused before admitting that there were no plans to interview him.[65] McCaughey has since died (of natural causes).

* * *

We move north now, from Armagh to the ancient town of Dungannon in South Tyrone on St Patrick's Day, 1976. The town, or at least the nationalist part of it, was celebrating the Irish national saint's day in customary fashion.[q] The Hillcrest Bar on Donaghmore Road, an

---

q   Both communities now celebrate St Patrick's Day, but in 1976 it was regarded as a mainly nationalist celebration.

ordinary town-centre bar, was busier than usual for the time of day, with customers coming in to 'drown the shamrock'. They included Joseph Kelly (aged fifty-seven), a mechanic who had just been to mass for the saint's day and was on his way to pick up his wife, Mary, at the end of her nursing shift at the local hospital.[66]

Andrew Small

Outside, Andrew Small (sixty-two), a married man with four children, had also just come from mass and was walking with Winifred (Winnie) his wife, in the spring air.[67] Andrew went into a shop while Winnie continued up the street past the Hillcrest Bar. She was waiting for him to catch up with her and turned round to see if he was coming.[68]

Patrick Barnard

Outside the bar, two thirteen-year-old boys, James McCaughey and Patrick Barnard, were dawdling idly past on their day off school. A green Austin 1100 drove up and parked at the kerbside. The driver emerged and got into a red Rover car parked nearby. John Fee, the manager of the Hillcrest Bar, was working on the first floor when he heard the explosion. He ran downstairs to find pandemonium. The noise was still echoing around the hills that circle Dungannon. Norbert McCaughey, James' father, heard it from his home and shuddered.[69] Closer to the detonation, four people were lying dead or dying: Patrick Barnard, James McCaughey, Joseph Kelly and Andrew Small. Winifred Small was knocked off her feet by the blast. Forty-nine people were injured, nine seriously.[70]

Joseph Kelly

Ambulances began to arrive. St Patrick's Day 1976 was well and truly over for the townspeople of Dungannon. James McCaughey's heart was lacerated in the blast. Norbert, his father, was inveigled by friends to the hospital (on the pretext of meeting a friend home from England for the holiday). No one wanted to scare him in case it was not his son lying in the morgue, but it was.[71]

'An RUC sergeant whisked off a white sheet and I saw the body of a thirteen-year-old boy. I couldn't recognise it as James and was relieved for a second or two. Then I saw that the Pioneer pin was attached to his jacket upside down – just like James' always was, despite Molly telling him to put it on the right way up. His hair was blown clear off his head. I went home to tell Molly.'

James McCaughey   Norbert McCaughey, father of James

The scene at the Hillcrest was one of 'total devastation'.[72] Apart from some pieces of shrapnel and pieces of James' clothing, little was discovered to assist the police in finding those responsible. That left the RUC with only intelligence reports. Early and, as it turned out, 'flawed' intelligence originating from the British Army held republicans to blame. The RUC acted immediately, raiding the McCaughey family home at 4.20 a.m. on 18 March – before James' broken body had even been returned to his grieving parents, brothers and sisters.[73] Leading the raiding party was the same sergeant who had thrown back the sheet over the boy's body so briskly, without any apparent concern for the feelings of his father. Norbert said, 'The police used the most disgusting, horrible, ignorant language. They busted in the front door, smelling of drink and claimed James had been involved in placing the bomb.' The McCaugheys' remaining children were 'bundled into the living room like cattle, they were terrified'.[74] The HET has apologised for this 'gross intrusion of the privacy of the family home at a time when everyone was grieving for the loss of James'.[75]

Six months later, the dead boy's bloodstained clothes, minus his Pioneer pin, were returned to his family. Norbert says they were just 'dumped' on the doorstep. He wondered for years about James' pin until, quite recently, Clarke Small, the son of Andrew who was killed in the same bombing, discovered it among his father's clothing and returned it.

The day after the explosion, a second piece of intelligence was received by police, blaming the Mid-Ulster UVF and providing details of possible suspects. In stark contrast to the immediate and enthusiastic action that police took in raiding the home of a bereaved family (where they found nothing) based on (flawed) intelligence that republicans were to blame, the HET can discover 'no record of any RUC action' taken specifically in response to this new and – as it turned out – accurate information implicating the UVF.[76]

Two months later, in May 1976, the name 'Garnet James Busby', plus an additional unnamed suspect, crops up in police files. Again, no police action was taken, and because there are no available papers, the HET Report says it is impossible to determine why this was the case.[r] Busby was arrested in 1980 (a full four years later), interviewed for six days and released without charge. Two others were arrested around the same time but also released without charge. Six months later, in December 1980, Busby was again arrested 'as a result of intelligence received'.[77] After twenty-four hours in custody he finally admitted his role in the Hillcrest Bar bombing.

The following day, 10 December 1980, Busby voluntarily made a statement to police under caution. 'I did not want to do it,' Busby said in his statement, 'but felt I had no option.' He said he drove the bomb to the Hillcrest Bar with a scout in front. He admitted leaving the bomb there and getting into another car driven by the scout, before returning to where he had left his own car at the cattle mart. 'At no time did I think or intend that anyone would be killed in the bombing,'

---

r   A possible explanation for the lack of files, says the HET Report, is that all pre-1978 custody records held at Gough Barracks, Armagh, the central point for their collection, were destroyed 'because of asbestos contamination'. This explanation for the missing papers is dismissed as unbelievable by many families seeking to discover the truth about their relatives' killings.

Busby told police. 'I know it's stupid to say that now.' His stupidity extended to contradiction. While Busby said in this statement that he had been out of the UVF for the two years before the Hillcrest bombing (i.e. since early 1974), he then admitted his direct involvement in murdering Peter and Jenny McKearney in October 1975.

Busby appeared in court at Belfast on 23 October 1981 and pleaded guilty to fourteen offences including six murders, four of them at the Hillcrest Bar. For these he received mandatory life sentences as well as multiple concurrent sentences for explosives and firearms offences. In total he received six life sentences and ninety-four years in jail. He served sixteen years and was released in February 1997.

The next attack came on 7 May 1976, close to the border in South Armagh, when loyalists targeted Tully's Bar in the village of Belleeks. It was yet another no-warning gun-and-bomb attack.[s] Fortunately, unlike the Hillcrest, there were no fatalities. In his 3 January 1999 affidavit, John Weir claims that the gang responsible believed they had an accurate floor-plan of the bar.[78] It showed no escape routes, thus making Tully's an attractive target. They intended to detonate the bomb and then '[shoot] the place up' as customers fled through the only exit – but their floor plans were inaccurate and people managed to escape into the bar's living quarters.[79]

In the same affidavit, Weir conjures up a surreal picture of Mitchell's farmyard on the night before the attack on Tully's. There were, he says, between eight and ten armed men dressed in camouflage, drilling up and down in the yard. He also claims that the British military had been tipped off about the attack, but failed to act on the information.

About an hour before closing time, a thirty-pound (14 kg) bomb of commercial explosives, contained in a gas cylinder, was left in a

---

s   At his February 2001 meeting with JFF in Paris, John Weir claimed that Mitchell kept a group of internal layouts of pubs on his window sill. These, Weir said, had been provided to the RUC annually for licence renewal purposes and were then passed to Mitchell for use in planning loyalist attacks.

hallway leading to Tully's lounge by a man who kicked the door before running off to a waiting car.[80] As customers were leaving through a rear door, the bomb exploded. The front door was blown into the pub by the blast and but for its steel reinforcements (added after the Donnelly's Bar attack), which took the full explosion, many of those inside might have been killed or seriously injured.[81] An ambulance was called, but, while many people were badly shocked, no one required hospital treatment. Troops found a green Volkswagen car burned out on the nearby Whitecross Road. There were no prosecutions for this bombing.[82]

There is a vital link between Tully's Bar and the other attacks. The gun used in the attack was the one stolen from Glenanne in May 1971 and subsequently used to murder eleven people: Denis Mullen, Peter and Jenny McKearney, the victims at Donnelly's Bar, the Reavey brothers, Fred McLoughlin and Patrick McNeice. Aside from the provenance of the gun, the Tully's Bar attack seems to have been planned in a similar way to the attack on Donnelly's Bar, seven miles (11 km) away and five months previously, and the Rock Bar attack which followed a month later.

It wasn't long before another bar was attacked. Just eight days after the Tully's ambush, loyalist sights turned to the little village of Charlemont, on the border of Counties Armagh and Tyrone. In 1976, Charlemont was hardly more than a road junction – just a few houses with Millar Hill Orange Hall perched on a hill looking down on them. Blink and you would miss Charlemont even today as you drive from Armagh city across a bridge over the River Blackwater and uphill towards Moy.

Long before May 1976, Charlemont had seen more than its share of bloodshed. The village is named after Charles Blount (1563–1606), Lord Mountjoy, who as Lord Deputy of Ireland wielded an iron fist. Part of his campaign to subjugate Ulster was fought around the River Blackwater.

On the night of 15 May 1976, Charlemont was the scene of two co-ordinated loyalist gun-and-bomb attacks intended to murder as many people as possible: not in one Catholic-owned bar, but in two. It started off as a normal Saturday night. Frederick McLoughlin

Fred McLoughlin

(aged forty-seven), a manager in the local dairy, had just returned from driving his friend Seán's children to a dance at Ardboe, County Tyrone. Fred had been born a Protestant, but married May, a Catholic, and converted. He was a happy-go-lucky character, the sort of man who would crack a joke so dry it would take a few minutes before everyone in the company started laughing. Fred and Seán decided to stop off for a drink at the Eagle Bar.[83] They were the last customers let in. It was a tense time and the landlord, Peter Hughes, was keeping a close eye on his bar and its twenty or so customers. At around 10 p.m., Peter placed timber security shutters over the two front windows, and fifty minutes later, the front door was closed and locked. Fred was sitting with Seán and another friend, Brian Donnelly. Fred was facing one of the windows and Brian had his back to it when the shooting started. Two gunmen – one using an SMG, the other a revolver – sprayed the window with gunfire.

Peter saw the flashes as the bullets smashed through his bar's security shutters. He heard the rattle of gunfire and shouted to everyone to get down. When the shooting stopped, he began helping the injured into a back room before hearing the massive explosion at nearby Clancy's Bar.[84] Fred had been hit once in the chest but remained conscious. Brian was seriously injured, along with two others.[†] Seán tried

---

† Brian Donnelly is on strong prescription painkillers and has been unable to work since this event. He received £1,000 in compensation for injuries caused by a serving RUC officer whose status was withheld from the courts. He has a case before the police ombudsman.

to stem the flow of Fred's blood from his right side with handker-
chiefs, lifting him against a pool table.[85]

Another customer, Marie O'Hagan, was shot in the head.
Miraculously, as a doctor in Craigavon Hospital removed the bullet,
he discovered her hair had wound itself round and round the bullet as
it spun, slightly cushioning it before it hit her head. Marie may be one
of very few people in the world whose life was saved by her own hair.[86]

The chaos at the Eagle was mirrored by frantic efforts to save the
injured at Clancy's Bar, a few yards up the road. The bomb that exploded
at its front door had killed three people: its owner Felix (Vincy)
Clancy, Seán O'Hagan (brother-in-law of Marie, who was shot in the
Eagle) and Robert McCullough. Witnesses speak of seeing a green or
a blue flash as the bomb detonated, bringing down the ceiling. People
screamed out from the rubble for help. One woman managed to get
two arms out above the rubble and was pulled free. Another woman
nearly suffocated in the debris.[87]

Felix (Vincy) Clancy   *Seán O'Hagan*   *Robert McCullough*

Many of the people sitting having a sociable drink that Saturday
night were seriously injured. Vincy Clancy certainly had the worst
luck of any. He had just returned from the Eagle to his own bar when
the bomb went off, killing him. Seán O'Hagan died from multiple
fractures of the skull. Broken bits of wood and other debris had struck
him all down his left side, killing him instantly.[88]

The injured from both bars were rushed to South Tyrone Hospital some five miles (8 km) away, where a bullet was removed from Fred McLoughlin's chest after emergency surgery. Fred died in hospital of his massive internal injuries some sixteen days later, in the early hours of 31 May 1976. 'The sixteen days and nights were a nightmare', remembers Jim McLoughlin. 'We knew Dad was fighting for his life. Some days he improved and the doctors would tell us to go home and get some sleep but we would be wakened up again in the middle of the night to get back to the hospital as his condition worsened.'[89]

The front of the Eagle had been hit thirty times with bullets from two guns – most of them directed through the window to the left side of the bar (where the majority of the customers were sitting); and seventeen more bullets were found on the pavement outside. Whoever was responsible knew the bar's layout. No group admitted responsibility, but the local UVF members were prime suspects.

There appeared to be a breakthrough in the investigation only twenty minutes after the attacks, when a Ford Cortina was reported smouldering close by and another car was reported as speeding away from it – a potential gold mine for any investigator.[90] Three masks were found in the getaway car, along with a 9 mm bullet. Three fingerprints were found on the driver's door surround.

Earlier in the day, police in Portadown had arrested Ronald John Hanlon (aged twenty) in possession of a stolen Ford Cortina (not the one used in the attacks at Charlemont). He was re-arrested later in the day under anti-terrorism legislation and questioned about a pipe-bomb attack at a Catholic church in nearby Blackwatertown, in which several people were injured.[u] He admitted his role, saying he had acted as a look-out. Hanlon was held in custody at Portadown for the remainder of Saturday 15 May 1976 and therefore could not have been involved personally in the Charlemont attacks. But the

---

u   A pipe-bomb had been put outside a Catholic church at Blackwatertown on 29 February 1976, injuring a number of people, some seriously.

fact that he had been in a stolen Ford Cortina clearly gave rise to police suspicions, and the following day he admitted stealing the car used in the attacks on the Eagle Bar and Clancy's Bar.

He told police he had been 'picked up' at his home, given a selection of car keys and had stolen a car from near Portadown swimming pool. He had then followed two men (whom he would not name) to Armagh and left the stolen Ford outside the city. The fingerprints found on the car abandoned after the Charlemont attacks were Hanlon's: 'However he was never charged in connection with the theft of that car or any offence in connection with the shootings and bombing at Charlemont.'[91] Instead, he was charged with the unrelated bomb attack at Blackwatertown. He was given fifteen-year and twelve-year sentences, to run concurrently, for wounding with intent and explosives offences.

Two days after the Charlemont attacks, police received intelligence about the possible involvement of three men in stealing the attack car (one of the three being Hanlon) and where the car had been held between its theft and the attacks. The following day, police searched a house occupied by a sixty-six-year-old former B Special, church elder and justice of the peace, Andrew Godfrey Foote (since deceased). There they found 695 rounds of .22 calibre and sixty-nine rounds of 9 mm ammunition. There is no record of the police checking these against the bullets used in the attack on the Eagle Bar.

Less than three months after the Eagle/Clancy's attacks, the police had a genuine breakthrough. On 27 July they were told that one of those responsible was Garfield Gerald Beattie, a nineteen-year-old labourer and a serving private in the TAVR, based in Portadown.[v] Beattie was arrested on 11 August, originally in connection with the murder of another local man, Patrick McNeice.[w] He was initially

---

v   Beattie joined the TAVR on 24 September 1974.
w   Shot dead at his home on 25 July 1976.

uncooperative, but eventually admitted his role in that murder. He then admitted his role in the attack at the Eagle in Charlemont, saying, 'I was on the SMG – it was a scare job.' Beattie went on to admit his role in the murder of SDLP branch chairman Denis Mullen in September 1975, and implicated others in the attacks on the Eagle/Clancy's, including David Henry Dalziel Kane, a twenty-eight-year-old local orchard owner and former UDR man.[92] Beattie took police officers to countryside locations around his home in Annaghmore, where he recovered and surrendered four guns and ammunition, including the SMG he had used in the attack on the Eagle Bar. The other three weapons were all .455 revolvers.

Kane was then also arrested, and four days later admitted to being a driver during the attack on the Eagle. He confirmed one of the gunmen was Beattie, but neither he nor Beattie would give the name of the second gunman. Beattie said he had been ordered to attack the bar by a man he refused to name, whom he had been with in a loyalist bar.[93] Kane denied UVF membership, but admitted going to the same bar as Beattie and paying UVF dues. He and Beattie were charged with Fred McLoughlin's murder, while Beattie was also charged with murdering Patrick McNeice and Denis Mullen. Neither admitted any involvement in the simultaneous attack on Clancy's.[94] Both pleaded guilty in court to Fred's murder and were given life sentences. Both also pleaded guilty to attempted murder and possession of firearms and received sentences of between fourteen and eighteen years. Beattie also got two life sentences for murdering Denis Mullen and Patrick McNeice.

That left significant unanswered questions about the third man, whom both said had been involved but both refused to name. The police still had no one accountable for the attack on Clancy's – where three men had lost their lives. Two years after the Eagle/Clancy's attacks and twenty-one months after Kane and Beattie were first questioned, police arrested a third man. It is unknown to this day what led police to arrest Dungannon man Joseph Norman Lutton, who eventually admitted involvement, implicating Beattie and Kane in both the Eagle Bar attack (for which both had already pleaded guilty) and in the simultaneous bomb attack on Clancy's Bar (in which Beattie and Kane had both denied involvement).[95] Lutton confirmed Kane had been the driver and said that Beattie had lit the bomb fuse at Clancy's before he and Beattie had both fired shots at the Eagle. He said a fourth man, who he did not name, then picked them up for their getaway.

Where Beattie described the attack at the Eagle as a 'scare job', Lutton stated that he believed it was a 'test run' before his acceptance into the UVF – but that he had only taken part because he was 'scared' the UVF would kill him.[96] Lutton was charged with murdering Fred McLoughlin and the three victims at Clancy's Bar, along with possessing offensive weapons and explosives with intent to endanger life.

When the case came to court, the 'officer in charge' of the investigation gave sworn evidence that Lutton had 'no part in the planning of the multiple murder'.[97] In contrast, the HET believes that Lutton was centrally involved.[98] He had admitted to police that he and Beattie (with whom he regularly drank in a UVF bar in Portadown) 'had fired the guns at The Eagle Bar'. It is unlikely that Lutton, having been told of the plans days earlier, had not enquired any further or been briefed in any way. The same officer claimed in court that Lutton had not thought 'anything sinister was going to happen' when he got into a car used in the attack. Again, this contradicts Lutton's statement to police in which he said that he 'had been recruited to take part in the attacks by Beattie two or three days before they occurred'.

As a result of the mitigating evidence given for Lutton by the lead investigating officer, Lord Justice Gibson made no recommendation on the life tariff Lutton had to serve because, he said, 'the police officer was convinced that Lutton "bitterly regretted" his involvement'.[x]

Vincy Clancy had always ensured Lutton was made welcome by the mainly Catholic clientele at Clancy's Bar.[99] Lutton reciprocated by taking part in a gun-and-bomb attack on the premises. The RUC took no action against Beattie and Kane, despite Lutton implicating them in the triple murder at Clancy's. There is no explanation for this failure, though 'Lutton's statements were new evidence that would have enabled them to be further arrested and interviewed,' the HET Report says. 'There is no record that this was considered at any stage; HET can find no satisfactory explanation for this lack of action.'[100] One gunman, Beattie, who had fired over thirty bullets into the bar full of customers, killing a father of four sons, was not even re-interviewed about Lutton's claim that he had lit the fuse of the bomb that devastated Clancy's Bar and killed three more people.

But the strange case of Joseph Lutton becomes even more murky. Beattie was a private in the TAVR, and Kane was a former UDR man. Lutton, throughout all his appearances in court and in all prosecution papers, is described as a 'cheese processor'. That may well have been Lutton's full-time job, but in his spare time he was a constable in the RUC Reserve. When the HET checked police records, they discovered that Lutton had joined the RUC Reserve in December 1974 and had resigned on 31 May 1978 – the very day he was arrested. The cause of his resignation is given in the official papers as 'personal reasons'. 'Given that he was arrested at 6.15 that morning, at his home address, it is reasonable to assume that his resignation was demanded whilst he was in police custody,' says the HET Report, diplomatically. Unless Lutton had, at some time between midnight and 6.15 a.m., handed in his resignation, this is the only possible explanation. After his early morning arrest, the HET continues, 'Lutton is identified

---

x   The officer in charge of the Eagle/Clancy's investigation declined to assist the HET's review of the case, and the officer with oversight, Detective Inspector Gilmore, is deceased.

only once in police papers as a member of the RUC Reserve. This happens when two detectives (one, a Detective Sergeant Beacom) had a general conversation … regarding his duties as a part-time member.' That record was omitted from the court file, and Detective Sergeant Beacom was not included in the court witness list. Rather less politely, the HET Report goes on to note that the clear inference from all this is that 'a conscious decision was made to withhold the fact that Lutton was a member of the RUC at the time of committing these murders'.[101]

It is not possible to say at what level within the RUC this decision was taken, nor is it possible to say whether the chief constable, the Office of the DPP, prosecuting counsel, or indeed the trial judge, was aware of that fact. Clearly, the HET Report infers, a decision was taken to remove Detective Sergeant Beacom's statement from the court files, thereby eliminating any trace of evidence that Lutton had ever been a constable in the RUC Reserve. It points out that Lutton's dual membership of the UVF and RUC might have otherwise influenced the judge when setting his life-sentence tariff. 'The fact that a defendant was working as a police officer whilst committing terrorist related murders would undoubtedly have been a factor for consideration. Any decision to withhold this information detail from the Court is an extraordinary matter,' the HET Report says.[102]

The McLoughlin family and those of the victims at Clancy's Bar were never informed that all three men convicted of murdering their loved ones were either serving or former members of various branches of state forces.[103] Jim McLoughlin, after being told that his father had been killed by (a) an RUC Reservist, (b) a member of the Territorial Army and (c) a former UDR man, spent many hours in Armagh public library looking up old newspaper reports to confirm what he had been told. He needed to see the evidence in black and white.[104]

The bullet used to kill Fred McLoughlin was never recovered. It was removed from his chest during emergency surgery soon after he reached the South Tyrone Hospital in Dungannon, but there is nothing in police files about what happened to it after that. With no bullet and therefore no ballistic evidence, and since Beattie admitted to using the Sterling during the attack on the Eagle while Lutton confessed to using a revolver, Fred's family are still unsure who killed their father: the RUC Reservist or the private in the Territorial Army. The HET concludes that, given the large number of bullets fired and the fact that a woman sitting near Fred had been hit with a bullet from the Sterling, it is most likely that Beattie fired the fatal shot.

As noted previously, there is no documentation to show what, if any, action was taken to investigate the Sterling's theft from the Glenanne UDR base, nor any explanation of the circumstances in which it was taken. In all of the shootings in which this SMG was used subsequently, there is, however, clear evidence of involvement by one branch of the security services or another, whether UDR, TAVR or RUC. The particular series of shootings in which Sterling SMG UF57A30490 was used began in September 1975 with the death of Denis Mullen and ended in July 1976 with the shooting of Patrick McNeice – eleven killings in eleven months.

Beattie admitted involvement in the first killing (Denis Mullen) and in the last (Patrick McNeice). Because of the absence of RUC interview records, it is not possible to say if Beattie was questioned about the other nine murders. As for motives, Beattie, Lutton and Kane never explained why they had set off, armed with a bomb and at least two weapons, to attack indiscriminately two Catholic-owned bars in a small village on a Saturday evening in May 1976. The UVF itself never admitted responsibility, nor did it provide a motive.

The HET Report criticises the police investigation into the Eagle/Clancy's attacks, saying, 'there are disconcerting issues in respect of the concealment of information and failure to act on evidential opportunities'.[105]

These issues are:

1. Hanlon admitted stealing the car used, corroborated by fingerprint evidence, yet was not charged and his involvement was withheld from court hearings.

2. Lutton's evidence implicated Kane and Beattie in the triple murder at Clancy's, yet they were not even interviewed, let alone charged.

3. All three were serving or former members of the security forces.

4. The murder weapon came from a UDR base and was used to murder eleven people, while an unfired bullet found in the getaway car was standard British military issue.

5. In 1978, the year of Lutton's arrest, other members of the RUC were implicated in serious crimes including murder, yet his membership of the force was concealed and his resignation contrived.

Arising from this, the HET says, in one of its most damning conclusions:

> It is difficult to believe … when judged in concert with other cases emerging at that time, that such widespread evidence of collusion in these areas was not a significant concern at the highest levels of the security forces and government. It may be that there was apprehension that confirming the suspicions of collusion and involvement, particularly of RUC personnel, would have fatally undermined the credibility of the organisation and increased the overall threat to political stability.[106]

Further, the HET states, while such ethical judgements have to be considered against a wider set of issues than it is reviewing: 'With the passage of time since this tragedy … the opportunity may exist for an honest disclosure of all relevant matters and considerations, without risk to individuals. This family – and all the others affected – deserve no less.'

Among all these high issues of justice, the role of the state, and the knowledge 'at the highest levels' of government about what was going on, it is important not to lose sight of the families who suffered so grievously. Fred McLoughlin, says the HET, 'was an honest, decent, family man who had called in to his local pub for a beer and a chat with friends when he was the victim of a sectarian attack'. Jim McLoughlin said, 'even when my mother knew that some of the gang responsible had been charged with Dad's murder, and were to appear in court, she kept it from us. She didn't want any more disruption in our lives. She never did recover from Dad's death and died still a young woman.'[107]

Two days after the twin attacks in Charlemont, in what looks very like a retaliatory action on purely sectarian grounds, the IRA killed the Dobson brothers a very short distance away in Moy. Robert Dobson (aged thirty-five) and Thomas Dobson (thirty-eight), both Protestants, died at their egg-packing factory, which had a mixed workforce. The brothers were both sitting at their desks when a gunman walked up to them and shot both dead. Thomas Dobson was about to visit his wife in hospital, where she had just given birth to their fourth child; and two months after Robert died, his wife gave birth to their first son. There is no evidence that either brother was involved in any loyalist activity. The probability is that they were killed in response to the double attack on the Eagle and Clancy's. Collusion and murder do not take place in a vacuum. Events spark other events. Every perpetrator must take responsibility for his or her own actions – but it is worth considering the ultimate result of the kind of collusion such as that catalogued here.

With the death of the two Dobson brothers, the story moves to the village of Keady, not far away, and to a connected but separate series of extraordinary events that eventually led some in authority to take action. But it was too little, and far too late.

'A POLICEMAN'S BOOTS'
(JUNE 1976–DEC 1977)[a]

It is difficult to conceive of a statement that could be more fundamentally flawed or calculated to destroy the confidence of a large section of the community in the court's independence and probity.[b]

The Rock Bar, Granemore, sits isolated in rolling countryside in mid-Armagh. Anyone not Irish might wonder how a bar could possibly be viable without any apparent customer base in the empty fields and lanes that surround it. But in the days before the enforcement of drink-driving laws, a bar such as the Rock could attract a loyal clientele because of its owner, its ambience, the entertainment it provided, or a combination of these.[1] The Rock was popular in the mid-1970s because of just such a mixture. Joe McGleenan, its owner, was a mild-mannered and popular man, active in the civil rights movement, who encouraged local amateur musical talent.[2] Even so, it was what it was – an obscure country bar that should never have become known outside a ten-mile (16 km) radius.

Saturday 5 June 1976 was bright and sunny. It was still light at about 10.30 p.m. when Michael (Mick) McGrath, a fifty-four-year-old single man who lived with his brother in the countryside nearby, arrived at the Rock Bar (he was related to Joe McGleenan by marriage).[c]

---

a   From Mick McGrath's statement to Belfast solicitors Madden and Finucane, 26 March 2002. On file with PFC.

b·   HET Report – Michael McGrath, referring to the summing up statement by the Lord Chief Justice, Lord Lowry, passing suspended sentences on the RUC officers convicted of involvement in the Rock Bar attack, 1976.

c   Joe's uncle was married to Mick's sister.

He had only come in for half-a-dozen bottles of Guinness to take home, but was prevailed upon by a friend to stay for a quick drink. Then, with Francis Powell, the barman, he made

The Rock Bar

his way past the seventeen customers and out through the front door (kept locked securely in those days because of fears of attack).[3] Francis and Mick paused beside the railings at the front of the bar for a short chat. It was closing time, so when Francis noticed a car approaching, and thinking it might be more customers hoping to get in, he quickly turned to shut the door again, leaving Mick outside to walk home. Then terrible events began to happen.

Three men in masks got out of the car. One walked towards Mick, stood in front of him for an instant and then began firing, hitting him in the stomach and hip. Mick fell to the ground, crawling under a

Mick McGrath

nearby car for protection, but kept watching as the three men ran towards the front door of the Rock Bar and one laid something at the building, which Mick correctly guessed was a bomb.[4] The gunman who had wounded Mick then began firing through the windows of the bar. Mercifully, no one was hit or injured – though the dartboard was riddled with bullets. Only the bomb's detonator exploded, not the full charge. Chunks of shrapnel were nevertheless blasted across the yard. The gang ran back past Mick and made their getaway.

Much later, Mick recalled that as he had lain injured in the road he had noticed that the boots on one of the men running past him looked remarkably like those of a police officer. And this was correct

– all of those who carried out the attack on the Rock Bar were serving RUC officers.[5] At the time, however, Mick was understandably preoccupied with his own survival and called out for help. His sister, Molly McGleenan, heard him shouting and came out of her house 10 yards (9 m) away. Mick managed to cry out, 'It's me, I'm shot', as she ran to his side. A local doctor gave him painkilling drugs and set up a drip. The next thing he remembered was being in hospital.[6]

Mick had surgery on two bullet wounds, which caused serious internal injuries. One bullet was removed from his body (though the police never requested it for forensic tests). An X-ray revealed that he had a piece of shrapnel near his right lung. He was in intensive care for five days but was well enough to be sent home six weeks later.[7]

Back at the Rock Bar, the British Army bomb squad had arrived. The bomb contained five two-pound (0.9 kg) packs of gelignite[d] wrapped in nails and shrapnel, and placed into a five-litre paint tin. All the bomb's components were later destroyed in an unexplained 'malicious fire' at the Forensic Science Laboratory in September 1976.[8] The HET says there can be no doubt that it was clearly intended to kill and would have done so, had the full charge exploded.[9] The HET notes that, given the determined nature of the attack and the attempt to kill as many people as possible, together with clear links to other similar events, the investigation should have been overseen by an officer above the rank of detective constable. But instead of being treated as a serious investigation into attempted murder, the attack prompted only a 'fairly standard response'.[10]

Francis Powell had heard two shots after returning inside the bar, followed by a hissing noise from the direction of the front door. He then heard five more shots from bullets coming through the windows. Most of the customers dived for safety. Some ran out of the side and rear doors or up the stairs – anywhere to get away from the bullets.

---

d   Commercial-grade nitroglycerine.

The customers all gave statements describing the noise, how they had run out of the bar and how they had found Mick lying shot.[e] Fourteen bullets or bullet fragments were recovered. The Webley revolver found in a car burned out by the attackers had not been fired and, in any case, was too damaged to be of any forensic use. The two weapons fired were a Luger 9 mm pistol and a 9 mm SMG. Both had been used in other paramilitary attacks.[f] The 9 mm Sterling used was apparently home-made, or at least doctored, and had also been used during the murder of the three Reavey brothers at Whitecross.[11]

One fingerprint was found on the paint tin, but the file was 'weeded' around 1990 and no copies are available. The HET calls this 'disturbing'.[12] John Weir claims:

> Armagh SPG alone carried out the gun-and-bomb attack on the Rock Bar at Keady. The SPG boys stole a Mini car from [a] car park … in Armagh. They used it to actually do the attack and then they used the police car as a getaway.
>
> They wore overalls for the job; their uniforms were under the overalls so, down the road, they just had to do a quick change. On the getaway that night they ran into an army road-stop but did a handbrake turn on the road and got away quite easily.[13]

The original RUC investigation, says the HET, was neither meaningful nor effective. 'In the light of subsequent events in 1978,' it says, 'this can be partly explained: the attack was carried out by members of the Royal Ulster Constabulary. At least one of the attackers was involved

---

e   All except Mick himself, an omission the HET describes as 'extraordinary' given that he was the one person who saw the offenders and observed the bomb attack on the bar.

f   The Luger had been used twice in earlier incidents that caused no injury and remain unsolved. Of far greater significance is its use in two fatal attacks in which five people were killed: Seán Farmer and Colm McCartney at Altnamackin, and John-Martin, Brian and Anthony Reavey at their home in Whitecross.

in subsequent "investigation" work; all were involved in "policing" the area. What is not explained by subsequent events, however, is the lack of co-ordination and control by senior officers.'[14]

The only inference that can be taken here is that the HET – all of whose staff are former police officers themselves and are vetted for sensitive work in Northern Ireland – believes the original police investigation was deliberately poor to conceal the direct involvement of police in the attack. The HET's use of quotation marks around the words 'investigation' and 'policing' clearly implies it dismisses the integrity of the investigation into the Rock Bar attack. This can only mean it believes senior officers deliberately down-graded the investigation. The Rock Bar report is also damning regarding the absence of oversight by senior supervisory officers who should, and could, have prevented more junior investigative officers covering up the involvement of RUC members.[g]

Six weeks after the attack on the Rock Bar and less than twenty miles (32 km) away, Patrick (Patsy) McNeice, a fifty-three-year-old labourer, was at home with his family. Patsy worked digging drainage ditches for the local council. The family lived in a modest bungalow on a small site almost entirely surrounded by large orchards belonging to David Henry Dalziel Kane, a former member of the UDR.[h] The McNeice family felt at the time that they were a thorn in Kane's side. Their home was a small corner among Kane's substantial orchards. The two neighbouring households were polite – but distant.[15]

Patsy McNeice

Patsy McNeice had five children aged from seven to twenty-four,

g   See Chapter 11: Ridding the Land of Pestilence for a full account of the legal and security implications of the Rock Bar attack.

h   The month after Patsy McNeice's murder, David Henry Dalziel Kane was implicated in the murder of Fred McLoughlin at the Eagle Bar. He had been dismissed from the UDR in 1973 for the negligent discharge of a weapon.

all but one of them boys. He was married to Josephine and was a quiet, well-respected family man who had no political or paramilitary links.[16] On a warm summer's evening, he was at home with his wife and two of his sons, John and Damien. At about 11.50 p.m. Josephine had made a cup of tea. As she went into the living room, she saw Patsy leaving to check on the dog, which was outside barking. Two waiting gunmen shot Patsy on the doorstep and left him bleeding to death as they escaped through the surrounding apple orchards.[17] Josephine heard a single shot, followed by others. Fearing the gunmen might try to kill all of them in the house (as had happened to the Reavey and O'Dowd families six months earlier), she, Damien and John ran into a bedroom to take cover under the beds.

Cowering in the bedroom a few minutes later, Josephine saw the motorbike headlights of her son, Patsy Junior, coming home. Patsy had seen what he now believes was the getaway car. But he was unable to describe the vehicle later because he did not know at the time that his father had just been murdered; in any case, he had a helmet on and was blinded by the lights. He arrived home and saw a shadow at the front door. Not realising it was his father, Patsy Junior went in through the back door to find his mother and brothers in a confused and distressed state. Josephine ran outside and discovered her husband's body lying in a pool of blood at the front door. Though they feared the gunmen might still be lying in wait outside in the dark, they ran to a neighbour's home (not Kane's) to call the police, a priest and an ambulance.

Once again, screaming sirens and blue ambulance lights, racing to and from hospital, disturbed the peace of the Armagh countryside. Two units of the Armagh SPG happened to be on duty not far away. They had finished work at midnight and were returning to base when they were redirected to the scene. An ambulance and two priests were already there. Patsy senior was lying dead on a stretcher at the side of the house.[18]

There were four bullet strike marks on the front porch and two firing points. A total of ten bullet cases were found in two groups of five, indicating two gunmen. One firing point had been on a tractor track running parallel to the side of the house. The second was on the other side of the McNeice's waist-high hedge, in Kane's orchard. A police officer found two woollen sleeves and a pair of woollen mittens discarded in the orchard. Red woollen fibres were found attached to a barbed wire fence 500 yards (457 m) from the McNeices' home, near the Ardress Mission Hall. A post-mortem report found that Patsy had died from gunshot injuries to his head, neck and trunk. Four bullets were recovered from his body. The usual lines of enquiry were followed: press appeal, house-to-house enquiries, etc. No group claimed responsibility. Patsy Junior says his 'mother never recovered from the shock of what had happened. She was a small woman anyway but lost about five stone in the months after Dad died. She was skin and bone.'[19]

The detective leading the enquiry was Maurice Neilly, then with the rank of detective inspector; this was one stroke of luck at least for the McNeice family (Neilly was one of the more efficient and determined detectives in the area at the time). Another stroke of luck was that, two days after Patsy's murder, on 27 July, police received intelligence naming Garfield Beattie as having been involved in the murders of Peter and Jenny McKearney the previous October, as well as the attack on Clancy's and the Eagle Bar just two months earlier. Beattie had just returned from a TAVR training tour in Germany and discovered that the finger of suspicion was pointing at him. Six days after the police received the intelligence, he was at the door of Portadown loyalist Dorothy Edith Mullan, telling her that 'a big lift' (arrest operation) was imminent.

In its report, the HET puts forward three options as to how Beattie discovered the police were on to him. The one they favour is that he had been 'tipped off by members of the security forces about the impending arrest of suspects'. Incriminating evidence was missing from Beattie's home after his arrest. The HET concludes that it was 'very likely he had been tipped-off', leading him to dispose of the clothes he was wearing when murdering Patsy. 'The source of this leak,' says the HET, 'is not known. It could have come from local security force members.' An independent observer might conclude it could *only* have come from that source. Beattie's exact words to Mullan were, according to police files quoted by the HET, 'There's going to be a big lift; I have got information. If they are round looking, yous [*sic*] better keep your mouth closed and say nothing or I'll be calling to give you a visit with a forty-five and that goes for the rest that talk. If anyone talks, I will clean out their whole house.'[20]

The police moved in to arrest Beattie on 11 August, and detectives, led by Neilly, interviewed him over the next six days. At first, he denied involvement in any murder – only admitting to taking part in illegal 'USCA' roadblocks about once every fortnight 'during which he stopped cars for the safety of the people in the area'.[i]

Still denying involvement in Patsy's murder, Beattie began to feed information to the police on a piecemeal basis. He led them to where the murder weapon, the Sterling SMG stolen from Glenanne UDR base in May 1971, was hidden in Annaghmore bog. This weapon had been used in seven different attacks, killing eleven people.[j] Patsy was its final victim. He also led police to the hiding place of two more guns – a Colt .45 and a Webley .455 – and later still, to thirteen rounds of 9 mm and twelve rounds of .455 ammunition.

Finally, on Friday 13 August, Beattie confessed to his involvement in Patsy's murder. Further, he said 'an old school-friend', Henry

---

i   USCA = Ulster Special Constabulary Association, a self-styled organisation of (mainly) former Ulster Special Constabulary members; see http://cain.ulst.ac.uk/issues/police/docs/usca80.htm (accessed 3 July 2013).

j   Denis Mullen, Peter and Jenny McKearney, Trevor Brecknell, Patsy Donnelly, Michael Donnelly, John-Martin, Brian and Anthony Reavey, Fred McLoughlin and Patsy McNeice.

Garfield Liggett, was the other gunman, and Liggett's girlfriend, Dorothy Mullan, was the driver.[k] The murder, he said, was planned in a bar in Portadown where he had been drinking with Liggett and Mullan. Beattie said Liggett asked him if there were any 'rebels' in the area; he replied that one of Patsy's sons 'was an IRA man'.[l] Liggett then told Beattie that they would 'do him'.[21]

The two men took an SMG and a .455 handgun over the fields towards the McNeice home. There, Beattie said, he had readied himself, cocking the SMG, when a dog began barking. He saw the shadow of a man at the side of the house. Liggett, said Beattie, fired the first shot and started to run away. Beattie admitted then firing a burst from his weapon and running after Liggett before meeting up with Mullan and driving away.

In the following days, Beattie also confessed to his role in Denis Mullen's murder and the shooting of Fred McLoughlin at the Eagle Bar in Charlemont. For an unexplained reason, he was never charged with the triple killing and bombing of Clancy's Bar in the same village around the same time. Beattie then led police to yet another weapon – a .455 pistol buried in his own back garden. The murder of Denis Mullen, he said, had been 'an initiation process' before his planned joining of the UVF[m] (he had later, he said, changed his mind about that).[22]

On the same day that Beattie made his admission of involvement in Patsy's murder, police arrested Mullan, whom Beattie named as their driver. She strenuously denied involvement. She did admit to attending the funeral of UVF bomber Wesley Somerville, whose

---

k   In various interviews Beattie contradicted himself on the extent of Mullan's involvement.

l   The HET Report says there is no record of any of Patsy's sons being involved with the IRA, and it has 'reviewed numerous murders where unfounded gossip and local speculation were accepted as reason enough to murder someone'.

m   At that time, the UVF was not a proscribed organisation. It was illegal from 28 June 1966 to 23 May 1974 and made illegal again on 4 October 1975.

widow was a friend.[n] On 21 August, she then told Neilly that she had driven Beattie and Liggett about on the night of the murder but she had not known what they had done. Liggett had been arrested on 17 August. Over five days he admitted doing 'welfare work' for the UVF, but denied involvement in Patsy's murder. On the sixth day, 21 August, he was informed of Mullan's admissions and he also confessed, under caution, claiming that Beattie had put him under pressure. Liggett said he had agreed to go with Beattie 'for some excitement' and 'for a laugh'. Mullan and Liggett were charged two days later with Patsy's murder.

On 27 August, after Beattie named Kane as the driver for the attack on the Eagle Bar, the former UDR man was arrested and confessed. He was questioned about Patsy's killing but denied involvement. The HET says that while Kane was clearly involved in one UVF sectarian shooting and other terrorist crimes, there was no evidence he was involved in killing his neighbour or was aware that Liggett and Beattie had used his land to make their approach and retreat.[23]

Given three life sentences and fourteen years, to run concurrently, Beattie served sixteen years and was released from jail on 29 March 1993. The prosecution dropped the murder charge against Mullan. She was convicted of possessing an SMG and .455 revolver, and of assisting offenders, and was sentenced to ten years for each offence, to run concurrently. She served five years and was released on 21 August 1981.

Liggett was convicted of murdering Patsy, possessing an SMG and a .455 revolver, and membership of the UVF. He was sentenced to life, fourteen years and five years in jail, respectively. He served fourteen years and was released on 28 December 1990.

---

n   Somerville, who was killed during the Miami Showband attack, was involved in a string of other sectarian loyalist murders.

The HET says the gang's shooting of Patsy had been 'casual'. They had no strategy to identify their supposed target, or even to ascertain whether he was at home when they arrived. 'This was irrefutably a callous, sectarian killing,' concludes the HET. '... they were content to shoot whoever came out ... it was a cowardly attack on an honest, hard-working man, loved by his family and respected in the community.' The HET wrote to all three gang members asking them to co-operate with the review on a non-evidential basis. Beattie refused point blank. The other two did not reply at all.[24]

* * *

Of all the horrific killings outlined here, the next is unique. There is clear and irrefutable evidence that this bombing could easily have been prevented, two lives saved and countless injuries avoided. Many other of these attacks, of course, were also eminently preventable. But in the case of the Step Inn bombing, the evidence is unquestionable. The Step Inn, surely, for even the most sceptical observer, metaphorically provides a smoking gun.

To begin at the beginning. By the time that Patsy McNeice's killers had set out from Portadown intent on murder, plans were probably already well under way elsewhere in County Armagh to bomb a bar just across the border in County Monaghan. According to John Weir, the plot was hatched at the Glenanne farmhouse, home of RUC Reservist James Mitchell.°

The group of loyalists, UDR men and RUC officers who met, drilled and conspired there on a regular basis in the 1970s had singled out a soft target: the Breaside Bar (also known as Renaghan's) in the village of Clontibret. They chose 15 August for their attack: the

o   PFC interview with John Weir and HET Report. The HET concludes that, though he was recalling events from over thirty years ago, some that he witnessed directly, others not, 'there is much in [Weir's] account that is factually correct and supported by the intelligence' (HET Report – Step Inn).

Catholic feast of the Assumption of the Virgin Mary, a big day for the Ancient Order of Hibernians when, after their annual parade, members would socialise and the bar would be full of people enjoying a day off work.

As the gang laid its plans to steal a car and transport the bomb south to blow up Renaghan's Bar, they had no idea they were being watched by the British Army. The RUC Special Branch had known since 5 August, ten days before the planned explosion, that a bombing was planned.[25] They had received intelligence from an informant, 'Source A', that a car would be stolen in the Armagh area and taken to a farm at Markethill. A bomb was to be placed in the vehicle and driven eighteen miles (29 km) on to Renaghan's after a 'dry run' to test security on both sides of the border.

On Friday 13 August, a second informant, 'Source B', told RUC Special Branch that the car was to be stolen in Belfast, rather than Armagh, for use by the Portadown UVF. The intelligence also named the Portadown UVF man involved.[p] On Saturday 14 August, 'Source A' notified the RUC that the planned bombing had been brought forward to that very evening. 'Source A' also named the same Portadown UVF man identified by 'Source B', plus he named two twenty-six-year-olds from Portadown and Tandragee, both Mid-Ulster UVF members.

The RUC had by then linked the information from their two sources and were aware that something very serious was afoot. Officers wrote up a 'situation report',[q] which detailed authorisation from the detective superintendent of RUC Special Branch (South Region) for military surveillance on the Glenanne farm owned by Mitchell. Inexplicably, the surveillance order given by the RUC to the British Army did not mention the rather salient fact, surely known

---

p   This man, whose name is still publicly unknown, was never arrested or interviewed about the subsequent bombing.

q   Situation reports, or for short, 'sit reps', were routine daily reports.

to the RUC at the time, that the farm the soldiers were being asked to watch was owned by an RUC Reservist. Nor did the surveillance authorised cover the entire weekend. There were gaping holes in the timetable during the hours of darkness – the likeliest time for the bombers to take the device from its staging post at Glenanne farm.[r] This, despite the RUC being warned that the bombing was unlikely during daylight hours.[26]

Three British Army units in the area at the time were available for surveillance duty: the 2nd Regiment, Royal Fusiliers (based at Armagh from June to October 1976) and the 2nd Battalion, Parachute Regiment (based at Bessbrook from April to August 1976). Then there was the SAS. The HET was unable to find any documentation identifying which unit was deployed to watch the Glenanne farmhouse, and the surveillance report itself does not name the unit responsible. (It is therefore possible that SAS men – fresh from their exploits in Dhofar – were deployed to watch Mitchell's farm.)[s] The surveillance report details 'some activity, with vehicles calling at the farm on 15 August'. The vehicles were logged but the report concluded 'there was nothing to suggest an operation was imminent'. The surveillance ended, as authorised, at 1.30 a.m. on Monday 16 August.[27]

Two of the vehicles spotted at the farmhouse were locally owned, but no evidence can be found that their owners had paramilitary connections. The third vehicle, however, aroused suspicion. That car, seen at Mitchell's farm on Sunday 15 August, was a Belfast-registered, blue Vauxhall Viva, registration number EOI 3377. Unknown to the RUC at the time, it belonged to John Weir, a serving member of the

---

r   Surveillance was authorised for late evening on Saturday 14 August until 11.30 p.m., and from late evening on Sunday 15 August until 1.30 a.m. Monday 16 August.
s   The SAS had been officially deployed to County Armagh since 7 January 1976 in response to the Kingsmill massacre.

RUC and former member of the Armagh SPG.ᵗ Weir had bought it two months previously from a relative.ᵘ

According to Weir, a 'few days' before the planned attack, he and an RUC sergeant, had selected the bar at Clontibret as the bomb target.[28] They originally intended to plant two bombs, the second with a longer timer, designed to kill rescuers and those congregating after the first bomb had exploded, to ensure maximum casualties. (The idea for the second-wave bomb was later dropped.) The planning meeting, held at Mitchell's farm, also involved two UVF men, who then left with Weir on a reconnaissance trip to Clontibret.[29]

On 14 August, at around 3 p.m., a part-time RUC Reserve constable, the owner of a blue Ford Consul car, was shopping on Belfast's staunchly loyalist Shankill Road.ᵛ When contacted by the HET many years later, he explained how he had been forced by a group of men into a nearby pub (a well-known UDA meeting place). The men took his car keys, held him at the pub for two to three hours and took his car. The hijackers told him they knew who he was and threatened his life if he went to his colleagues in the police. He recognised the faces of four of the five men involved, one of whom, he said, was the local UDA 'commander' (he gave this man's surname to the HET) who he believes is now dead. He had reported the theft of his car and its keys immediately – but was never asked to make a formal statement or attend an identity parade. He said the incident was the final straw for his family, who had recently lost a young child, and they emigrated two months later.

---

t   At the time of this attack, John Weir was a member of Castlereagh SPG. He was transferred to Omagh SPG on 1 September 1976. He was promoted to the rank of sergeant on 11 October 1976 and transferred to Newry RUC station.

u   HET Report – Betty McDonald. By October 1976 the RUC Special Branch in Belfast had discovered that this car belonged at the time to RUC officer Weir. He was not, however, questioned about why his car was at the home of an RUC officer where a loyalist bombing mission was under way.

v   The policeman's name has been withheld in the HET Report.

In Glenanne a bomb was constructed in McClure's repair garage and loaded into the police officer's stolen Ford Consul.ʷ Carrying out the 'dry run' on Sunday 15 August, however, Weir found to his dismay that Clontibret was cordoned off with garda activity on roads leading into the village.ˣ Stopped at a garda checkpoint, Weir flashed his RUC warrant card. The gardaí told him they were anticipating a bombing. Weir did a U-turn, returning by the previously agreed route so he could warn the bombers if they approached from the opposite direction. He drove straight to Mitchell's farm to raise the alarm. He then discovered that Mitchell already knew they were being watched. Mitchell told Weir that the UDR captain who had supplied the explosives for the bomb had informed him of the surveillance, and that he (the UDR captain) had already called off the attack on Clontibret.ʸ

At this stage, with a bomb on the farm and the bombers knowing they were being watched, the obvious next move should have been to clear the area as rapidly as possible to avoid arrest and to dump incriminating evidence. This, however, is not what happened. Despite knowing there had been surveillance on the farm, the gang simply carried on with their plans that Monday as if nothing had happened. Why did they not clear the scene? Apparently, they did not fear detection or arrest. The possible implications of that are immense.

Weir's direct involvement with the bombing, he says, ended there, but he claims he has since been told that on Monday 16 August, at another meeting in Mitchell's farmhouse (which he says he did not attend), the Step Inn, Keady, was chosen as the new target.[30] Keady was, and remains, a predominantly Catholic town. The Step Inn was

---

w   McClure's repair garage was located 500 yards (457 m) from Mitchell's farm in Glenanne but he was on holiday in Scotland for the weekend.

x   It appears that gardaí took the bomb warning received from the RUC more seriously than their northern counterparts did.

y   The UDR man's name is known but cannot be disclosed for legal reasons. Weir claims this man supplied the explosives for many of the bombings detailed here and was working for British military intelligence.

frequented mainly, but not entirely, by Catholics. It was not a haunt of local republicans but simply a small, town-centre bar.

Surveillance having been lifted twenty hours earlier, the UVF gang was at liberty to transport their bomb to its new target. A gang of four men drove the blue Ford Consul, carrying a false registration number BIB 4502, to the Step Inn and parked between two other vehicles on a slight incline.[31]

Malachi McDonald, the bar owner, remembers it was a lovely evening. Two of his sons, Gerald and Vincent, were staying with relatives south of the border. His wife, Betty, was serving customers in the bar. Leaving through a side door, he walked towards a friend's house intending to borrow a trailer. Passing the bomb-car parked outside his bar, Malachi remembers that he unwittingly put his hand on it briefly to steady himself as he squeezed between it and another car to cross the narrow street.

Moments later, there was a huge explosion.

Forty yards (37 m) away, Malachi was knocked off his feet by the blast. He saw black smoke and flames shooting from the Step Inn. Then, he says, it was as if 'a black hole' just opened up where he lived with his wife and three young boys.[32] It was a massive blast. Police later noted that larger pieces of the bomb-car were catapulted thirty yards (27 m) while smaller pieces were found hundreds of yards away. The bomb contained somewhere between twenty and fifty pounds (9–23 kg) of commercial explosive, or the equivalent in home-made materials.

A police inspector described the scene as one of 'devastation'. There was a gaping hole in the side of the Step Inn, the remains of the car lay in pieces, and soldiers, firemen and local people were 'frantically digging through rubble, looking for anyone that may have been buried underneath'.[33]

At 10.08 p.m., Malachi's wife, Betty, lay mangled in the wreckage of her family's home, with Laurance, her four-year-old son, crying over her body, calling 'Mammy'. She had been serving customers when the bomb caused the bar's exterior walls to disintegrate from ground to roof. The family's living quarters, on the first floor, collapsed into the bar area, burying Betty and the customers below.

'Betty was an incredibly caring person and loved a bit of craic. She loved Irish dancing. She never lost her temper, either with me or the children. I am not the easiest person in the world to get on with – but the two of us just clicked. That was the way of it. She was kind and gentle and methodical. What more can you say?'

Malachi McDonald, Betty's husband

Betty McDonald

Gerard McGleenan was just leaving his front door opposite the bar to go for a quick evening's pint. He was spun round by the powerful force of the blast as pieces of metal pierced his body and he fell to the ground. Shards of the bomb-car had sliced through his lungs and heart. He, too, called out for his mother.

In addition to the two dead, twenty-two people were seriously injured.[z] Shrapnel from the blast flew everywhere. There was the usual horror of sirens, blue lights and people moaning while others tore at the rubble to reach the dead and injured. Malachi found Betty in the rubble and handed Laurance to a friend to care for. He carried Betty to a neighbour's house, comforting her and waiting for the doctor. Today, he realises she was probably dead when he first reached her, but at the time he held her in his arms and prayed she would live. Less than half an hour after the explosion, a doctor confirmed she was dead. The post-mortem examination listed Betty's cause of death as internal bleeding due to inhaling blood from a throat lacerated by shrapnel wounds to the neck, causing 'her rapid collapse and death'.

---

z   One of those injured, Maria McShane, who was pregnant, lost an eye. The son she gave birth to later, Gavin McShane, died at the hands of the UVF in a sectarian shooting in Lower English Street, Armagh city, on 18 May 1994.

Gerard McGleenan's brother, Robert, and father, Paddy, carried his body from their shattered home to a house nearby, where he was confirmed dead. A police officer noted two penetrating wounds to his chest. Gerard's cause of death was given as internal bleeding due to bomb explosion shrapnel lacerating his heart and lungs. The pathologist removed eight pieces of shrapnel, each measuring between an eighth to three-quarters of an inch in size from his upper body. One of the larger pieces had lodged in his heart.

Gerard McGleenan

'Gerard had just left the house. One foot was on the street. Then he fell at my feet saying, "Mummy" over and over again.'

Maureen McGleenan, Gerard's mother

'The windows came in around me. I went to the front door and Gerard walked towards me, saying he was hit and clutching his stomach. He collapsed on his knees. Daddy and I lifted him out of the wrecked house and carried him to a neighbour's to wait for the ambulance. But he was dead by the time it arrived.'

Robert McGleenan, Gerard's brother

No group admitted responsibility. The RUC investigation began, such as it was. On 17 August, Special Branch received intelligence that the bombing had been carried out by the Portadown and Belfast UVF – a lethal pairing that had also been responsible for the Dublin/Monaghan bombings.[aa] The confidential report accurately stated that the target had been changed from Renaghan's Bar in Clontibret to the Step Inn because of unexpected security activity on the southern side of the border. It also named three people allegedly involved – the same three men named by 'Source B' on 13 August, three days before the bombing.

Inexplicably, the RUC record linked to this intelligence contains a decision not to approach Mitchell's farm or any of the suspects

---

aa   This new intelligence came from an informant other than 'Source A' or 'Source B'.

involved, without naming the officer who took that decision. The HET, commenting, states, 'It is presumed that, as this was an intelligence operation already under the authority and supervision of the Detective Superintendent Special Branch (South Region), it must have been made at least at a similar senior RUC [CID] level.'[34]

On 19 August, an RUC intelligence document was created confirming for the first time that the occupant of the farm was James Mitchell, but while it mentions that Mitchell's brother (who lived nearby) was a member of the RUC Reserve, it curiously fails to mention that James Mitchell himself was an RUC Reservist.[ab] The HET remarks that enquiries had been carried out by that stage and 'it is incomprehensible that Mitchell's security force status had not been established'.[35] Either that or it had been established and was already the subject of a cover-up.

On 20 August, the RUC received intelligence identifying the four men who had stolen the police officer's Ford Consul on the Shankill Road. Among the papers accompanying this, the HET discovered a handwritten note containing the names and Belfast addresses of all four men responsible for the theft, along with an official arrest photograph of one of them. However, 'There is no record that any of the men were specifically interviewed or arrested in connection with the theft of the car'; clearly, the HET says, Armagh CID knew of the men, but what (if any) investigative action they took against them is not documented 'and cannot be established'.[36]

On 21 August, an eighth piece of intelligence was received by Special Branch, naming the four men who drove the bomb to Keady – three of whom had been implicated previously by Sources 'A' and 'B' in the days before the lethal explosion.[37] The fourth man named was a twenty-three-year-old member of the UVF from Portadown.[ac]

---

ab Reserve Police Constable James Mitchell (No. 3604) had been a member of the force since 24 September 1974.

ac Identity known but cannot be given for reasons of confidentiality.

He was arrested and interviewed, but released without charge. There is no police record that the other three men were ever arrested or interviewed about the Step Inn bombing, or any reason given why they were not.

On 4 September, a ninth intelligence report created by Special Branch officers, based on intelligence received, named two of the men who drove the bomb to Keady, and stated that the explosives came from a quarry in Loughgall. The report further stated that the bomb had been hidden, in a shed or barn, six or seven miles (10–11 km) from Keady. It also revealed that, after Clontibret was determined as a non-starter, there were discussions about bombing the home of a nationalist politician before it was agreed to target the Step Inn.[38] One of the two men named in this final RUC intelligence report had been implicated four times (twice before the bombing, and twice after). The other was a thirty-three-year-old Portadown UVF man not identified in earlier reports.[ad]

Summing up, all of this intelligence material establishes that, both before and after the bombing, RUC Special Branch had built up a comprehensive picture of who was involved, as well as detailed information regarding the planning and planting of the bomb. All this information, however, was withheld from the police investigating team, says the HET Report. It adds that it is 'confident that original investigators were committed to undertaking diligent investigation into this crime', but intelligence was critical as there was little else for the CID team responsible to investigate as 'no meaningful forensic evidence' was recovered at the scene.[39]

---

ad Among those believed to be involved in the Step Inn bombing (the bomb-makers, scouts, the four men in the bomb-car and at least one getaway driver) were two Portadown brothers and a prime suspect in the Kay's Tavern bombing. They cannot be named here to avoid prejudicing future legal action. Judge Barron's 2006 report stated that they were 'reliably said to have had relationships with British intelligence and/or RUC Special Branch' and 'exchanges of information took place' (p. 135).

Fingerprint analysis of the bomb-car's registration plates, discovered still attached to the wreckage of the car, revealed nothing. There was also no forensic evidence to confirm either the nature of the explosives or the timing device used in the bomb's construction. Other forensic exhibits included swabs for traces of explosives from a wall, debris from the seat of the explosion and even shrapnel taken from Gerard McGleenan's body and a glass shard removed from Betty McDonald's body. None of them yielded any useful results. With essentially no forensic evidence available, the success or failure of the enquiry, says the HET, was dependent almost entirely on the extent to which Special Branch did, or did not, share information.[40]

One person was arrested, a twenty-three-year-old UVF man from Portadown, but he was released without charge. The HET has been unable to find any record of the circumstances of his arrest or interviews with him, though it is known that he was one of those named in intelligence. The HET comments that it is 'surprised that the circumstances surrounding this arrest and the interviews following it are not recorded with greater prominence in the case files'.[41]

Four months after the bombing that killed Betty McDonald and Gerard McGleenan, the police sent a file to the DPP's office informing them that they had no suspects. This despite Special Branch knowing the names of most, if not all, of those involved. The McDonald and McGleenan families were never informed of any background information about the surveillance or suspects; they were simply left to mourn.

Malachi McDonald later discovered the bumper of the bomb-car in a roof-valley of his bar. He told the RUC, but they made no effort to retrieve it for forensic, or any other, purposes. Three years later, he disposed of it himself.

Robert McGleenan, some time after the bombing, steeled himself to begin tackling the heap of bomb rubble dumped in the backyard of the family home. There he found the shattered interior door of their old front porch, against which his younger brother had staggered when hit by the force of the blast. It had been a lovely door, he remembers, with old stained glass in its upper half. As he uncovered the now-useless piece of door frame, he came upon a hand imprint his dying brother had left as he fell backwards into the hallway of their home. The bloodied mark looked, he said, like the 'Red Hand of Ulster'.[42] Horrified, he carried the door frame up the garden and burned it so that none of the rest of the family would ever have to see it.[43]

Gerard's mother, Maureen, visited her son's grave every day for over thirty years until she became too infirm. The entire family – Maureen, Paddy and their children, Robert, Frances, Mildred and Barry – was frozen in grief for decades. They asked for an RUC review in 1990 and were told that a number of people had been interviewed at the time, but with negative results. The only material made available to the detective chief inspector who carried out this review, however, was a three-line report submitted by the original investigating officer, Detective Inspector Maurice Neilly, three months after the explosion.[44]

Twenty-eight years after the bombing, the PFC requested a review (again, on behalf of the McGleenan family) and the case file was dusted off by the new PSNI SCRT. They assessed the papers and solemnly concluded that no further progress could be made, bearing in mind the 'limited records'. This falls far short of the truth. The HET's review produced dramatically different results. Both families bereaved by the bombing were finally accorded the dignity of knowing at least part of the truth – though there remain huge questions hanging over why the tragedy was not prevented and why no arrests were made afterwards. HET officers were deeply troubled by what they uncovered. It appears that Special Branch kept the detective who led the original investigation (Detective Constable Elder) and the officer who supervised him (Detective Inspector Maurice Neilly), both of whom are now dead, almost totally in the dark.

The RUC's failure to interview the police officer whose stolen car was used in the bombing is also significant. The first investigators might not have considered his potential evidence worthy of consideration, but the HET did. It claims the officer could have 'greatly assisted' the investigation and that 'a major opportunity was apparently ignored'. This prompts another question: were senior officers worried that others within the RUC would betray him to the loyalists who had taken his car (and who had threatened him if he reported it)? The HET follows this theory. It points out that the Step Inn attack came two months after the gun-and-bomb attack on the Rock Bar near Keady, and eight months after the Kay's Tavern/Donnelly's Bar bombing in Dundalk/South Armagh, in both of which serving RUC officers were centrally involved.[45] A pattern had clearly emerged of police collusion with loyalist bombers, already an open secret within the force.

When intelligence was received of loyalist intentions to bomb a target using a policeman's car stolen in Belfast, the alert level should have gone through the roof, says the HET. When further intelligence emerged that the attack was imminent, it rightly triggered a surveillance operation and a warning to the Garda Síochána. What, then, caused that surveillance to be lifted? 'There is no reasoning or rationale anywhere in the papers examined for leaving the bomb unrecovered,' states the HET Report, 'it may have been a speculative decision, hoping for more exact intelligence, it may have been about protecting the identity of informants; if so it was a huge gamble which went catastrophically wrong.'[46] There is an alternative which appears almost too appalling a scenario to consider: that police officers deliberately allowed the bombing to proceed.

Once again, ordinary people paid the price. The Step Inn was bombed. Two people lost their lives. Malachi lost his wife, Betty. His three young sons – Gerald (seven), Laurance (four) and John (twenty-one months) – lost their mother. The McGleenans lost

Gerard despite 'clearly reliable intelligence available to the police that could have prevented the bombing of the Step Inn bar ever taking place'. As to reasons why this happened, the HET has no answers:

> … given the history of previous attacks, it was never likely that the bomb would simply be abandoned. In the circumstances, the selection of a secondary target was highly probable. There are no records of any efforts to disrupt or prevent this event.[47]

RUC man James Mitchell's central involvement was 'evident' says the HET. That Mitchell remained on as a serving RUC Reservist for a further ten months is unconscionable. It wasn't until after his arrest in December 1978 that police finally raided his home, finding two home-made SMGs, reels of Cordtex,[ae] ammunition and other related items.[48] Incredibly, for these very serious offences – perpetrated by a former RUC officer – a one-year sentence was imposed by the courts, suspended for two years.

The RUC knew of John Weir's involvement in the double murder at the Step Inn by October 1976, the same month as he received a promotion to sergeant. Yet, also incredibly, he was not arrested until two years later, nor dismissed from the RUC for his role in the Step Inn conspiracy.[af] When police did finally arrest Mitchell, Weir, Laurence McClure and other RUC men, says the HET, despite obvious links to other attacks such as Donnelly's Bar, 'only cursory efforts were made to investigate them further'. The limited interview records show 'no determined efforts were made to investigate them in a meaningful fashion, despite the recovery of explosives and weapons from Mitchell's farm and despite all the intelligence that was available'.[49] The families have lodged an official complaint with

---

ae   Cordtex is inflammable bomb fuse wire used to detonate bombs.
af   Weir was dismissed, however, after his role in the murder of William Strathearn became known.

the NI police ombudsman, to whose office the HET has also referred its findings.

The ramifications from the Step Inn bombing continued. In the early 1980s, the then RUC Chief Constable, Sir Jack Hermon, unexpectedly asked to see the Step Inn file.[50] Why? Had he heard of RUC involvement? Why else would he ask for this particular file? What he was given, it appears, was the date-limited intelligence ending in September 1976 – coincidentally or not, the month before the RUC says it became aware of Weir's involvement. Even then, disturbingly, Hermon neither ordered a thorough re-investigation of RUC involvement in the Step Inn attack or a high-level external, possibly public, enquiry into why and how intelligence had been suppressed from the original police investigation.

Paddy McGleenan, Gerard's father, discovered years after his son's death that a police officer who had taken a statement from him after the bombing had been involved in the Rock Bar gun-and-bomb attack two months previously. Paddy and RUC Constable Ian Mitchell had travelled together to Dungannon for work years previously. Paddy considered him a friend. It was a shocking discovery that a man, to whom he had spoken privately of the death of his beloved son, had been involved in bombing a local bar.

Both the McGleenan and McDonald families, whose lives have been irretrievably damaged by the Step Inn explosion, have found it difficult to come to terms with the revelations contained in the HET Report. Those who investigated the case within the HET are also stunned at what they discovered. During a meeting with the McGleenan family (held in the Keady GAA club named after Gerard) an HET investigator bluntly summed up his own response: 'This is as bad as it gets.'[ag]

* * *

---

ag   For further analysis of the Step Inn bombing, see Chapter 9: The 'Short Arm' of the Law.

Two months after the Step Inn bombing, farmer Peter Woolsey (aged forty) had finished his dinner and was in his milking parlour about 200 yards (183 m) from his home in Cornascreibe. Peter was married to Anne and they had one son, Peadar (aged five). When Peter did not return as usual, Anne went to look for her husband and found him lying motionless on the milking parlour floor. Both she and the first RUC man on the scene thought he had died in a farming accident, but at 12.30 a.m. it was discovered that Peter had been shot. Two guns had been used in the attack, a shotgun and a .38 revolver.

'Peter's murder had a terrible effect on the whole family. He was a hard-working dairy farmer and kept himself to himself. Peadar found it particularly hard when the HET review meant we had to revisit everything, but I was grateful for their work.'

Anne Woolsey, Peter's wife

Peter Woolsey

In May 1981, three men were convicted of Peter's murder. They were Portadown loyalists John Raymond Porter, Robert Turner and Samuel Whitten. Porter admitted using his car to drive the killers and was charged with murder (and another attempted sectarian murder). Turner admitted firing a shotgun from the milking parlour door (though the pathologist's report suggests that the gun was fired from close range). Whitten, like Turner, tried to limit his involvement, only admitting to firing one shot from the doorway with the .38 revolver (again, the pathologist's report suggests two shots were fired at Peter from the revolver at close range). All three were convicted of murder and sentenced to life imprisonment.

Whitten was also named in Judge Barron's 2003 report as a suspect for the Monaghan bombing. One eyewitness, the report says, who probably saw the bomb-car, 'picked out a photograph of Samuel Whitten (UVF) as resembling a passenger'. Another witness identified Whitten as the driver of a red sports car in Monaghan town the previous evening.[51] Whatever the forensic and perpetrator links, Peter Woolsey's death, like all the others, was a personal tragedy for his family.

Some deaths in the conflict are long-remembered, whereas others seem unfairly to disappear from public discourse as soon as the victim is in the grave. The circumstances in which father-of-eight, shopkeeper and Gaelic footballer William Strathearn died ensure he remains in the first category. He was thirty-nine when he was shot at his home in the village of Ahoghill, County Antrim, in the middle of the night of 19 April 1977. Almost from day one, journalists called it the 'Good Samaritan' killing, as the gunmen appeared to rely on William's compassionate nature in their plans to kill him.

On the night he was murdered, William had gone to bed as usual but was woken at around 2 a.m. by a knock at the door of his village shop. He leaned out of the window to ask who was there. A man explained he had a sick child and needed aspirin. When Strathearn went downstairs, he was shot twice at his own doorway.

Seamus Heaney remembers William in his poem 'Station Island' as:

> … that same
> Rangy midfielder in a blue jersey
> And starched pants, the one stylist on the team.[52]

There was no breakthrough in the case until twenty months later – and one might not have come at all if an RUC man called William Alexander McCaughey had not got himself arrested through his erratic behaviour late in 1978. Ultimately this led to the case breaking open.[ah] McCaughey and John Weir, both RUC officers, were

---

ah McCaughey has since died.

eventually arrested, tried, convicted (in April 1980) and sentenced to life imprisonment for Strathearn's murder.[ai] McCaughey claimed to have been an active loyalist paramilitary since 1969, but Weir for a much shorter period.[53] Neither of them fired the fatal shots, however. The killers were Portadown loyalists Robin Jackson and R. J. Kerr.

Postscript

Three years after William Strathearn's murder, a young father was making his way to work in Belfast. Brendan McLaughlin was thirty-five and married with three young children. He worked for the Housing Executive in the lower Falls Road area of the city.

On 28 February 1980, as usual, Brendan had been walking around the corner into Clonard Street when, without warning, gunmen opened fire on him from the back of a van. Joe Austin, who daily opened the Sinn Féin offices near the scene, cradled the young man's head until the ambulance arrived. Austin said, 'He only had what I thought was a spot of blood on his cheek.'[54] Brendan was given a cigarette to calm his nerves as he waited for an ambulance to arrive from the nearby Royal Victoria Hospital. But the 'spot of blood' on Brendan's check was actually a bullet wound. He died in hospital later that day.

The gun used to kill him was the same weapon used to kill Daniel Hughes in Boyle's Bar in Cappagh (April 1974); James and Gertrude Devlin near Dungannon in May 1974 (for which a UDR man received two life sentences);[aj] Arthur Mulholland and Eugene Doyle in Hayden's Bar, Pomeroy in February 1975 (where two UDR men and an RUC officer were suspects); the Miami Showband massacre in July 1975 (at least two UDR men involved); and three members of the O'Dowd family in January 1976 – a total of twelve murders, in

---

ai   For an account of their trial for the murder of William Strathearn, see Chapter 11: Ridding the Land of Pestilence.

aj   William Leonard.

every one of which a member of either the UDR or RUC (or both) was either suspected or convicted. Brendan was the last person to die at the hands of the Parabellum Sterling SMG, with its serial number carefully removed, which had been used across Mid-Ulster, causing so much death and misery.

'Brendan loved football. He was a thoroughly unselfish man who would do anything to help other people out and was great company. He was a deep thinker but loved a good joke.'

Joe Austin, Brendan's work-mate

Brendan McLaughlin

Brendan's son Ciaran McLaughlin (who never knew his father) now works for a cross-community project linking Protestant and Catholic working-class areas of West Belfast. There can be no stronger contrast between the loyalists who used a single gun to devastate nine families, on both sides of the border, and Ciaran, the son of their last victim, who works to prevent sectarian hatred ever destroying another family.

Bombs Know No Borders

The butcher's bill for that dreadful day was worse than anything that any of us had encountered before … surely the story would run and run? It didn't.

Broadcaster Derek Davis[1]

Though the majority of people killed by loyalists from Mid-Ulster in the mid-1970s died in Northern Ireland, nearly forty (roughly a third) died south of the border. Bereaved families living in the Republic have felt neglected and sometimes even ignored, as if their very existence was an embarrassment both to the state and to their fellow citizens. It is no accident that the campaign group representing them chose the name 'Justice for the Forgotten' (JFF).[2]

They found it particularly hurtful that, at a time when London is still ignoring repeated cross-party Oireachtas (national parliament of Ireland) demands for even restricted access to the Dublin/Monaghan security papers, Queen Elizabeth II's advisers did not realise or think to check that she would arrive in the Irish capital for her successful 2011 visit on the thirty-seventh anniversary of the bombings.

The UVF's first foray south was in October 1969, when it bombed an electricity generating station near Ballyshannon, County Donegal, killing one of its own members in a premature explosion. Its next attempt was markedly bloodier. The first time loyalists brought death to the Irish capital was at 7.58 p.m. on a winter's evening in 1972. People were preparing to celebrate Christmas when a car bomb exploded on 1 December near Dublin's then sole skyscraper, the sixteen-storey Liberty Hall (the newly built headquarters of the Irish Transport and General Workers Union, now SIPTU).[3] Exactly a minute earlier, the

Belfast office of the *Belfast Newsletter* had received a warning about two bombs.[4] The caller spoke with a 'Belfast/English type accent'.[5]

Though dozens of people were injured, there were no fatalities from the first bomb that exploded. However, Dublin's luck didn't last. Gardaí evacuating a canteen serving Dublin's bus workers, unwittingly sent them into the path of the second car bomb, which exploded at Sackville Place, a lane off O'Connell Street. It killed bus driver George Bradshaw (aged thirty) and bus conductor Tommy Duffy (aged twenty-three).

The bombs appeared to have been planned for a specific political purpose. On the same evening, the Dáil was in session a mile away, debating a particularly controversial amendment to the Offences Against the State Act (1939). If passed, the Fianna Fáil-sponsored amendment would provide for the conviction and imprisonment of members of paramilitary organisations – not just on the word in court of a garda chief-superintendent, but on the word in court of a junior officer, based on the word of a chief-superintendent. A defeat for then Taoiseach Jack Lynch's Fianna Fáil government appeared inevitable as the opposition parties – and even some members of the government party – were opposed to the amendment. Human rights groups and supporters had been protesting for weeks. It looked certain that the amendment would fall. But that evening the two car bombs altered the course of history.

As the news broke in Leinster House, the political focus was diverted from civil liberties. Public opinion moved towards a need to confront the violence that had spilled across the border and onto the streets of the capital. Fine Gael politicians, despite their previous objections, abstained. The bill was passed.[6]

Were the bombs solely the responsibility of loyalist paramilitaries? Or were British security services involved? Eight months after the bombing, on 11 August 1973, the (by then) former Taoiseach Jack Lynch, in an interview on ITN network television, expressed the opinion that British agents had been involved.[7] The incoming Fine Gael Minister for Foreign Affairs, Garret FitzGerald, no conspiracy-theorist and regarded by many throughout his political career as an optimistic judge of British *bona fides*, also clearly suspected the same. A detailed telex report sent by British Ambassador Sir Arthur Galsworthy on 17 August 1973 to his bosses in London reported as much, stating that FitzGerald had expressed concern 'it was possible that some disreputable characters in our [British] employ, or in some way associated with us, might have acted on their own authority'.[8]

FitzGerald had also told the ambassador that 'he knew that one of the Irish newspapers was conducting its own investigations into the Dublin bombings of last December and January and that shortly they would be coming out with fresh allegations that British agents had after all been responsible'.[9]

In this, at least, FitzGerald was correct. Later that month, more than one journalist made claims of British involvement: Kevin Myers, Jim Cantwell, Conor McAnally and Hugh McKeown. Myers wrote that 'DI6'[a] agents were responsible,[10] while Cantwell claimed that the government had evidence connecting the SAS with the bomb blasts, adding that Special Branch had passed a dossier to the government.[11]

On 30 August, McAnally and McKeown of the *Irish Independent* wrote to the Irish Minister for Justice, Paddy Cooney, claiming that they had 'come across certain information ... which casts a blanket of doubt over denials that any British Agency was involved'. They also claimed that they were 'being met with serious attempts by Government Departments and agencies to divert us from this course'.[12]

When JFF contacted Conor McAnally several years ago, he could not recollect the information he had in 1972 or the difficulties encountered in their investigation. He did, however, recall that soon

---

a   Defence Intelligence Service, linking the British Ministry of Defence with MI6.

after corresponding with the Department of Justice, he was on night duty at the *Independent* offices when a death notice arrived that surprised him. The 'death notice' was for his colleague, Hugh McKeown, who was very much alive. Both he and McKeown took this as a serious threat to their lives and work on the story stopped.[13]

Sackville Place was bombed again – on Saturday 20 January 1973, just seven weeks after the first blast. At 3.20 p.m. a parked car exploded. It killed Tommy Douglas (another bus worker, aged twenty-one, and from Stirling in Scotland). Douglas' mother was from Achill Island in County Mayo. He had been living in Dublin for just four months.

The bomb-car, a hired Vauxhall Victor, had been hijacked from its driver that morning at Agnes Street off the Shankill Road in Belfast. The driver was reported to have been held until shortly after 3 p.m., about the time the bomb exploded.[b]

The garda investigations into both these bomb attacks came to nothing. No one was ever charged, much less convicted.

In between the Dublin bombings of 1 December 1972 and 20 January 1973, Fermanagh-based members of the UDR and UVF carried out three bombings within an hour – in Clones (County Monaghan), Belturbet (County Cavan) and Pettigo (County Donegal) – all on 28 December 1972. Two teenagers, Geraldine O'Reilly (aged fifteen) and Paddy Stanley (sixteen), were killed in Belturbet. Again, no one was brought to justice.

In January 1974, then Garda Commissioner Patrick Malone met RUC Chief Constable James Flanagan and issued a statement on harrying IRA men of violence south of the border. In utter frustration, two Catholic priests in Northern Ireland, Fathers Raymond Murray and Denis Faul, wrote to *The Irish Times*, demanding to know what the Irish authorities had yet done to 'protect the legal rights of a

---

b   In almost every detail, the hijacking of the car that exploded in South Leinster Street on the day of the Dublin/Monaghan bombings (17 May 1974) resembled this earlier hijacking.

minority in the North'.[14] In Mid-Ulster, they said, loyalists were walking freely around 'in their sanctuaries after the murder of Catholic householders, the bombing of Catholic churches, schools, halls, parochial houses, public houses'.[15]

On Sunday 12 May 1974, in an RTÉ interview, Vanguard leader William Craig described the spate of sectarian murders in Northern Ireland as 'understandable' and 'excusable'. Further, Craig said in a BBC interview on 16 May, 'The British Government will have to recognise that it cannot ratify the Sunningdale Agreement or im-plement it in any way. If they do there will be further action taken against the Irish Republic and those who attempt to implement it.'

The next day, the same group of loyalists that was engaged in an all-out sectarian campaign in Mid-Ulster inflicted the worst single day of violence in the entire conflict – on people south of the border. Journalist Vincent Browne, already a veteran of the Northern Ireland conflict, happened to be close by when the bombs exploded on what he remembers was, until then, 'a magnificent summer's afternoon' in Dublin.[16] He recalled first hearing the dull thunder of the blasts and then finding body after body lying in Talbot Street near his workplace just off O'Connell Street. There was, he says, a stillness early on, broken only by groans coming from the piles of debris. He describes a man lying with a car fender sticking into his side, bleeding profusely, and a woman, barely breathing, who disintegrated in his arms. Her body 'simply fell apart inside her clothes'.[17]

Journalist Frank Connolly also witnessed the carnage. As he walked across the open green space within the grounds of Trinity College, he heard one of the three blasts and saw clouds of smoke rising. He heard screams and sounds of panic as he headed towards the scene of the South Leinster Street explosion:

> It was a scene of utter chaos and destruction, with dozens, maybe hundreds, of people wandering around in shock. The remains of a car

were in flames near the college railings. What looked like a foot, or an arm, and other body parts, were strewn close to the burning vehicle. A woman was lying nearby in the centre of the road. I went to her assistance. She was badly injured and clearly confused. She was crying for help. It seemed like an age before the ambulances, sirens blaring, neared. She was still alive when they lifted her from the road.[18]

The basic facts of the slaughter are well established. The first of the three Dublin bombs went off at 5.28 p.m. on Parnell Street, near its junction with Marlborough Street. Shops and cars were destroyed, and bodies were strewn about the street. The bomb-car was a metallic-green Hillman Avenger, hijacked in Belfast that morning. Eleven people were killed in this explosion, including two baby girls and their parents, and a First World War veteran. Many others were badly injured.[c]

The second bomb went off at about 5.30 p.m. at 18 Talbot Street near its junction with Lower Gardiner Street. The bomb-car was a metallic-blue Ford Escort, stolen that morning in the docks area of Belfast. Eleven people were killed outright in this explosion, and another two died over the following days or weeks. Twelve of the thirteen victims were women, including one who was nine months pregnant.[d]

The third bomb went off at about 5.30 p.m. in South Leinster

---

c   Those killed in Parnell Street were: Marie Butler (aged twenty-one), John Dargle (eighty), Patrick Fay (forty-seven), Elizabeth Fitzgerald (fifty-nine), Antonio Magliocco (thirty-seven), Edward O'Neill (thirty-nine), Breda Turner (twenty-one), and John (twenty-four), Anna (twenty-two), Jacqueline (seventeen months) and Anne Marie (five months) O'Brien.

d   Those killed in Talbot Street were: Josie Bradley (aged twenty-one), Anne Byrne (thirty-five), Simone Chetrit (thirty), Concepta Dempsey (sixty-five), Colette Doherty (twenty), Baby Doherty (full-term unborn baby), Breda Grace (thirty-four), May McKenna (fifty-five), Ann Marren (twenty), Dorothy Morris (fifty-seven), Marie Phelan (twenty), Siobhán Roice (nineteen), Maureen Shields (forty-six) and John Walshe (twenty-seven).

Marie Butler   *Patrick Fay*   *Antonio Magliocco*   *Breda Turner*

Josie Bradley   *Anne Byrne*   *Simone Chetrit*   *Concepta Dempsey*

Anna and John O'Brien   *Jacqueline O'Brien*

Colette Doherty   *Breda Grace*   *May McKenna*   *Ann Marren*

Dorothy Morris   *Marie Phelan*   *Siobhán Roice*   *Maureen Shields*   *John Walshe*

Street (almost simultaneously with the Talbot Street bomb), near Trinity College. Two women were killed instantly. The bomb-car was a blue Austin 1800 Maxi. It too had been hijacked in Belfast.[e]

Ninety minutes later, at 6.58 p.m., one more car bomb exploded, outside Greacen's pub in Monaghan. The bomb-car was a green 1966 model Hillman Minx. It had been stolen from a car park in Portadown that afternoon. As in Dublin, no warnings had been given. This bomb killed five people almost instantly, while another died four days later, and a seventh on 23 July.[f]

Paddy Askin   Tommy Croarkin   Archie Harper   George Williamson

Jack Travers   Peggy White   Christina O'Loughlin

The Garda Síochána sealed the border, but the damage had already been done.

Paddy Doyle of Finglas, who lost his daughter, son-in-law and two infant granddaughters in the Parnell Street explosion, described the scene inside Dublin's city morgue as being like a 'slaughterhouse', with workers 'putting arms and legs together to make up a body'.[19]

Iris Boyd told the Joint Oireachtas Committee in 2004 that she had accompanied her father, Archie Harper, into Monaghan on the afternoon of the bombing and had gone to visit a sick aunt while he went shopping. The bomb exploded as she was saying goodbye to her aunt. Iris stated, 'I went down town, where there was devastation … There were bodies everywhere – it was terrible.' Archie survived until the following Tuesday, but never spoke during that time. 'We were with him in the end but life has been very tough. It has never been the same for us as a family. Everything changed.'[20]

That night, the then Fine Gael Taoiseach, Liam Cosgrave, spoke in a TV and radio broadcast of the 'revulsion and condemnation felt by every decent person in this island at these unforgivable acts'. Cosgrave's fury, however, was directed not only at the loyalists responsible for the bombings, but also at focusing southern minds on republican violence: 'Everyone who has practised violence or preached violence or condoned violence must bear a share of responsibility for today's outrage.' He argued that the bombings 'help to bring home to us … what the people in Northern Ireland have been suffering for five long years'.[21] By 26 June, some politicians had shifted the blame completely onto republicans, with Fine Gael's Paddy Harte declaring in the Dáil, 'Does anyone believe that Northern Irish Protestants, or Loyalists, or anyone else who would plan such a terrible deed, would have come down here if the IRA were not bombing in the North of Ireland?'[22]

The leader of Fianna Fáil, Jack Lynch, also widened the blame to include republicans: 'Every person and every organisation which played any part in the campaign of bombing and violence … shares the guilt and shame of the assassins who actually placed these bombs on the streets of Dublin and Monaghan last Friday.'[23]

Unionism was unequivocal in its condemnation. Brian Faulkner, then head of the power-sharing Executive at Stormont, sent a message to Cosgrave expressing 'deepest regret' on behalf of himself and his Executive colleagues.

Whatever the political fall-out, relatively few politicians visited the families of the dead and injured.[g] There was no national day of mourning as there had been for Bloody Sunday. Nor was there an Irish government fund for the dependants of those murdered. The government did not even contact the families to offer sympathy.

So who was responsible for the bloodshed on the streets of Dublin and Monaghan in May 1974? Both the UDA and UVF initially denied responsibility, though the then UDA press officer, Samuel Smyth,[h] said he was 'very happy about the bombings in Dublin. There is a war with the Free State and now we are laughing at them.'[24]

At this remove, all sides agree that the UVF carried out the actual bombing. (The British government announced its de-proscription just three days before, on 14 May.) But did they act alone? Until 1990, it seemed that they had. Then people began to ask questions. Rumours began to spread that there might have been British involvement. Journalists began sniffing around. At first sight, it seems an outlandish allegation that the single greatest loss of life in any one day in the conflict could be in any way connected to the servants or agents of one of the two democratically elected governments most closely involved. The British political establishment still firmly contests any claim of responsibility. The UVF also claims to have carried out the atrocity on its own – but questions raised by a British television documentary still remain unanswered. Nearly twenty years after the explosions (on 6 July 1993), Yorkshire Television broadcast 'Hidden Hand: The

---

g   Eddie McGrady of the SDLP did visit one constituent, Nora Fitzsimmons, who had been injured in the Monaghan bombing, at her home in County Down.
h   Smyth was also a spokesman for the Ulster Workers' Council (UWC). He was killed by the IRA on 10 March 1976.

Forgotten Massacre'.[25] The television documentary quoted evidence from George Styles, former head of the British Army's bomb disposal network worldwide, who had served in Northern Ireland from 1969–72.[i] Styles concluded that whoever had planted the bombs certainly knew what they were doing. Getting any bomb onto four wheels, he said, was difficult enough, but 'the organisation of getting three cars into the centre of a city – all going off at roughly the same time – that smacks of some pretty good administrative ability. Whatever organisation therefore that was behind this outrage, you could say they were not low down on the learning curve, they were high up on it.'[26]

Irish Army Commandant Patrick Trears told the programme's producers, 'It was a very sophisticated operation, a very military type operation. The terrorist group had to be well-trained to carry this out so smoothly and without a flaw.'[27] 'Hidden Hand' concluded that the two explosives experts, British and Irish, believed it was highly unlikely that an attack of this complexity could have been mounted by the UVF alone. Styles was blunt about his views on loyalist expertise at handling explosives: 'I have no high regard for their [UVF] skills in 1974. I don't think they were at a level that would equate to the sort of techniques that were used here in Dublin.'[28]

Samples taken from the scene were dealt with in a cavalier fashion. The debris was not properly handled or stored and, apart from a few samples, it was not examined in Dublin (there was no dedicated forensic laboratory in the Republic at that time). According to the first Barron Report (2003), it was instead delivered to the forensic science laboratory in Belfast – a full eleven days after the atrocity. Forensic analysis was fatally compromised by the delay.

---

i   Lieutenant Colonel George Styles, G.C., Royal Army Ordnance Corps, author of *Bombs Have No Pity: My War Against Terrorism* (1975), which, *inter alia*, wrongly claimed the 1971 McGurk's Bar bomb that killed fifteen Catholics was an IRA 'own-goal'. Many years later this theory was dismissed.

JFF has since commissioned a former British military explosives ordnance disposal officer, former Lieutenant Colonel Nigel Wylde, to examine photographs and forensic reports. He concluded that the explosives in the Dublin bombs were of the kind typically used by the IRA, raising obvious questions as to how loyalists could have acquired them.[j] Wylde suggested that unexploded IRA bomb-making material, captured by the British Army, may have been provided to the UVF. The IRA had developed a method of re-crystallising ammonium nitrate from fertiliser to boost its explosive power. There is, says Wylde, no evidence that loyalists knew of or used this technology at the time. He believes fragments of the explosives can still be seen in some of the photographs supplied to him by JFF.[29] Wylde also contrasts the three bombs with those he typically dealt with in Belfast between June and October 1974. The loyalist devices were far less sophisticated. The Monaghan bomb, however, was contained in a beer barrel (unlike the devices in Dublin), says Wylde, which was more typical of loyalist bomb-making at the time.

The 'Hidden Hand' producers had the co-operation of a number of retired garda officers and named a number of UVF men it claimed were involved. These included former British soldier (Royal Ulster Rifles and UDR sergeant) Billy Hanna,[k] David Mulholland, Robert McConnell (a UDR corporal), Harris Boyle and a key loyalist whom the producers referred to only as 'the Jackal'. The last-named was, of course, Robin Jackson. ('Hidden Hand' declined to name him at that time for legal reasons.) William (Frenchie) Marchant was also named as the leader of the Belfast UVF gang that had hijacked the cars used.

More seriously, however, the documentary also claimed loyalists

---

j   IRA explosives generally consisted of ammonium nitrate and fuel oil, a combination commonly referred to as 'AnFO'.

k   Hanna was later shot dead, reportedly by Robin Jackson or Harris Boyle, two associates, on his doorstep in Lurgan, according to *The Sunday Times*, 7 March 1999.

had been assisted by unidentified British security force members,[30] based on information given to them by former senior British Army information officer Colin Wallace, British Army intelligence officer Fred Holroyd, and other sources, including former RUC officer John Weir.[31]

'Hidden Hand' disturbed many people. Questions began to be asked in the Dáil. The government ordered the Garda Síochána to examine the programme's evidence. The UVF, while belatedly admitting its role for the first time, vehemently denied that it had obtained assistance from anyone. The UVF statement read:

> … the entire operation was from its conception to its successful conclusion, planned and carried out by our volunteers aided by no outside bodies. … The type of explosives, timing and detonating methods all bore the hallmark of the UVF. It is incredulous [*sic*] that these points were lost on the Walter Mittys who conjured up this programme. To suggest that the UVF were not, or are not, capable of operating in the manner outlined in the programme is tempting fate to a dangerous degree.[32]

Trade unionist Kevin Walsh, from the working-class Dublin suburb of Ballyfermot, had witnessed the carnage on 17 May 1974 while on his way to a meeting in Liberty Hall.[1] When he saw that no memorial had been erected, even after ten years, he began to lobby Dublin City Council, and on the sixteenth anniversary, in 1990, organised the first commemorative mass in the city's Pro-Cathedral, which brought some of the families together for the first time. The then Fianna Fáil Lord Mayor of Dublin, Seán Haughey, listened, and the city council paid for a memorial to be erected outside the Garden of

---

1   Kevin Walsh died on 12 November 2007. He had been involved with JFF's campaign for several years.

Remembrance in Parnell Square. It was unveiled on the bombing's seventeenth anniversary.[m] In January 1996, JFF was formed and began lobbying for a public enquiry. Its primary demand was, and is, for the release of Irish and British files.

Three years later, the then Taoiseach, Bertie Ahern, ordered an enquiry – but it was to be in private and with no powers to subpoena witnesses. It was, however, unique in that JFF was able to consult with the judge and suggest lines of investigation and witnesses he might question.[n] The 2003 Barron Report reached a series of disturbing conclusions, including:

- The bombings had been carried out by two UVF gangs, one based in Belfast and the other around Portadown/Lurgan.

- It was 'neither fanciful nor absurd' to believe that members of the Northern Ireland security forces could have been involved. It was likely that individual members of the UDR and RUC had participated, or were at least aware at the planning stage.

- On the other hand, loyalists were capable of carrying out the bombings on their own without assistance from the security forces, though this did not rule out the involvement of individual RUC, UDR or British Army members.

- RUC Reservist James Mitchell's farm at Glenanne was likely to have played a significant part in the preparation for the attacks.

- Within a short time, the RUC had good intelligence to suggest who was responsible and 'a number of those suspected were reliably said to have had what it called "relationships" with British intelligence and/or RUC Special Branch officers'.

---

m   This memorial was later moved to Glasnevin Cemetery. A much larger memorial stone bearing the names of all the Dublin and Monaghan victims was unveiled in Talbot Street in 1997.

n   Unable to intervene or cross-examine witnesses, JFF's legal team (headed by Cormac Ó Dúlacháin and Greg O'Neill) made over fifty submissions to the inquiry.

- Whatever assistance the RUC might have offered the gardaí may have been compromised by these 'relationships' and the garda investigation ended prematurely.

- The Irish government had 'showed little interest in the bombings. When information was given to them suggesting the British authorities had intelligence naming the bombers, it was not followed up.'

It was not all the families wanted, but it was a huge step forward. Facts, particularly ballistic links, that otherwise would never have seen the light of day are now on the public record and could form the basis for making links between attacks on both sides of the border.

One of the Barron Report's most startling findings was that the garda investigation was wound up in a matter of weeks, with the final report for Monaghan written on 6 July and that of Dublin on 9 August 1974 – before three months had elapsed – with no charges and no convictions.

After years of research in the British National Archives, some of the context can be seen, and while answers are still not on the public record, inferences can be drawn. From early 1974, the British government was determined to secure the support of the Irish government in its battle against the IRA. As a result, the gardaí should have been in a strong position to demand co-operation from the RUC to locate and charge those who bombed Dublin and Monaghan. It appears that they failed to do so. The British were pushing for a high-level meeting with their Irish counterparts to establish channels of communication, not only between the gardaí and the RUC, but also between the gardaí and the British Army. Merlyn Rees declared that this was very much in the British interest.[33] The British noted privately that their wishes would have to be 'forcibly brought home to the Irish to move them from their ivory tower'.[34]

On 13 May, a Northern Ireland Office official noted that one reason why Dublin was resisting cross-border security co-operation was that it tended to be a one-way street: 'because all the violence takes place in the North, the demands for assistance are usually one way and it is seldom that the RUC gets an opportunity to reciprocate the assistance given by the gardaí.'[35] After the Dublin/Monaghan bombings, the one-way street could have become a six-lane highway. For once, the shoe was on the other foot, and London could have shown Dublin the kind of assistance it was always demanding from the Irish security forces.

Also on 13 May, documents purporting to suggest an all-out offensive by the IRA against the Protestant community in Belfast were presented dramatically to the Taoiseach by the British Ambassador.[o] While the British were suggesting imminent republican violence (making lurid headlines in Ireland and Britain), they were ignoring advance intelligence on the threat posed by the Ulster Workers' Council whose strike began two days later, on 15 May.[36]

In the wake of the 17 May bombings, the British Ambassador reported back to the Foreign Office on the mood in Dublin, remarking that the reactions of the Irish government and public, from the British viewpoint, were 'healthy and helpful', adding, 'There is now a much keener realisation of the Republic's vulnerability to acts of terrorism spilling over from the North and recognition of the direct connection between this and continued violence by PIRA'.[37]

The final remark of British Ambassador Sir Arthur Galsworthy was that 'Protestant opinion in the North must feel with some bitterness that it is only now that the South has experienced violence that they are reacting in the way the North has sought for so long', but warned against rubbing in this point, saying, 'the Irish have taken the point'.[38] Similar disturbing remarks were made in a briefing for

---

o   They had been found in the possession of leading IRA man Brendan Hughes, in an apartment in South Belfast, and were doctored by the British to appear offensive when, in reality, they were a defensive blueprint in case of major anti-Catholic pogroms in the city.

a British cabinet meeting the following day. It was stated that 'this lesson' should help co-operation, but again warned against the British 'rubbing it in'.[39]

The real reason for the abject failure, and the short duration, of the garda investigation may possibly be found by examining contemporaneous statements made by the Taoiseach, Liam Cosgrave, and the Minister for Posts and Telegraphs, Conor Cruise O'Brien. Both condemned the IRA vociferously as causing the collapse of power-sharing. In a press conference on 14 June, Cosgrave said, 'The violence which characterises the North should be prevented from spilling into the Republic – the best way to do this is to offer all possible assistance in reducing violence in the North and to end any support for violence in any part of the Republic.'[40] These remarks suggest that the top priority for the state was not pursuing the bombers of Dublin/Monaghan, but defeating the IRA.

This view is reinforced by comments made by the British Ambassador in his annual review for 1974, reporting Dublin as adopting a low profile on Northern Ireland. The Irish government, he said, has decided its most effective contribution is to promote reconciliation between the two communities and refrain from any action that would exacerbate the situation.[41] At a meeting between both governments on 11 September 1974, Merlyn Rees said he believed people interned during the UWC strike were responsible for the 'Dublin bombings'. He also provided names, but no action was taken.[42]

A long-demanded (by the British), high-level meeting took place on 18 September 1974, at Baldonnel military aerodrome in County Dublin. Attendees included Northern Ireland Secretary of State Merlyn Rees, Irish Minister for Justice Paddy Cooney, RUC Chief Constable Sir James Flanagan, Garda Commissioner Patrick Malone and senior civil servants from both sides. The minutes are remarkable for the unwitting testimony they provide of Irish ministers and senior gardaí failing to raise the Dublin and Monaghan bombings, which had occurred only four months previously – or to express any concerns about loyalists crossing the border into the Republic. Instead, Minister for Justice Paddy Cooney invited suggestions from the British on measures the Irish government might take against IRA bombers.[43]

As a result of the meeting, formal and powerful structures, known as 'technical panels', were quickly put in place between the RUC and the gardaí on communications, advance planning, exchange of information on ballistics and explosives, and the detection of sources of supplies of arms, ammunition and explosives.[44] The new structures worked very well for the British side, with the gardaí providing full information on explosives finds in the Republic and passing on captured weapons for ballistic examination. There is no evidence of any reciprocal response or even any request for such a response. It is hard not to conclude that the Dublin and Monaghan bombings, and other bombings in the Republic in the 1970s, proved advantageous to British government policy.

In contrast, the four Barron Reports failed to provide the answers needed to set the past to rest for families south of the border. The 2003 Barron Report named several suspects who were listed in the garda files: David Mulholland, Sammy Whitten,[p] Stewart Young, Nelson Young, Ronald Michael Jackson, Charles Gilmore, Billy Fulton and William (Frenchie) Marchant. Billy Hanna and Robin Jackson were added to the garda list only in 1993.[q]

'Only the greatest possible disclosure of what led to the bombings and who was truly responsible, will allow the families to lay down the heavy burden of searching for the truth. A sixteen-page synopsis, written by those with most to lose from disclosure, hardly fits that bill,' says Margaret Urwin of JFF. A Dáil committee scrutinising the

---

p   Whitten was a UVF man from Portadown convicted of murdering Catholic farmer Peter Woolsey in October 1976.

q   Other suspects, not on the garda file and including members of the RUC and UDR, cannot be named here for legal reasons.

report said: 'There is no way of knowing what might be contained in documentation which exists in Northern Ireland and the UK without gaining access to that documentation.'[45]

Judge Barron also conducted a review into the bombing of Kay's Tavern, Dundalk, and concluded that there was extensive collusion involving many of those it had already identified as being responsible for the Dublin/Monaghan bombings. Quite apart from their disturbing conclusions on events south of the border, the Barron Reports also found a chain of ballistic history linking many attacks in Northern Ireland, specifically in Mid-Ulster, as well as the murder of John Francis Green in County Monaghan.

Two years on, on 10 July 2008, a Dáil all-party resolution urged the British government 'to allow access by an independent, international judicial figure to all original documents held by the British government'. Yet another, almost identical, resolution was passed unanimously on the thirty-seventh anniversary of the bombings. These calls for disclosure, backed by the families and JFF, have fallen on deaf ears. How, they ask, even if Britain believes public disclosure might jeopardise its national interests, can it oppose an agreed, security-vetted judicial figure viewing the documents?

JFF lodged two complaints with the European Court of Human Rights against the United Kingdom, alleging collusion and failure to co-operate with an investigation. The ECHR, however, deemed (for reasons unknown) that these complaints had originated from the 'Hidden Hand' programme, rather than events in 2003 at the Barron inquiry. As a result they were never considered, the court ruling that they should have been lodged within six months of the original broadcasting of the programme in 1993.

There are few in Britain prepared to fight the cause of the thirty-four victims. One indication of the prevailing attitude at Westminster is reflected in a report in *The Times* (London) of 11 December 2003. Flying in the face of the Barron Report's damning findings, the article cheerily claimed that he had failed to prove 'the involvement of senior members of the security forces in the planning and execution' of the Dublin and Monaghan bombings.

At the time of writing, then, there are two starkly contrasting analyses. In one camp sit the UVF, the RUC, the British security services, the British press and the British government, all continuing to deny responsibility – the press calling Barron's conclusions merely 'well-worn allegations'.[46] The UVF, they all say, carried out the bombings on their own with no state assistance.

In the other camp are the victims' families and JFF, Judge Henry Barron, Colin Wallace, Fred Holroyd, former RUC sergeant John Weir and retired RUC detective Gerry McCann, who all believe the evidence does point to some level of collusion.

As Derek Davis[r] wrote in his 2011 letter to *The Irish Times*, the timing of the royal visit on the anniversary of the outrage 'served to remind people of an atrocity that might otherwise be allowed to pass unnoticed'.

And there it sits.

* * *

The next killing carried out by loyalists south of the border was the shooting dead of John Francis (Francie) Green, who had escaped from Long Kesh internment camp in 1973. Francie was married to Ann and they had three children. He was a trade unionist in his home town of Lurgan. He joined People's Democracy,[s] and later became involved in the IRA. The garda investigation report into his shooting on 10 January 1975 said he was a 'staff captain' and intelligence officer for the IRA. His brother Leo acknowledges that, on escaping from internment Francie 're-engaged with the IRA'.[47]

---

r   In 1974 Davis was working for RTÉ and the BBC, just a year after leaving Northern Ireland.

s   A left-wing group of students and workers involved in the civil rights movement.

John Francis Green

'We had a brother, Gerard, a priest who used to say mass in the camp every Sunday. This week, they overpowered him, tied him up, Francie put on his clerical garb and he walked out of the jail,' said Leo.[48] Francie was spirited across the border and set up home in Castleblayney, driving every day to a rundown cottage in the countryside at Comaghy for meetings and other IRA activity.

He made occasional visits back to Lurgan, however, and on one of these – at Christmas 1974 – the house was surrounded by a large force of British soldiers. Expecting a house raid and arrest, Francie and his family were amazed when the soldiers politely knocked on the door and then retreated. He had intended to spend a few more days at home, but almost immediately after the soldiers' visit left Lurgan to return to Castleblayney. His family never saw him alive again. On 10 January, at the house in Comaghy, he was shot with two pistols – a Luger and a Star revolver.[t] He sustained several head wounds at close range and died almost instantly.

The farmhouse he was visiting at Comaghy belonged to Gerry Carville, a republican sympathiser who was, according to RUC Special Branch detective Sergeant Drew Coid, the intended target. Green's death had been 'an unexpected bonus' for the killers.[49] John Weir also says that Carville was the intended victim. The Green family do not believe this.

On the day of Green's funeral, crowds lined the streets of Castleblayney as the cortège moved north. Across the border in Lurgan, large crowds also came to pay their respects. As far as the Green family is concerned, the SAS and unknown loyalists were responsible for his death.

---

t   This Luger was also used in the Miami Showband massacre and was recovered on the farm of Edward Sinclair in May 1976. The Star had been stolen from a UDR member in March 1973. It was used in the attempted murder of Patrick Turley and the murder of Dorothy Trainor.

For investigating gardaí, the most important lead was a red Ford Escort, registration number BIB 1291, seen on both sides of the border within a mile of the murder scene on different occasions between 1 and 14 January 1975. Two days after the murder, the car was seen in Keady RUC barracks, and on 14 January, two garda officers spotted it crossing the border. On seeing the garda patrol car, the driver of the Escort stopped, reversed back over the border, then turned and drove towards Keady. When the gardaí checked with the RUC, they were told that the number plate was false and had not been issued to any vehicle. They were also told that two RUC patrols in the vicinity had not seen the car, and that the British Army, who had also been in the area, had not noticed it either. However, later that evening, the British Army in Armagh rang the gardaí at Castleblayney, admitting the vehicle was one of theirs, and that two plain-clothes soldiers had been in the car when it was seen by the two gardaí.[50] Barron found no evidence of any follow-up by the garda investigation team.

During enquiries into allegations made by Fred Holroyd in the 1980s, it emerged that the vehicle had been allocated to 3 Royal Tank Regiment. The regiment had served in Armagh from 9 September 1974, but left on 4 January 1975, six days before Green was killed.[51] On reviewing the case at that time, Assistant Garda Commissioner J. P. McMahon was inclined to believe some of Holroyd's claims because of the numerous sightings of the Escort. He stated that there was 'one set of suspects, i.e. the occupants of the British Army car'.[52]

John Weir claims that UDR corporal Robert McConnell was involved in the attack, and probably also Robin Jackson. He supports a claim made by Fred Holroyd that Robert Nairac may have been present at the shooting. Weir also alleges that the Star pistol was McConnell's 'personal' weapon, and that he was regularly in the company of undercover soldiers.[53] No one was ever charged with killing Green.

The next killing in the south came in Dundalk, just south of the border. The town suffered both economically and socially as a result of the conflict. Pejoratively labelled 'El Paso' by some newspapers because of its reputation as a bolt-hole for fugitive republicans, its citizens greatly resented that reputation.

On Friday 19 December 1975, as people were beginning to wind down for Christmas, the horror of the conflict hit the town hard. People were enjoying the company of friends and work colleagues in the town's bars – among them, Kay's Tavern in the town centre. At about 6.15 p.m., a red car with false number plates exploded, virtually

demolishing two houses and setting Kay's Tavern on fire. The car had been stolen from the Shankill Road in Belfast.

Two men were killed: Hugh Watters, a sixty-one-year-old tailor and married father of four described by his family as very quiet, gentle and deeply religious,[54] and Jack Rooney (aged sixty-two), an 'outgoing and popular' married father of two, a fireman for the local council.[55] Jack had been walking close to Kay's Tavern. Amid the smoke and panic after the bomb, he lay fatally wounded on the pavement. Hugh was trapped inside the burning tavern, unconscious and unable to escape, breathing in poisonous fumes. (The landlady, Kathleen

Hugh Watters

Jack Rooney

McErlean, told an inquest hearing of how, while upstairs cooking dinner for her two daughters, she had seen a 'blue flash'.)[56]

In a co-ordinated attack, north of the border, three hours after Dundalk was hit, Donnelly's Bar in Silverbridge, County Armagh, suffered a gun-and-bomb attack in which three men lost their lives.

In Dundalk twenty people were injured, many severely. Nearly 100 rescuers rushed to the scene, including civil defence volunteers. One volunteer described the wounded as stumbling out of the wrecked bar, bleeding and dazed:

The rescuers had to wait forty-five minutes so that the [Fire] Brigade could bring the fire under control. We scraped through the debris and we found a tall, elderly man covered in rubble.[u] He must have felt the explosion coming because he had his hands up to his face. The skin was completely burned off his face and hands. He was in a terrible mess. A Garda felt his pulse and said he was barely alive but when he arrived in hospital, he was dead.[57]

Jack was taken to hospital with massive injuries.[58] There he contracted peritonitis and died three days later. Hugh died from inhaling smoke in the wreckage of the bar.

Margaret Watters had been sent to find her father by her frantic mother who already feared the worst. Margaret could not find him at the scene of the bombing and, when other family members went to the hospital, they were not allowed in. Her sister had to climb through a window, only to find that their father had died.[59]

Jack's family could not find him in his usual haunts and also hurried to the hospital. There was a patient called 'Mooney' on the list of injured and they realised this was a misspelling, and that Jack had been hurt. Initially he appeared to be doing well, talking in bed, so the family believed he would recover and even brought him in cigarettes.[60] However, Jack died on 22 December from his injuries and was buried on Christmas Eve.

At the inquest, the coroner commented on what he said could be seen as a third victim of the bombing: a young, married telephonist, Margaret Brennan, who died in a car crash, driving to answer the emergency call-out from Dundalk telephone exchange on the night of the attack.[61]

There were contradictory claims on who had carried out the bomb-

---

u   Hugh Watters.

ing. *The Irish Times* on 22 December claimed the UDA[v] was responsible, but McKittrick, in *Lost Lives,* blames the Red Hand Commando (RHC),[w] which was an 'integral part of the UVF'.[62]

After the bombing at Kay's Tavern, the gardaí interviewed eye-witnesses, gathered what little forensic evidence remained, and set up an incident room where bereaved families hoped that the optimistic sounds coming out of Dundalk garda station were genuine. Superintendent Dan Murphy, head of the special unit of the Garda Technical Bureau, said he was hopeful of finding the bombers;[63] 1,600 people had been interviewed and the gardaí had taken 475 statements.

However, nothing much happened until Detective John Courtney was appointed as border superintendent in September 1978. He renewed his contacts with the RUC and began to press for information about Kay's, which led to a meeting in January 1979 with the head of the RUC CID, Bill Mooney, at its headquarters in Belfast. Mooney took Detective Superintendent Courtney and Detective Sergeant Owen Corrigan to Tennant Street RUC station, where they were due to meet an officer who had information on the car that exploded at Kay's. On arriving at Tennant Street, the two gardaí were asked to wait while Mooney went to find the officer with information. When he returned, his friendly attitude had gone. The gardaí would not, after all, be allowed to interview the officer.[64]

While co-operation between the two police forces on the island is officially highly praised, this incident appears to be a deliberate failure to co-operate in a murder enquiry – a stark reminder of the RUC Special Branch being seen as 'a force within a force'.[x] Without

---

v   The UDA was then still a legal organisation.

w   The following year, the RHC claimed responsibility for the murder of forestry worker Seamus Ludlow, who was hitching a lift home after a night out just north of Dundalk in May. Two of his killers were UDR members.

x   The phrase 'a force within a force' was coined by former Deputy Chief Constable of the Greater Manchester Police, John Stalker, while heading a stymied 1982 enquiry into alleged RUC 'shoot-to-kill' incidents. It was also used by Chris Patten the full co-operation of the RUC and Northern Ireland authorities, the gardaí stood little chance of finding those responsible for the attack on Kay's Tavern.

Barron named the Dundalk suspects as Robin Jackson, Stewart Young, Ivor Young, Nelson Young, Sammy McCoo,[y] John Somerville and Sammy Whitten, although this list is not exhaustive and there were others involved whom he does not name.[65] On 29 November 2006, a Dáil committee considering the Barron Report on Kay's (and other related attacks) did not mince its words, stating that, taken with other events, the bombing amounted to 'international terrorism'. It concluded that:

- Information had been withheld from Barron by the RUC, giving rise to 'a suspicion' that its actions 'were designed to limit information relating to security forces collusion in terrorist activity from reaching the public domain'.

- The gang based at former RUC Reservist James Mitchell's farm at Glenanne 'contained members of the RUC and UDR'.

- Northern Ireland authorities knew the Glenanne farm was a 'centre for illegal activities as early as January 1976, yet those activities were allowed to continue for another two years'.

- Senior members of the security forces allowed 'a climate to develop in which loyalist subversives could believe they could attack with impunity'.

- Some loyalists, notably Robin Jackson and the Young brothers, 'were reliably said to have had relationships with British intelligence and/or RUC Special Branch and exchanges of information took place'.

- People employed by the British state ostensibly to preserve peace

---

in his 1999 report on reforming the RUC.

y   Sammy McCoo was also named by Weir (Barron Report, 2006, p. 97), as a suspect for the gun-and-bomb attack on Donnelly's Bar, Silverbridge.

and to protect the public were instead 'engaged in … the butchering of innocent victims' (the committee was 'horrified' at this).

• The British cabinet was then 'aware of the level at which the security forces had been infiltrated by terrorists' and that its refusal to act 'permitted the problem to grow'.

The committee did not spare Irish embarrassment either, concluding that gardaí and judicial authorities south of the border 'at all levels could have been far more vigorous in their attempts to identify and bring to justice the perpetrators'.[66]

* * *

Patrick (Packie) Mone and his wife, Anna, lived peacefully in a cottage in the townland of Tattinclave, County Monaghan, until March 1976. Packie was a bicycle mechanic, aged fifty-six. He and Anna shared the cottage with her elderly aunt, Margaret, tending a smallholding of cattle, pigs and chickens. The couple had married about seven years earlier after a long courtship. Packie had moved out of his family home to live with Anna and the aunt she cared for in the cottage tucked into the hillside. He travelled to work every day fixing bicycles in Castleblayney. The couple had no children and the evenings would be spent *céilidh*-ing (having get-togethers in friends' homes). They were happy and contented, working together in the fields with their animals. It was a quiet country life.

Packie Mone

Everything changed on 7 March 1976. That Sunday evening, Packie and Anna left their home to drive Mary, a friend of Anna's, into Castleblayney to catch a bus home to Dublin. On the way into town, they were waved through a garda checkpoint; a car with Northern Ireland registration plates was being searched.[67]

Fifteen minutes later, Packie was parking their car on the town's main street outside the Three Star Inn, manoeuvring it into a better spot nearer the bus stop for the convenience of their guest, before the three of them waited for the Dublin-bound bus. There was another car parked beside them: a metallic-blue Ford Cortina about which one of the barmen in the Three Star Inn was already slightly suspicious. It had four digits after the Monaghan registration letters (JBI) instead of the maximum three. The car had been stolen on the Shankill Road in Belfast,[68] but, in a terrible twist of fate, the barman decided to wait for his boss to arrive before clearing the bar and alerting the authorities. The bar manager walked into the packed bar just as the car bomb exploded.

Anna later said that, as they waited for the bus, 'Packie got out of the car and went to the front of it. According to the post office clock the time was just after 8.20 p.m. I saw a blue flash which seemed to light up the place and I heard a very loud bang. The car was turned over on its side and glass came in on top of us. The street went into darkness and the car was filled with dust and smoke.'[69]

Years later, Anna still recalls the terrible smell:

> Like when an electric plug gets over-heated. Everything went black and I found I was kneeling on the door of the car. The car windscreen was shattered. I crawled through from the back of the car to the front seat and followed Mary out through the windscreen, cutting my arm. I saw Packie, lying [in the roadway] beside the car with his feet towards the footpath … His leg was blown off but I think he was still breathing. I can remember screaming and rushing to try and help him but a passer-by grabbed me and pulled me away.[70]

Packie had been standing directly between his car and the no-warning car bomb. Two nurses were on the scene within minutes and the ambulance arrived within five to ten minutes, but despite this immediate medical assistance, Packie died from his injuries in the ambulance.

Seventeen other people were injured by the bomb, which caused extensive damage to nearby buildings. It seemed a miracle to local people that more had not died.[71] It is believed that the intended target was the bus to Dublin. It was said that you 'could set your clock by it', but on this occasion it was two minutes late because it had been held up at the garda checkpoint on the way into town. Huge loss of life may have been avoided as a result, although this is no consolation to Anna.[72]

No group claimed responsibility for the attack, though reliable loyalist sources have claimed that the UVF was responsible.[73]

In the immediate aftermath, extra security checkpoints were set up around Castleblayney and on both sides of the border. The following weekend, garda officers, backed up by soldiers, visited many houses in the area, including the homes of Protestant families.[74]

Photographs taken in the aftermath of both the Dundalk and Castleblayney bombings show garda officers handling parts of timing and power units (TPUs) without gloves. Former British Army bomb explosives expert Nigel Wylde noted the missed forensic opportunity: 'The construction of TPUs was invariably undertaken at this time by a bomb maker who was not wearing gloves. In my experience it was always possible to find fingerprints on this type of evidence. By their actions, the police could well have destroyed any such evidence.'[75]

When the state pathologist, Dr John Harbison, visited the scene the day after the bomb explosion, he found 'a battery with a wire attached to it and the works of a clock, which may have formed part of the timing mechanism of the bomb'.[76]

According to former RUC Sergeant John Weir, UDR Sergeant Robert McConnell and RUC Reserve Constable Laurence McClure were involved in planting the Castleblayney bomb;[77] and a UDR captain supplied the explosives for it, which were stored at Mitchell's farm in Glenanne – as well as for all the bombings carried out by the gang.[z]

---

z   The UDR captain cannot be named here to avoid prejudicing future legal action

Anna will never forget Packie and the quiet country life they had once enjoyed: 'I still see that blue flash to this very day. Even when I am digging in the garden or busy at something, I see that blue flash.'[78]

– though he allegedly also supplied the explosives for the Dublin and Monaghan bombings.

'Acquainted with Grief'ᵃ

Every night when I go to bed, I hope that I may never wake again, and every morning renews my grief.

Franz Schubert, Composer, 1797–1828[1]

Grief caused by the traumatic death of a loved one, especially at the hands of an unknown and irrational aggressor, lasts forever. No one 'gets over' such a loss; those who have lost a loved one merely become used to living with it. Grief, like everything else in life, is relative. The grief of losing a parent is hard, but can at least be understood. The psychological furniture in the dining room of the mind can, with time, be rearranged so that the parent is never really gone – just sitting in a different part of the room. The grief of losing a close relative in an accident is far harder to bear, but imagine being a child witnessing your father bleeding to death or your mother screaming in pain as she dies. Then imagine discovering that those responsible were not psychopaths, but those who were entrusted and paid to protect life and uphold the law.

Imagine if, after thirty-five years of believing that your father was shot dead by a 'cheese processor', you discovered he was actually shot dead by a serving police officer and that this had been hidden from the court, and your family, by other, more senior, police officers.

Imagine believing for thirty-five years that your mother had been killed by a telephone engineer only to find out that he was a serving

a   From Isaiah 53:3: 'He is despised and rejected of men; a man of sorrows, and acquainted with grief ...', Authorised version, King James Bible. The official King James Bible online is available at: http://www.kingjamesbibleonline.org; accessed 18 April 2013.

member of a regiment of the British Army – and that this had also been kept from the court.

Imagine learning in mid-life that the beautiful mother you adored, who had disappeared from your life before you were ten years old, could have been saved by the stroke of a policeman's pen. Or that the father you barely knew – the tall, dark presence who was part of your daily life, and for whom your mother grieved so sorely – was first shot and then blown up by a gang including a police officer living down the road. Or that your unborn baby daughter was blown to pieces by a UDR man, before she could take her first breath.

Then imagine how the mere knowledge of this puts you into an 'Alice in Wonderland' existence where you dare not speak your mind, fearing that blank eyes will return your gaze, evidence you are not believed ('Sure, the grief has got to him').

Those left behind will always have agonising memories of the person they lost. Not a day goes by without them being remembered. The annual routine brings it all back: Christmas, birthdays, the date of the killing. Children who were toddlers at the time their parent was killed may have no clear memory of what he or she looked like and have to rely on fuzzy black-and-white photographs and family stories.

Perhaps the family never speaks at all about the relative they loved and lost; it is simply too painful to put into words. Mothers sometimes decided, soon after their bereavement, not to speak of their children's murdered father in case it made them bitter enough to become paramilitaries. Children, anxious not to cause their grieving parent even more pain, would keep silent – despite longing to speak about the father they never (or hardly) knew.

Most of those who have been through this experience are bemused. At first they cannot believe what has happened. Then they become angry. The grief can turn from a familiar dull ache into fury. Then it deposits an unwelcome burden on their shoulders. The heavy burden of trying to find out the truth about what happened.

The people whose murders are recounted in this book (with the exception of Francie Green) had no paramilitary connections. Most of the families had, and have, no active political affiliations either. Some people had SDLP connections: people like James and Gertrude Devlin,[b] who were both active party members,[2] or Denis and Olive Mullen[3] or the Reavey family,[4] who were friendly with Seamus Mallon of the SDLP.

Many families went to GAA matches and social events. James Devlin played for his county (Tyrone). Francis McCaughey had bought some land and intended giving it to the GAA.[5] Owen Boyle sat on his local GAA committee. William Strathearn played for the County Derry senior football team. An analysis of all those who died (excluding those killed in bars mainly serving the Catholic community, such as Donnelly's, the Eagle, Clancy's or Traynor's) shows one very significant pattern. In cases where the killers deliberately singled out their victims they were almost exclusively from that increasingly confident, emerging Catholic middle class, reflecting the social change that was spurred by the British 1947 Education Act providing secondary-level schooling for all children from the age of eleven. In all cases, with one or two exceptions,[c] targeted victims appear to have been selected because they were doing well, moving up, prospering economically, building a new home or renovating an older one, or setting up in business.

In some cases the victims had inherited property (Francis and Bernadette Mullan, for example), recently had a business success (Owen Boyle), had been promoted (Denis Mullen) or owned property (James and Gertrude Devlin). They were nurses, shopkeepers, farmers, publicans, engineers, factory workers, plumbers, joiners, coal-deliverymen, mechanics, parents. The overwhelming majority,

---

b   The couple had inherited forty acres and a substantial home. Gertrude was a librarian, James a publican.

c   Such as John Francis Green, targeted because he was a republican.

whether random victims or targeted specifically, were simply ordinary Catholics living ordinary lives. At least seven random victims were raised as Protestants and were killed in indiscriminate attacks.

News of death could hit in any number of ways. Those who were informed by friends or priests at least had the dignity of privacy – unlike those who witnessed the actual event. Some had to identify the bodies of their loved ones in the morgue. Others were kindly prevented from doing so – particularly if the body was very mutilated by either bomb or bullets. Some bereaved relatives were themselves so badly injured that they were not immediately told the truth or allowed to attend funerals (Patricia Devlin, Winnie Small, Margaret and John Taylor, among others). For most, the funerals passed in a blur of tears. On a personal note, I believed, after thirty years covering the conflict as a journalist, that no story was capable of surprising me. I was wrong. Here are just some of the accounts of the bereaved.[6]

Helen McCoy, on her husband, Brian (trumpeter and singer with the Miami Showband): She heard he had died on the 8 a.m. news. 'I was totally devastated, left with two small children. The word on the street was that a higher force was involved. The government did not seem interested and did not care. It is not really justice my family and I crave at this stage; perhaps just an apology and an acknowledgment of what happened, from the right people.'[7]

Michael O'Toole (RIP), on his brother, Fran: 'Fran was generous, charming and blessed with both good looks and good nature. Fran's mother never left the house again, her anguish was awful and she died of a broken heart. Two of the men sentenced were part of the state security forces (UDR) which made the entire episode much worse. After all, states are meant to protect innocent civilians, not set them up and murder them. The day Fran died, a star went out of the sky.'[8]

Winnie Boyle, on her husband, Owen: 'I thought he was handsome with his auburn hair. He was a Pioneer and he didn't smoke but he was a good singer and ballroom-dancer. He could fix any kind of machinery or anything needed on a farm; cattle grids, trailers, tractors, railings – anything.'

Barney O'Dowd, on his brother, Joe: 'He was not a physically large man – but he was resolute and hard-working. Anything he set out to do, he did well. He was gradually buying up more land round about, using it to raise cattle, pigs and poultry.'

Noel O'Dowd, on his brother, Barry: 'He was a great guy, very easy-going and popular. He worked incredibly hard on the oil-rigs and would come home for the weekend and go a bit wild. He loved playing the banjo and enjoyed Johnny Cash long before anyone else did.'

Barney O'Dowd, on his son, Declan: 'He never had any time for chatting. Delivering coal was hard work. He kept the books right too, he had a head for business but he could still be charming and easy going.'

Deirdre McKee, on her husband, Martin McVeigh: 'He dreamed about one day going to live in New Zealand. I remember the row when he let his brother's pet dog out of the garage and she became pregnant. The day the puppies arrived, Martin was killed.'

Dessie Small, on his father, Andrew: 'He was very much the man of the house. It would be "You wait until your father gets home." He made sure we had our favourite comics every week. You won't get anyone in Dungannon saying a bad word about him.'

Clarke Small, on his mother, Winnie: 'She changed completely. The smallest thing would alarm her, even the closing of a car door. She developed a fear of strong wind, as if she would be lifted up in the air again like she was on the day of the bombing.'

Ann Brecknell, on her husband, Trevor: 'I was immediately worried that Trevor might have been injured. I couldn't conceive it could possibly be any worse. I stood at the window looking at the ambulances arriving. As time went on, I became more scared. Then the doctor who had delivered Róisín arrived along with the hospital priest. The doctor said he knew I was a brave woman and I would need to be to get through this. I knew instantly that Trevor was dead.'

Donna Barry, on her father, Patrick Campbell: 'He had always been opposed to sectarianism in any form at the shoe factory. He was affectionate and loving, but his word was law. That night, he told me to go to bed and, as usual, I obeyed him. I was sleeping when I heard the first bangs and he said "My God, not this" as they shot him in the hallway.'

Tony Connolly, on his brother, Patrick: 'Patrick loved his red Suzuki motor-bike, his two Alsatian dogs, The Beatles, The Stones and Jimi Hendrix. I can remember the grenade, shaped like a pineapple, and smoking – before the flash and huge explosion. I never saw Patrick again. All I can remember is the blood running down my head, and a lot of people standing around. Then I was in hospital.'

Nishi Farmer, on his brother, Seán: 'It was a sunny Sunday morning. The two set off for Dublin and all seemed well. He left home laughing, joking and full of life. We never saw him alive again.'

Seán McCartney, on his brother, Colm: 'He couldn't wait to leave school and start work. He was always tinkering about trying to fix friends' and neighbours' cars. He was young and carefree and loved going to dances. When the police broke the news to our mother, Marie, a uniformed police officer came to the door. He told her, bluntly, that her son was dead before turning on his heel and walking back through the gate.'

Sally Mulholland, on her father-in-law, Arthur: 'He wasn't a huggy-cuddly sort of man. What he really liked was a game of cards with his friends and a quiet pint and digging turf.'

Norbert McCaughey, on his son, James: 'He was into all kinds of sports but it was music where he was specially gifted. He could hear an air just once and play it perfectly on his recorder. His favourite tunes were "The Irish Soldier Boy" and "Noreen Bawn".'

Malachi McDonald, on his wife, Betty: 'The last conversation I saw Betty having was with a customer at the bar. His wee boy had been taken into hospital and she was asking after him. I had barely left the bar, walking only about forty steps, when the explosion went off. I turned, or was spun, around. When I turned, the bar had disappeared and a black hole had opened up.'

Maureen McGleenan, on her son, Gerard: 'He was an incredibly sunny, cheerful boy. I can honestly say he never answered me back or got into a bad temper. He was always smiling and joking. He was also a "hugger" – an affectionate child. He had just walked out the front door, and had a foot on the pavement. He fell at my feet saying "Mummy" over and over again.'

Jim McLoughlin, on his father, Fred: 'Dad was happy-go-lucky, a real character. His friends loved to see him coming. He would have pulled their leg but he had such a dry sense of humour they wouldn't have known it until long after he had left.'

Brian Donnelly – survivor of the Eagle Bar attack: 'I was shot twice in the back and I have a ricochet wound to my arm and nose. I have never recovered. I was sitting with my back to the wall when the shooting began. Both sides of my coat were holed by bullets. Only the tin plate in the chair saved my life. I went to the hospital in the same ambulance as Fred McLoughlin and I was the last person to speak to him.'

Aileen White, on her father, Pat Molloy: 'Daddy was always smartly dressed, his shirt always ironed and his shoes shining. He loved watching cowboy movies and wrestling on the TV. He was witty and funny and protective in an old-fashioned way. He might have been the life and soul of the party in Traynor's Bar [where Patrick was killed] but at home he had strict rules for running the family home.'

Anna Mone-McEneaney, on her husband, Packie Mone: 'We worked hard but we were used to it. Packie was a good dancer and he liked playing the occasional game of cards but that was about it.'

Tommy Mone, nephew and best man to Packie: 'Packie was a quiet man, a countryman. An easy man to work with.'

Olive Mullen, on her husband, Denis: 'August Bank Holiday was our last day out together. We had gone to Arklow for a short break. Denis was on the point of going to the All-Ireland semi-final at Croke Park but changed his mind to stay with the family. I took the children out for a walk that Sunday afternoon. As I left the hotel, I turned and saw Denis looking at us from a window. I wonder now if he was thinking "That is how they would look, as a family" if he was killed and we were left on our own.'

Eugene Reavey, on his brothers John-Martin, Brian and Anthony: 'John-Martin was a placid, gentle boy. He was an exceptionally good son to my mother, Sadie. He would take her shopping every week to Newry in his car. He had a quiet, uneventful life and never caused anyone any harm or annoyance. Brian trained as a joiner and was always making something lovely for the house. He could have become an artist, an engineer, or even a PE teacher, if he had had the chance. Anthony was a different character, tall – with red, wiry hair and aged only seventeen when he was shot. Even before he left school, he was raising turkeys to make some extra shillings.'

Kevin Trainor, on his mother, Dorothy: 'My father was grabbed from behind and pulled to the ground. Shots rang out and my mother fell. He tried to crawl towards my mother but lapsed into unconsciousness. They lay for nearly two hours before they were discovered, covered in blood – my father lying on the path and my mother on the grass verge.'

* * *

With the funerals over, each of the families had to struggle to come to terms with life again, often on their own and with children to bring up. Donna Barry remembers her mother, Margaret Campbell, being 'distracted with grief and on sedatives for weeks'. Margaret was once so befuddled that she put a duster in the fridge and milk in the hot-press. A friend, who was a nurse, talked her into gradually coming off the tablets. 'She told Mummy she had to come off the drugs to look after us, that she had to face reality and get back to normality for our sake. How she coped, I'll never know.'

Dessie Trainor, speaking of the aftermath of the murder of his mother, Dorothy, said, 'Dad was in a state of shock for years. He never worked again. He was overwhelmed with what had happened. He would sit quietly in the back living room and listen to country music. He was a broken man. It was the worst thing that could have happened to all of us. A nightmare. I cried myself to sleep for a long, long time afterwards. The centre of our family had gone.'

In many families, grief was endured alone. In one family, the children say, their mother 'was a private and proud woman, she cried alone in her room'. Following the murder of his brother, one man said that for the best part of a year he was in a daze, until his mother gently remonstrated with him: 'We can't all die, son.'

However they dealt with their grief – whether it overwhelmed them or not – all the families had to adjust to their new and invariably more difficult circumstances. Compensation often amounted to barely enough to bury the dead. Clothes, some still carrying the lingering scent of their wearers, had either to be thrown away or passed on. Photographs were hunted out and framed. The double bed in many homes became a place of loneliness and sorrow rather than warmth and companionship.

Margaret Campbell and her three children could not bear to step on the bit of carpet where Pat had lain dying. But, to use the bathroom, they had to step over it. None could find it within themselves to do that on their own. So, day or night, the four of them held hands and went to the bathroom together.

A family, whose home was destroyed in an explosion, had to start again from scratch and were moved into another housing estate, virtually destitute. Those whose loved ones had been killed in the sanctity of the family home sometimes decided to move out, then and there, never to return.

In some families the dead loved one is spoken of easily and frequently: 'Your father would have loved …' or 'I wish your father was here to see you graduate/marry/the birth of your first child …' Much-loved black-and-white photos hang in pride of place on the walls or are carefully dusted on mantelpieces or the top of the TV.

In other homes, however, the dead person is rarely, if ever, mentioned. Some children have chosen deliberately to 'move on' and not to dwell on the circumstances in which they were bereaved. The impact on children varies from some who appear to have emerged relatively unscathed to others who still live with, and suffer from, the consequences. The first problem facing the surviving parent, if there was one, was how to break the news to their children.

In some cases that task fell to the parish priest: 'He took one of them on each knee and reminded them that their Dad had gone out the night before to see me and the baby in hospital. The boys replied, yes, they knew that – and where was their Daddy? The priest told them he wouldn't be coming home. One of the boys then simply responded that this couldn't be true.' One of those two boys, Alan Brecknell, is now a case worker with the PFC and has spent nearly fifteen years, along with others, researching the series of murders described in this book, including his own father's killing. Ann, his mother, takes a quiet pride in her son: 'It was a big decision to make. I am so proud of him – although I worried for a long while how he would make ends meet.'

Many children live on a daily basis with the grief that was inflicted on them at a young age: 'Maybe because I was his only daughter, his wee girl, he saved one knee for me to sit on. My two brothers had to share his other knee.'

Many widows, whose husbands were killed, say their children suffered badly psychologically and should have been given counselling:

'There was no such thing available at the time. All of us would probably have benefited from help,' says one.

One man took two nephews back to where their uncle was murdered: 'They were asking us about what had happened, so we took them there. It is a lonely, eerie spot. It always seems unnaturally silent. Nothing seems to be moving. Not even the birds sing. It's a scary place.'

The mere presence of friends, family and neighbours at funerals helped many families, at least temporarily, deal with their loss. In some cases, that solidarity went further. When a family friend found out how paralysed with fear one family was, she insisted that the mother and the three children move into her maisonette, doubling- and tripling-up in two bedrooms.

The damage is not only psychological. One man still suffers from wounds sustained in the same attack that killed his brother. He had injuries to every part of his body: head, neck, chest, abdomen, arms, legs. His front teeth were also blown out. He lives in relative poverty now, though the grenade that caused him such grievous injury was of British Army issue.

All of the families found it hard to pick up the pieces financially. The O'Dowd family decided to sell their various businesses and land and move south, buying a house in Navan, County Meath.[d] Realising it would be a wrench to leave their home, they delayed for a while until they were stopped at an illegal loyalist roadblock on their way home from a day out six months after the shooting. 'That was it,' says Barney O'Dowd. His wife announced, 'We're leaving.' They were gone within a month.

It was particularly hard for other families. A mother and her nine children struggled for years to get by on her widow's pension.

---

d   Four members of the O'Dowd family (Noel, Loughlin, Ronan and Damien) who were on the murder scene within minutes were refused compensation on the basis they had not witnessed the shootings. They won on appeal in 1983, paving the way for other families in the same position.

The children all took turns in the evenings in a cold, dark outhouse peeling apples for a local canning factory to make a few extra pounds.

On receiving her widow's pension, explained one mother, her children's free school meals ended. Without a driving licence and with three young children, she stood no chance of getting back into full-time employment. So, she took driving lessons in her dead husband's old car and began to get bits and pieces of work locally as a home help. Another woman describes how for six months she lived on nothing but family hand-outs while the state decided whether or not she was entitled to a widow's pension.

When the four Devlin children were orphaned, an elderly uncle was made one brother's legal guardian while two more were cared for by an aunt before being put in the care of two other uncles, single men in their sixties, ill-equipped physically or emotionally to parent two adolescent boys so recently and violently bereaved. Despite this, all four have been successful in their different professional and business lives. Had Gertrude and James survived, they would have been immensely proud of their children.

Once sympathetic crowds had departed, mass cards thinned out and phone calls became less frequent, bereaved families had to try to get on with their lives, but they could never return to their old ways. There were no counselling services then. Anyone who believes a person cannot die of a broken heart has no experience of truly traumatic grief. Barney O'Dowd, who lost two sons and a brother, began taking long walks at night when he couldn't sleep: 'I would walk out into the night, hoping for wind and rain. I would set my face into the wind and walk up the lane a mile, then back. The cold, wet and wind would give me some satisfaction.' But arriving home was difficult after his long walks: 'Going into the bedroom and looking at the bed … you might as well ask me to walk into hell. I used to sit at the kitchen table, drinking cups of tea and bent over double to try and get rid of the pain in the centre of my body. Then I would go out and walk again until dawn.'

Anthony Connolly describes how his mother later died of grief after her son's murder, when still a relatively young woman of sixty-one: 'My mother was worth nothing afterwards. She was a wee, small woman. Ever afterwards, she couldn't abide being in crowds. My father always said he couldn't understand why we were targeted. He had fought for his country in the war and survived – but he was unable to protect his family in our own home.' Another bereaved parent did not go out of the house for a full eight years after her son was killed. Grief drew some families together, others drifted apart. One mother says, despite the murder of her husband, leaving her to bring up eight children on her own, 'It was a happy home. They all went to the school nearby and came home to me for their lunches.'

And the police? Most families had little or no contact with them, in contrast to any normal society where families seeking justice would regard them as allies. A disturbing absence of any real inquiry or investigation prompted massive doubt and distrust. Many families were never informed that anyone had been charged in connection with the killings of their relatives. Andrew Small's family, for example, only discovered on the evening news that a man had been convicted of murdering their father, and that he had been living close to them. When Deirdre McVeigh went to ask the RUC if abusive graffiti about her murdered husband could be taken off a wall in the factory where he had worked, the officer on duty had asked her, 'How do you spell "shit"?'

'I never went back to give them another chance to humiliate me,' she said.

When relatives in England (of a man killed by a gang comprising UVF and RUC/UDR men) phoned Newry RUC station to ask about the funeral, they were led to believe he had been killed by the IRA. His mother went to her grave believing it. Another widow was advised by police, within weeks of her husband's killing, that she would find it 'easy to find another husband' as she was a 'good-looking woman'.

A bereaved mother was so desperate for information about her son – any information – she wrote to the then RUC Chief Constable, Sir Jack Hermon. The only response she received was a letter that misspelled his name and got the date of his murder wrong. 'We always knew there was no real investigation into the killings,' she says.

For many families, their first experience of any serious police investigation came when, thirty-five years later, they were contacted and advised that the HET was reviewing the case. At the end of that process, the doubts of several families had become even further entrenched, their grief and bitterness intensified. There are other, more positive, outcomes, however. Some families – such as those discouraged by their parents' generation from talking openly about their loss – found the HET process broke the floodgates, leading to open discussion about the murders for the first time. Brothers, sisters, aunts, cousins and uncles have found themselves sharing long-hidden and unspoken memories. The experience, while not risk-free and potentially painful, has also been healing.

One family left disillusioned about the HET says: 'They asked the right questions but the report was mainly just another whitewash. We didn't expect anything from the police but the HET were little better.'

The daughter of one murder victim feels disappointed that their final HET Report did not identify who singled out her father to be ambushed and killed. They had hoped the HET would state definitively that Robin Jackson, 'the Jackal', had been responsible and that he was an RUC Special Branch agent. The HET Report certainly infers Jackson's involvement, but stops short of accusing him directly, even though he is now dead and they are therefore not precluded from doing so by Article 2 of the European Convention on Human Rights.[e] Nevertheless, she has no regrets about engaging with the HET.

---

e   Article 2 commits the state and its agencies to protect the individual's right to life.

The nine children of one victim are also underwhelmed by their experiences with the HET. Other than being informed about the involvement of a former B-Special in the manufacture of the bomb, they say there was little in the report they did not know already.

One woman, whose grandfather was shot dead, decided to go along to a PFC/family meeting. 'You heard terribly sad stories of mothers losing sons, of wives losing husbands. I realised we were not alone … When the HET Report was finally released, showing there was collusion in the murder, I kinda said to myself "Hurrah!" We were right all along.'

The Mulholland family discovered for the first time, through their HET Report, that the gun used to murder Arthur was also used in the Miami Showband massacre, while Angela McKenna, daughter of Owen Boyle, says their family meetings with the HET were worthwhile: 'at least they listened to us'.

One woman welcomed the HET inquiry into the killing of her brothers and sister: 'At least someone cared enough to let us know more.'

On occasion, an apology has poured healing balm on old wounds. The Reavey family, for example, greatly appreciates the regrets offered by the head of the HET, Dave Cox, for the depraved and hostile way they were treated after the murders of Brian, John-Martin and Anthony. Eugene Reavey says that engaging with the HET was difficult at first: 'I came close to ordering them out of my home. They were unable to believe my account of events. But they do now.' When the HET apologised to his mother, Sadie, he says, she reacted as if a physical burden had been lifted off her shoulders. 'She was sitting in a chair, the wee woman, and a great peace seemed to descend over her. The wrong done had been acknowledged. She seemed suddenly very calm.'

Another family would never have known of collusion in their father's death, had it not been for the HET. While it came as difficult news, the four sons say they are grateful to have discovered the truth, but they still have unanswered, and probably now unanswerable, questions. How can it be, they ask, that police officers, senior commanders, judges and politicians have, to date, escaped accountability for their actions in Mid-Ulster in the 1970s?

Norbert McCaughey says that the HET at least established that the RUC had raided the family home on the same night as James' death. That led directly to an apology from the then British Secretary of State for Northern Ireland for the 'gross intrusion' at a time of grief.

The nine children of one victim found themselves talking about their father for the first time in thirty-four years because of the HET investigation. Sisters and brothers sat up long into the night, comparing stories. One daughter has now become a bit of a sleuth, digging in databases and libraries to try to make some sense of their loss. 'At least the HET review meant we began talking about Daddy as a family, sharing our memories and how it affected us.'

Donna Barry says that when her mother, Margaret Campbell, began talking about it, she asked why she had kept it to herself for all those years. 'That was one effect the HET process had on us, it meant we talked to each other.'

Malachi McDonald says his wife, Betty, was 'the love of my life. I could face anything with her by my side. Now I walk alone. She had put her chosen career, nursing, to one side to raise our family. I cannot bear to dwell on that terrible night. I found her dead – her mouth wide open, her blue eyes wide, staring from a distressed face. Our four-year-old son beside her in the rubble. You try to block it out, but we need an explanation.'

For many families, the ability to 'move on' is regarded as a grace to aim for.

The 'Short Arm' of the Law

There is no human situation so miserable that it cannot be made worse by the presence of a policeman.

Brendan Behan, Irish writer (1923–64)[1]

The police are the public and the public are the police; the police being only members of the public who are paid to give full time attention to duties which are incumbent on every citizen in the interests of community welfare.

Robert Peel (1788–1850), British Prime Minister who,
as Chief Secretary in Ireland in 1814, founded the Irish Constabulary
(the 'Peelers')[2]

From its creation in June 1922 until it was replaced by the Police Service of Northern Ireland in 2001, the RUC was a controversial force, as its duties were to protect the stability and laws of a state that was regarded, by at least a third of its population, as illegitimate. Originally, the RUC was intended to be 3,000-strong and roughly one-third Catholic. Fewer Catholics than the expected numbers joined at the new force's inception, however, and even that number dwindled as they retired and were not replaced. With the birth of the civil rights campaign and the escalation of violent conflict, relations between the Catholic population and the RUC deteriorated rapidly. London decided, in August 1969, to deploy the British Army to assist an exhausted RUC, and the die was cast. After RUC men led a loyalist mob as it attacked civil rights marchers at Burntollet on 4 January 1969, and officers were also witnessed joining other mobs attacking Catholic housing on the Falls Road and at Ardoyne in Belfast, many nationalists neither trusted nor wished to become members of the RUC.

Early on, there was undoubtedly a sense of complacency in the upper echelons of the RUC that it was faced with a very serious problem of civil unrest and bitter sectarian tensions. While nearly five hundred (496) people died in 1972, undoubtedly the worst year of the entire conflict, the RUC denied there was a sectarian problem until 1973. On 13 November 1974, at a meeting in the NIO office in London (held to discuss the Irish government's case against London at the European Court of Human Rights), an official from the British attorney general's office asked, quite reasonably, why 'only Roman Catholics had been interned before 1973'. A Treasury solicitor[a] replied that it was the view of the RUC that there was 'no serious Protestant threat in that period that led to death or serious injuries'.[3] The RUC was, then, denying that the 143 loyalist killings carried out during 1971 and 1972 were motivated by sectarian hatred, and telling the ECHR there was no problem of sectarian loyalist killings.[4]

The RUC, of course, suffered quite terribly during the conflict. Over 300 of its members were killed and almost 9,000 injured in paramilitary attacks, mainly by the IRA. The HET, in all its reviews of police enquiries, acknowledges the pressures the force faced. Most HET Reports include references to the pressure of work and other difficulties facing the force. Those sections vary in detail from report to report, but in general the HET acknowledges that 'applying modern standards to contrast earlier enquiries is potentially misleading and can be viewed as unfair'.[5] It also accepts that policing has changed, and 'officers involved in investigations of the time will point to an atmosphere of fear that sometimes precluded the passing of information to the security forces'.[6]

The RUC also faced fearsome enemies, says the HET: 'proficient

---

a   Treasury solicitors act for the British government in such cases.

and professional assassins with a support network designed to eliminate forensic evidence opportunities and defeat investigations by the provision of look-outs, get away arrangements and safe houses'.[7] Having said all that, in report after report, the HET goes on to criticise successive RUC enquiries.

Some will argue that the RUC put many loyalist perpetrators behind bars. That is beyond doubt, but an in-depth analysis shows that many of those convicted of the most serious offences such as murder were small fry (Joseph Lutton, William Leonard, William Parr) compared with those directing the campaign (Edward Sinclair, James Mitchell, Robin Jackson). In other cases, loyalists were convicted for relatively minor offences and not questioned at all about more serious similar and possibly linked crimes (for example William John Nimmons, Laurence Tate and Howard Henry McKay were convicted for a non-fatal attack at Derrymeen but not questioned about the similar Killyliss bombing nearby in which four people died).

The key question when examining the RUC's record is whether the lack of convictions in some of these cases – or even a failure to investigate – indicate incompetence or collusion? Where does a surprising absence of documentation lead to justifiable suspicions that paperwork has either been deliberately destroyed or removed? HET officers acknowledge that when they take some murder enquiry files down from the shelves, their weight tells them almost immediately they are going to find very little of any substance to review. Some officers apparently took papers home when they retired and these are now stored in lofts and garages or lost. In too many cases families are told their questions can never be answered because the paperwork is absent – for whatever reason.

Arguably the most serious questions arise from the RUC's prior knowledge of (and later investigation into) the Step Inn bombing. Senior officers had ordered British Army surveillance before the attack. After the bombing, not only did Special Branch fail to give

CID officers the information required to make arrests – but two police officers known to be involved remained in the force.[b]

Though it was known in August 1976 that Mitchell's farm was the bombers' staging post, it was not raided until December 1978. A decision was taken, and recorded, not to raid the farm immediately. The name of the person who made this decision is not recorded but, the HET says, the operation was 'already under the authority and supervision of the Detective Superintendent (South Region); it must have been made at least at a similar senior RUC level'.[8]

Jack Hermon

In the early 1980s, the then Chief Constable, Sir Jack Hermon, asked for a report on the Step Inn attack, but he was never told that military surveillance on James Mitchell's farm had, by October 1976, revealed that RUC SPG member John Weir's car had been on the farm only hours before the bombing. Even so, Hermon knew that a farmhouse belonging to a part-time RUC Reservist had been used to launch a bomb attack in which two people were killed, and that the man had remained an RUC officer for a further ten months. Why did he not order further investigations? It could have led to additional revelations and charges against other officers. In October 2000, there was another review of the Step Inn case, but according to the HET Report, only a three-line 'Investigative Update Report' was provided, stating 'a number of suspects have been interviewed with negative results'.[9]

The police investigation into the Rock Bar gun-and-bomb attack is equally disturbing. The RUC failed to interview the only victim and main eyewitness, Mick McGrath, who, even as he lay injured, realised that his assailants were wearing standard-issue RUC boots. They also

---

b   James Mitchell remained a paid RUC Reservist for a further ten months, while John Weir, who admits preparing the aborted attack on Renaghan's, was forced to resign after he was arrested in 1978 – two years after the Step Inn attack.

failed in their duty to inform Mick when the case against the four officers came to court, so he was prevented from giving evidence that the police officer who shot him had aimed to kill.

To be fair, at the time that Constable Ian Mitchell took a statement from an eyewitness to the Rock Bar attack, it is possible that the RUC was unaware of his active involvement in it, so no one could have prevented him from taking part in an investigation into an attack in which he had just been personally involved. It is still, however, an indictment of senior management that the entire case was not reviewed when it was realised that this had contaminated the original investigation.

Equally worrying, in two other cases, RUC officers deliberately concealed from the courts and the public that offenders were members of the security forces. Joseph Lutton was involved in the near-simultaneous attacks on the Eagle and Clancy's Bars in Charlemont on 15 May 1975 (when four people were killed and others seriously injured), yet his profession was suppressed, and he was described in court as a 'cheese processor' though he was, until the morning of his arrest, 31 May 1979, a serving part-time RUC Reservist.[c]

The HET concludes that the circumstances show a conscious decision was made to withhold this salient information and the decision could only have been made by a senior officer as a police statement (identifying Lutton as an RUC man) was still in the file when it left the divisional commander's office for that of the chief constable.[10] The statement was 'weeded' from the record, though by whom and why is unknown. Were the prosecution service and the courts effectively lied to? It stretches credulity to believe that a choice item of news like that would not have spread at all within the RUC.

The HET is in no doubt, saying a 'clear inference ... is that a

---

c   Lutton was in the RUC Part Time Reserve from December 1974 to 31 May 1978 – the day of his arrest. His record shows he resigned for 'personal reasons'.

conscious decision was made to withhold the fact that Lutton was a member of the RUC at the time of committing these murders'. Lutton's status as a police officer would surely have affected his tariff. 'Any decision to withhold this information detail from the Court is an extraordinary matter,' says the HET.[11] Even more seriously, the HET believes the decision was taken at a very high, even political, level. 'It is difficult to believe,' says the report, 'when judged in concert with other cases emerging at the time that such widespread evidence of collusion in these areas was not a significant concern at the highest levels of the security forces and of government. It may be that there was apprehension that confirming the suspicions of collusion and involvement, particularly of RUC personnel, would have fatally undermined the credibility of the organisation'.[12]

The RUC's 'credibility' within the nationalist community was already shaky, to say the least. Unionists, on the other hand, regarded the force as their main bulwark against violent republicanism. Hard evidence of collusion, the HET concludes, may have forced London's hand to take action to reform the force.

The killing of James and Gertrude Devlin on 7 May 1974 is a second case where a defendant's security force links were deliberately withheld from the victims' family, the courts and the public. William Leonard was a serving member of the UDR at the time he took part in the killings, but this salient fact 'does not', says the HET, 'feature in his antecedents in the RUC Prosecution Case File dated September 9 1974; neither is it included in his Estimate of Tariff of Life Sentence Report dated November 16 1982'.[13] Given the nature of the offences, and the public, political and media concerns about UDR links to terrorist activities, it goes on to say that this is 'inexplicable'.

There are also cases of an inexplicable failure by RUC officers to question people already in custody about related events. For example, when detectives investigating the Miami Showband attack arrested Howard Henry McKay, Laurence Tate (a UDR man) and William

John Nimmons, all admitted bombing a partially built cottage at Derrymeen on 30 May 1975. However, while the Derrymeen bombing was similar to that at Killyliss, none of the three were questioned about that outrage. The two attacks were six miles (10 km) and six weeks apart. Both involved booby-trap devices and both targets were young Catholic families either building or renovating cottages. Had police questioned their suspects rigorously, they might have admitted to Killyliss (as well as Derrymeen). As it was, all three admitted only to involvement in one, non-fatal, attack.

Police had a suspect in the Devlin case, a part-time UDR man.[14] When he was finally arrested, police found three handguns, ammunition and two home-made bombs at his home. He denied involvement in the Devlin murders and was not questioned about either the Derrymeen or Killyliss bombings, despite being found in possession of explosives and the two attacks taking place less than three months previously (and in one of them a known associate was already implicated).[d] Even more astoundingly, all this suspect's court records have disappeared. The last time he surfaced was on 9 September 1975, when he was refused bail. After that he disappeared off the judicial radar.[15] The only detail that remains within his record is an informal note that he was convicted. Enquiries conducted by the HET have established that the charge and sentencing details have since been removed ('weeded') from the system. It seems an interesting coincidence that a suspect's records: (1) disappear from all police databases, (2) are absent from the Criminal Records Office and (3) are 'weeded' from the system, and that he was not charged with possession of the two home-made bombs found at his home.

Then there is the perennial problem of Special Branch failing to share intelligence with officers in the CID. The most immediate and

---

d   Nor was he ever charged with possessing the bombs, though he was charged with possessing the three handguns and ammunition.

pressing question is over the actions of RUC agent Robin Jackson. The action that led to RUC Chief Inspector Ernest Drew revealing that Jackson received inside police information is detailed in Chapter 4: Turning to Murder and need not be rehashed here. A failure to even interview Jackson about the Miami Showband killings, despite his fingerprints being found on a gun silencer used in the atrocity, certainly points to Jackson being a protected agent or informer. Luck alone cannot explain why he did not spend most of the mid-to-late 1970s and 1980s in jail.

On 9 October 1979, for example, Jackson was arrested in possession of the Lee Enfield .38 pistol used to kill Martin McVeigh four years previously. The pistol had been stolen in 1973 from an armoury servicing Jackson's own UDR unit in Portadown (a raid in which, the HET says, there are 'grounds to suspect that those responsible were helped by members of the UDR').[16] Jackson, it appears, was never questioned about the original raid and neither was he asked about Martin McVeigh's murder, circumstances the HET calls 'inexplicable'.[17] He was never prosecuted for his role in Patrick Campbell's murder in 1973, nor was he prosecuted at that time for possessing illegal ammunition at his home, or for a notebook containing details of over two dozen republicans (from as far away as County Meath and Derry city). He was merely dismissed from the UDR. These circumstances either point towards levels of almost unbelievable police incompetence or, much worse, that Jackson's many murders were either tolerated or even encouraged by some within the RUC.

There are serious questions hanging over other police decisions. On 15 May 1976, the RUC in Portadown arrested Ronald John Hanlon (aged twenty) in possession of a stolen Ford Cortina. Questioned about a pipe-bomb attack, he admitted his role, and the following day also admitted stealing the car used in the attack on the Eagle and Clancy's Bar.[18] Fingerprints found on the car abandoned after the two attacks were Hanlon's but he was never charged in connection with the theft of that car or any offence in connection with the attacks on the two bars.[19] Instead, he pleaded guilty to the unrelated bomb attack on the Catholic church in Blackwatertown and was sentenced to fifteen years and twelve years to run concurrently. He served only seven years (a far shorter sentence than he would have served had he been convicted of four murders).

The relatively lenient sentences handed down by the courts to certain defendants raises the possibility that some may have been RUC 'assets'. After his enquiries, Judge Barron was in no doubt that some were actively protected by police: 'Some loyalists, notably Robin Jackson and the Young brothers,' his report states, 'were reliably said to have had relationships with British intelligence and/or RUC Special Branch officers. It is reasonable to assume that exchanges of information took place.'[20]

Hanlon's arrest led to another surprising development. On 18 May 1975, acting on information received about where the car he had stolen was stored before the Eagle/Clancy's attacks, police searched the home of Andrew Godfrey Foote, where, as noted in Chapter 5, they found 695 rounds of .22 and sixty-nine rounds of 9 mm ammunition. They failed, however, to check the find against the bullets used to attack the Eagle Bar, or for any other attacks. Foote was charged with unlawful possession of the ammunition, pleaded guilty in Belfast in February the following year and received a conditional discharge.[21] He claimed he had 'forgotten' about the ammunition, which he said must have been held over from his time as a B Special. That force, however, had been disbanded in 1970 and the bullets were of 1974 manufacture – details that must have been familiar to RUC officers. It hardly even made the papers that a justice of the peace had pleaded guilty to the possession of over 700 rounds of ammunition.[e]

---

e   Six paragraphs buried in the *Irish News* and five in the *Belfast Telegraph* (4 February 1977).

There are other puzzling cases where seemingly obvious lines of questions are inexplicably not followed up. Six months after the murders of Peter and Jenny McKearney, soldiers searching Ted Sinclair's land found guns, ammunition, commercial explosives and other bomb-making materials. One of the guns was a .38 Colt automatic pistol and magazine, found in Sinclair's bedroom, and forensic tests showed it was the weapon that killed the McKearneys. Sinclair, caught red-handed with a murder weapon in his bedroom, claimed he had bought the gun for £10 and had lent it to a 'boy' for five months. He would not name the 'boy'. The HET says the obvious line of questioning would have been for the RUC to ask Sinclair about Peter and Jenny's murders, but 'it appears it did not'.[22] As a result, instead of a murder charge, Sinclair was accused only of possession and was sentenced to a mere six years in jail. The year after he was released, Sinclair was finally questioned about the McKearney murders and agreed with a detective superintendent that 'he drove the car used in the murders' and went on to say 'he could not admit to it'. The HET says, however, that this line of questioning 'did not continue'.[23]

After the McKearneys were shot, a routine British Army patrol in Portadown stopped four UVF members, detaining two, both of whom tested positive for firearms residue. One was released because he was a UDR man (and could explain the residue) while the other was freed because he might have shaken the first man's hand. Despite being detained within an hour of a double murder, and close to the scene, police benevolently accepted both men's explanations.

In some cases, the RUC took an extraordinarily casual attitude towards alibis. After the double killing at Hayden's Bar in February 1975, for example, several items of intelligence led to the finger of suspicion pointing at the two Somerville brothers, Wesley and John, both already notorious loyalists. Wesley's alibi was that he had been attending a UVF prisoners' meeting, but he declined to name anyone else there. John said he was at a political meeting in Moygashel Orange Hall, similarly declining to provide any evidence. The alibis were not even tested, something the HET says, with its habitual understatement, was 'a missed opportunity'.[24]

In the same case, RUC detectives checked out the alibi of a fellow officer named in intelligence reports and discovered he had left his Liverpool hotel earlier than he had stated. They then appear to have failed to consider the implications of this discrepancy – that he could, therefore, have taken part in the attack.[25]

The police investigation into an alibi given by a man identified by an eyewitness to the three O'Dowd family murders is similarly open to question. All three supposed witness statements were vague. None of the three could account for where the named suspect was at the time of the murders but the suspect was still released without charge.[26]

Sometimes the RUC did excellent police work – but then failed to follow through. In the case of Martin McVeigh's murder, for example, the police discovered that only 157 cars fitted the description of one seen by two eyewitnesses as it sped from the scene. This became the only significant line of enquiry.[27] The murder team identified all 157 car owners. When none said they were near the scene, however, the police failed to follow through. They would otherwise have been led to Garfield Gerald Beattie, later convicted of three murders: Denis Mullen, Patsy McNeice and Fred McLoughlin.[f] After RUC Reservist Joseph Lutton said Beattie and Kane had been involved with him in the bombing of Clancy's Bar, no action was taken. This despite the two men having admitted their role in the near-simultaneous attack on the Eagle, and Lutton claiming that Beattie had lit the fuse at Clancy's.[28]

---

f   There is strong evidence for believing Beattie was also involved in the murders of Vincy Clancy, Seán O'Hagan and Robert McCullough in the near-simultaneous bombings at Clancy's and the Eagle Bar in which Fred McLoughlin was killed.

Some aspects of policing have not changed down the years. All police forces, in the past as now, know the value of a meticulous scenes of crime officer (SOCO). Most of us would assume that, even in the 1970s, any SOCO attending a house where three members of the same family had been gunned down would carry out a fingertip search. Not so, it appears, when three members of the O'Dowd family were slaughtered on 4 January 1976. Two bullet heads were discovered a month after the attack where they had been hidden by a settee. Bullet casings were also discovered by the family of Patrick Campbell after his murder in Banbridge in October 1973, at the bar in Aughamullan after the murder of Patrick Falls, and at the house where the three Reavey brothers were shot dead. The bullet-riddled dartboard in the Rock Bar was not examined at all. In that gun-and-bomb attack every one of the perpetrators was a member of the RUC – are these two facts coincidental? When a SOCO searched the outside of the house where Owen Boyle was killed in April 1975, no casts were taken of suspicious footprints at the firing point. The HET says it would have been 'reasonable to expect' this to be done.[29] Nor is there any record of an examination of the external window panes for fingerprints,[g] or of any tyre prints being taken of the getaway car used in the murders of the three Reavey brothers.

These were elementary mistakes in multiple-murder cases at a time when the RUC knew there was a dangerous gang on the loose determined to inflict more bloodshed on an already terrified community. But perhaps the most shocking failure at any scene-of-crime was the RUC's failure to recover a large piece of the bomb-car after the Step Inn bombing. Malachi McDonald reports that he found the car's front bumper, months after the explosion, lying in a roof-valley of his stricken bar. Malachi informed his local police station on

---

g   This apparent failure to try to find fingerprint evidence is repeated in other reports, e.g. at Bleary Darts Club, where three people were shot dead in April 1975.

several occasions, but they did not respond and he finally gave up and disposed of the bumper himself.

Police appear also to have been insouciant about taking statements. After loyalists threw a grenade into Patrick Connolly's house, killing him and seriously injuring members of his family, police failed to take statements from eyewitnesses. Known eyewitnesses to the double shooting of Colm McCartney and Seán Farmer were ignored – 'inexplicable' says the HET.[30] No statement was taken from Mick McGrath, the only victim and sole eyewitness to a gun-and-bomb attack on the Rock Bar – carried out by at least four RUC officers. Nor was he given advance warning of the trial or asked to give evidence.[h]

A vital part of any police enquiry is also, of course, to check statements for discrepancies. Yet the police made no apparent attempt after Laurence McClure's contradictory statements (on whether the same group of people were involved in both the Rock Bar and Donnelly's Bar attacks) to exploit this. The HET is puzzled about why the RUC did not explore this, and other, evidential opportunities. As a result, McClure was only charged with withholding information about the Donnelly's Bar attack, which, ironically, led to a search for the truth and, ultimately, to this book. McClure and Lily Shields claimed to be unaware of the attack on Donnelly's Bar, though they were in the getaway car.[i] An effective RUC interview strategy would have disproved this, paving the way for prosecutions, but that, in the end, never happened.[31]

The RUC appears to have failed in the case of Dorothy Trainor's murder in April 1975 to circulate the photofit that her husband, Malachy, had helped to compile and which had created a strong image. A good photo-fit was also created of one of the suspects

---

h   Mick McGrath was finally asked to make a statement to the second enquiry in 1978 – two years after he was shot.

i   Ian Mitchell offered the same implausible defence about driving the getaway car after the Rock Bar attack.

for the Donnelly's Bar gun-and-bomb attack.[32] Despite the lack of feedback from Special Branch, when the detective in charge took an eyewitness to identify the suspect, he had substantially changed his appearance. Suspicions, to say the least, must arise that someone within Special Branch had tipped the loyalist off.

After the killing of four people, including two thirteen-year-old children, in the Hillcrest Bar bombing in March 1976, a detective was appointed to head the murder team even though he was due to leave Northern Ireland for training in Britain two weeks later, inevitably disrupting the investigation.[33]

One aspect of modern policing is that grieving families are shown respect and kept informed about investigations. In no case included in this study has a family praised the RUC for keeping them updated as to the scope and progress of investigations. In several cases, families were not informed about inquest hearings.[j] In other cases, families were insulted by police,[k] and in yet others they were abused when they visited their local police station.[l] These and many other complaints are currently being investigated by the office of the NI police ombudsman.

The home of James McCaughey, one of the children killed in the Hillcrest Bar, was raided while his body still lay in the morgue. Similarly, the home of Eugene and Eileen McCann was raided on the night Eileen's father, Joe Toman, was killed at Bleary Darts Club in April 1975. Both the McCaughey family and the Reavey family have received apologies for the way the security forces treated them.

Other families are also left asking questions. On the night of the

---

j   Nora Molloy was informed of her husband's inquest on the day it took place. She had to stand at the back and was unable to hear the proceedings.

k   Officers advised the grieving Olive Mullen that she 'would find another husband soon enough' (interview with author, 2011).

l   Police officers in Portadown asked Deirdre McVeigh to spell 'shit' when she complained to them about graffiti relating to her dead husband (interview with author, 2013).

gun-and-bomb attack in which John McGleenan and two others were killed, four police officers were sent to check bars in Armagh city and outlying areas for under-age drinking. While the HET has found copious notes (time, name of bar, outcome of visit) relating to that relatively low-priority police operation, virtually no papers could be found relating to the police enquiry into the triple murder gun-and-bomb attack on John McGleenan's bar. Seán and Mary, two of his children, have asked about the whereabouts of the records. Was the attack simply disregarded? Or has someone removed the notes? And if so, why?[m] The Connolly family still wonder whether, if the RUC had listened seriously to their concerns that they were being harassed and intimidated in Portadown in 1972, would Patrick still be alive?[34]

Some police investigations closed down before they ever really got under way. It took just two weeks for the RUC to decide that there was no point continuing with the investigation into the triple murder at Bleary Darts Club.[35] It has distressed many families that the HET has often been unable to find enough information in the RUC's files and records to come to any meaningful conclusions. It openly refers to the investigation into the murder of John Mallon at Hughes' Bar, Newry, in November 1974 as 'shambolic'.[36] Such is the paucity of police detail relating to the double murder of Colm McCartney and Seán Farmer (two GAA supporters returning home from a match), says the HET, that it is 'difficult to ascertain that any investigation took place at all, after the initial scene examination'.[37] Because this was no isolated incident and UDR uniforms were worn, so soon after the Miami Showband killings during which uniforms were also worn, says the HET, 'this should have triggered a major response from the security forces. Nothing was done.'[38]

---

m   This is far from being unique. The HET believes some officers simply took case papers home with them when they retired.

The HET also reports other 'disturbing omissions ... the lack of any structured investigative strategy' and voices a view that the killings 'should have rung alarm bells all the way to the top of Government. Nothing was done; the murderous cycle continued.'[39] The HET Report concludes:

> Members of the Nationalist community, and relatives of the victims in cases such as these, are convinced that investigations were not rigorously conducted in a deliberate effort to conceal security forces' involvement and perpetuate a campaign of terror by loyalist paramilitaries against Catholic citizens. The HET is unable to rebut or allay these suspicions.[40]

At the time of these killings, the RUC was urged over and over again to take more robust action. Fathers Raymond Murray and Denis Faul were not alone in remarking on the RUC's lack of success in bringing the perpetrators to justice. On 14 April 1975 (a week before the Killyliss bombing), Cardinal Conway, the head of the Catholic Church in Ireland, and a delegation of nine bishops raised concerns with the British government. Accusing the RUC of 'virtually ignoring' the eighty killings of Catholics over the previous three months, the bishops said a legal organisation (the UVF had been de-proscribed the previous year) was openly boasting of its murders.

Seamus Mallon, then chairman of the SDLP parliamentary group, called a meeting of people living in the villages of Moy and Annaghmore in March 1975, afterwards issuing a statement pointing to eight recent murders, fourteen attempted murders and nineteen bomb attacks in the area. 'This must surely be the highest incidence of sectarian attacks considering the size of the minority community in the whole of the North,' Mallon said. 'It is highly significant that not one person has been charged with having been responsible for these heinous sectarian crimes. Beyond any shadow of doubt, there is a highly-organised sectarian murder gang operating against the Catholic minority.' He added that people 'failed to understand this ridiculously low rate of detection'.[41]

John Weir
Courtesy of Crispin Rodwell

John Weir's explosive allegations, on his release from jail in February 1993, that senior RUC officers had colluded with loyalists in Mid-Ulster, and that some had even known of plans to bomb Dublin and Monaghan in May 1974, finally prompted an official internal enquiry. The RUC called it 'Operation Nantucket' and it is regarded by those who have analysed it, including some officers within the HET, as frankly risible. Eyebrows rise whenever it is mentioned.[42] Rather than being an honest assessment, it was a damage limitation exercise, more intended to harm Weir (to the point of prosecuting him should he ever return to Northern Ireland) than to honestly assess his credibility.

Some, but not all, of the outcome of Nantucket was shared with the gardaí, though the two forces came to very different conclusions on Weir. Put bluntly, the gardaí believed Weir's claims while the RUC did not – at least in public. On 14 February 2000, the RUC sent the Nantucket report to the garda team that had been asked to look into Weir's allegations. Judge Barron found a number of glaring errors. According to Nantucket, Lily Shields (the live-in housekeeper at James Mitchell's farm at Glenanne, South Armagh) was dead. However, garda enquiries found her not just to be alive, but still living at Mitchell's farm. The RUC report also claimed that William McCaughey had served with Weir in the Armagh SPG. Again, this was inaccurate. Nantucket said Weir had pleaded guilty at his trial – but he had not. On Billy Hanna, the UVF commander in Mid-Ulster, Nantucket denied he had ever served in the UDR and claimed there was no information linking him to Mitchell's farm at

Glenanne. Both of these statements were untrue; Hanna had served in the UDR as a weapons instructor. The RUC also knew, dating back to 1978, that Hanna had been the first person to ask Mitchell to store weapons and explosives on his farm.

Nantucket, however, was prepared by an RUC CID officer who had no access to the RUC Special Branch daily record sheets relevant to Weir's claims. When Judge Barron finally accessed them, they showed that in at least two cases they contradicted Nantucket (both cases relating to the discovery of arms and ammunition on James Mitchell's farm in December 1978). Nantucket played down Weir's allegations by saying that Mitchell had no idea who had asked him to store the weapons on his land. But the daily record sheets established that Mitchell knew the names of ten loyalists who had moved arms and explosives to and from his farm. Of those ten, six appear in Weir's statements, accused of participating in other attacks, thus corroborating his claims.

Nantucket made no mention of evidence from RUC interviews with some of the officers who had carried out the attack on the Rock Bar. The missing information included confirmation of Weir's account about those involved in the Donnelly's Bar attack, the double murder of Seán Farmer and Colm McCartney, and the Reavey and O'Dowd killings. One of those interviewed, an RUC officer, also confirmed Weir's story of the RUC constable who was producing home-made machine guns. Finally, two of those convicted for the Rock Bar attack suggested that the fourth person named by Weir (Sergeant Gary Armstrong) was indeed involved, though he made no admissions and was never charged.[43] In short, Nantucket was laughable to anyone with any knowledge of the facts.

The failings listed here point to convincing questions that must be answered. Collusion, as defined by the Canadian Supreme Court's Judge Peter Cory, is to connive, to turn 'a blind eye; to wink; to excuse; to condone; to look the other way; to let something ride'.[44]

RUC officers were not always incompetent and inefficient, though. In 1979, for example, a man was found guilty of murdering former UDR man William Corrigan[n] and his son three years earlier through teeth marks found in an apple left at the scene.[o] Loyalists, however, seem to have been able to slip repeatedly through the net, particularly the big fish such as Sinclair, Mitchell and, above all, Jackson. Was this because of institutional failings, or a deliberate conspiracy? And if so, at what level, and how pervasive?

At the time, British and unionist politicians were routinely praising the RUC for its professionalism and courage, and the force easily shrugged off criticism. For example, the SDLP and Irish government had for a number of years demanded the disbandment of the RUC Reserve. In May 1976, Sir James Haughton, Chief Inspector of Constabulary for England and Wales, carried out a detailed inspection of the RUC Reserve and warned London that they appeared to be exclusively Protestant and were 'in truth merely paid vigilantes'.[45] The Reserve, however, continued to exist until 2001.

For many years, the SDLP and others had asked if the protection of informers was given greater priority than the solving of multiple murders, and raised concerns that Special Branch was keeping intelligence to itself. Why, in so many of these murders, were alibis unchecked? Why was forensic and ballistic evidence ignored? Why was relevant evidence kept from the courts?

There is more than enough evidence that the police shielded killers. Even before the Step Inn bombing, the RUC, at the level of superintendent, knew that an RUC Reservist (James Mitchell) was deeply implicated in vicious sectarian gun and bomb attacks. The same RUC hierarchy also knew that another officer (John Weir) was present at Mitchell's farm as a bomb that killed two civilians

---

n   A suspect for the murder of Denis Mullen.
o   A plaster cast was made of the suspect's jaw and compared to the marks on the apple (*The Irish Times*, 18 January 1979).

was being primed. Why did the RUC not re-open and re-investigate every case in which they had been involved?

At least two chief constables, Sir Kenneth Newman (May 1976–January 1980) and Sir Jack Hermon (January 1980–June 1989), must have known that important investigations were contaminated, yet neither did anything. The RUC failed the nationalist community in Mid-Ulster during the 1970s, just as Fathers Faul and Murray, Cardinal Conway and the SDLP alleged at the time.

Excuses about pressure of work do not wash (the RUC was generously funded and staffed). Its workforce lived within the unionist community. They knew who the killers were – yet they failed to put them behind bars, thus paving the way for more killings (including many of their own officers) and prolonging the conflict.

BRITANNIA WAIVES THE RULES

Nobody has a more sacred obligation to obey the law than those who make the law.

Sophocles, 497–406 BC[1]

It may be true that the law cannot make a man love me, but it can keep him from lynching me, and I think that's pretty important.

Martin Luther King, Jr[2]

From its inception, the Northern Irish state tested liberal legal principles to the limit and beyond. Its heavily armed police had – and still has – powers far beyond those in other Western European democracies. Juries were abolished in conflict-related cases, and remain so, leaving judges to decide guilt or innocence. In 1963, J. B. Johannes Vorster, the then South African Justice Minister, remarked that he would trade all the coercive powers at his disposal 'for one clause of the Northern Ireland Special Powers Act'.[a]

Article 7 of the United Nations' *Universal Declaration of Human Rights* declares: 'All are equal before the law and are entitled without any discrimination to equal protection of the law.' That holds whether you are a soldier, a loyalist, a republican paramilitary, a police officer, a judge, a general or even a prime minister. A cornerstone of any liberal democracy is that the law exists to protect the rights of the citizen without fear or favour.

Now that the conflict in Northern Ireland appears to have drawn

---

a   Such as the power to detain without warrant or to jail someone 'suspected of having acted or being about to act in a manner prejudicial to the preservation of the peace and the maintenance of order in Northern Ireland'.

to a messy conclusion, lessons for the future can only be learned if a clear eye is cast over how the institutions of state administered the law. To take the police first, the RUC is coming under some scrutiny from the police ombudsman, while the HET (despite its many and deep-seated inherent weaknesses) is reviewing individual murder investigations, albeit with mixed results.[b] The UDR and the British Army's role, however, are under far less rigorous scrutiny, and there is no sign at all of any mechanism being introduced to examine the record of the judicial system.

On the contrary, after the HET made some mild criticisms of the DPP's office (in one late-2010 Derry-based case), the DPP's office responded by refusing to share its files with the HET for a year. The DPP then demanded prior access to HET Reports, presumably to 'vet' them, before they were provided to families. Since these undeclared hostilities ended, the HET (coincidentally or otherwise) has not repeated its criticisms of the DPP. The practical outcome in more recent HET Reports has been that, whenever obvious questions loom over action (or lack of it) by the office of the DPP, they are simply left unanswered – and sometimes even unasked.

Despite these problems, and the thoroughly opaque way justice was administered during the conflict, there is still value in looking at the outcome of some prosecutions and asking questions about the judicial system, even if the answers have to be inferred from circumstances. To begin with, one of the most prolific killers (if not *the* most) of the entire conflict – Robin Jackson. On at least five separate occasions (that we know of) he was the beneficiary of legal rulings and decisions (on other occasions he struck it lucky because of police failures). One of his

Robin Jackson

---

b   An Amnesty International report, under preparation at the time of writing, is expected to level strong criticisms at the British government for failing to establish independent and equitable truth-recovery mechanisms.

early victims was Patrick Campbell, the Banbridge trade unionist shot dead in October 1973. Had Jackson been convicted of this murder, he would have been in jail instead of pursuing a very active career as a loyalist killer throughout the 1970s and 1980s. For that reason, the legal decisions made when he was first arrested for Pat Campbell's murder in late 1973 are worth examining in some detail.

To briefly recap: at the time he shot Pat Campbell dead, Jackson was a private attached to D Company 11 UDR and a UDA member (joint membership of both organisations was not illegal and was viewed as a 'safety valve').[3] At the conclusion of an ID parade, Pat Campbell's widow, Margaret, said that 'within reason' she was satisfied she could identify Jackson.[4] He had then become distressed and subsequently changed his mind about knowing Margaret when witnesses contradicted his statements to police. To cap all this, the RUC had found illegal ammunition and a notebook at his home containing (with no reasonable explanation) the names of over two dozen people, their addresses and vehicle details. Taken together, this evidence should have allowed them to charge him with murder, and a junior RUC officer recommended this course of action. A detective superintendent, however, disagreed, and the DPP concurred that the murder charge should be dropped: Jackson's first escape from the courts.

The DPP then went even further, ruling against prosecuting Jackson even for the relatively minor charge of illegally possessing the forty-nine bullets above his UDR allowance and the notebook. By this stage, the DPP must have known that the reason police had originally searched Jackson's house was because he had been named by a man on whose land a major arms haul was recovered (after a raid on Jackson's UDR armoury in Portadown – itself an apparently collusive act).[5] This was the second time Jackson escaped from the courts.

He was also lucky to escape conviction for his undoubted involvement in the Miami Showband attack. This, despite his fingerprints being discovered on the barrel of a metal silencer specifically adapted to fit the Luger used in the attack. In court, Jackson claimed that his fingerprints had been transferred from insulating tape wrapped around the silencer onto the silencer itself. (A forensic expert said this was technically possible, though he had not come across such an incidence in thirty years of fingerprint examination.)[6] The judge rejected Jackson's defence but, in a ruling that stretches credulity, found the fingerprints on the silencer were not sufficient evidence to convict as they 'did not prove that Jackson knew he was in possession of a Luger silencer, nor did it show that he assented to such possession'.[7] So, despite this time finally being brought before the courts, Jackson walked free for the third time.

When he was arrested red-handed in possession of the pistol used to shoot dead Martin McVeigh (a gun that itself had been stolen from his old UDR armoury) he was not even questioned about the shooting (and may not even have been questioned about the original theft), though this time he was sentenced for possessing the weapon. That was his fourth stroke of luck.

Jackson was then named by two police officers (William McCaughey and John Weir) as having taken part (along with another notorious loyalist R. J. Kerr) in the killing of William Strathearn in April 1977. The allegations on their own were insufficient evidence to bring charges, but one obvious way of supporting them would have been for the police to interview the two loyalists to see if they made any admissions. The RUC, however, decided against this course of action, because they considered Jackson and Kerr as being 'virtually immune to interrogation', and arresting 'either man is a waste of time'.[8] (In contrast there is little evidence that such a defeatist attitude was taken at the time towards republican suspects, who were frequently arrested and subjected to week-long interrogations at Castlereagh Holding Centre.)

If Weir had made a sworn statement against Jackson, he might have been charged with Strathearn's murder, but he refused to do so unless the murder charge he himself faced was withdrawn. It is understandable that the assistant DPP would have considered this deal (in which a murder charge against a police officer would have been dropped in favour of a similar charge being proffered against a known loyalist) insufficiently advantageous. The assistant DPP had the power, however, to insist that the police interview Jackson and Kerr, once Weir and McCaughey's trial was over. According to evidence given by an RUC officer to the Barron Enquiry, both Weir and McCaughey refused to turn Queen's evidence after their trials, but this did not preclude the RUC from at least asking Jackson questions about the Strathearn murder. They did not, however. This was Jackson's fifth stroke of luck – and there are likely to have been many others for which as yet we have no evidence. Jackson continued to kill people with apparent impunity right through the 1970s and 1980s.

There are many other valid questions about the role of the DPP. Patricia Devlin and her parents, Gertrude and James, were all attacked in their family car on a lane leading to their home. William Thomas Leonard, a twenty-three-year-old post office engineer (and a private in the UDR), was charged with murdering James and Gertrude, but he was not charged with attempting to murder Patricia, despite a recommendation from the senior investigating officer, Detective Inspector Harold Colgan. The DPP decided that Leonard could not have known Patricia was in the car along with her parents and there was insufficient evidence of intent.[9] He did not, it appears, take into account the evidence that the killers had been watching the pattern of the Devlins' movements, and would have known that Patricia always drove with Gertrude to collect James. In addition, the DPP dropped a series of charges against Leonard, including bombing a bar in Dungannon in August 1973, in which five people were injured; hijacking a car and bombing Quinn's Bar, Dungannon, the same year, when one person was injured; abducting two bread-deliverymen, stealing their vehicle and bombing a housing estate at Coalisland in March 1974; and bombing a house at Orpheus Drive, Dungannon, in April 1975. All the HET can say about these four attacks is that the DPP took the decisions as Leonard 'was already serving two life sentences for the murders of James and Gertrude'.[10] This is on top of Leonard's exceeding 'good fortune' in managing to hide from the court the very relevant fact of his employment as a part-time member of the UDR.

Another loyalist kingpin in Mid-Ulster who, like Jackson, also largely escaped jail, was Ted Sinclair. Just to cite one inexplicable decision: in May 1976, a .38 Colt automatic pistol was found in Sinclair's bedroom. It was one of the guns used to murder Peter and Jenny McKearney. Sinclair was convicted (of possession only) and served three years in jail. Re-arrested in December 1981, he was questioned about these murders again and told police he had driven the car but 'could not admit to it'.[11] Questioned further, Sinclair said, 'I'm not denying I wasn't involved' and, asked further about this ambivalent response, 'I'm not saying anything. I can't afford to.'[12] These admissions were enough for the police to charge him four days later with murdering the McKearneys. In April the following year, however, the DPP dropped the charges on the grounds of insufficient evidence.[13]

Sometimes it is difficult to decide whether the police or the DPP is at fault for failing to bring miscreants to court. Three years after the triple killing at Donnelly's Bar on 19 December 1975, for example, RUC SPG member Laurence McClure and Lily Shields (housekeeper to RUC Reservist James Mitchell at the Glenanne farm) were charged with failing to give information. McClure and Shields claimed to have been unaware of the exact target while admitting they realised that the men they ferried about were involved in illegal acts.[14] McClure had admitted that while he was at Mitchell's farm an associate (UDR corporal Robert McConnell) had asked to be collected. He also admitted to posing with Shields as a courting couple at an Orange Hall eight miles (13 km) from Donnelly's for half an hour until McConnell and two other men returned to the vehicle; he had then dropped them off near Mitchell's farm.[15]

McClure appeared in court in June 1980 charged in relation to the Rock Bar attack. After a suspended sentence was imposed on him for that offence, he should surely have faced charges for his role in the Donnelly's Bar attack – at which point the suspended sentence would have been converted automatically into a custodial one. Fortunately for McClure, there were interminable legal delays. The legal system then deemed these were unfair to McClure and ruled that the charges should be dropped. The DPP said the case would have been solely dependent on the couple's own admissions and 'there was insufficient admissible evidence their associates had carried out the attack, despite their belief that they had'.[16] This stretches credulity, given the known facts from their evidence.

In 2007 the Brecknell, Reavey, O'Dowd and McCartney families, along with Mick McGrath (who had been injured in the Rock Bar attack), won an important legal victory after taking a case to the European Court of Human Rights (ECHR). The court ruled that the RUC was not the appropriate body to investigate claims against itself.[17] Article 2 of the ECHR stated that only an independent enquiry could do that with any credibility.[18]

We now come to the perennially vexed question of perceived lenient sentencing. Judges jealously guard their prerogative on sentencing as justifiable, but it is still legitimate to question some decisions. When Sinclair pleaded guilty (see above) to possessing firearms, ammunition and explosives with intent/in suspicious circumstances, he received sentences amounting to only six years in jail.[c] With 50 per cent remission, this meant that he served only three years behind bars.

---

c   Two pistols, two home-made machine guns, a stick of gelignite, a detonator and forty bullets found on his farm on 18 May 1976.

After a 1978 raid of the Glenanne farmhouse, where police officers found home-made SMGs, ammunition and explosives, James Mitchell, a former RUC Reservist was given a one-year sentence suspended for two years, despite it being by then 'evident', says the HET, that his farm was also used to relay a bomb that killed two people in Keady (the Step Inn).[d]

Another example of an apparently ludicrously light sentence is that imposed on Andrew Godfrey Foote (aged sixty-six). Despite being found in possession of illegal ammunition in May 1976, and charged with three counts of unlawful possession, the judge said the accused was a man who had given service to the community and the country, and it was also 'obvious' he was not a common terrorist and had been 'totally misguided'. A custodial sentence, said the judge, would 'positively damage his health'.[19] Foote was given a conditional discharge.

In their 1973 work *Justice in Northern Ireland – A Study in Social Confidence*, Tom Hadden and Paddy Hillyard pointed controversially to inconsistencies in the sentences given to Protestants and Catholics on apparently very similar charges.[e] They clearly touched a nerve, as an angry riposte, though not a rebuttal, was published the following year by the Great Britain Law Officers' Department, entitled *Prosecutions in Northern Ireland: A Study of Facts*. This claimed that Hadden and Hillyard had included 'incorrect statements of fact' and 'faulty interpretations', but the two academics are not the only ones asking questions.

This analysis comes without the benefit of access to any documents giving reasons for the above decisions. Those papers are gathering dust in the vaults of the office of the Public Prosecutions Service for

---

d   Mitchell had been allowed to remain in the RUC for ten months after the attack.
e   Though the authors accepted it would be 'highly dangerous' to conclude definitively that the sentences varied because of sectarian bias, they recommended that judges should make clear in open court the reasoning behind sentencing. There has been no comparable analysis since, though there is plenty of anecdotal evidence to back Hadden and Hillyard's findings.

Northern Ireland (as the office of the DPP for Northern Ireland has been called since 2002). In deciding whether to put evidence before a court, the DPP must assess the strengths and weaknesses of the case and weigh up whether there is a good chance of a conviction against the cost of a failed prosecution. The DPP, however, must also give due consideration to the over-riding public interest – particularly in cases where there is evidence that police officers, tasked with enforcing the law, have broken it. The dangers of weakening public confidence in the judicial and security apparatus, particularly at times of civil conflict, must also be taken into account.

In the cases under examination, where hardened loyalists such as Robin Jackson, well known to the police, were involved, that surely should have been a very significant factor weighing in favour of prosecution and allowing a court to decide guilt or innocence in public. Custom and practice in the British legal system dictates that the more serious the offence, the more likely it is that a prosecution will be needed in the public interest, particularly if a weapon was used or violence threatened.[20] In Jackson's, James Mitchell's and Ted Sinclair's cases, police were well aware of their activities as loyalist ringleaders involved in organising others ready and willing to carry out shootings and bombings against vulnerable Catholic targets. This should have been a strong factor mitigating in favour of prosecutions rather than decisions made in private. There were the strongest grounds for believing that these men were likely to continue to commit further very serious crimes, and encourage others to do the same. This should surely have spurred the DPP to take a more robust stance.

The PFC, accompanied by Mick McGrath, had a meeting with a senior director at the DPP's office on 18 January 2008, seeking an explanation for the apparent bizarre decision-making process before – and during – the trial relating to his case. Far from making a genuine attempt to explain its reasoning, the DPP's representative adopted a defensive approach and failed to offer any explanation. A new DPP has since been appointed. Barra McGrory, as a solicitor and QC, had an exemplary record of defending human rights. Perhaps, a new spirit of transparency will develop in his office and those families who are pursuing the truth about past DPP decisions will be afforded more respect. Some decisions not to prosecute may not be as perverse as they appear. Others may be even more perverse. Until then, it is difficult to argue with the conclusion reached by Professor Bill Rolston in his paper 'An Effective Mask for Terror: Democracy, Death Squads and Northern Ireland': 'Although the law was sometimes used against state forces, it was used leniently, even when they acted independently outside of their special units.'[21]

11

RIDDING THE LAND
OF PESTILENCE

... more than ordinary police work was needed and was justified to rid
the land of the pestilence which has been in existence.

Lord Chief Justice Lowry, 1980[a]

When those who make the law, break the law, there is no law.

Graffiti, Divis Flats, Belfast, 1982

Starting in 1977, a series of bizarre events were set in train when the
actions of an alcoholic, possibly psychopathic and certainly sectarian
police officer, brought the sequence of killings and attacks described
in this book to an end. William McCaughey from Ballymena, in
Ian Paisley's 'Bible Belt' constituency and a former member of the
Armagh SPG, was suspended from duty as an RUC officer. He was
drinking too much, had become estranged from his wife, whom he
was accused of assaulting,[1] and was charged with theft and drink-
driving.[b] He was also a killer.

Living at his parents' home in Ahoghill, County Antrim, Mc-
Caughey was disintegrating psychologically and acting unpredict-
ably. In September 1978, he was finally taken to court, jointly charged
(alongside notorious Portadown loyalists Philip Silcock and R. J. Kerr)
with 'going equipped to steal'.[2] McCaughey, who had been driving a
car at the time of the arrests, had run away from police. When Silcock

---

a   Lord Chief Justice Lowry's judgment at the end of the trial of four officers
charged with a gun-and-bomb attack on the Rock Bar in June 1976.
b   McCaughey was charged with drink-driving in March 1978. He was convicted
and suspended from driving for fifteen months in November 1978.

and Kerr appeared in court, their defence solicitor said McCaughey, by that time in a psychiatric ward, would exonerate them.^c An RUC officer was dispatched to speak to McCaughey and returned to confirm the solicitor's account. Silcock and Kerr were bailed.

William McCaughey
© *BBC*

For a police officer, albeit a suspended one, being charged with 'going to steal' was not good – but of even greater concern to those within the RUC who knew of McCaughey's activities was that he was speaking openly to other officers about his loyalist career, including his involvement in the blatantly sectarian murder of William Strathearn. This posed clear and obvious dangers, not only for those with whom he had been colluding, but also for senior ranks within the RUC who were either already aware of his past actions or were rapidly becoming so. This could spiral out of control. It was a watershed moment.

The HET Report into the Rock Bar attack deduces that McCaughey 'was no doubt already a source of concern to his employers; he was known to be drinking heavily on regular occasions, he had matrimonial difficulties and was estranged from his wife'. There must have been many within the RUC hierarchy who realised that they had to take action to prevent McCaughey's activities becoming public. The decision to arrest him may even have been taken because of a plot to kill a fellow police officer. Kevin Sheehy, former head of the RUC Drugs and Anti-Racketeering Squad, claims he was told in September 1978 that 'a group of uniformed police officers attached to Armagh station had planned to kill Detective Inspector Maurice Neilly, the head of CID in that region, that very evening by placing a booby-trap bomb under his car'. Neilly, wrote Sheehy, had 'discov-

---

c   Solicitor Gus Campbell told the bail hearing he had spoken to McCaughey, who was prepared to accept responsibility for the hatchet, etc., found at the arrest scene.

ered that a number of local police had taken part in serious terrorist attacks in the area' (this must have included the Rock Bar attack). Sheehy then described his role in interviewing some of the officers arrested, including Constables Ian Mitchell and Laurence McClure – whom he describes as 'not difficult subjects' to break.[3]

McCaughey had been in the UVF since 1969[d] and was a prime mover in the June 1976 gun-and-bomb attack on the Rock Bar. He was also centrally involved, along with Robin Jackson, R. J. Kerr and former Armagh SPG member John Weir, in the murder of Strathearn. He later admitted privately that he had been involved in the killing of the three Reavey brothers.[4]

Given that something had to be done about McCaughey, those in a leadership position within the RUC were faced with a clear choice. If they were genuinely appalled by what they knew (and they feared that even worse revelations lay ahead), they could – and should – have invited the Police Complaints Board or an outside force to investigate fully. While this would have been the ethically correct decision, it would have caused a political storm. The enquiry's outcome would have been unpredictable and could have resulted in proposals for radical reforms of both the RUC (including Special Branch) and the UDR. An alternative to this unpleasant option would be to try to keep a lid on the scandal through a damage limitation exercise. If they could bring a few of the more blatant culprits to court on relatively minor charges, perhaps it would avoid a major political row, averting calls for a full inquiry. Neither course of action was risk-free.

The first option risked those in authority losing their jobs and reputations. They could try, of course, to manipulate any enquiry's terms – but nothing could be guaranteed. Whatever had taken place, after all, had happened on their watch. A full internal, or external, review would, at least temporarily, blacken the force's reputation –

d   McCaughey interview on BBC NI *Spotlight*, broadcast 25 May 2004.

and that of the British Army (including the UDR), the two frontline forces fighting the organisation the security establishment regarded as its main enemy, the IRA.

The damage limitation option was also not without risk. Information might leak out through court appearances and nationalist alienation from the UDR and the RUC might intensify. The Catholic Church, the SDLP and the Irish government were already accusing the RUC of failing to take the loyalist threat seriously.[5] A minimalist strategy would depend on a low standard of legal scrutiny. If the guilty parties could be persuaded to accept plea-bargaining deals and keep their mouths shut, however, it would certainly reduce the chances of the truth being aired publicly in the courts. The authorities would have to hope that no one in politics or the media would hold them to account.

It is not hard to fathom which option appeared the more attractive. The upper echelons of the political and security establishment could not have spent much time agonising before making their decision.

To understand the outcomes of that decision, we need to begin with the events of 17 June 1978, when the IRA ambushed an RUC car at a spot called Sturgan Brae, close to Camlough in County Armagh. Gunfire hit the vehicle over twenty times. One RUC officer, Hugh James McConnell (aged thirty-two), a married man with two children, was killed instantly.[e] A second RUC constable, William James Turbitt (aged forty-seven), a married man with four children, was hit in the head and probably died very soon afterwards.[f] The IRA, however, took his body away and hid it in a bog or in water of some kind. In the

---

e   McKittrick, in *Lost Lives*, says he went to school and played football with some of the Kingsmill victims. Former RUC officer Kevin Sheehy, in his book *More Questions than Answers*, says McConnell was a 'quiet, lovely guy' and a skilled footballer.

f   McKittrick, in *Lost Lives*, quotes a pathologist's report saying that Turbitt was unlikely to have survived for long after he was wounded. His body was recovered on 9 July 1978 and a post-mortem examination revealed he had died at around the same time as McConnell.

public mind, as there was no body, the missing officer might be alive. Police officers flooded into South Armagh to conduct a search.

The following day, at around 7.30 a.m., Fr Hugh Murphy, OBE (a former Royal Navy chaplain),[g] parish priest in Ahoghill, County Antrim, was alerted by knocking and, dressed in pyjamas and a dressing gown, opened the front door of the parochial house to be confronted by an armed man wearing a balaclava. A second man blindfolded Fr Murphy and forced him into the rear seat of a waiting car. The two men were Constable William McCaughey and Sergeant Gary Armstrong. They drove the priest to an outhouse on a farm less than a mile away, which belonged to McCaughey's father, Alexander. Fr Murphy was left hooded, with his hands bound, and tied to a ring that hung from the wall and was normally used for tying up cattle.

Meanwhile, Constable Turbitt's grief-stricken wife made a public plea for the release of both her husband and the kidnapped priest, as did the DUP leader, Ian Paisley. Following Paisley's appeal, Fr Murphy was released, unharmed, by his captors. Shortly afterwards, the priest appealed for the IRA to release the kidnapped RUC man, thanking Paisley for his intervention.[6] Turbitt's body was subsequently discovered.

Police believed their chief suspects for the Murphy abduction were loyalist paramilitaries but, three months after the episode, newspapers began reporting that the RUC authorities had set up 'a special team of detectives' to investigate the kidnapping.[7] On Monday 11 December 1978, 'as a result of extensive and protracted enquiries four persons were arrested and taken into police custody at Castlereagh'.[8] So far, so predictable, but the reports went on to give the sensational news that: 'Of the four persons arrested two are policemen – a sergeant and a constable[h] – and the two others are the father and mother of the

---

g   *The Irish Times*, 17 June 1980.
h   Armstrong and McCaughey, who were arrested on 11 December 1978.

constable.[i] The civilians have now been released but a report on them is being furnished to the DPP for his consideration.' The report went on, 'The policemen are still in custody and it is expected that a charge will be proffered against them. Both officers have been suspended from duty', and concluded by adding that one of the policemen was also being questioned about the murder of William Strathearn, and again it was stated that it was expected that a charge would be proffered.[9]

Someone, somewhere within the RUC had made the critical decision to arrest McCaughey. He was taken in for questioning after a raid on his parents' home, which began at 6.30 a.m. on 11 December 1978 – six months after the Murphy kidnapping. A series of arrests followed – William McCaughey, both his parents and RUC Sergeant Gary Armstrong were all taken into custody; Sergeant John Oliver Weir was arrested on 13 December; RUC Reserve Constable James Mitchell and his housekeeper, Sarah (Lily) Shields on 14 December; Constable Laurence McClure and another police officer who cannot be named on 15 December; Constables Ian Mitchell and David Wilson on 16 December; and an officer who cannot be named on 18 December.[j]

Within six hours of McCaughey being taken from his home, according to the HET Report on the Rock Bar, the RUC had found (unspecified) 'strong evidence' linking him to the priest's kidnapping. McCaughey's mother had, meanwhile, also implicated both her son and a 'police sergeant' in the murder of Strathearn. McCaughey went on to admit his involvement in that murder and then implicated RUC Sergeant John Weir, who was then arrested.[10]

---

i   McCaughey's parents – his father was a Presbyterian church elder.
j   Armstrong, McClure, Mitchell and Wilson were all serving members of Armagh SPG, while Weir was at that time based in Magherafelt SPG. James Mitchell was a former member of the RUC Reserve. McCaughey had been a member of Armagh SPG until his suspension in 1977.

The net widened to include renewed criminal investigations, not only into the Rock Bar attack, the Strathearn murder and the kidnapping of Fr Murphy, but also into the triple murder at Donnelly's Bar in December 1975. A search of James Mitchell's farm on 14 December, led by Maurice Neilly, led to the discovery of weapons and bomb-parts. Seven of the nine police officers subsequently arrested were convicted of various offences.[k] McCaughey's parents and James Mitchell's housekeeper, Lily Shields, make up a total of twelve. All this must have been of major interest to the Chief Constable, Jack Hermon: 'It was a case of the most vital importance, so much so that the Chief Constable was kept informed of developments', according to prosecuting counsel during McCaughey's trial.[11]

On the third day of his questioning, McCaughey 'intimated'[12] that he wished to make admissions to crimes other than the priest's kidnapping – including involvement in the Rock Bar attack. On his fourth day in detention, McCaughey was questioned at length about that attack. Incontrovertible evidence was emerging of RUC involvement in a serious paramilitary attack. A corner of the veil was slowly being lifted. What the HET calls 'a significant and major investigation' began. The twelve people arrested were interviewed a total of 126 times over the next eleven days, by a team of fifty-eight detectives. The various admissions made by the other police officers[l] on their differing roles in the Rock Bar attack merit attention because of their significance when examining the charges facing them at their later trial, and the highly controversial comments made by the Lord Chief Justice, Lord Lowry, as he passed sentence.[13]

k   McCaughey, Ian Mitchell, Laurence McClure and David Wilson were convicted for their roles in the Rock Bar attack. James Mitchell was convicted of possessing ammunition and explosives, Gary Armstrong of false imprisonment and kidnapping and John Weir got a life sentence for murder. The other two were a constable and a sergeant (identities known but they cannot be named for legal reasons), who were subjected to internal RUC disciplinary procedures.
l   Laurence McClure, Ian Mitchell and David Wilson.

McCaughey admitted carrying out the attack on the Rock Bar, claiming it had been an act of retaliation against republicans, but was unable to give any reason as to why it had been selected.[14] He admitted stealing one of the two cars used in the attack and of going to a safe house with two other men he did not name, one of whom produced three guns along with a bomb, masks, gloves and overalls.[m] He said the conspirators were joined by another man in a second (blue) car and the gang drove to the Rock Bar using both cars – three of them in the stolen Mini along with the bomb (and McCaughey carrying a 9 mm pistol). The driver of the blue car went ahead to rendezvous with them later. On arriving at their target, McCaughey said he got out of the Mini and saw a man (Mick McGrath) coming towards him. On an order from another gang member, McCaughey said he fired two shots – he claimed at Mick's legs – and had then fired repeatedly through a window into the bar, while another gang member (McClure) placed the bomb against the bar door. During this shooting and attempted bombing, according to McCaughey, two other police officers were circling to warn of any police patrols. The two groups were in radio contact, 'the clear inference being that both of these vehicles were police, or security force, vehicles'.[15]

For his part, Laurence McClure denied any involvement in the Rock Bar attack until he was told of McCaughey's and Ian Mitchell's admissions. He then made a written statement, under caution, in which he claimed the target of the attack had been Dessie O'Hare, a republican on the RUC wanted list who, he claimed, drank in the Rock Bar, which McClure said was a 'den of Provos'. There is nothing in any database or document examined by the HET or from any other source to support either of these assertions.

McClure also named Gary Armstrong and said the attack had been planned in Armstrong's house, where it had been decided to

---

m   A 9 mm pistol, a home-made SMG and what he described as a .45 handgun.

'fire a few shots into the bar and put a small bomb beside it'. He admitted that he, McCaughey and Armstrong had stolen the Mini; that McCaughey had been carrying the gun that was used to fire at Mick McGrath, and that he (McClure) had driven an official blue police car during the attack (its registration plate altered with insulating tape). Once at the scene, said McClure, they were joined by Ian Mitchell, who seems to have taken over driving the blue police car when he had joined the others in the attack. McClure admitted placing the bomb beside the bar door, lighting its fuse and running back to the Mini, before driving away and setting the car on fire.[16] The overall plan, he said, had merely been to 'hunt these boys back into the Free State and there would be no more killings'.[17] McClure added, of course, that he deeply regretted the part he had played.

Ian Mitchell said he had unwittingly taken part after 'a few drinks', realising too late that his colleagues had been, as he put it, 'up to something'. He admitted driving the blue police car to a spot three miles (5 km) from the Rock Bar and waiting there for fifteen minutes before driving McClure, McCaughey and Armstrong away from the scene of the attack. Only the reaction of his fellow officers, when they came upon a British Army vehicle checkpoint on the road back towards Armagh, said Mitchell, had indicated they had been involved in anything illegal. He had not, he said, seen any guns or the bomb, or been aware of the attack. He had not even known of the attack until the following day and had not reported his role because he was 'in fear of his life'. The HET, however, concludes that discrepancies between Mitchell's account and that of the others show he was deliberately lessening his true role. Evidence from another officer indicates that Mitchell went on duty as station officer at Keady a few hours after the bombing/shooting (and later took a statement from at least one witness), contradicting his account of being unaware of the attack until the following day. Mitchell's claim that his suspicions were not aroused when his fellow officers burned the vehicle in which they'd arrived, is hardly credible.

David Wilson similarly denied any knowledge before finally admitting he had been asked to take part, but had refused. His account was that Armstrong had called to tell him they were going to 'do the Rock Bar'. Wilson told detectives he had told Armstrong he was 'mad for having anything to do with it' and that he was not interested himself because he had too much to lose. While admitting he should have reported the conversation to his superiors, he said he had not because he had feared McCaughey and his associates.[18]

Armstrong denied any involvement during 'rigorous' police questioning and never faced charges despite being named by two of those involved (McClure and Wilson).[19] The HET says case papers from the time show detectives believed that Armstrong was 'a principal offender' in both the planning and execution of the attack.[20] The RUC report submitted to the DPP's office in July 1979 recommended Armstrong be charged with involvement, including the attempted murder of Mick McGrath and others, but the DPP disagreed.

One option considered was to drop all charges against the officer considered the least culpable – Wilson – and instead deal with him through internal police disciplinary procedures. That would have allowed him to be subpoenaed as a prosecution witness against Armstrong. The DPP rejected this course of action and the net effect was that a junior officer, Wilson, who had refused to take part in the attack, was prosecuted, while an RUC sergeant, Armstrong, whom police believed was a main protagonist in a gun-and-bomb attack, escaped prosecution. This seems an extraordinary outcome at such a critical trial for the RUC's integrity. Was there a hidden plan to protect the force's reputation, and was someone sending directions to the DPP to 'use a light hand'?

The only charges Armstrong eventually faced were for the unlawful imprisonment of Fr Murphy and possession of a firearm during the kidnapping. He received a two years' suspended prison sentence. Interviewed for a final time while on remand in prison during February 1979, he told police he would say no more as he had 'come to know Jesus' and 'his sins had been purged'.[21]

While he was never charged for the attack on the Rock Bar, Armstrong gives an account of a very similar incident in his book, *From the Palace to Prison*. In a chapter entitled 'Unfulfilled Potential', he wrote:

> One night I was at the scene of an incident when a bomb was planted outside the door of a Roman Catholic owned pub. A five gallon tin had been packed with gelignite and a fused detonator. Shots had been fired from machine guns and handguns to introduce the arrival of the gang who proceeded to plant the bomb at the door of the pub. Having shot one man they fled the scene to allow their bomb to go off, causing maximum injury and devastation. The fuse had been lit. The fact is that the bomb failed to go off because only the detonator exploded – not the bomb! The plan had gone wrong and the purpose was thwarted because the bomb failed to explode – unfulfilled potential.[22]

The HET concludes that 'there can be little doubt Armstrong is referring to the Rock Bar attack' and that Armstrong was, indeed, a key player in the whole affair.[23] Judge Barron made similar remarks.[24]

Describing how he felt at the moment the Lord Chief Justice, Lord Lowry, passed sentence for the kidnapping of Fr Murphy, Armstrong wrote:

> He looked compassionately on the actors ... Before he ever got to the stage of passing sentence, I excitedly nudged Barry (Armstrong's pseudonym for his co-defendant) and said, 'He's going to let us out!' ...

Lord Robert Lowry

Sure enough, against all the predictions and to the amazement of prosecution and defence, he gave us all suspended sentences for our acts of terrorism. None of us would serve any prison sentence. We were free! Without any thought and quite loud, I shouted 'Praise the Lord' … What a joyous occasion that was when we all shook hands with Officers and Defence and were madly embraced by weeping loved ones and overjoyed friends.[25]

What appears to have been entirely overlooked by the prosecution during the Rock Bar affair, are the ballistic links between the gun used by the policemen who mounted the attack, and a series of previous killings and shootings that brought Northern Ireland close to outright civil war. The police officers could only have obtained these weapons from loyalist paramilitaries. Even more alarming is the possibility that the SPG officers implicated in the attack on the Rock Bar were actively involved in these earlier sectarian murders.

Were they questioned about their associations? Were they ordered to name those from whom they obtained the weapons? If they were not asked such obvious questions, why weren't they? And if they were, and they refused to answer, why weren't they charged with conspiring to pervert the course of justice? The only answer currently available is that one of the RUC men, William McCaughey, was asked about the origin of the weapons used at the Rock Bar – and he refused to answer.[26] He was not, however, charged as a result of this refusal.

The 9 mm Luger pistol used at the Rock Bar had already been used in two non-fatal attacks during 1974. Far more seriously, it had also been used in attacks that resulted in the deaths of five people (Seán Farmer and Colm McCartney as they returned from a GAA match on 24 August 1975; and the three Reavey brothers on 4 January 1976). The 9 mm SMG used at the Rock Bar had also been used in the Reavey killings. Neither of these weapons was ever recovered – which can only mean that the RUC officers either destroyed the evidence or returned the weapons to the source from which they originally came – the UVF.

The only weapon recovered from the scene of the Rock Bar attack was a Webley .455 Mk VI revolver. It was found in the burnt-out Mini, but was too badly damaged to be test fired and so no one will ever know its ballistic history. Its serial number had been removed, presumably to prevent its provenance being established.

The complete lack of any curiosity on the part of the prosecution or the trial judge in respect of the bomb raises similar questions. Who supplied the explosives, who possessed the know-how to assemble a bomb, and how could it be that these people were associates of serving police officers?

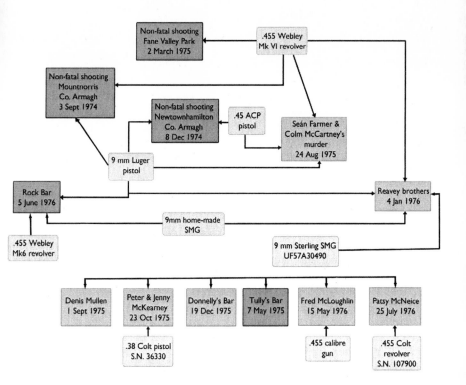

Ballistic links to the Rock Bar attack

With the facts at its disposal, and the admissions made by the seven officers over the course of dozens of interviews, the DPP levelled a number of charges:

- Constable William McCaughey was charged with the murder of William Strathearn, the kidnapping of Fr Murphy, the attempted murder of Michael McGrath and of the seventeen people inside the Rock Bar, causing an explosion, possession of explosives and possession of firearms.

- Sergeant John Oliver Weir was charged with murdering William Strathearn.[27]

- Constable Ian Mitchell was charged with the attempted murder of Michael McGrath, the attempted murder of the seventeen people inside the Rock Bar, causing an explosion, possession of explosives and possession of firearms.[28]

- The sole charge against Sergeant Gary Armstrong was the kidnapping of Fr Murphy.[29]

- Constable Laurence McClure was charged with the attempted murder of Michael McGrath, the attempted murder of those inside the Rock Bar, causing an explosion, possession of explosives, possession of firearms and withholding information about the attack on Donnelly's Bar.[30]

- Former Reserve Constable James Mitchell was charged with having at his home, on 14 December 1978, two home-made SMGs, two home-made magazines, assorted ammunition and three reels of (Cordtex) detonating cord.[31]

- RUC Reservist David Wilson was charged with withholding information about the planned attack on the Rock Bar.

- Civilian Sarah Elizabeth (Lily) Shields was charged with withholding information about the attack on Donnelly's Bar.[32]

These were the gravest charges each individual faced. Over the following months, however, the DPP decided not to proceed with many of the most serious of these charges. Those decisions remain to be explained.

At the sentencing hearing, all the attempted murder charges against McCaughey, McClure and Mitchell were dropped when the DPP entered a *nolle prosequi*. A similar direction was given by the DPP in the case of the wounding with intent charges against McClure and Mitchell (other charges were also dropped).[n] Later, all the charges against three of the police officers for the attempted murder of Michael McGrath were dropped after the DPP once more entered a *nolle prosequi* – without giving any reason.

Despite an unprovoked gun-and-bomb attack, intended to cause mass murder, carried out by police officers and causing serious injuries to Mick McGrath, this meant that none of the accused faced any charges of attempted murder. The only person who faced any charges of even wounding McGrath was McCaughey. His defence counsel then began to argue that McCaughey had aimed only at McGrath's legs, intending to wound, not kill. This defence argument was accepted by the trial judge – Lord Chief Justice Lowry. He stated in his summing up that McGrath had been shot in the legs – though McGrath had without doubt been shot in the stomach (and was prepared to give witness evidence that his assailant had aimed the gun at his heart).

McGrath has stated clearly that, as he left the bar, 'they open[ed] up with guns … aimed at my heart, one fired with a revolver out of the car and then another came out of the car and fired at me from a longer gun'.[o]

---

n   Counts seven, nine and ten – which remain a mystery as they were not specified in court during the sentencing hearing and neither was any reason for the DPP's *nolle prosequi*. They may relate to the theft of the getaway car as no one ever faced this charge, or possibly the use of one or more police vehicle(s) in the commission of the crime.

o   Statement of Michael McGrath, taken by Fr Raymond Murray, 11 September 1980, on file with the PFC.

It would, of course, have been standard practice for McCaughey's defence counsel to minimise the gravity of his client's actions. Quoting from McCaughey's statement, however, it was the prosecuting counsel who said: 'He [McCaughey] admits that he fired two shots at the man, who must have been Mr McGrath, aiming at his legs.' Though Lord Chief Justice Lowry, the most senior judge on the Northern Ireland bench, said this was a 'very serious offence', he went on to add that he accepted it did not amount to attempted murder.

McCaughey was a police officer with many years' experience of firearms. He knew where he was aiming and why. Seconds after shooting McGrath, McCaughey had gone on to fire shots through the window of the bar, clearly intent on killing whoever was inside: 'McCaughey admitted firing a number of shots through a window into the bar – a confined space where he would have anticipated people were socialising. The area around the dartboard was riddled. The bomb was wrapped in nails and pieces of metal.'[33] Those who attacked the Rock Bar not only carried guns but also a bomb consisting of five packs of nitro-glycerine high-explosives inside a paint tin that would have turned into shrapnel, intended to kill as many people as possible.

On 12 May 1980, faced with his own admissions, McCaughey pleaded guilty to murdering William Strathearn. He was sentenced on 16 June, but two weeks later the court dropped the charge he faced of attempting to murder Michael McGrath, although his earlier conviction had clearly exposed him as capable of murder. No mention in court was made of McGrath's assertion that two men had fired at him (one from the car).[p]

The Rock Bar trial took place in tandem with McCaughey's trial for the kidnapping of Fr Hugh Murphy. Crown counsel inaccurately

---

p   HET Report – Michael McGrath.

claimed in court that the Rock Bar attack occurred just thirteen days before the kidnapping. This was repeated in all the newspaper coverage. In fact, the two incidents were separated by more than two years. Prosecuting counsel may have been mistaken – but the unchallenged assertion that all police criminality was telescoped into a brief two-week period of 'madness' is likely to have influenced Lord Chief Justice Lowry.

Those who gave character evidence in support of the police officers included a Church of Ireland minister and a former senior member of the Ulster Unionist Party, John Taylor. Both they and the defence counsel referred to the undoubted difficulties facing RUC officers. McClure, it was said, had been on duty at the scene of the Kingsmill massacre. There were also allusions to the murder of five men at Tullyvallen Orange Hall the previous August.

While giving character evidence is quite proper, it must be set against the fact that neither the victim nor the civilian eyewitnesses, including the customers and the bar staff, were ever called to give evidence. According to McGrath, a policeman called on him in early April 1980 and served him with a summons to appear at the Crown Court in Belfast on 23 April. The case was delayed on several occasions, but when it finally went ahead, McGrath was not informed. Witnesses were never contacted again and only discovered the outcome of the case when they heard a radio report. McGrath thought this strange, because the policeman who called on him on four occasions had said it was an important case.[q] The shocking fact is that the chief witness, and main victim, in a case where four police officers mounted a bomb-and-gun attack on a busy country pub, was only belatedly asked to provide a statement and not called at all to give evidence at the trial that one had tried to kill him.

q   Statement of Michael McGrath, taken by Fr Raymond Murray, 11 September 1980, on file with the PFC.

The Lord Chief Justice, Lord Lowry, imposed the most lenient of sentences; his comments merit repeating in detail:[34]

> I must now deal with … a type of offence which is mercifully rare in our community. I refer to the involvement of members of the Royal Ulster Constabulary in crimes arising out of the terrible experiences to which this country has been subjected without respite for something like eleven years.
>
> It is a matter for admiration that this disciplined force has withstood so successfully the temptation to resort to unauthorised force under the continual strain of the threats to their wives and families and the sight of their neighbours and colleagues being attacked and in many cases killed.
>
> All of the accused, except the accused Alexander McCaughey, have awaited trial in custody, itself a sorry ordeal and humiliation for an officer of the law to undergo.[r] [This was not quite correct, as David Wilson had been on bail.]
>
> All of the accused have admitted their offences[s] and all of them have acted either wrongly or emotionally under the same powerful motives,[t] in one case the mortal danger of their service[u] and in the other the feeling that more than ordinary police work[v] was needed and was justified to rid the land of the pestilence which has been in existence.

---

r   Alexander was William McCaughey's father.

s   While this is technically correct, this was only after they had pleaded not guilty to a number of charges which the DPP then withdrew in unexplained and disputed circumstances.

t   The reference to 'powerful motives' is likely to mean Lowry excluded from his mind one strong possibility – that their motivation was sectarian hatred.

u   In mitigation, it was said that McClure's identity and address were known to the IRA.

v   Lowry here attributes mitigating circumstances to the accused while ignoring the evidence. No suggestion was ever made that criminal activities were being co-ordinated at the Rock Bar which 'ordinary police work' was unable to address. The indiscriminate nature of the attack does not support a claim that anyone was targeted.

It does not seem realistic to believe that after all that they have endured – some with their careers in ruins, others with their careers in jeopardy – that they require much by way of deterrent or by way of reform, and no proper sentence which I pass will make an impression on terrorists while other members of the police force are no doubt already sufficiently embarrassed and shocked by what has ... been seen to happen to their colleagues. It can be said of each of the accused that he has done the State some services. Ordinary people can only imagine what is being done for them by the police in these days and at what cost to themselves.

Not only that but counsel for the accused have painted a very fine and eloquent picture of what these individual men and their families have had to go through regarding their past and their hopes for the future.

So far as I can temper justice with mercy I am resolved to do so. It is the duty of judges to uphold the law as it is that of police officers. But I do not propose to vindicate my own reputation for justice and impartiality at the expense of these misguided but above all unfortunate men.

I must remember that whatever sentence is just it would follow that it would be imposed on a different and lower scale from that appropriate to terrorists,[w] no matter whichever side, whose aim is to achieve their political ends by violence and to attack the very fabric of society.

These were extraordinary comments from the most senior judge on the Northern Ireland bench. At the time of this summing-up, the Lord Chief Justice knew that one of the RUC men centrally involved in the Rock Bar attack (McCaughey) had also been involved in killing

---

w This apparently overlooks the possibility that police officers may also be 'terrorists'.

William Strathearn. He also knew that McCaughey had done so alongside two of Northern Ireland's most notorious loyalists, Robin Jackson and R. J. Kerr. And he knew McCaughey and Armstrong had been centrally involved in the kidnapping of Fr Murphy, and must also have known that all five officers were linked to RUC Reservist James Mitchell, who was before the courts for sentencing on explosives and weapons charges.

Nevertheless, Lord Chief Justice Lowry proceeded on the basis that all the officers charged (with the exception of McCaughey) had been involved in one incident only and, having advised himself thus, he handed down the following sentences:

- Constable Ian Mitchell: two-year sentence, suspended for three years, for causing an explosion, possession of explosives with intent, possession of a firearm with intent.

- Reserve Constable Laurence McClure: two-year sentence, suspended for three years, for causing an explosion, possession of explosives with intent, possession of a firearm and ammunition with intent.

- Constable William McCaughey: seven-year sentence for wounding, two years for causing an explosion, four years for possession of explosives, and three years for possession of a firearm and ammunition with intent, all sentences to run concurrently with his sentence for the murder of William Strathearn.

- Auxiliary Constable David Wilson: one-year sentence, suspended for two years for concealing an offence.[35]

This bizarre outcome means that the police officer who lit the bomb fuse and placed it at the bar (McClure) was given a lighter sentence – two years, suspended for three years – than McCaughey, who did not place the bomb (but who was sentenced to four years to run concurrently with his life sentence for murdering Strathearn).

On concerns over the lenient sentencing, the HET responds un-equivocally to Lowry's explanation that the RUC officers were merely trying to 'rid the land' of 'pestilence'. That, says the HET:

> ... is simply staggering. It is difficult to conceive of a statement that could be more fundamentally flawed or calculated to destroy the confidence of a large section of the community in the court's independence and probity ...
>
> This outcome was palpably not justice for Mick ...
>
> The shooting down of a member of the public, and the placing of a large bomb (modified to become, in effect, an anti-personnel device) would represent the gravest of circumstances that a court would have to consider.
>
> Added to that, the fact that the perpetrators were all police officers, betraying the trust of their office, and utilising their position to facilitate the offences and their escape; would normally be exceptionally aggravating features.[36]

The HET points out that the attack was carried out by a group of police officers, with the intention of causing death and serious injury, motivated by sectarianism. They had betrayed their positions of trust as police officers and misused police equipment (including a police car and radios).

Then there are the cases of the two other police officers, neither of whom has been named publicly, who were arrested in December 1978, at the same time as McCaughey and the others. One was a sergeant and the other a constable. Neither was charged with criminal offences, though both faced internal disciplinary procedures for failing to report the criminal conduct of their colleagues (Armstrong, McCaughey and McClure). On the day of their disciplinary hearing, evidence was heard before the Chief Constable, Sir Jack Hermon. After the lunch recess, all the charges were dismissed, when the

RUC tribunal ruled their transgressions amounted to 'mistakes' and not 'wilful neglect'. How, it might be asked, does using a police car and communications equipment to ensure a clear path for a gang of bombers and gunmen to attack innocent civilians in a bar amount to 'mistakes' and not 'wilful neglect'? We know the chief constable sat on the disciplinary panel along with two others, but we may never know the full details of the involvement of these two officers in the attack on the Rock Bar.[37]

The HET Report makes the following observations about the Rock Bar:

> It is useful to reflect on all the outcomes at this point. A busy country pub, frequented by honest, decent working people was a target for a sectarian attack; a member of the public in the street outside was callously gunned down without warning; a powerful explosive, wrapped in nail and metal fragments to ensure the maximum numbers of people would be killed or maimed, is detonated at the door; the police investigation is cursory, ineffective and even fails to interview the only witness, who survived being shot down.
>
> The fact that the attack was part of a linked series is apparently ignored. Subsequently, as a result of other matters, it is found that local police officers planned and committed this outrage; it seems that they stole the getaway car used but utilised at least one police vehicle and police radios in the commission of the offence to avoid being disrupted or thwarted; one officer at least was part of the original investigation; and others knew about the actions of their colleagues and did nothing.
>
> With the exception of one officer, who was already convicted for murder (which carries an automatic sentence fixed by law) everyone else involved walked away with either a suspended sentence or no finding of guilt.
>
> Frankly, this scenario beggars belief and cannot be explained. Small wonder that the families of those affected have an enormous sense of

grievance ... This was a terrorist attack on a community pub, with a purely sectarian motive.[38]

The HET agrees with an *Irish News* article, printed in 2008, describing Mick McGrath as a 'quiet, unassuming man who had harboured no bitterness about the attack' – a judgement with which, the HET says, it agrees, having found him 'gentle and reserved with a wry sense of humour'.[x] The HET Report recalls that Mick had personally told them of his suspicions at the time of the shooting that police officers were to blame. As he lay wounded on the ground, he had seen what he thought were police boots and trousers. This only serves to underline the RUC's inexplicable failure to take a statement from him in 1976 or call him as a prosecution witness.

Put in a sharper context: Mick McGrath was a better detective than the RUC. The HET apologised to him for the 'insensitive' failure of the RUC to provide the truth of what it knew about his attackers: 'The system had failed him completely. This was unforgiveable, especially considering the nature of the case and the identity of the defendants; it robbed him of any chance of making his views felt on the nature of the pleas being offered, or of any sense of resolution over the incident by seeing offenders convicted.'[39]

The HET sought to interview officers from the original investigation. One had retired and another did not respond to a letter inviting him to an interview, a third was killed in a 1994 Chinook helicopter crash, and a fourth has since died. Those officers to whom the HET did manage to speak, however, gave a common view that the entire 1978 police investigation was overseen by the then Chief Constable, Sir Kenneth Newman.

---

x   Mick McGrath met the head of the HET, Dave Cox, and his then deputy, Phil James, at Benburb Servite Priory in May 2006, along with Alan Brecknell of the PFC and Joe McGleenan, a relative of Michael's and the proprietor of the Rock Bar at the time of the attack.

It is hardly a huge leap of the imagination, considering the direct involvement of police officers in the most serious of crimes and the 'flawed, cursory and ineffective' nature of the original 1976 investigation, to conclude that the investigation was poor because the investigators knew of police involvement. The HET makes this leap, and goes further, saying, 'The only question that remains is whether it [the original 1976 enquiry] was deliberately sabotaged by serving officers who had been amongst the perpetrators.'[40]

Answering this question, however, is problematic, as the papers are almost entirely missing. Certainly, the HET says, the police officers involved would themselves have 'tried to obstruct any enquiries that might have implicated them', but all were relatively junior staff. It claims, 'There is no satisfactory explanation for why this attack was not overseen by a senior officer, or why there was no linking of this

investigation to other similar offences in the region.' It is, then, unsurprising, says the HET, that the most senior officer available, the chief constable, took a close supervisory role in the second (1978) enquiry, given that: 'An objective observer might have considered that the whole reputation of his organisation was at stake.'[41]

Kenneth Newman

The second RUC enquiry (after the discovery of McCaughey's involvement in the Strathearn murder), in comparison with the first, says the HET, is well documented and there seems 'at last' to be a degree of co-ordination – including linking the Rock Bar attack to the similar one at Donnelly's Bar, Silverbridge, six months previously and only fifteen miles (24 km) away, in which three people were killed.

In stark contrast to the HET's conclusions, some commentators have praised the RUC investigation into the murder of Strathearn and the linked trial into the attack on the Rock Bar, saying it exemplified the force's determination to root out 'rogue' officers. One is journalist

Chris Ryder[y] (now retired but formerly a long-standing *Sunday Times* correspondent in Belfast and former member of the Northern Ireland Police Authority). 'The Rock Bar trial,' wrote Ryder, resulted in the RUC receiving 'widespread acclaim for digging the "bad apples" out of its own barrel'. It was seen by senior officers, he said, 'as marking significant milestones along the road to making the RUC evidently impartial and professional, and therefore acceptable to both sections of the community'. While the police did not expect it 'would change attitudes dramatically', they hoped that 'fair-minded people would recognise the achievement and credit the force for it'.[42]

Similarly, Martin Dillon, in *The Dirty War*, praised the 'excellent detective work' that brought Weir and McCaughey to trial for the murder of William Strathearn. While conceding that they, and their accomplices, had damaged the reputation of the RUC by operating within it 'with impunity for years', Dillon added that other considerations also applied. 'After all,' he wrote, 'it was the RUC which unflinchingly detached them from its midst and prosecuted them.'[43]

But is the 1980 prosecution of four members of the Special Patrol Group (an elite anti-terrorism unit disbanded in 1980) truly an example of impartial police investigation and a willingness to apply the rule of law without fear or favour? Are the HET's conclusions or Ryder's and Dillon's more convincing?

The HET's concerns extend more widely than its sense of grievance on behalf of Mick McGrath[z] and point in the direction

---

y   Author of *The RUC: A Force Under Fire* (1989) and *The Ulster Defence Regiment: An Instrument of Peace?* (1991). Commenting on the former, Sir Kenneth Newman, former Chief Constable of the RUC/Commissioner of the London Metropolitan Police, wrote that the book is 'an account which gives full credit to the extraordinary courage, dedication and professionalism of the men and women of the RUC' (back cover).

z   McGrath was shot twice – in the abdomen and hip. He spent over a month in hospital and carried a bullet fragment for the rest of his life.

of both the judicial and political authorities. The legal outcome of the Rock Bar trial, it says, prompts questions about what really lay behind the lenient sentencing, which it calls 'deeply troubling', and goes on to state: 'It promotes consideration of whether other factors were taken into account, apart from the circumstances of the case.' In 1978, it concludes pointedly, Northern Ireland was in the midst of conflict. London depended on the RUC, supported by the British Army, to maintain the rule of law: 'It is an interesting consideration as to what level of political involvement was attached to this case. Certainly the Chief Constable was personally overseeing matters; he would undoubtedly have been reporting on developments to government.'[44] Here, again, questions remain about the involvement of politicians at the highest level.

The dropping of the charges against McClure relating to the triple murder at Donnelly's Bar and those against Armstrong of involvement in the Rock Bar attack meant that both came before the court on one charge only – paving the way for their suspended sentences. It is difficult to avoid the conclusion that all this good fortune may have served as a powerful incentive to both officers, discouraging them from speaking out about other cases in which police officers might also have been involved.

In the light of past and future events, says the HET, the trial and its outcome 'raised anew suspicions of state collusion and cover-up. Again, this is perfectly understandable … the HET has no convincing evidence which can satisfactorily rebut such accusations.'[45]

Concerns at the time, says the Rock Bar report, must have spread outside the RUC to the political establishment, which, it says, may actually have influenced the astonishing legal outcome: 'The question arises as to whether political approaches were made to the court, proposing a "low key" response and minimising public attention to the case. This is a suspicion held within the Nationalist community.' The HET also suggests a reason why there may have been a cover-up:

The revelation that members of the RUC were routinely consorting with loyalist paramilitaries, and actually planning and executing terrorist shootings and bombings, would have had a dramatic impact on public confidence and the reputation of the force.

This in turn would have had massive implications for government; the loss of public support for the RUC would have rendered Northern Ireland ungovernable.

Members of the Nationalist community had been making allegations of widespread involvement and collusion by members of the security forces with loyalist paramilitaries. These claims were ridiculed, and individual instances previously uncovered had been dismissed by reference to 'rotten apples'.

This investigation in 1978 revealed a much more disturbing picture; the Rock Bar case had the potential to validate claims of widespread and routine collusion.

As well as the Rock Bar, there were [ballistic] links to other offences such as the murders of the Reavey Brothers, the victims at Donnelly's Bar, and Mitchell's Farm – reputedly the hub of collusion between members of the security forces and loyalist paramilitaries, notably the Mid-Ulster UVF.

This last link opened the way for consideration of scores of links between weapons used, involvement of known UVF paramilitaries and similar attacks. ...

It is difficult to believe, when judged in concert with other cases emerging around that time, that such widespread evidence of collusion was not a significant concern at the highest levels of the security forces or government.[46]

Underlining the potential political disaster facing the RUC, should the facts ever have been aired in open court, and had not the court viewed the facts with such extraordinary leniency, the HET says: 'It may indeed be that there were fears that to confirm suspicions of collusion and involvement of RUC and security forces personnel in these terrorist crimes would have fatally undermined the credibility of the organisation, and possibly compromised overall political stability. It may have been viewed as seriously as that.'[47]

The HET Report refrains from making any final judgement on this possibility, saying events have to be set against wider political judgements, but it then challenges the present British government, clearly pointing to the need for further action: 'With the passage of time since these shocking, shameful and disgraceful crimes, the opportunity should exist for an honest disclosure of all relevant matters and considerations, without risk to individuals or of prejudice to the reputation and standing of new law enforcement arrangements. The families of those affected in this case – and in the linked cases – have received no justice to date.'[48]

Aside from the sentencing, and the rationale behind it, there are other, equally disturbing, issues raised by the way the legal system dealt with the Rock Bar assailants. Had the full implications of the role of the RUC, the DPPs and the Lord Chief Justice in the Rock Bar trial been known, it is likely that a scandal of unprecedented proportions would have ensued.

We have the Barron Enquiry and its reports, ordered by the Irish government into the Dublin/Monaghan bombings (and related attacks), to thank for the further evidence that gives rise to these questions. Judge Barron had unprecedented access to some of the written statements taken during the police interrogations of the four police officers, as well as some RUC Special Branch 'daily record sheets' that noted items of specific intelligence interest arising from the interviews. In examining these accounts of the allegations and cross-allegations made by police officers about the Rock Bar, Barron concludes that claims made by Weir of widespread collusion were corroborated in four cases, involving the murders of no fewer than eleven people. Barron is unambiguous:

... what can be said is that in relation to the attacks on Donnelly's Bar (Silverbridge), John [Seán] Farmer and Colm McCartney, the Reavey family, and the O'Dowd family, information was given by one or more of the interviewees which confirmed Weir's account of who was responsible in each case. One of those interviewed, an RUC officer, also confirmed Weir's story of the RUC constable who was building home-made machine guns for loyalist extremists. Finally, two of those convicted for the Rock Bar attack gave information which suggested that the fourth person named by Weir was indeed involved, although he made no admissions and was not charged.[49]

The obvious question arises: why, if police had information in 1978 relating to the Farmer/McCartney, Donnelly's Bar, Reavey and O'Dowd murders (a total loss of eleven lives), did the RUC fail to pursue those responsible? Did the RUC baulk at the awful truth? Or did it fail to forward updated files to the DPP, despite prior directions from the DPP's office to do so, should further information come to light?[aa] Barron says that statements from a number of serving police officers, made to investigating detectives, were available in 1978 pointing to the officers being involved in a number of other murders and bombings.

The evidential trail was strengthened considerably with the availability of ballistic evidence that demonstrated clear links between a number of fatal attacks. The apparent response of the RUC and DPP's office, rather than making a concerted attempt to bring prosecutions for these murders, was to limit the damage done to the force's reputation by focusing on one attack – the Rock Bar, one murder outside County Armagh – William Strathearn, and less serious offences. The focus on the Rock Bar attack may have been deliberate because

---

aa As stated repeatedly in letters to the PFC, on file, including correspondence to Madden and Finucane, solicitors, from the DPP, 19 April 2004.

no one died and it was carried out solely by police officers without the involvement of loyalist paramilitaries. It could, still, therefore, in theory be denied that members of the security forces colluded with loyalists.

When McCaughey and Weir named Jackson and Kerr as their co-conspirators in murdering Strathearn, neither loyalist was even interviewed, let alone arrested or charged, further lending support to the theory that the RUC was trying desperately to put as much space as it could between its employees and the UVF, whatever the cost in prosecutions.

Weir offered to testify against Jackson and Kerr, on condition that the charge of murdering Strathearn was withdrawn, but this was refused by the assistant DPP. Kerr and Jackson, he said, were not interviewed by the police:

> … because the police state they are 'virtually immune to interrogation' and the common police consensus is that to arrest and interview either man is a waste of time. Both men are known to police to be very active and notorious UVF murderers. Nevertheless the police do not recommend consideration of withdrawal of charges against Weir. I agree with this view. Weir and McCaughey must be proceeded against. When proceedings against them are terminated the position may be reviewed in respect of Jackson and Kerr.[50]

One can see the sense in that. There was nothing, however, to prevent these two prolific killers, named by a police officer (albeit a collaborator) as having killed the 'Good Samaritan' Strathearn, being questioned, robustly, after Weir and McCaughey's convictions (as recommended by the assistant DPP).

The RUC is not the only authority with questions to answer. The DPP's role between late 1978 and the trial in 1980 is one which, to paraphrase the European Court of Human Rights in a separate case, 'cries out for explanation'. With a new dispensation and a new Public Prosecution Service, the time is surely now right to ask its new director, Barra McGrory, for an independent review of the decisions taken which resulted in what appears to be a blatant cover-up.

The HET notes that Mitchell's farm was the centre of allegations, which are still 'the subject of continuing research … that loyalist paramilitaries used it as a base for planning and launching terrorist attacks, and that members of the security forces – both police and military – colluded with and actively engaged in these activities'.[51]

These uncomfortable facts throw up another question: in what other Western European democracy would any prosecution case make so very little of the ballistic evidence linking a gang of serving police officers, supposed upholders of the law, to five high-profile sectarian murders and two other attacks?

HER MAJESTY'S MURDERERS

…the Protestant groups – UDA and UVF – see themselves as defenders
of the status quo threatened by a culturally and socially inferior minority
sub-group, which is identified by the Catholic religion. This justifies
random attacks on Catholics as a group to 'keep them down'…

> *Excerpt from letter, Sir Frank Cooper (Permanent Secretary,*
> *NIO) to Lt Gen. Sir Frank King (GOC), 15 May 1975*

It would be wrong to suppose that the loyalist gunmen and bombers
who killed so many decent people are the real villains of this book.
While they all had an individual's moral responsibility to choose
between right and wrong, it could be argued that many loyalist
paramilitaries were brought up in a tradition where Catholics were
almost invariably seen as the enemy. For the true villains, perhaps
look to some of the names on the British honours lists of the last few
decades, and old gentlemen living comfortably on civil service and
political pensions in the English shires.

One wonders if they ever look back on their time in Northern
Ireland, at what they did and who they encouraged and manipulated
– and then examine their consciences. Could they have in some
way imagined that their actions were defensible? While asking
pertinent and searching questions of those who ran the Irish counter-
insurgency campaign at Westminster and Stormont over thirty-five
years of conflict, however, it is also useful to look at the calibre of the
individual loyalist paramilitaries they exploited.

Who were the people who carried out these terrible deeds? And
why? If the rest of this book deals with 'what', 'where', 'when' and
'how', this chapter deals with 'who' and 'why'.

To begin with 'why'. First, because they could. Loyalists certainly had the weapons, as the British Army's own internal analysis detailed: 'Since the beginning of the current campaign the best single source of weapons (and the only significant source of modern weapons) for Protestant extremist groups has been the UDR.'[1] They also had the will to bomb and shoot people quite indiscriminately: people they knew had taken no action against either themselves personally or the Protestant/unionist community in general.

The victims of every single attack detailed in this book were either killed at random (because they were in a public place associated with the Catholic community) or targeted because they were Catholic and upwardly mobile.[a] Without access to weapons, Catholic non-combatants were defenceless, with no ability, or particular desire, to retaliate. Individual families living in the countryside of Counties Armagh and Tyrone were vulnerable targets. It did not take a great deal of courage to drive up to their cottages and farms with an SMG.

Protestants, it is sometimes forgotten, are in a minority on the island of Ireland. Many of their ancestors arrived in recent centuries from England and Scotland. A residual fear that the Gael[b] might sweep down from the hills upon the Planter[c] is understandable, along with the perennial fear of all 'colonials' that the 'mother country' will eventually desert them; that they are unloved and unlovable.

Tom Allen, a loyalist character in Graham Reid's play *The Hidden Curriculum*, expresses well that lack of self-esteem and fear of imminent betrayal:

---

a   The one exception was John Francis Green, an IRA fugitive shot dead in County Monaghan on 10 January 1975. See Chapter 7: Bombs Know No Borders.

b   The Merriam-Webster dictionary defines 'Gael' as 'a Celtic especially Gaelic-speaking inhabitant of Ireland, Scotland, or the Isle of Man'; see http://www.merriam-webster.com/dictionary/gael.

c   'The Plantation of Ulster' which began in 1609, bringing settlers from both Scotland and England; see http://www.plantationofulster.org; accessed 3 July 2013.

They don't know about us in 'The Guardian' or 'The Sunday Times' ... We're just Loyalist extremists. We're never right, we're never reasonable and we're never recognised. They think that there are a million of us swarming all over the place, smothering all the wee innocent Catholics. But there aren't. There's a handful of us and we're just fighting to survive.[2]

To 'fight' and 'survive', loyalist paramilitaries formed themselves into two main groups. The larger of the two, the Ulster Defence Association (UDA, founded in August 1971) was legal until 1992, despite its members' direct involvement in hundreds of sectarian murders (carried out under its *nom de guerre*, the 'Ulster Freedom Fighters', declared illegal in November 1973). In 1972 it issued a public statement complaining that loyalists were perceived as 'second-class Englishmen and half-caste Irishmen ... betrayed and maligned' by 'flabby-faced men with pop-eyes and fancy accents'.[3] For 400 years, the statement went on, 'we have known nothing but uprising, murder, destruction and repression', and ended with a plea to 'send the soldiers home and leave us the weapons and we will send you the IRA wrapped-up in little boxes and little tins like baked beans'.[4]

The Ulster Volunteer Force (UVF) was formed in 1912 to frustrate the implementation of Home Rule by organising the training of volunteers (primarily from the working class) and to obtain guns, should they be needed. On the outbreak of the First World War in 1914, the UVF joined the British Army en masse and were the first troops ordered over the top at the Somme on 1 July 1916.[d] The British government's October 1920 mobilisation of the UVF (in the Ulster Special Constabulary or USC) was intended to counter the IRA through a predominantly Protestant militia, paving the way

---

d   Of the West Belfast Battalion of the UVF, known as the 'Shankill Boys', 760 men left for the trenches. When the slaughter was over, only 76 had survived.

for the creation of the Northern Ireland state.[e] The UVF was not outlawed until June 1966,[f] then legalised again in May 1974 before being banned again on 4 October 1975, over eighteen months later.[g]

As for the IRA, whatever its stated aims of attacking what it called 'combatants' (a varying definition, but including the RUC, British Army and, in the 1980s, even those who cooked their food or maintained their barracks), as well as killing 474 members of the security forces, it also killed 358 Protestant civilians during the conflict.[5] The IRA sometimes accused police of failing to clear an area fast enough, or said a bomb had detonated earlier than expected, or pleaded mistaken identity. This made no difference, of course, to the dead. They had still lost their lives and their families mourned them just as much as if they had been killed deliberately. Most unionists pay no heed to what they see as self-serving IRA 'excuses' and accuse republicans of targeting Protestant civilians for sectarian motives.

Sympathy for and understanding of the loyalist predicament, however, tends to dissipate when one contemplates how it expressed itself. Loyalists openly admitted that a key strategy was to terrorise ordinary Catholics into repudiating Irish republicanism through a campaign of indiscriminate violence. This was not unique to Mid-Ulster during the 1970s. In *The Red Hand*, academic Steve Bruce admits that throughout the conflict 'a very large proportion of loyalist victims were Catholics who were not active republicans ... they killed "any oul Taig"[h] who had the misfortune to fall into the hands of a team out for a kill'.[6]

---

e   The B Specials were disbanded on 30 April 1970 and replaced by the UDR.
f   In 1971 John Taylor (UUP), then Northern Ireland Minister for Home Affairs, told Gerry Fitt (SDLP) 'there was no evidence that it [the UVF] was involved in anything illegal that would enable it to be said conclusively to exist as an organisation'.
g   The UVF was re-proscribed after twelve people were killed in a spate of bombings and shootings across Northern Ireland on 2 October 1975. During the eighteen-month period that UVF membership was legal, the organisation killed over seventy-five people, on both sides of the border.
h   'Taig' is one of many abusive terms used by some loyalists to refer to Catholics.

These attacks were 'believed to be one way of isolating the IRA within its own community. If loyalist paramilitaries could not shoot the fish, they would poison the water. Eventually, they reasoned, this would ineluctably drive the nationalist community to pressurise the IRA to stop its campaign'.[7] A spokesman explained the UVF strategy at that time: 'We believed, rightly or wrongly, that the only effective way to beat the terror machine was to employ greater terrorism against its operative ... By bombing the heart of Provisional enclaves we attempted to terrorize the nationalist community into demanding that the Provisionals either cease their campaign or move out ... we hoped to crack their morale and destroy their chain of command.'[8]

In 1973 the UDA appealed to Catholics to 'break' with the IRA, warning its campaign would otherwise continue. 'Throw these gangsters out of your midst,' said the statement. 'Until you do this you must bear the agony. Our fight is not with you but with the animals you shelter.'[9] In September 1976, a UDA commander, writing in *Combat*, said there is only one way to control 'an area or a ghetto that harbours terrorists and insurgents and that is to reduce its population to fear by inflicting upon them all the horror of terrorist warfare. Where these means cannot, for whatever reasons, be used, the war is lost.'[10]

Many loyalists viewed their own violence as an extension of state actions against republican paramilitaries. This is hardly surprising, given the private views expressed by senior civil servants, British Army officers and government ministers themselves. In September 1971, when the loyalist threat was already well established, Brian Faulkner met British Prime Minister Edward Heath to urge the creation of UDR units in places such as the Harland and Wolff shipyard, as a 'means of avoiding further pressures for the formation of irregular Protestant armed groups'.[11]

Three days later, when considering the danger of a Protestant backlash, a senior British Army officer accompanying the chief of the general staff of the British Army wrote: 'they [the GOC, the Commander of Land Forces and the head of MI5 in Northern Ireland] certainly convinced me that if we do not harness their [loyalist] energies the Protestants will fight the republicans and consider themselves right to do so'.[12]

As for the UDA threat, the GOC wrote to Secretary of State William Whitelaw in July 1972 proposing a possible handover of entire Protestant areas to 'a combination of the UDA, Orange Volunteers and RUC'. He did not, apparently, see any difficulty in the three groups working together: 'It may even be necessary to turn a blind eye to UDA arms when confined to their own areas.'[13] Responding to repeated unionist demands for the creation of 'Home Guard' type units, British civil servants dismissed the idea, as 'security-minded' men could already offer their services to either the UDR or the UDA.[14]

This attitude was hardly a secret to Catholics. The SDLP and Cardinal Conway, in repeated meetings with British ministers, complained about a perceived RUC reluctance to come down hard on the UDA and UVF. In April 1975, Conway said it was 'intolerable that ... the UVF remained a legal organisation when they give press conferences in the Shankill at which they openly boast about killing Catholics'.[15] In response to the cardinal's angry outburst, two days later an internal memo from an A. G. Turner of the policy department was sent to the Northern Ireland Office repudiating Conway's views and claiming Protestant attacks were provoked by IRA kneecappings and bombings.[16] The following month, officials at Stormont decided to suppress a paper giving statistics on violent deaths and murder conviction rates. The paper showed that, of 346 deaths classified as sectarian, 290 remained unsolved, and these unfavourable findings should not be sent to Dublin.[17]

On 15 May 1975, a time when the UVF and UDA were both legal organisations, a paper prepared for the British government concluded that 'Waves of sectarian assassinations seem to start from the Protestant side. When the Protestants feel threatened ... they turn to a campaign of murder.'[18] Two weeks later, possibly stung by this incontrovertible evidence of loyalist sectarian killings, civil servants met Secretary of State Merlyn Rees, who commented that there was 'a marked tendency for the Army to leave the problem of sectarian murders to the RUC so they could concentrate on fighting the PIRA which they saw as their main task'.[19]

Meanwhile, it offended loyalist paramilitaries (as with republicans) that they were seen as criminals at all. A writer in the UDA magazine, *Ulster*, in September 1974, complained: 'To call them criminals is in itself a crime because the 41 [*sic*] who still remain in Compound 17 are former members of the RUC, British Army, UDR and Orange Order. (22 Orangemen, 4 RUC, 5 UDR, 9 British Army, 2 Prison Officers and 6 T. & A.V.R. [*sic*]). Facts speak for themselves.'[i]

The web of individual loyalist perpetrators is inextricably tangled. Killers swapped weapons and partners in their dance of death around Counties Armagh and Tyrone. What follows shows how intimately they were linked.

Robert (Robin) John Jackson was born on 27 September 1948 and brought up in the County Down village of Donaghmore, where he is now buried, between Banbridge and Newry. Though he is said by some writers to have been the most prolific loyalist killer during the conflict, very little has been written authoritatively about him.[20] Newspaper reports have called him a 'psychopath' with a visceral hatred of Catholics, while others claim that he worked as a hit-man for British military intelligence and for the RUC. The number of people he killed ranges from a conservative estimate of fifty up to a hundred, and even more. Certainly, if he did not pull the trigger himself, he is estimated to have been involved in the murders of scores of ordinary

---

i   'Compounds' was the name given to the part of Long Kesh where detainees were interned without trial in Nissan huts. Copy on file with PFC.

Catholics. To avoid libel action, he became known by the soubriquet 'the Jackal' to the readers of Northern Ireland's tabloid newspapers in the late 1970s and 1980s.

Jackson's cited motivation varied from his hatred of Catholics to a devotion to his concept of 'Britishness'. What is not conjecture is that he had a corrupt and indefensible relationship with enough RUC officers to protect him from ever facing a murder charge, leaving him free to continue killing people for over two decades (from 1973 to the 1990s). The only known victim to have questioned him directly was the son of a Catholic police officer, Joe Campbell, shot dead in Cushendall, County Antrim, in February 1977. Joe junior went to Jackson's home shortly before he died to ask if there was any truth in John Weir's claim that he had been involved in his father's murder. Jackson brusquely denied it.

The facts, as far as they can be ascertained, about Jackson's career are that he joined D Company of 11 UDR, based at Scarva Barracks, Banbridge, in August 1973. After the 23 October 1973 arms raid at the armoury used by his unit, he was named by a man on whose property police discovered a significant arms cache.[j] It was, however, two weeks before the police searched his home in Lurgan. Between being named and the raid, Jackson is believed to have shot dead Banbridge trade unionist and father of three, Patrick Campbell.

In Jackson's house, the RUC found forty-nine more bullets than his UDR entitlement and a notebook containing details of over two dozen people, including their car registration numbers. Despite all the evidence, all charges against him of murder and possession of ammunition were dropped the following January. The only action taken against him was his dismissal from the UDR on 4 March 1974. If more determined action had been taken, dozens of lives could have been saved.

---

j   For a more detailed account, see Chapter 1: Blooding-In.

Was it at this stage that Jackson was 'turned' by the RUC? At the end of June 1974, Colin Wallace, then a senior British Army military intelligence officer, sent a memo to an A. H. Holman at British Army HQ in Lisburn. It asked which of a list of loyalists that Wallace's 'Psy-Ops' unit wished to target was working for military intelligence and therefore immune from his attentions. Next to Jackson's name, a note in Wallace's own handwriting says: 'Robin Jackson was charged with the murder of Patrick Campbell in October last year. Charges were dropped following RUC SB[k] intervention.'[21]

On 14 August 1975, Wallace wrote again, this time to his former mentor in the British Army's public relations unit, Major A. H. Staughton, giving a list of people he claimed had been involved in the 17 May 1974 bombings in Dublin. Those listed include Jackson, 'Mulholland, Hanna, Kerr and McConnell' (all known loyalists) who, Wallace says, were 'working closely with SB and Int.[l] at the time'.[22]

Three months later, within hours of the shootings of Peter and Jenny McKearney on 23 October 1975, British soldiers came to Jackson's house (clearly by then he was on the list of 'usual suspects') and there found James Roderick Shane McDowell, a UDR man, who was later linked to the Miami shootings by his strong prescription spectacles, fragments of which had been found at the scene.

On 18 May 1976, police found a Luger weapon on Ted Sinclair's farm, close to where Peter and Jenny McKearney had been killed. It had been used in the Miami Showband attack and in the killing of Francie Green in County Monaghan. Jackson's fingerprints were found on its silencer and, while the detective questioning him did not believe his concocted explanation, and he was charged with possessing the silencer (but not the gun), a court cleared him of even this relatively minor charge. His prints on the specially adapted silencer,

---

k   RUC Special Branch.
l   British military intelligence.

said the judge, were insufficient to prove his knowing possession of it.

While the Jackal was again free to go on his way, papers detailing his claim about being tipped-off by two police officers about the fingerprints unaccountably disappeared. No disciplinary action was taken against the two officers.

Jackson's next arrest came in May 1977 during the second, failed, UWC strike. Reliable security sources say he was taken into custody but the reason for this is not known. The outcome is known, however. Nothing came of it.

On 9 October 1979, Jackson was caught red-handed in possession of one of the weapons taken by the UVF from his former UDR armoury six years previously (October 1973). In the car in which Jackson was travelling, police also discovered balaclavas and gloves. Police knew the .38 Enfield revolver had been used to kill Martin McVeigh in 1975. There is no evidence that Jackson was ever questioned about the shooting. His luck held once again.[m]

On 24 April 1980, Jackson was named in court along with loyalist R. J. Kerr for the murder of William Strathearn. RUC officers William McCaughey and John Weir claimed they had only a peripheral role in Strathearn's murder, and that the gunmen had been Jackson and Kerr. McCaughey and Weir (who had driven the car to Strathearn's home) offered to turn Queen's evidence against Jackson and Kerr – but only if charges against them were dropped. The DPP considered this deal to be unacceptable, but said Jackson and Kerr would be questioned later (after the courts had dealt with Weir and McCaughey). This, unaccountably, never happened.

It is believed that Jackson was arrested twice more; once in January 1991, shortly after a fatal shooting of Gervais Lynch in Magheralin (between Moira and Lurgan), and again in October 1993 after two

---

m This is the subject of a current complaint by the McVeigh family to the police ombudsman.

brothers were attacked south of Lurgan.[n] In neither case was he charged. Five years later, in June 1998, having watched as power-sharing was established by the Good Friday Agreement, Jackson was dead from lung cancer, aged forty-nine. His luck had finally run out.

On 4 June 1998, speaking within days of 'the Jackal's' death, Colin Wallace (who had known as far back as June 1974, twenty-four years previously, that Jackson was under the wing of the RUC Special Branch) gave him a eulogy of sorts:

> Everything people have whispered about Robin Jackson for years was perfectly true. He was a hired gun. A professional assassin. He was responsible for more deaths in the North than any other person I knew. The Jackal killed people for a living. The state not only knew he was doing it, its servants encouraged him to kill its political opponents and protected him.[23]

One of Jackson's close loyalist associates was Wesley Somerville, born in 1940, from Moygashel outside Dungannon, County Tyrone. The Moygashel unit of the UVF was particularly active throughout the 1970s. It is believed to have carried out the following attacks in which ten people and one unborn baby girl died: Patrick Campbell, (October 1973); Boyle's Bar, Cappagh (one dead, January 1974); the killings of James and Gertrude Devlin (May 1974); Patrick Falls (November 1974); the killings at Hayden's (two dead, February 1975); and the bombing at Killyliss (four dead, April 1975).

Described as a 'lieutenant' in the UVF newsletter, *Combat*, Wesley's career came to a bloody end at the scene of the Miami Showband shootings. He was certainly well known to the police by then, though. He, like Jackson, had also led a charmed life. The one time he faced

---

n   Rory (aged eighteen) and Gerard (aged twenty-two) Cairns were killed when gunmen broke in and shot them in front of their sister, Róisín, who was celebrating her eleventh birthday.

charges was after two bread-deliverymen were abducted and their van used to ferry a bomb to Mourne Crescent in Coalisland on 5 March 1974. The van-bomb exploded, seriously injuring three people and causing major damage to property. Somerville was arrested and charged, along with his brother John, but was acquitted.[24]

John Somerville was another a loyalist of some note. Later convicted for his role in the Miami Showband killings and the murder of Patrick Falls, he had earlier been charged alongside his brother for the bread-van bombing – and like Wesley appears not to have received a jail sentence. John was convicted of bombing Devlin's Bar, Dungannon, in April 1973 and of hijacking a CIÉ bus at Aughnacloy two months later, alongside William Thomas Leonard, a UDR man later convicted of murdering James and Gertrude Devlin. Leonard also admitted to being involved in hijacking the bread van that was blown up. John Somerville has since found God.

When Leonard was brought to court charged with murdering James and Gertrude Devlin, a statement he had made to police was read out in court. In it, Leonard says that Wesley Somerville had ordered him to drive the car carrying the gunmen on the night the couple were shot dead.

The Miami Showband ballistic evidence establishes links between the UVF unit at Moygashel led by Wesley Somerville and Robin Jackson, the UVF's most prolific killer in Counties Armagh and Down. Add up the number of people killed by the Moygashel unit and others murdered with the guns used in the Miami Showband attack and the total is twenty-three people.[o]

Wesley Somerville's status as a 'godfather' is underscored by testimony given that one of his UVF duties was to swear in recruits, one of whom was Stuart Ashton, convicted of twenty-eight offences. These included the attempted murder of Marian Rafferty and Thomas

---

o   See the figure on page 107 showing the Miami Showband weapons links.

Mitchell in November 1974, the attempted murder of shopkeeper Paul McNeice in March 1975, the Traynor's Bar bombing in which Patrick Molloy and Jack Wylie died, and explosions too numerous to list here. Jointly charged with Ashton in relation to an attempted bombing of a house in Moy in 1975 was Samuel McCartney, who joined 2 UDR in 1977 and pleaded guilty to possession of explosives in 1981.

Along with Ashton, also convicted of attempting to murder Marian Rafferty and Thomas Mitchell was Derek McFarland.[25] He is unique among the gang of killers listed here because he was a member of not one or two, but three different units of the security forces in Northern Ireland. He was a constable in the RUC from May 1969 to October 1970; was employed as a Ministry of Defence police constable at Castledillon British military base from 9 July 1972 to 24 October 1975;[p] and was in the UDR from November 1975 to 1977, when he was dismissed (for reasons unknown).

Among those named by Ashton during interviews with police was Ted Sinclair. As we have seen, Sinclair was arrested in connection with the bombing at Traynor's Bar, but released without charge. During the three years he spent in jail (after the gun used to shoot dead Peter and Jenny McKearney was found in his bedroom) there was a remarkable reduction in the number and frequency of attacks against Catholics in the area. This could have been entirely coincidental, of course, but it seems unlikely.

In 1980 Sinclair was again arrested and charged with murdering the McKearneys. On the direction of the DPP, however, who considered there was insufficient evidence to sustain a trial, he was released again.[q] Though Sinclair escaped conviction for murdering

---

p   Castledillon, the home of Four Field Survey Troop, was a key base for covert forces working in the County Armagh area in the 1970s. Captain Robert Nairac, for example, was based at Castledillon.

q   See Chapter 10: Britannia Waives the Rules for more details of the DPP's decision.

the McKearneys, bread-deliveryman Garnet James Busby was not so fortunate. Busby was also convicted of bombing the Hillcrest Bar in March 1976 (when four people were killed).

The gun used in the McKearney killings was also used to kill Denis Mullen in 1975. Two men were convicted: William Parr and Garfield Beattie, the latter a member of the TAVR. Beattie was also convicted of the shooting at the Eagle Bar, Charlemont, in May 1976 (killing Fred McLoughlin and seriously wounding several others) and the murder of Patsy McNeice in July of the same year. He led the RUC to three arms caches.

David Henry Dalziel Kane, a former UDR man, was convicted alongside Beattie of the attack on the Eagle. When RUC Reservist Joey Lutton admitted his role in the shooting at the Eagle, he implicated both Kane and Beattie in the simultaneous attack on the bar next door, Clancy's. Inexplicably, neither Beattie nor Kane was re-arraigned for that attack, in which three people died (Seán O'Hagan, Robert McCullough and Vincy Clancy). Kane had been discharged from the UDR for the negligent discharge of a weapon.

Joey Lutton was a member of the RUC Reserve convicted for his involvement in the bombing at Clancy's Bar and the shooting the same night at the Eagle Bar in the same village. Ted Sinclair also told police that he saw Lutton carrying a gun across his land shortly after he heard gunfire on the night Denis Mullen was shot dead (1 September 1975). Lutton was never questioned about Mullen's murder.

William Corrigan, a former member of the UDR, was also involved in murdering Denis Mullen. He had been spotted by Denis' wife, Olive, a week before the attack, in disguise, scouting the house.

This sequence of shootings and bombings centres on Moygashel and Ted Sinclair's farm, but it stretches as far as Portadown, ten miles (16 km) away. On the night that the McKearneys were shot dead, a known loyalist, Sammy McCoo, was stopped in a car there but allowed to go. The crimes for which he is suspected include the attack on Donnelly's Bar in South Armagh, where three people were killed (Trevor Brecknell, Michael Donnelly and Patsy Donnelly).[26] McCoo was also convicted of robbing Richhill post office, County Armagh, on 11 November 1976, when a .765 Sauer pistol was recovered. The same gun had been used to rob Scarva post office and was also used to attack the Miami Showband and in an attempted murder in Rathfriland, County Down.

Another suspect, alongside McCoo, in the Donnelly's Bar attack was one Philip 'Shilly' Silcock, also of Portadown. He was named as being involved by one of the police officers arrested. Barron also notes that there is information that suggests he may have been involved in the double killing of Seán Farmer and Colm McCartney.[27] Silcock was arrested on numerous occasions throughout the Troubles, on arms, explosives and other charges. He was charged with the attempted murder of Paschal Mulholland in February 1984 (along with R. J. Kerr and Ernest McCreanor, the only one convicted). In 1981, Silcock was convicted, along with Robin Jackson and Robert Joseph Thompson, for possession of the gun that had been used to kill Martin McVeigh on 3 April 1975, which had been stolen in October 1973 from Jackson's UDR unit.

Another prominent Portadown loyalist was Billy Hanna. With a fascination for guns, Hanna joined the Royal Irish Fusiliers as a teenager and served as a lance corporal in Korea. Back in Portadown, Hanna joined the Territorial Army and B Specials.[28] On the disbandment of the latter, he joined the UDR and was promoted to sergeant and weapons instructor at Gough Barracks in Armagh.[29] In 1973 he was charged with the possession of bomb-making material and was dismissed from the UDR, but his involvement with the UVF is believed to long pre-date this. In his report to the Oireachtas, Judge Barron noted an RUC report that stated Hanna had not served in the UDR and there was nothing to link him to RUC Reservist James Mitchell's farm at Glenanne. Both of these RUC statements, however, are untrue. Hanna was the first person to have asked Mitchell to store weapons and explosives on his farm according to RUC Special Branch notes on interviews with Mitchell, supplied to Barron.[30] John Weir claims that Hanna was the main organiser of the Dublin/Monaghan bombings. Colin Wallace also named Hanna to the Barron Report as having led the Dublin/Monaghan bombings, along with Jackson.[31]

Former British military intelligence officer, Fred Holroyd, writes in his notebooks that Hanna, whom he was watching, 'gave instructions in bomb-making on Monday nights'.[32] He joins Wallace in citing Hanna's role in the Dublin/Monaghan bombings. Hanna was shot dead on 27 July 1975, allegedly by Robin Jackson and Harris Boyle, after a loyalist internal power battle just before the Miami Showband killings. The Webley revolver used was recovered by the RUC after McCoo's armed robbery at Scarva post office, along with the Sauer pistol used in the Miami Showband killings.

Harris Boyle first came to public attention in September 1972 when he was arrested with fellow loyalists R. J. Kerr and William Ashton Wright, a member of 11 UDR, and was charged with having firearms and ammunition in suspicious circumstances. He was named by 'Hid-

den Hand' as a suspect for the Dublin/Monaghan bombings, and his name occurs in several of Fred Holroyd's notebooks. He was killed when the bomb he was loading into the back of the Miami Showband's minibus exploded prematurely on 31 July 1975, also killing Wesley Somerville. He was named as a 'Major' in the UVF in its *Combat* newsletter, which also carried a sympathy notice from the UDR in Portadown.

Harris Boyle

The three Young brothers were active loyalists for decades. The eldest, Ivor Dean Knox Young, served with the Royal Ulster Rifles in Cyprus. He was arrested in September 1972 for robbing a post office in Portadown. Around the same time, he faced a charge of attempting to murder another man at a UDA recruitment 'open night' in

Portadown.[33] In January 1973, he faced a charge of robbing a post office van. Appearing before Armagh County Court, Young was described as a former British Army corporal who had become a colonel in the UDA. Young then told the jury that he was 'the commander of the UDA' in the area. On leaving court, he was re-arrested by police and became the first UDA man from the Portadown area to be interned.[34]

In January 1976, the RUC chief constable wrote to then Assistant Garda Commissioner Larry Wren, and implicated Ivor Young and his brother Stewart in the December 1975 bombing of Kay's Tavern.[35] Stewart Young, who also served with the Royal Ulster Rifles in Cyprus, is listed as a garda suspect in the Barron Report for the Monaghan bombing of May 1974. He was described as Officer Commanding the Portadown UVF in a memo from a garda detective to his superintendent colleague in Monaghan in 1974.[36] Stewart is also named in the Barron Report as one of ten men who took arms/explosives to James Mitchell's farm at Glenanne.[37]

Stewart Young
© *BBC*

Nelson Young, the youngest of the three brothers, is also listed in a garda investigation file about the Monaghan bombing. Two girls picked him out independently as a man they saw emerging from public toilets opposite Greacen's Bar in Monaghan where the bomb later exploded.[38] He was also picked out from photographs by seven eyewitnesses after the Kay's Tavern bombing on 19 December 1975.[39] Seven people died in the Monaghan bombing and two died at Kay's. Nelson was never brought before a court.

Now we come to the police officers who were variously charged with involvement in the gun-and-bomb attack on the Rock Bar (June 1976) and in the abduction of Fr Hugh Murphy (June 1978).[r]

---

r   For a full list of all the RUC men and UDR soldiers whom we can name publicly, see Appendix.

William McCaughey was an RUC man at the time he was involved in both attacks, and in the killing of William Strathearn.

Laurence McClure was an RUC man at the time of the attack on the Rock Bar. He also admitted involvement in the attack on Donnelly's Bar, Silverbridge, in December 1975. Ian Mitchell was also an RUC man at the time of his involvement in the assault on the Rock Bar, and went directly from there to work a shift at Keady police station, taking at least one witness statement relating to the attack in which he had been involved.

Laurence McClure
© BBC

Gary Armstrong was an RUC sergeant at the time he kidnapped Fr Hugh Murphy. He was not charged with any offence in relation to the Rock Bar attack. David Wilson was an RUC man at the time he knew of plans to attack the Rock Bar. He was only charged with failing to disclose information. The guns used in the Rock Bar attack were used in a string of other killings and attempted murders at around the same time.[s]

Gary Armstrong
© BBC

John Weir was an RUC sergeant at the time of his involvement in Strathearn's murder. He was also directly involved in planning a bomb attack on a bar in County Monaghan. After that bombing was aborted, the same device was used in the bombing of the Step Inn, in which two people died.

As for the UDR, Robert McConnell, a serving member of that regiment at the time of the murders of Seán Farmer and Colm McCartney, fell under suspicion for their murders after he was

---

s   The same guns were used to kill the three Reavey brothers, and Seán Farmer and Colm McCartney. Guns used in those attacks were also used to kill Denis Mullen, Peter and Jenny McKearney, at Donnelly's Bar, at the Eagle and Clancy's Bars, and Patsy McNeice: a total of sixteen killings.

killed by the IRA.[40] He was also involved in the attack on Donnelly's Bar,[41] and named in the YTV documentary 'Hidden Hand' as having been involved in the Dublin and Monaghan bombings. He is also believed to have been one of the gunmen who shot the three Reavey brothers dead.

Robert McConnell

There are two men whose farmhouses are critical to the murders recounted here. The two farms were places where conspirators met and plotted shootings and bombings, where they stored guns, explosives and bombs, and which served as safe meeting places for loyalists and members of both the RUC and UDR. One of the houses is tucked into a hillside in South Armagh. It belonged to one-time RUC Reservist James Mitchell. The other belonged to Edward (Ted) Sinclair. Neither man was ever convicted of murder and neither ever served a significant prison sentence. The longest sentence either was given in the courts was Sinclair's six years for the possession of guns (he was freed after three years). Mitchell was sentenced to one year, suspended for two years, when guns and bomb-making equipment were found on his land in 1978. Both could be described as 'godfather' types: men who directed and controlled rather than pulling the trigger or lighting the fuse themselves. Their victims were ordinary men, women and children whose names the two probably never knew before condemning them to an early death.

Of the two men, Mitchell is the better known. Towards the end of his life, the occasional reporter would turn up on his doorstep – only to be turned away roughly with a 'No comment'. His farmhouse is a nondescript pebble-dashed building, but its walls could tell many an ugly tale. Mitchell was an RUC Reservist from September 1974 to June 1977, during the time that his farm was used extensively by loyalists. Among the attacks that are known to have been planned and carried out from his home were the Dublin and Monaghan bombings (34 dead), Donnelly's Bar (three dead), the Reavey brothers (three

James Mitchell
© BBC

dead), the Step Inn (two dead), Seán Farmer and Colm McCartney (two dead), McArdle's Bar (one dead) and the Miami Showband (three dead). The list could be much longer, but the deaths listed here alone total forty-eight.

Ted Sinclair is a more mysterious character. His family were settlers who obtained land in 1642 in the Kinneary area (now known as Canary) near Moy, County Tyrone, and who were also involved in the linen industry. Born in 1936, Ted Sinclair married and had three sons. He died in 1985. He managed to keep a low profile throughout his career, though his name still evokes contempt when mentioned to older Catholics in Moy, Dungannon, Armagh and Portadown. The attacks mounted from his farm include Traynor's Bar (two dead), Peter and Jenny McKearney (two dead), the Hillcrest Bar (four dead), Denis Mullen, the Eagle and Clancy's Bars (four dead) and Killyliss (four dead). There are likely to be others of which we do not yet know, but that alone is a total of seventeen.

Both Mitchell and Sinclair were named repeatedly in admissions to police. Questions must be asked about how they escaped jail sentences on so many occasions despite the RUC knowing the serious and lethal activities being carried out, year after year, on their farms. Whatever the reasons for the two men's striking good fortune, they have taken their secrets to their graves.

From Dhofar to Armagh

The British have succeeded in counter-insurgency where others have failed because history has given them the kind of military establishment and colonial administrative experience necessary to defeat revolutionary movements.

Thomas Mockaitis[1]

What are states without justice but robber bands enlarged?

St Augustine: The City of God[2]

As the sun finally started to set over the British Empire, and London began the slow and bloody process of disengaging from its colonies, a recurring military strategy emerged: recruiting locals to conduct the more unsavoury operations. It may have started in Ireland.

In the Irish War of Independence that followed the 1916 Easter Rising, and to good effect, the British authorities based in Dublin Castle liberally deployed Irish-born spies and surrogates against the IRA. This is unlikely to have caused much soul-searching in London. Ireland had, after all, struck a first blow against the British Empire, demonstrating 'even to the most unimaginative English mind that the deepest Irish loyalties were altogether alien to their own. Irish patriotism might be nonsense, was certainly treasonable, but was evidently true.'[3]

The Irish insurgency 'rankled with the English ... that the most persistent threat to their omnipotence should come from this sister isle, whose people were not even black, brown or yellow, nor even exactly pagan'.[4] Seeking an explanation, British writers tended to decry the Irish rather than examine their own record, as exemplified by Captain Hugh Pollard (1888–1966, a British 'special operations executive' during the Irish War of Independence), who wrote: 'movements which would be abortive failures among the nordic races of Europe achieve success in Ireland, where credulity and fanaticism are still dominant factors in spite of a century of well-meant British endeavour'.[5] (Pollard either overlooked the British reaction to the Great Famine or interpreted it as a 'well-meant' endeavour.)

In true imperial style, the 1916 Rising steeled London's future resolve to deal with unruly subjects by suppressing dissent while forging a veneer of political legitimacy for whatever tactics this might require, including the use of proxies to carry out the less savoury tasks.

London is not alone in its use of surrogates to carry out duties with which it would rather not sully its hands publicly. Throughout history, informers, spies and renegades have been used by sheiks, tzars, rajahs, sultans, emperors and führers (when putting 'The Final Solution' into awful practice, the Nazis set up special units of Jewish concentration camp prisoners, called the *Sonderkommandos*,[6] who were forced to lure fellow Jews into the gas chambers and help to dispose of their bodies).[7]

At the time of writing, the British Army reckons that since the Second World War it has engaged in seventeen rebellions; seven successful,[a] one a draw[b] and five failures[c] (the rest are either ongoing or thought to be unquantifiable).[8] Disengagement with honour may have been the goal, but British strategists at more than a few outposts used distinctly morally questionable means to quell revolts. In Palestine, Britain's first post-war counter-insurgency offensive ended poorly. Between 1945 and 1948 Britain was pitted against an impassioned Zionist underground movement fighting to establish a new state of Israel, as well as pan-Arab nationalist forces. With no allies among the local population and repression a non-runner because of US objections, Britain experienced a 'humiliating defeat'.[9]

---

a   Malaya, Kenya, Brunei, Malaysia, Radfan, Dhofar and Northern Ireland.
b   Cyprus.
c   Palestine, Egypt and Aden (on three occasions).

If Palestine was Britain's first post-war colonial conflict, the Mau Mau rebellion in Kenya was the bloodiest. It was here that Frank Kitson (then a young captain) redefined the concept of surrogacy.[d] As a military intelligence officer in Kenya from 1953 to 1955, he organised 'counter-gangs', as he called them. They consisted of former Mau Mau members, or sympathisers, persuaded to change allegiance and become intelligence-gatherers and later agents provocateurs mounting offensive operations.[e] They were 'captured rebels who were prepared to change sides, pretending to be still loyal to the revolutionary movement in order to make contact with the surviving rebel bands so they could be broken down and eliminated. Kitson believed this to be the most effective way to kill rebels.'[10]

Kitson later wrote in his memoirs, *Bunch of Five*, 'Most soldiers [regarded the] finding and disposing [of Mau Mau] in the same way as they would regard the hunting of a dangerous wild animal.'[11] Still, Kitson complains in *Gangs and Counter-gangs*, British forces 'had firmly fastened one of their hands behind their backs with the cord of legal difficulties'.[12] Oxford University historian David Anderson, in his history of the Kenyan colonial war, says Kitson produced 'remarkable results'.[13] The country, he says, became 'a police state in the fullest sense of that term', while British justice in 1950s Kenya was 'a blunt, brutal and unsophisticated instrument of oppression'.[14] Over 30,000 Mau Mau were killed in combat;[f] 1.5 million of its supporters were interned,[15] captives were routinely tortured[g] – sometimes to

---

d   From 1952 to 1960, the British Army backed white settlers and loyal Kikuyu tribal chieftains in crushing nationalist Kikuyu who were being pushed off their land and deported to reserves.

e   In Kitson, F., *Gangs and Counter-gangs* (1960), he writes that persuading a rebel to join a counter-gang using incentives, threats and persuasion was doing 'nothing dishonourable'.

f   John Newsinger, in *British Counterinsurgency: From Palestine to Northern Ireland* (2002), estimates that 50,000 Kikuyu rebels were killed.

g   Including US President Barack Obama's paternal grandfather, Hussein Onyango Obama, who was arrested in 1949, tortured by having pins inserted under death[16] – and 1,090 Kenyans were hanged on a portable gallows that toured villages and towns.[17]

In contrast, while Kikuyu insurgents certainly committed atrocities, fewer than 200 British soldiers and police and only thirty-two white settlers were killed – nearly the same as were killed in traffic accidents in the Kenyan capital, Nairobi, during the same period.[18] Harvard historian Caroline Elkins says Britain first denied abuses, then, when presented with evidence, blamed the beatings, hangings, torture and forced removals on 'bad apples'.[19] 'Duplicity at its finest,' she calls it, adding that the British held bonfires of official papers[h] as they left in an attempt to cover their tracks.[20] Meanwhile, Kitson was promoted to captain on 15 December 1953,[21] and on 1 January 1955 received the Military Cross 'in recognition of gallant and distinguished services'.[22]

In 1950s Malaya (now Malaysia),[i] Sir Gerald Templer, the British High Commissioner, was so determined to see 'fanatics' of the (mostly ethnic Chinese) Communist Party 'exterminated' that he called in Dayak head-hunters from Borneo to track down and, where necessary, decapitate anti-British rebels.[23] Of the 4,000 Malayan rebels who surrendered or were captured, 2,700 became informers.[24] They were 'known as "Surrendered Enemy Personnel" and were encouraged by generous rewards'.[25] One leading communist, Lai Tek, was revealed to be a British agent. He disappeared just before he was exposed, taking with him most of the Communist Party's funds.[26] Here again, Kitson could be found at the forefront of the action,

---

his fingernails and into his buttocks, and imprisoned for two years (*Daily Mail*, 3 December 2008).

h   Not all were burned. *The Guardian* reported on 18 April 2012 that 8,000 files from thirty-seven colonies, discovered at the Foreign and Commonwealth Office property at Hanslope Park, Buckinghamshire, are being examined by Tony Badger, master of Clare College, Cambridge, as five Kenyans (two of whom were castrated) sue the British government for compensation.

i   Malaya remained a British colony until 1948. It gained its independence from the Commonwealth of Nations in 1957.

where he honed and adapted the techniques learned in Kenya.[j]

The late 1950s also found the British in Cyprus[k] fighting Greek Cypriot demands for Enosis (integration with Greece) and the underground fighters of Ethniki Organosis Kyprion Agoniston (EOKA).[l] Cyprus was strategically imperative to the UK's military capabilities in the Middle East.[27] The British Parachute Regiment's 2nd Battalion 'effectively eliminated the organisation in one area' through the use of agents and 'Q Patrols' to capture both men and guns.[28] Q Patrols evolved when Greek police officers came to be seen as overly sympathetic to EOKA. The British recruited Turkish police officers to serve in the frontline and a separate 'Special Mobile Reserve' unit was created, recruited exclusively from among the Turkish community.[29] Kitson served in Cyprus as second-in-command of 3 Royal Green Jackets between 1962 and 1964.[30] According to Elkins, the Q Patrols worked alongside British snatch squads and interrogation teams, earning themselves the nickname of 'HMTs', or 'Her Majesty's Torturers': 'Like the pseudo-gangs in Kenya,' she says, 'they operated with a free hand in a police state.'[31]

Despite all this, says author and historian John Newsinger, 'The British with overwhelming strength, 40,000 men at one point, signally failed to eradicate a guerrilla force a few hundred strong led by a sixty-year-old man[m] on an island half the size of Wales.'[32]

In the mid-1960s, Britain (in alliance with Saudi Arabia and Jordan) joined royalists trying to quash a republican uprising in North Yemen that coincided with a deadly guerrilla insurgency against the British to the south, in the colony of Aden – the 'cornerstone of British military policy in the Gulf region'.[33] Publicly, the Prime Minister, Sir Alec

---

j   According to the RAND Corporation (1963), an influential US global policy think-tank linking the US military and corporate sectors, Kitson was able 'to apply this [Kenyan] experience in the [Malaya] anti-terrorist campaign'.

k   Cyprus did not gain its independence from the UK until 16 August 1960.

l   National Organisation of Cypriot Fighters.

m   The extreme right-wing EOKA leader, George Grivas.

Douglas-Hume, told parliament on 14 May 1964: 'Our policy towards the Yemen is one of non-intervention in the affairs of that country. It is not therefore our policy to supply arms to the Royalists.'[34] But, in secret documents unearthed by author and historian Mark Curtis, British Defence Minister Peter Thorneycroft privately called for 'tribal revolts' so that the British could initiate 'deniable action … to sabotage [pro-Yemeni Republican] intelligence centres and kill personnel engaged in anti-British activities'.[35] British tactics included arming Yemeni royalist forces against the new republican government, as well as enlisting sympathetic Arabs into Special Branch in 'an integrated repressive apparatus combining police, Army and civil administration along the lines pioneered in Malaya'.[36] The British Army, including the SAS, also deployed small mobile patrols, 'sometimes operating disguised as Arabs', known as 'Special Branch Sections'.[37]

When the South Arabian Federation Army and police mutinied in June 1967, it took the Battle of Crater (also called 'The Last Battle of the British Empire') to restore order – bringing the 1st Battalion Argyll and Sutherland Highlanders and its regimental commander, Lieutenant Colonel Colin Campbell (Mad Mitch) Mitchell, to the fore.[n] The imposition of what Mitchell called 'Argyll Law' (described elsewhere as rule by 'a bunch of Glasgow thugs'[38]) against 'dirty, smelly people'[39] translated in practice to sniper-shooting anyone who looked like a threat. 'It was like shooting grouse,' Mitchell claimed.[40]

Mitchell, who later served in Northern Ireland, once expressed his preference for dealing with the IRA to *Guardian* journalist Terry Coleman:

'I would send round a list of 100 suspects and then just start shooting them; by the time you've knocked off ten of them the rest will be in

---

n   So-called because of his recklessness and bravery under fire. Mitchell also served in Palestine, Korea, Cyprus and Borneo.

Killarney … I'd like to have a machine-gun built into every TV camera
and then say to the IRA, "Come out and let's talk" … and then shoot
the lot.'

'After a trial?' asked Coleman.

'That would be a complete waste of time,' Mitchell replied.[41]

While claims of the use of such tactics by the British Army in Northern Ireland may seem fanciful, more information is now emerging
about the 'shoot-first-ask-questions-later' activities of the Military
Reaction Force in Belfast during the early 1970s.[42]

In January 1981, two soldiers from the Argylls were convicted of
killing two Catholics in County Fermanagh.[43] The convictions led to
the *Glasgow Sunday Mail* on 26 April and 10 May 1981 exposing
how British soldiers were involved in unprovoked killings in Aden.
In the chilling 2004 BBC2 documentary film *Empire Warriors*,
another veteran states that if he told the truth about Aden, 'half the
battalion would be done for murder'.[44] British forces finally withdrew
from Aden – a territory since 1839 – on 30 November 1967, and the
independent People's Republic of South Yemen was declared.

While the British government had no jurisdiction over Oman,
this was the territory in which it fought its last counter-insurgency
campaign before deploying troops to Northern Ireland.° The local
sultan of Muscat and Oman paid British forces to fight left-wing
rebels threatening to overthrow his rule. The sultan, fabulously rich,
exploited his absolute power by lodging oil revenues into Swiss bank
accounts, spending his summers in London hotels and outlawing all
twentieth-century development for his people. Only 5 per cent of
Omanis were literate, there was a 75 per cent infant mortality rate,
no electricity supply until 1971 and 'There were hardly any schools or

---

o   The Dhofar Rebellion was fought from 1962 to 1976. It ended with the defeat
of the rebels, but Oman was radically modernised.

health care and diseases were rampant.'[45] The rebels controlled a fertile plain, which the RAF bombed and the SAS invaded. They were, says writer and professional soldier Phillip Allfree of their arrival in Oman, 'the coolest and most frightening body of professional killers I have ever seen'.[46]

In 1971 the SAS began training 'surrendered enemy personnel' (SEPs) in Dhofar, along similar lines to those that the British Army had employed successfully in Kenya and Malaya. The units of SEPs, or 'firqats'[p] as they became known locally, were 'one of the main factors in winning the war' and their success was regarded as 'a great tribute to the training and professionalism of the SAS'.[47] Eventually, 3,000 firqats fought against their former comrades. Organised along tribal lines, they acted as guides and patrols, lured enemies into ambushes, gathered intelligence and executed covert assassinations. The combined power of air-bombardment and SAS firqat counter-gangs crushed the poorly organised left-wing rebellion.

Frank Kitson, meanwhile, went from strength to strength. By 1958 he held a post in the War Office, having argued successfully for the deployment of the SAS to Oman. The following June he was awarded an MBE.[q] In all these conflicts – especially Kenya, Malaya, Cyprus and Oman – his name crops up repeatedly. He did not invent, and does not claim to have invented, the concept of pseudo-gangs.[r] But he certainly elevated it into an established, if grubby, British military tactic.

---

p   Firqats were defectors from the main rebel group, the Popular Front for the Liberation of the Occupied Arabian Gulf (PFLOAG), who were disillusioned with its socialist secularism.

q   Member of the Most Excellent Order of the British Empire (MBE), a royal award for service to the United Kingdom.

r   Fr Raymond Murray, in *The SAS in Ireland* (Mercier Press, Dublin 1990), wrote: 'He [Kitson] is not to be credited as an innovator. British colonial policy and principles of counter-insurgency go back a long time before him' (p. 41). Fr Murray does, however, concede that Kitson 'researched its workings, updated it and commented intelligently on it'.

In the years since, Kitson has assumed the status of 'bogeyman', cited by a succession of conspiracy theorists as being responsible for many of the plentiful examples of British dirty tricks in every dark or bloody corner of the globe. This tends to obscure his factual record and writings from mainstream scrutiny, which is regrettable, as he indubitably had a malign influence on security policies in Northern Ireland, particularly at the start of the three decades of conflict.[48] Follow his career and a pattern emerges: dispatch Kitson to various parts of the globe to quell anti-colonial forces, then on his return home heap honours on him. He was promoted to brigadier before his deployment to Northern Ireland in spring 1970 as Commander of the 39th Brigade area – the youngest at that rank in the British Army.[s] The year before, the British Army's *Land Operations Volume III – Counter-Revolutionary Operations* (1969) stipulated that one SAS task was 'liaison with, and organisation, training and control of, friendly guerrilla forces operating against the common enemy'.[49] 'Friendly forces' could only, in the Irish context, mean loyalist paramilitaries.

'Colonel Kitson developed and perfected a novel approach and technique for the collection and utilisation of the special kind of intelligence that is indispensable in guerrilla warfare,'[50] noted the RAND Corporation.[t] In *Low Intensity Operations*, Kitson himself has defined counter-insurgency as 'military, paramilitary, political, economic, psychological and civic actions taken by a government to defeat subversion and insurgency'.[51]

Kitson left Northern Ireland in October 1971 but returned in April 1972, three months after Bloody Sunday.[u] Details of his second

---

s   From August 1969, the 39th Brigade of the British Army took responsibility for Belfast and the eastern side of Northern Ireland, excluding South Armagh. From September 1970 it was commanded by (then) Brigadier Kitson.

t   This US global policy think-tank was formed during the Second World War and played an important role in developing Cold War strategy.

u   Bloody Sunday was 30 January 1972, when fourteen civil rights protesters were shot dead by soldiers of the Parachute Regiment.

tour of duty remain elusive, but his standing in London apparently rose, as he was awarded a CBE.[v] Among the military tactics that Kitson entertained, but ultimately dismissed, was the option of using defoliating chemicals to force insurgents out into the open, as US forces had done in Vietnam. Such methods, he wrote in *Low Intensity Operations*, would have 'a greater adverse effect on world and domestic opinion in relation to the advantages gained'. Dropping Agent Orange defoliants onto South Armagh might have been a step too far for Kitson, but he was a keen advocate of the use of 'special forces'who can 'operate in a more unobtrusive way than regular troops' – an important factor 'if the insurgents were trying to exploit world opinion against their government'.[52]

The use of surrogate or proxy forces is invaluable, wrote Kitson: 'there are innumerable ways in which the principle [of counter-gangs] can be applied and it is up to those involved to invent or adapt such methods … as may be relevant to the situation.'[53]

Kitson also saw the importance of propaganda. As historian Bernard Porter[w] noted, 'Between 1970 and 1972 Kitson … may have been largely responsible for the setting up and development of "Psyops" units [in Northern Ireland].'[54] Kitson also turned his mind to the law, which, he wrote, could be 'used as just another weapon in the government's arsenal, and in this case it becomes little more than a propaganda cover for the disposal of unwanted members of the public … For this to happen efficiently, the activities of the legal services[x] have to be tied into the war effort in as discreet a way as possible, which in effect means that the member of the government responsible

---

v   Commander of the Most Excellent Order of the British Empire (CBE), a royal award for service to the United Kingdom.

w   Professor Bernard Porter of Newcastle University is the author of *Critics of Empire: British Radicals and the Imperial Challenge*. (2008) and *The Absent-Minded Imperialists: Empire, Society and Culture in Britain* (2006).

x   Note here the term 'legal services', which could include not only the courts but also the office of the DPP.

for law either sits in the supreme council or takes his orders from the head of the administration.'[55] Though Kitson repeatedly speaks of the importance of upholding the rule of law impartially, this is conditional, Porter says, on new 'tough' legislation being introduced as and when needed.[56] Even this, says Kitson, though morally preferable, might prove 'unworkable' as it can be 'politically impossible' to introduce new laws speedily enough.[57]

Kitson's concept of discreetly modifying the law to suit military aims is exemplified in a letter dated 17 January 1974 from Lieutenant General Sir Frank King (then GOC in Northern Ireland) to General Sir Cecil Blacker (Adjutant-General) addressing concerns that Blacker had raised on the possible prosecutions of soldiers. 'He [the then Attorney General, Sir Peter Rawlinson] assured me in the plainest terms' wrote King:

> … that not only he himself but also the DPP and senior members of his staff, having been army officers themselves, having seen active service and knowing at first hand the difficulties and dangers faced by soldiers, were by no means unsympathetic or lacking in understanding in their approach to soldier prosecutions in Northern Ireland. Rather the reverse, since directions not to prosecute had been given in more than a few cases where the evidence, to say the least had been borderline.[58]

From early on in the Northern Ireland conflict, senior security appointees were frequently the veterans of previous British colonial conflicts. The first police officer to hold the title of Chief Constable of the RUC (formerly, 'inspector general') was Sir Arthur Young (1969–70), who had previously served in both Kenya and Malaya,[59] where he had commanded a 500-strong counter-insurgency unit.[60] Other British counter-insurgency officers dispatched to Northern Ireland with hard-won experience in previous colonial wars included

Sir Timothy Creasey, GOC of the British Army in Northern Ireland (1977–9), who had fought the Mau Mau in Kenya, the IRA border campaign in 1956, and in both Aden and Oman, where he had made full use of firqats.[61] So Frank Kitson was not philosophically isolated during his years in Belfast – a time when both the UDA and the UVF were expanding exponentially and ripe for exploitation.

As defined by Bruce Campbell and Arthur Brenner in *Death Squads in Global Perspective*, paramilitary groups can interpret their existence as one primarily loyal to the state, 'operating with the overt support, complicity or acquiescence of government'.[62] If you were a loyalist and believed – as most did – that the link with Britain required robust defence to defeat republican political objectives, you had the first option of enlisting in state forces dedicated to that aim (the RUC or the British Army). If, however, your application was rejected, or should you regard the state's forces to be ineffective against the threat, there was an alternative option: loyalist paramilitary groups. On one key point, state and loyalist forces were united: their mutual enemy was republican insurgency – the Provisional IRA.[63]

Kitson had theoretical back-up. In *Bunch of Five* he wrote of how, in Malaya,[y] he had discussed his counter-insurgency theories with Lieutenant Colonel (later Major General) Richard Clutterbuck:[z] 'one of my instructors at the Staff College ... [and] one of the seminal counter-insurgency theorists of the 1960s and early 1970s'.[64] Clutterbuck was for thirty-five years a professional soldier, serving in thirteen post-war colonial conflicts before becoming an academic and writer.[aa]

---

y   Kitson had wanted to write about his experiences in Northern Ireland 'but at the time of first publication that was too sensitive' (see http://www.faber.co.uk/catalog/bunch-of-five/9780571271351; accessed 23 January 2013).

z   Major General Richard Clutterbuck (1917–98) was chief army instructor at the Royal College of Defence Studies (1971–2), having served in the Second World War (France, Italy, Sudan, Ethiopia, Western Desert), Palestine (1947), China (1957) and the Far East (1956–8). He wrote in *Kidnap and Ransom* (1978, p. 181): 'History has shown that terrorism can be and has been eliminated by a ruthless response.'

aa   For a list of just some of Clutterbuck's works, see the bibliography.

His standing became such that in 1981 the SAS commissioned him to analyse 'their likely tasks in the coming five or ten years'.[65] He also taught politics at Exeter University and served on the Advisory Council of the St Andrews Centre for the Study of Terrorism and Political Violence from its inception in 1994 until his death in 1998.[66] Unlike Kitson,[67] however – who may now regret his relative transparency in some of these matters – Clutterbuck rarely indulged in similar indiscretions.[ab] As late as April 1981, the Foreign and Commonwealth Office was recommending Clutterbuck as an expert speaker to the US organisers of an international conference on terrorism.[68]

A third military strategist with experience in Ireland was Robin Evelegh, who served in Cyprus during the late 1960s.[ac] After service in Northern Ireland he wrote *Peace-Keeping in a Democratic Society: The Lessons of Northern Ireland*, which influenced later security operations.[69] In his book, Evelegh bemoaned 'shortcomings in the laws governing the operation of the Security Forces [in Northern Ireland] to suppress terrorism and disorder' which – if only they could be corrected – could 'succeed in ending these horrors'.[70] Echoing Kitson, he thought such limitations necessitated civil, policing and military powers being united to 'weld all the efforts of the Government into a machine directed at one end, the defeat of the insurrection' – a call, in effect, for martial law.[71] Evelegh supported Kitson's lead on turning paramilitaries into allies who 'have to be consciously created' and then indemnified with immunity 'for the crimes he will have to commit'.[72] On agents provocateurs infiltrating enemy ranks, Evelegh says openly

---

ab Clutterbuck was also a member of the Institute for the Study of Conflict until the end of 1997.

ac Colonel Robin Evelegh, 1932–2010, served in Penang, Brunei, Borneo, Indonesia, Cyprus and Belfast, where he commanded the 3rd Battalion, The Royal Green Jackets in 1972 and in 1973–4. He retired in 1977. With two other ex-officers from the Royal Green Jackets, Evelegh set up 'Ridgeway International' specialising in the international transport and shipping of explosives and ammunition. He was also a member of the Conservative Party in Oxford.

that the agent should 'clearly play his part in terrorist activity which will almost inevitably involve him in committing further crimes'.[73] He quotes Lord Widgery[ad] in a 1974 High Court appeal as also acknowledging this fact.[74]

Robin Ramsey, author and joint founder of the British intelligence watchdog publication, *Lobster,* describes Evelegh's proposals as even more draconian than Kitson's, and suggests that Evelegh's book is 'a long wistful look at the powers available in previous *real* colonial wars *not* available in Northern Ireland'.[75]

Kitson, Clutterbuck and Evelegh were just three members of the British military/security/political establishment grappling with the challenges of defeating insurgent forces in colonial conflicts – including Ireland. Their printed works mirrored private debates in the early and mid-1970s as military commanders, politicians and police twisted and turned to think of new ways to defeat the IRA and reduce its support base. Their counter-terrorist theories are still taught to aspiring British officers before they embark on tours of duty to Iraq, Afghanistan and elsewhere.[76] The British Conservative MP and 'defence expert', Patrick Mercer, who followed his father into the Sherwood Foresters (Nottinghamshire and Derbyshire Regiment) and served in Northern Ireland (completing nine tours between 1979 and 1992) and Bosnia, states that at the British Army military college at Sandhurst, a 'generation of young officers that was being prepared for the Troubles was drilled and schooled in the idea that counter-insurgency warfare was never won by force of arms alone'.[77]

British counter-insurgency tactics moved seamlessly from the Far East and Africa to Northern Ireland. In declining Margaret Thatcher's request in September 1979, for example, to become overall 'Security Co-ordinator' in Northern Ireland (a role subsequently accepted by

ad Lord Widgery conducted the first, now-discredited, Bloody Sunday Enquiry into the events of January 1972.

Sir Maurice Oldfield), a senior civil servant cited the 'real difficulty' he felt he would have in putting into practice 'the kind of thing we had to do in Malaya under Sir Robert Thompson'.[78] Meanwhile, the rules governing the 'deep interrogation' of suspects in Northern Ireland were governed by experience in 'many previous internal security situations' and in 'the light of experience gained since the last [Second World] war', which were further revised in 1967 after British experiences in Aden.[79] Collusion, likewise, between state forces, the British Army and locally recruited paramilitaries, was not unthinkable in past and partly parallel colonial-style conflicts. Why should it be different in Ireland – other than the added imperative for secrecy because of its geographical location? While proximity to the 'mother country' has led to little academic scrutiny, the police have not been entirely immune. In *State Crime: Governments, Violence and Corruption*, authors Penny Green and Tony Ward conclude that there was a 'substantial overlap between the membership of the UDA and the part-time Ulster Defence Regiment'.[80] UDR soldiers, they say, 'moonlighted' as paramilitaries.[81] The UDA and UVF similarly easily infiltrated the UDR, whose 'willingness to allow dual membership of the regiment and the UDA clearly facilitated the UDA's murderous activities'.[82]

US academic Jeffrey Sluka[ae] wrote *Death Squad: Anthropology of State Terror*, having lived in Belfast periodically between 1981 and 1996, and pulls no punches, accusing London of ignoring and misrepresenting the nature of loyalist violence.[83] He claims that British authorities 'insist that they have nothing to do with … individual acts by rogue soldiers and policemen' which are 'not a reflection of government policy or military strategy'. Sluka goes on to say that this is 'Lies. All lies.'[84]

---

ae Sluka is currently an associate professor in the Anthropology Department of Massey University, New Zealand.

The debate over the legitimacy of using surrogate forces in conflicts around the globe is far from over. Terrorism was always news, but the World Trade Center attack in New York on 11 September 2001 pushed the debate on how to combat terrorism far higher up the political agenda. Few academics with first-hand experience of the interaction between conflict and the state have offered any analysis. But there are exceptions. In 2005 Professor Bill Rolston published 'An Effective Mask for Terror: Democracy, Death Squads and Northern Ireland', pointing to the relative absence of any international academic work on collusion as a 'missed opportunity to understand Northern Ireland's dirty war', threatening 'to perpetuate the fallacy that real death squads only occur in non-democratic societies'.[85] He adds that both the UDA and UVF in the early 1970s, when 'both engaged in terror for pro-state ends', viewed their respective violence as 'taking the war to republican insurgents'.[86]

Another key paper based on the Northern Ireland experience was 'State Crime by Proxy and Juridical Othering', by Ruth Jamieson and Kieran McEvoy.[87] A long-standing strategy for state evasion of responsibility for actions carried out in pursuance of its 'organisational goals', the authors say, 'is for state agencies to put distance between themselves and actors responsible for conducting illegal activities on their behalf. States routinely develop spoken and unspoken arrangements for concerted and deliberate ignorance concerning such actions as part of broader strategies of denial.'[88] Evasion strategies might include (a) 'resort to perfidy'; (b) the expanded use of specialist forces; (c) collusion with indigenous paramilitaries; or (d) use of private-sector mercenaries.[89] Each of these tactics can blur the relationships between the state and perpetrators of illegal, violent acts, but points (a) and (c) are the most relevant here. Jamieson and McEvoy propose that the most corrosive legal outcome occurs when 'prosecutors and indeed the judiciary may become tainted by fairly naked efforts to prevent state collusion being unearthed in open court'.[af] And if states use native paramilitaries or surrogates, argue the authors, they render 'the task of identifying and prosecuting the planners and perpetrators of violations particularly difficult'.[90] Most pointedly, Jamieson and McEvoy state that the 'key tactical advantage' of surrogates is 'Terror is fought with terror'.[91] Thus, 'innovative sadism' – terrorising the target community while making any link appear unlikely to onlookers – assists the state in denying responsibility.

Just as the use of surrogate killers by governments intent on covering their tracks pre-dates the modern Irish conflict, so it continues into the decades beyond. The US-backed and US-funded Nicaraguan Contras, who fought the Sandanista government, have been described as a 'proxy army'.[92] The Contras killed an estimated 29,000 people by 1989 (half of them civilians), and the US government's actions were ruled illegal by the International Court of Justice in June 1986.

During the twelve-year-long civil war in El Salvador between the US-backed government and left-wing Farabundo Marti National Liberation Front (FMLN) guerrillas, an estimated 75,000 people lost their lives to death squads. Since 2010 the tortured corpses of an estimated 300 Baloch insurgents in Pakistan have been flung on roadsides, 'victims of a "kill and dump" policy run by the Frontiers Corps (FC), a paramilitary force that works with the Inter-Services Intelligence (ISI) spy agency.'[93] And the Spanish government has employed permutations of the surrogate concept against ETA (Euskadi Ta Askatasuna) Basque separatist paramilitaries – though not the identical tactics of Kitson's pseudo-gangs in Northern Ireland.[ag]

---

af   This is precisely what occurred in the Rock Bar trial; see Chapter 11: Ridding the Land of Pestilence.

ag   The Grupos Antiterroristas de Liberación (GAL) murdered twenty-five people between 1983 and 1987, including a journalist and a paediatrician. An estimated third of the victims had no connection with ETA.

In 2008 the RAND Corporation published *Rethinking Counter-insurgency*, a work that drew heavily on British lessons first learned in Malaya and then in North Borneo, Oman and Northern Ireland.[94] Its authors concluded that, while the British experience in Malaya 'did not change the course of history', it provided Britain with a *modus operandi* for subsequent campaigns, emphasising the importance of separating the insurgents from their indigenous supporters.

John Arquilla, a professor of defence analysis at the US Naval Postgraduate School in Monterey, California, has urged the US to examine carefully British imperial counter-insurgency efforts in 1950s Kenya. This experience, Arquilla argued, could teach the US how to fight insurgents in Iraq and deal with global terrorism.[95]

There is also an alternative viewpoint. In 2005 Caroline Elkins, author of *Britain's Gulag: The Brutal End of Empire in Kenya*, wrote in *Atlantic Magazine* that Kitson's pseudo-gangs could not have succeeded in Kenya, Northern Ireland or anywhere else without the use of 'severe and overarching measures' which she characterises as 'police-state control'.[96] Such tactics set up a framework for future instability, breaches in human rights, communal divisions, violence and repression.[97]

One of the documents unearthed by the PFC at the National Archives in Kew, London, gives details of the official deployment of the SAS into South Armagh (after the murders of the O'Dowds, the Reavey brothers and the Kingsmill massacre). The eighty-five SAS men came to the fields around Crossmaglen and Newtownhamilton directly from the mountains and deserts of Dhofar. No one can, of course, draw a direct parallel between the SAS fighting alongside the Dhofari firqats and the SAS fighting alongside the UDR, but in both theatres of conflict there were similar aims – the defeat of local insurgents. The SAS and the UDR in South Armagh shared Bessbrook barracks and the SAS routinely patrolled alongside regular units of the British Army and the UDR.[98] In London's view, SAS 'knowledge of counter-insurgency operations' made them 'an ideal choice' for deployment in South Armagh.[99]

The use of surrogate or proxy forces against insurgents, then, is now an established practice in counter-insurgency operations. The main difference in Northern Ireland was its proximity to Britain, and the consequent requirement for 'maximum plausible deniability' – as well as a limit on the numbers of people who could safely be killed to hundreds rather than thousands.[100] The imperative for secrecy was paramount – a special unit was set up in Britain to destroy the trail of evidence leading to those responsible for outrages in Kenya: 'Thousands of documents detailing some of the most shameful acts committed during the final years of the British empire were systematically destroyed'.[101]

The Second World War was possibly the last war where two armies faced each other across a 'no man's land' on the field of battle. Collusion has become, and will continue to be, an ever more central strategy of warfare. Pitched battles have been, if not replaced, joined by a battle for hearts and minds.[ah] Wars in the twenty-first century will not be fought on battlefields – but street-by-street, village-by-village in the hearts of men and women. Pitted against these 'special forces', and the powerful governments and agencies who deploy them, are a handful of poorly funded investigative journalists, human rights activists such as Amnesty International and Human Rights Watch, and the families of their victims. Their only recourse is to the long, lonely and expensive process of taking cases to international courts and to the court of public opinion.

Governments that declare themselves to respect the rules of

---

ah US President Lyndon B. Johnson said of the war in Vietnam: 'the ultimate victory will depend on the hearts and minds of the people who actually live out there'. 'Hearts and minds' then became known as 'WHAM' (Win Hearts And Minds): US policy to win over the Vietnamese people. The phrase is believed to be based on a quote by John Adams, second President of the USA, who wrote in a letter dated 13 February 1818: 'The Revolution was in the minds and hearts of the people.'

international law, such as the British government, and yet covertly allow their servants and agents to employ some very dirty tricks, are forced to twist and turn, and above all use delaying tactics, to avoid admitting the truth. This is exemplified by the continuing dispute between the British government and the family of a murdered Belfast solicitor, Pat Finucane. In October 2011 – rather than provide the full, independent, public enquiry the previous Labour government promised – the British coalition government ordered a mere review of the Finucane case papers. When the man chosen for this task, Sir Desmond de Silva, QC, reported in December 2012, he singularly failed to allay public concerns, quoting the security service (i.e. MI5) conclusion that 85 per cent of UDA intelligence in 1985 originated from sources within the security forces. Amongst de Silva's most damning conclusions was the following: 'The real importance, in my view, is that a series of positive actions by employees of the State actively furthered and facilitated his [Finucane's] murder and that, in the aftermath of the murder, there was a relentless attempt to defeat the ends of justice.'[102]

Pat Finucane's widow, Geraldine, called the de Silva Report a 'whitewash' and accused the British government of 'engineering a suppression of the truth'.[103] Just as a previous report into the Finucane murder, under Canadian High Court Judge Peter Cory, revealed details withheld from three previous police investigations carried out by the former Commissioner of the London Metropolitan Police, Sir John Stevens,[ai] so de Silva has revealed alarming new details withheld from Judge Cory.[104]

Dragging the truth out of the British government is indeed a Sisyphean task.

---

ai Sir John Stevens' three reports remain unpublished. His conclusion, however, was that there was collusion in the murder of Pat Finucane.

CONCLUSION

You have, in order to beat off your enemy in a war, to suspend some of your civil liberties for a time.

Margaret Thatcher, The Times (London), 26 October 1988

It is the fundamental duty of the citizen to resist and to restrain the violence of the state. Those who choose to disregard this responsibility can justly be accused of complicity in war crimes.

Noam Chomsky, At War with Asia, 1970

It is easy for those who have not suffered bereavement and injustice to lecture those, who have, about 'moving on'. Easy and insulting. Moving on is impossible when the truth lies buried in a barren field in County Armagh without a headstone. Clichés are not enough for families who were not only bereaved but also ignored for nearly half a century and then fed lies. What future does any community have that refuses to uncover or understand the truths of its recent past?

The inescapable fact, established beyond doubt by these events, is that successive British governments and their law enforcement agencies entered into a collusive counter-insurgency campaign with loyalist paramilitaries. It was thoroughly unethical – and it failed dismally. It was also illegal under international law.[1]

Families, and some politicians, who endured those dark days of the 1970s, say the 'Murder Triangle' killings were recognised even then for what they were. Far from bleeding support away from militant republicanism, collusion fed the conflict. Francie Molloy, Sinn Féin MP for Mid-Ulster since March 2013 and assembly member for Mid-Ulster since 1998, says loyalist killings made 'absolutely no difference' to the level of republican support.[2] Sinn Féin's electoral support increased steadily throughout the 1970s and 1980s, even in those areas worst affected by sectarian killings. Molloy, who lived at the very epicentre of the 'Murder Triangle' throughout the conflict, remembers mourners at the funeral of Fred McLoughlin in June 1975 shaking his hand and telling him they 'knew what was going on'.[a] He says collusion merely served to further alienate people from the RUC and the state. 'People well knew who was behind the killings. And they knew the police knew too,' he says.[3]

Leo Green, now a Sinn Féin adviser at Stormont, spent seventeen years in jail from 1977, including fifty-three days on hunger-strike, having been convicted of killing an RUC man. His brother, Francie, was an IRA member shot dead in County Monaghan in January 1975, but in County Armagh, he says, it was obvious that loyalists were targeting non-combatants: 'They were just killing ordinary people. It didn't make the slightest bit of difference to our support base.'[4]

This is no new revelation. In the 1970s, even as the events in this book were unfolding, senior IRA leaders were unperturbed by the random sectarian assassination of their co-religionists. Dáithi Ó Conaill (1938–1991), a prominent republican and long-standing member of the IRA 'army council', told journalist Kevin Myers that, on the contrary, such murders could even be beneficial for the IRA. First, said Ó Conaill, because hardly any IRA men were ever killed; second, because they acted as a recruiting sergeant; and third, because they added to the general sense of anarchy that was 'vital,' Myers quotes Ó Conaill as saying, 'to the IRA campaign'.[5]

By 1979 the British were forced reluctantly to conclude that nothing they had done, or were able to do, could eliminate the IRA. When Margaret Thatcher became Prime Minister, the British Army received a private assessment from the then Brigadier of the General

---

a   Molloy's belief that ordinary people understood the killers' agenda is mirrored elsewhere. In El Salvador, for example, the aims of the 'Black Shadow' and 'White Hand' death squads (who had the tacit support of the government in the mid-1990s) were well known to target communities.

Staff (Intelligence), James Glover, who had reached the gloomy conclusion that the IRA could not be defeated militarily.[6] Ten years later,
an unrepentant Glover repeated this assertion in a BBC *Panorama*
documentary.

The kind of brutal, unethical and cynical British government
tactics inflicted on people in Kenya and Oman, then, had no more
chance of establishing peace and democracy in Northern Ireland
than they had done in those far-flung places.

* * *

Over 120 people lost their lives in attacks attributed to permutations
of the 'Glenanne Gang' and their associates between 1972 and
1977. At least sixty-five separate families lost loved ones. They were
bereaved by loyalists, aided and abetted by state forces. A terrible
price was paid, but not by those in London or Stormont who devised
or indulged this strategy, and who went on to receive royal honours
and enjoy peaceful retirements on generous state pensions.

It may be too late, for many, but the truth is gradually emerging
and the families have the right to as much truth as can be uncovered.
Most do not want prosecutions or costly Bloody Sunday-style public
enquiries. They deserve, however, a fair and prompt mechanism by
which the truth can be established, as far as possible after so many
years. They also deserve acknowledgement, apologies and reparations.

One of the great unanswered questions they ask is 'why?' Only one
of the over 120 people killed in these events was an active republican.
Almost the entire IRA leadership escaped the conflict very much
alive. If the purpose of loyalist collusion during the Northern Ireland
conflict in the 1970s was not to eliminate the IRA leadership, then
what was its purpose?

Among London's uppermost priorities were ending IRA violence,
reducing support for Sinn Féin and persuading nationalists to settle
for a compromise within the existing borders of Northern Ireland.

Arguably, however, London's top priority has always been to portray itself internationally as an honest broker between two rival, incomprehensible and irrational religious tribes. Loyalist priorities were to lower nationalist aspirations and persuade the Catholic community to abandon both the political aims and methods of the IRA. If the British carrot held out to the Catholic/nationalist community was the promise of increased political influence, including a possible consultative role for Dublin, then the existence of a loyalist stick was a useful tool in its box – so long as it had gloves to keep its hands clean.

As pointed out in Chapter 8, the overwhelming majority of those specifically targeted were people who were progressing economically, socially and politically – people with aspirations their parents could only have dreamed of. They were a new generation of Catholics: well-educated, articulate, upwardly mobile people who were improving their families' prospects through their own hard work and initiative. Inspired by civil rights movements abroad, and determined that their financial and political aspirations would be respected and valued by the state and their Protestant neighbours, they were the ones targeted.

In the 1970s, then, London and the loyalists had a confluence of aims: 'The fact is that the British and loyalist campaigns were symmetrical ... The Protestant murder gangs helped wear the Catholic working class down.'[7] Unlike the loyalists, however, the British state had to give the impression to the outside world that it was just as determined to defeat the UDA and UVF as it was to vanquish the IRA. In Mid-Ulster, this fooled no one. Fathers Murray and Faul, made repeated, if vain, attempts to persuade London to put pressure on the RUC to arrest those responsible. In addition to writing angry letters to the newspapers, they raised their concerns at every other possible opportunity. The governments, said Fr Faul in the *Irish News* of 26 April 1975, were teaching:

... a deadly lesson to the people – that power came out of the barrel of a gun, that the ballot box is powerless against force, that police and army can betray their trust and not be the impartial servants of government and people, that the judiciary can fail to oppose tyranny and protect life.

He was correct: 'For they who sow the wind ... shall reap the whirlwind.'[8]

The RUC, Fr Faul said, were refusing to 'search certain wooded plantations and houses, even when these were pinpointed for them'. The evidence was clear in every graveyard in North Armagh and South and East Tyrone. All anyone had to do was to take a cursory glance at the identities of those who were being murdered – farmers,[9] publicans,[10] small businessmen,[11] young couples renovating derelict homes,[12] a trade unionist,[13] a librarian.[14] The bars and pubs attacked were invariably those where ordinary nationalists socialised, sometimes with a sprinkling of Protestant patrons.[15] They were not shebeens or clubs from where republican songs echoed out across the streets and countryside.

As for Dublin, its priority was not, as unionists imagined, the constitutional imperative of a united Ireland, but rather preventing, at almost any cost, the contagion of violence from sliding across the border into the south and rocking the economic boat. It could be argued that, in failing to pursue the loyalists behind the Dublin bombings of December 1972 and January 1973 (and the Belturbet bombing of the same month, in which two teenagers perished), the Irish security forces left the door wide open for the loyalists who killed thirty-four people on 17 May 1974.

If they are honest, many politicians in the Republic will admit they had suspicions about collusion. Some, realising its corrosive effect on nationalist confidence in the rule of law, such as Garret FitzGerald, did raise such concerns during meetings with British ministers. Others, however, whatever they believed, failed to make an effective case with London. Even an arch-critic of the IRA and Sinn Féin, Conor Cruise O'Brien (the architect of Section 31 censorship in the Republic)[16] recognised collusion existed, writing in 1992:

> What the Provisionals have succeeded in eliciting, however, is a tacit alliance between loyalist paramilitaries and significant elements in the security forces. In the circumstances, it is not surprising that some members of these forces should regard the loyalist paramilitaries as their allies against a common enemy.[17]

If Cruise O'Brien knew, then so did others. It is as indefensible for the Irish state to hold its hands up and say it didn't know as it is for the Catholic Church to plead ignorance about its appalling record on the clerical abuse of children in past generations. It was Dublin's responsibility to find out what the British state was up to in Northern Ireland. When the Catholic Church has attempted to hide behind the doctrine of mental reservation, it has, rightly, been repudiated.[b] Just as the Catholic Church has had to accept its faults, so the British and Irish states cannot credibly attempt to hide behind a similar casuistry.

In the papers seen so far from the National Archives of Ireland, collusion was rarely an issue in meetings between successive Irish governments and British ambassadors to Ireland, or at summits in Dublin and London. All the focus was on the IRA and what could be done to defeat it. Meanwhile, ordinary citizens suffered and died.

Despite this, the truth is slowly emerging, though it is happening too slowly and only for some. There are currently three ways for families in Northern Ireland to try to discover the truth. If they have

---

b   'Mental reservation' has been defined as a concept which permits a churchman knowingly to convey a misleading impression to another person without being guilty of lying.

sufficient resources or qualify for legal aid, they can go to the courts –
lengthy, expensive, harrowing and unpredictable. If they allege RUC
wrong-doing, they can take a case to the NI police ombudsman (and
many of the families named here are). Again, a lengthy and harrowing
process.[c] Currently, only the prohibitively expensive legal action
route is open to families in the Republic. Neither is there any form
of redress (other than a civil action) on whichever side of the border
they live, if a family wishes to find out the truth about a relative's
death at the hands of the UDR, any other British Army regiment or
if their case is against Westminster itself.

There is a third option, again only available in the North, which
is even more unpredictable – and in many cases has been a bitter
disappointment – and that is to engage with the Historical Enquiries
Team. The HET calls itself independent within the meaning of the
European Convention on Human Rights – but it reports to (and in
future will be funded by) the chief constable of the Police Service
of Northern Ireland. The HET's investigatory staff are themselves
usually former police officers.[18] The HET can only review (not re-
investigate) previous police investigations and its reports can be, and
often are, contrary and inconsistent. HET conclusions are sometimes
ambiguous or understated. There are important questions about the
gatekeepers who provide the HET with documents and who decide
what is disclosed. Former police officers can decline to be questioned.
It is a flawed and unpredictable mechanism totally dependent on
what papers can still be found in RUC safe storage, and on the relative
determination and intelligence of the individual officers involved.

It is not all bad news, though. Generally speaking, dog is reluctant
to eat dog. Even so, despite the strong natural instinct of professional
police officers not to criticise each other in public, in many cases the

c   Some families were recently informed by the NI police ombudsman that
investigations into their complaints would not start for an estimated two years.

HET is unambiguous about what it has discovered: 'Indisputable evidence of security forces' involvement with loyalist paramilitary murderers ... should have rung alarm bells all the way to the top of Government. Nothing was done. The murderous cycle continued,' it says in one report.[19] In another it notes: 'Members of the Nationalist community had been making allegations of widespread involvement and collusion by members of the security forces with loyalist paramilitaries. These claims were ridiculed, and individual instances, previously uncovered, dismissed by reference to "rotten apples".'[20] It also says, regarding the same case (the 1976 Rock Bar attack), 'This investigation ... had the potential to validate claims of widespread and routine collusion', adding that the ballistic evidence linked police officers to scores of other incidents.[d]

It is difficult to believe, says the HET:

> ... when judged in concert with other cases emerging around that time, that such widespread evidence of collusion was not a significant concern at the highest levels of the security forces or government. It may indeed be that there were fears that to confirm suspicions of collusion and involvement of RUC and security forces personnel in these terrorist crimes would have fatally undermined the credibility of the organisation, and possibly compromised overall political stability ... It may have been viewed as seriously as that.[21]

In several reports, the HET suggests that, after the passing of so many years, the time may now be right to re-open these cases:

---

d   The HET does not suggest that all, or nearly all, RUC officers or UDR men were complicit in murder, either directly or indirectly. It does, however, say repeatedly in reports on, for example, the killings of Seán Farmer, Colm McCartney, Betty McDonald, Gerard McGleenan and the attack on the Rock Bar that senior officers must have been aware of collusion and yet failed to act.

With the passage of time since these shocking, shameful and disgraceful crimes, the opportunity should exist for an honest disclosure of all relevant matters and considerations, without risk to individuals or of prejudice to the reputation and standing of new law enforcement arrangements. The families of those affected in this case – and in the linked cases – have received no justice to date.[22]

It is important to note that, although the Rock Bar attack is believed to be unique, in that all those involved were police officers (and not just some of the gunmen and bombers), the HET has reached the same conclusion in several other cases (notably the killings of Seán Farmer and Colm McCartney and the murder of Fred McLoughlin at the Eagle Bar). The HET clearly sees no merit in a 'do nothing' option.

For those readers who still doubt systemic collusion, consider all the evidence in the Mid-Ulster series, but before you do, answer the following questions. By mid-1976 (and – if you believe former RUC Sergeant John Weir – months earlier), the RUC knew that the farmhouse of one of its Reserve officers, James Mitchell, had been put under military surveillance and had been used as a staging post for a bomb in transit that killed two people at the Step Inn, Keady. Yet he remained on in the force for another ten months until he resigned in July 1977 (for 'personal reasons'[23]). Why?

By October 1976, the RUC knew that the car of another officer, Weir, a member of its supposedly 'elite' Special Patrol Group, had been spotted there by the same surveillance team at the time the bomb was present. Yet he remained on as a member of the force for another two years. Why?

Why was there no enquiry into the many 'disappearances' of weapons taken from UDR men's homes or in major raids on military armouries in Portadown and Lurgan in October 1972 and October 1973, respectively? This, despite ballistic evidence to show that they were used repeatedly to kill young men and women, mothers and fathers. This was at a time when the British Army knew it had a problem with loyalist infiltration. Its own 1973 internal report said: 'It seems likely that a significant proportion (perhaps 5% – in some areas as high as 15%) of UDR soldiers will also be members of the UDA, Vanguard Service Corps, Orange Volunteers or UVF.'[e] Yet, the document concludes, little should be done about it: 'The discovery of members of para-military or extremist organisations in the UDR is not, and has not been, a major intelligence target', and the UDR will remain, 'wide open to subversion and potential subversion'.

The British acknowledged the existence of collusion as long ago as 1972.[24] In document after document, the word crops up, particularly in relation to monthly tallies of weapons 'losses' from the UDR in the Armagh and Dungannon areas. Without new mechanisms to seek out the truth, these concerns are unlikely ever to be laid to rest. The events and analysis offered here are the closest anyone has so far got to a smoking gun. London's refusal to release the intelligence files relating to the Dublin and Monaghan bombings, even (so far) to an agreed judicial figure of international standing, shows how determined the British political, civil service and security establishment is that the truth should never be told.

On one level this is understandable. Britain is geographically adjacent to Northern Ireland, so the imperative for discretion is particularly vital. While the principles remain the same, it is one thing to admit to running 'counter-gangs' on the faraway grasslands of Kenya or in the mountains of Oman, but quite another around the farmlands of Dungannon.

Collusion, being intrinsically covert, leaves no fingerprints, no DNA. You will not find 'collusion' logged at inquests as a cause of death. It will not be written down in post-mortem reports. Genuine

---

e   'Subversion in the UDR', August 1973. Copy on file with PFC.

whistle-blowers run the risk of being smeared by the same powerful forces they seek to expose.[f] Nevertheless, look at those who are convinced. A 1994 Amnesty International report, 'Political Killings in Northern Ireland', concluded unambiguously:

> Such collusion has existed at the level of the security forces and services, made possible by the apparent complacency, and complicity in this, of government officials. This element of apparent complicity has been seen, for example, in the failure of the authorities to take effective measures to stop collusion, to bring appropriate sanctions against people who colluded, or to deploy resources with equal vigour against both Republican and Loyalist armed groups that pursue campaigns of political murder.[25]

The US academic and historian, J. Bowyer Bell, says:

> The lack of very much hard data about British covert actions in Ireland is hardly a matter of chance. A great deal of care, trouble, intimidation and influence has been expended to keep British secrets secret … The resources of the British government to restrict revelation have been available across an entire spectrum of assets: money, force, loyalty, greed, disinformation, the law, patriotism, fear all have been deployed for the Crown. And if in the end nothing works, then firm denial, regardless of the evidence. And for a generation the British security forces have largely kept their secrets, given the nature of an open society, a curious press, and, in Ireland, a suspicious arena.[26]

This is a debt the British government owes to the entire Northern Ireland community. Not only Catholics and nationalists died as a result of this Irish mutation of British counter-insurgency strategy.

---

f   John Stalker, Colin Wallace and Fred Holroyd.

Protestants and unionists died too – and not only the ten who died at Kingsmill in the IRA response to the deaths in the Reavey and O'Dowd families. Hundreds of RUC officers and UDR men died at the hands of young IRA recruits alienated from the state. Were they, too, regarded in London as merely 'collateral damage'?

Some will argue that the wealth of forensic evidence presented in the HET Reports, along with the testimony of family members and revelations from official documents, only goes to prove that a small number of state servants broke the law. This, they may contend, is disgraceful and outrageous – but nothing else. Professor Paul Wilkinson, CBE, dubbed Britain's 'foremost authority on terrorism',[27] probably gave the establishment (and the British public's) view fairly accurately when he wrote in 1986, 'The British Army[g] ... is steeped in the democratic ethos ... it is doubtful whether any other army in the world could have performed the internal security role in Northern Ireland with such humanity, restraint and effectiveness.'[28] Many British soldiers no doubt served to the best of their ability in Northern Ireland, and some paid with their lives, but Wilkinson's words conflict sharply with the experience of many in the nationalist community.[h]

British politicians, of whatever hue, constantly urge people in Ireland to 'move on', to forget the past, to abandon demands for enquiries and to build a new future together. A realisation of the impossibility of this, however, must eventually dawn on even the most obtuse mind at Westminster. A shared future in Ireland will never be built on a bitterly divided view of a shared past. If there is to be such a

g   The British Army killed 301 people in Northern Ireland during the conflict. Four soldiers were convicted of murder. All served less than three years in jail and returned to their regiments. See http://www.thedetail.tv/system/uploads/files/274/original/King%20letter%20to%20AF.pdf?1365767205 (accessed 3 July 2013) for evidence of how soldiers were protected from prosecutions.

h   In April 1981, a civil servant at the Foreign and Commonwealth Office recommended both Wilkinson and Richard Clutterbuck (see previous chapter) as speakers at an international conference on terrorism in April 1981 (Source: NAUK CJ4/3349).

shared future, inevitably there will have to be a truth recovery process that can attempt to lay the past to rest.

After the deeply flawed investigation into the killing of Stephen Lawrence in April 1993, a British public inquiry exposed 'institutionalised racism' in the Metropolitan Police and led to significant improvements in policing.[i] The episode was described by Jack Straw in 2012 as 'the single most important decision I made as Home Secretary'.[29] On 15 June 2010, the British Prime Minister, David Cameron, made a heartfelt apology for Bloody Sunday,[30] and more recently said he was 'profoundly sorry' for the lies told by the South Yorkshire Police in the wake of the Hillsborough football stadium tragedy, in which ninety-six people perished.[31] None of these generous-spirited apologies led to the sky falling in. Instead they have each begun a process of healing old wounds and a slow lifting of the burden of history from the shoulders of both the victims and the state alike.

Over 120 people died in the Mid-Ulster sequence of killings – more than eight times the number killed on Bloody Sunday and more than twenty more than died at Hillsborough. Not every life might have been saved, but a good many certainly could have been. Their still-grieving families deserve better than more retrenchment, more sophistry and years of legal circumlocution. These are not just questions about Northern Ireland's past. They impinge critically on the future – and not just the future of the Irish peace process. They have both British, Irish and international implications. Governments which claim to uphold the rule of law must lead by example. This is even more important during times of civil conflict. Ultimately, there can be no short-cuts. Breaking the law to defend the law simply does not work. The hard lessons learned in Armagh and Tyrone have a

---

i   The 1998 Stephen Lawrence Enquiry headed by High Court Judge Sir William Macpherson.

relevance as far away as Afghanistan, Iraq and other modern theatres of war.

Shortly before the completion of this book, a joint *Guardian*/BBC report, under the headline: 'Revealed: Pentagon's link to Iraqi torture centres' documented appalling human rights abuses. It named two US 'special forces' personnel, Colonel James Steele ('a 58-year-old retired special forces veteran') and Colonel James H. Coffman (also a retired 'special adviser'), who reported to US Defence Secretary Donald Rumsfeld and General David Petraeus respectively. They had, said the report, enlisted Shia militias to combat Sunni insurgents, which led to an acceleration of 'the country's descent into full-scale civil war'.[32]

In February 2013, the Afghan President, Hamid Karzai, ordered US 'special forces' to leave a province south of the capital, Kabul, claiming that US Afghani recruits were 'harassing, annoying, torturing and even murdering innocent people'.[33]

The US-Spanish philosopher George Santayana (1836–1952) famously said that those who cannot remember the past are doomed to repeat it. The reason his words are repeated so often is that many people recognise the truth behind them. For the health of the British body politic, quite aside from pressing questions of justice and fair play in Ireland, those in London who have the power to set the truth free should now take the first step.

Appendix

Known serving (or former) Security Force Members
involved in murder and other serious criminal offences
– Mid-Ulster 1970s

Gary Armstrong: an RUC sergeant when he kidnapped Fr Hugh Murphy and at the time of his alleged involvement in the attack on the Rock Bar.

Garfield Beattie: TAVR man when involved in the simultaneous gun-and-bomb attacks on Clancy's (three dead) and the Eagle Bars (one dead), and the shooting dead of Patsy McNeice, for which he was convicted.

Thomas Crozier: UDR man at the time of his involvement in the Miami Showband attack.

Andrew Godfrey Foote: former B Special, church elder and justice of the peace who allowed his farm to be used for storing a stolen car later used to kill four people at the Clancy's and Eagle Bars attack and where a large quantity of ammunition was discovered (some issued to the British Army within the twelve months beforehand).

William Hanna: former UDR sergeant and weapons instructor, who had served with the Royal Irish Fusiliers in Korea, involved in the Dublin/Monaghan bombings and many other attacks.

Robin Jackson: part-time UDR man (also RUC agent) expelled for illegal possession of ammunition. Involved in the shooting dead of trade unionist Patrick Campbell, the Miami Showband murders, the Dublin/Monaghan bombings, at least one raid on a UDR armoury when SMGs were stolen and in the murders of three members of the O'Dowd family.

David Kane: former UDR man at the time he was convicted for his part in the attack on the Eagle Bar. A neighbour of murder victim Patsy McNeice.

William Leonard: UDR man at the time of his involvement in the murders of Gertrude and James Devlin. Also believed to have been involved in at least three other bombings in the Dungannon area.

Joseph Lutton: an RUC Reservist at the time of his believed involvement in the shooting dead of SDLP official Denis Mullen. He was convicted for the attacks at Clancy's and the Eagle Bars (Charlemont) in which four died, although his employment as an RUC man was deliberately concealed from the court.

'Man B': RUC man who cannot be named for legal reasons but was a chief suspect in the murders of Arthur Mulholland and Eugene Doyle at Hayden's Bar.

Samuel McCartney: former UDR man convicted for possession of explosives.

William McCaughey: RUC man convicted of shooting dead William Strathearn and the gun-and-bomb attack on the Rock Bar; believed also to have been involved in the shooting of the three Reavey brothers and many other offences.

Laurence McClure: RUC man at the time of his involvement in the attack on the Rock Bar (for which he was convicted), the Donnelly's Bar gun-and-bomb attack and was a suspect for the murders of Seán Farmer and Colm McCartney.

Robert McConnell: UDR man at the time of his (believed) involvement in the attack on Donnelly's Bar, the murders of Seán Farmer and Colm McCartney, and the Dublin/Monaghan bombings.

James Roderick Shane McDowell: UDR sergeant at the time of his involvement in the Miami Showband attack.

Derek McFarland: had served as a member of the RUC, the UDR and the Ministry of Defence police, convicted of the attempted murder of Marian Rafferty and Thomas Mitchell – named by a convicted UVF bomber as involved in numerous other attacks.

Ian Mitchell: RUC man at the time of the Rock Bar attack for which he was convicted. Took statements in his capacity as a police officer at the scene of this attack.

James Mitchell: RUC Reservist when involved in the Step Inn and Donnelly's Bar attacks in which five people died. His farmhouse was used to plan the Dublin/Monaghan bombings, in which thirty-four people were killed. He was only ever convicted of possession of weapons and explosives for which he received a one-year suspended sentence.

Edward Sinclair: former B Special who became UVF quartermaster. The gun used to murder Peter and Jenny McKearney was discovered in his bedroom, making him a prime suspect; convicted for possessing a gun used in the Miami Showband killings; and believed to have been involved in the Traynor's Bar bombing in which two men died. The HET believes his farmhouse was used in the planning and execution of many attacks between Dungannon and Portadown.

'Suspect 2': UDR man who cannot be named for legal reasons but was a chief suspect in the murders of James and Gertrude Devlin and in the murders of two men at Hayden's Bar.

Laurence Tate: UDR man arrested after the Miami Showband murders who confessed to involvement in a non-fatal explosion.

John Weir: RUC sergeant at time of his involvement in William Strathearn's murder and planning of the aborted attack on a bar in County Monaghan (the target was then switched to the Step Inn, where two died).

David Wilson: RUC man at the time of the attack on the Rock Bar.

Stewart and Ivor Young: both served in the Royal Ulster Rifles. Stewart is named by the Barron Report (2006) as being involved in the Monaghan bombing and suspected of involvement in the Donnelly's Bar bombing. Ivor is also suspected of involvement in a variety of attacks.

NOTES

GLOSSARY

1   http://cain.ulst.ac.uk/othelem/chron/ch1800-1967.htm; accessed 3 July 2013.

INTRODUCTION

1   HET Report – Colm McCartney and Seán Farmer.

CHAPTER 1: BLOODING-IN

1   Kipling's poem 'Ulster, 1912' can be found at: http://www.kipling.org.uk/rg_ulster1.htm; accessed 3 July 2013.
2   Portadown is regarded as the birthplace of the Orange Order.
3   See: 'Northern Ireland – The Plain Truth', Campaign for Social Justice for information on Unionist domination of the Northern Irish government. Available at: http://cain.ulst.ac.uk/events/crights/pdfs/csj179.pdf; accessed 28 May 2013.
4   Heath, E., 24 March 1972. Available at: http://cain.ulst.ac.uk/events/abstract/72storm.htm; accessed 3 July 2013.
5   Faulkner, B., 28 March 1972. Available at: http://cain.ulst.ac.uk/events/convention/back.htm; accessed 3 July 2013.
6   Sutton, M., *An Index of Deaths from the Conflict in Ireland 1969–1993*, 1st edn (Beyond the Pale, Belfast 1994).
7   McKittrick, D. *et al.*, *Lost Lives*, 1st edn (Mainstream, Edinburgh 1999). Reported testimony of a police inspector at Paul Beattie's inquest.
8   *Portadown Times*, 14 July 1973.
9   McVeigh, J., *Garvaghy – A Community Under Siege*, 1st edn (Beyond the Pale, Belfast 1999).
10   *Portadown Times*, 8 August 1973. The alleyway was between 290 and 292 Churchill Park, according to police evidence at the inquest.
11   Author interview with anonymous source.
12   PRONI: ARM/6/1/1/20, *Report of Autopsy*, 13 July 1972.
13   *Portadown News*, 21 July 1972.
14   McKittrick *et al.*, *Lost Lives*.
15   *Portadown News*, 21 July 1972.
16   McKittrick *et al.*, *Lost Lives*.
17   *The Irish Times*, 9 and 16 October 1973.
18   *Ibid.*
19   *Portadown News*, 6 March 1973.
20   *Ibid.*, 16 March 1973.
21   *Ibid.*, 18 May 1973.

22   Operation Motorman on 31 July 1972 was a British Army move into areas
      controlled by republicans in Derry, Belfast and some other large towns.
23   *The Irish Times*, 11 December 1973.
24   Author interview with Christopher Connolly, 2011.
25   HET Report – Patrick Connolly.
26   *Ibid.*
27   NAUK: DEFE 24/835, *UDR: Arms and Armouries; Theft and Loss of Weapons*,
      August 1973.
28   NAUK: DEFE 24/822.
29   NAUK: DEFE 24/835, 'Subversion in the UDR', August 1973. Prepared for
      the Joint Intelligence Committee. Copy on file with PFC and available at:
      http://www.patfinucanecentre.org.
30   NAI: *Schedule of Facts and Statements Relating to Loyalist Groupings and Acts
      of Violence Perpetrated by Loyalist Para-Military Forces, January 1972–December
      1973*.
31   Deutsch, R. and Magowan, V., *Northern Ireland 1968–1973: A Chronology of
      Events*, Volume 2, 1972–73 (Blackstaff Press, Belfast 1974)
32   NAI: Military Archives, 2003/15/G2/C/1660.
33   NAUK: *Security Forces and the UDA, Background Brief*, 23 November 1972.
      Copy on file with PFC.
34   Seanad Éireann debate on an amendment to the Offences Against the State
      Act on 2 December 1972.
35   Faul, D. and Murray, R., *The Triangle of Death: Sectarian Assassinations in
      the Dungannon–Moy–Portadown Area* (self-published, 1975). A remarkably
      prescient early account of events in Mid-Ulster.
36   NAUK: DEFE 24/824.
37   *Ibid.*

CHAPTER 2: 'MY GOD, NOT THIS'

1   *The Armagh Guardian*, 15 March 1973.
2   In Loughgall on 24 March 1973.
3   Boulton, D., *The UVF 1966–1973: An Anatomy of Loyalist Rebellion* (Gill &
      Macmillan, Dublin 1994), p. 48.
4   HET Report – Dorothy Trainor.
5   *Ibid.*, but with no date or provenance for the intelligence report.
6   Wood, I., *Crimes of Loyalty: A History of the UDA* (Edinburgh University Press,
      Edinburgh 2006).
7   *The Irish Times*, 7 August 1973.
8   *Ibid.*, 9 August 1973.
9   Faul and Murray, *The Triangle of Death*.
10   NAUK: DEFE 24/835.
11   NAUK: Memo to Lieutenant Colonel J. L. Penal (OBE), July 1972. Copy on
      file with PFC.

12   *Ibid.*

13   NAUK: *Development of the Ulster Defence Regiment,* confidential letter from Headquarters Northern Ireland to Ministry of Defence, 12 June 1972. Copy on file with PFC.

14   HET Report – Charles John McDonnell.

15   John Weir's 1999 affidavit, available at: http://www.patfinucanecentre.org/collusion/weir.pdf; accessed 3 July 2013.

16   NAUK: DEFE 24/822, *Theft of Weapons from UDR Armoury on 23 October 1973.*

17   *Ibid.*

18   HET Report – Patrick Campbell.

19   *Banbridge Chronicle,* 2 November 1974.

20   HET Report – Patrick Campbell.

21   Author interview with Margaret Campbell, 2011.

22   HET Report – Francis O'Toole, p. 24: Jackson was 'suspected by security forces of a significant number of UVF attacks and murders'.

23   HET Report – Patrick Campbell.

24   Royal Highland Fusiliers Privates John and Joseph McCaig and Dougal McCaughey in Belfast three years earlier, on 9 March 1971.

25   Author interview with Margaret Campbell, 2011.

26   *Ibid.*

27   Author interview with Margaret Campbell, 2012.

28   HET Report – Patrick Campbell.

29   *Ibid.*

30   Author interview with Margaret Campbell, 2012.

31   Verbatim account from Quinn's statement, from HET.

32   HET Report – Patrick Campbell.

33   *Ibid.*

34   *Ibid.*

35   *Ibid.*

36   Author interviews with Margaret Campbell, 2011 and 2012.

37   HET Report – Patrick Campbell.

38   *Ibid.*

39   For details of McCartney's conviction see *Belfast Telegraph,* 28 May 1981, and *Armagh Guardian,* 29 May 1981.

40   HET Report – Francis McCaughey.

41   *The Irish Times,* 13 November 1973.

CHAPTER 3: 'KILLING THE NEIGHBOURS'

1   *Tyrone Courier,* 23 January 1973.

2   HET Report – Daniel Hughes.

3   *Tyrone Courier,* 23 January 1973.

4   HET Report – Patrick Molloy.

5   *Ibid.*
6   Author interview with Molloy family, 2011.
7   HET Report – Patrick Molloy.
8   *Ibid.*
9   Identifiable from cross-referencing several HET Reports.
10   HET Report – Patrick Molloy.
11   Author interview with Patricia Casey (née Molloy), 2011.
12   *The Irish Times*, 2 August 1975.
13   *The Times* (London), 19 March 1974.
14   NAUK: PREM 16/154, 2 April 1974.
15   Bew, P. and Gillespie, G., *Northern Ireland: A Chronology of the Troubles 1968–1999* (Gill & Macmillan, Dublin 1999), pp. 83–4.
16   NAUK, 17 April 1974. Attached Minutes from Vice-Chair of General Staff to Under Secretary of State (Army). Copy on file with PFC.
17   *Tyrone Courier*, 8 May 1974.
18   *Ibid.*, 15 May 1974.
19   HET quotation from DPP's decision.
20   Leonard was joined in hi-jacking the CIÉ bus by John Somerville.
21   HET Report – James and Gertrude Devlin.
22   *Ibid.*
23   *Ibid.*
24   NAUK: DEFE 24/875.
25   NAUK: CJ 4/842.
26   Dillon, M., *The Dirty War* (Arrow, London 1991).
27   NAUK CJ 4/645, 'Public Statements and Reaction to Provisional IRA Plans to Destroy Parts of Belfast', 13–17 May 1974. See also http://hansard.millbanksystems.com/lords/1974/may/13/northern-ireland-ira-plans; accessed 28 May 2013.
28   JFF interview with Brendan Hughes, 2003.
29   NAUK, 13 May 1974: Note of meeting between Secretary of State, Graham Shillington Chief Constable of RUC and General Officer Commanding the British Army in Northern Ireland, 13 May 1974. Copy on file with PFC.
30   *Ibid.*
31   *Ibid.*
32   Available at: http://cain.ulst.ac.uk/events/uwc/docs/hw25574.htm; accessed 21 January 2013.
33   *Portadown News*, 25 April 1975.
34   *The Sunday Times*, 15 March 1987. Holroyd also says Duffy's killers were involved in the Dublin/Monaghan bombings.
35   Available at: http://cain.ulst.ac.uk/othelem/chron/ch74.htm; accessed 31 January 2013.
36   HET Report – Pat Falls.
37   *Ibid.*

38 Available at: http://cain.ulst.ac.uk/othelem/chron/ch74.htm; accessed 31 January 2013.

39 Author interview with Michael Mallon, 2012.

40 HET Report – John Mallon.

41 HET Report – Thomas McNamee.

42 John Weir's 1999 affidavit is available at: http://www.patfinucanecentre.org/collusion/weir.pdf; accessed 3 July 2013.

43 NAUK: DEFE 24/835, 'Subversion in the UDR', August 1973. Prepared for the Joint Intelligence Committee. Copy on file with PFC and available at: http://www.patfinucanecentre.org.

Chapter 4: Turning to Murder

1   NAUK: 'Secret. UK Eyes Only', 9 May 1975. Copy on file with PFC.

2   McKittrick *et al.*, *Lost Lives*.

3   HET Report – Arthur Mulholland.

4   *Mid-Ulster Mail*, 14 February 1975.

5   *Ibid.*, 17 February 1975.

6   HET Report – Arthur Mulholland.

7   *Ibid.*

8   McKittrick *et al.*, *Lost Lives*.

9   NAUK: CJ 4/838.

10 Malachy's own account as recalled by his son, Kevin.

11 HET Report – Dorothy Trainor.

12 *Ibid.*

13 HET Report – Martin McVeigh.

14 Author interview with Maura Martin, Thomas Bowen's sister, 2013.

15 *Ibid.*

16 *Ibid.*

17 *Irish News*, 26 April 1975.

18 HET Report – Marian Bowen, Seamus and Michael McKenna.

19 Author interview with Winnie Boyle, 2010.

20 HET Report – Owen Boyle.

21 Author interview with Boyle family, 2010.

22 HET Report – Joe Toman.

23 Author interview with Eugene McCann, 2013.

24 HET Report – Joe Toman.

25 Author interview with Eugene McCann, 2010.

26 PFC interview with John Weir, 2001.

27 Dillon, M., *The Trigger Men* (Mainstream, Edinburgh 2003), p. 25.

28 NAUK: FCO 87/423, 12 September 1975.

29 NAUK: CJ 4/1156, 8 August 1975.

30 NAUK: FCO 87/422, 13 August 1975.

31 HET Report – Francis O'Toole.

32   *Ibid.*

33   *Ibid.*

34   NAUK: 'Guidance to Overseas Posts on Sectarian Assassinations', July 1975. Copy on file with PFC.

35   *Ibid.*

36   Harnden, T., *Bandit Country* (Hodder & Stoughton, London 1999), pp. 140–1.

37   HET Report – John McGleenan.

38   *Ibid.*

39   *Ibid.*

40   *Ibid.*

41   *Ibid.*

42   NAUK: FCO 87/476.

43   HET Report – Colm McCartney and Seán Farmer.

44   *Ibid.*

45   *Ibid.*

46   *Ibid.*

47   Houses of the Oireachtas, Joint Committee on Justice, Equality, Defence and Women's Rights, *Interim Report on the Report of the Independent Commission of Inquiry into the Bombing of Kay's Tavern, Dundalk*, July 2006 (henceforth Barron Report, 2006) p. 115 names 'Suspect T' as being a suspect in these murders. 'Suspect T' is identified as Philip Silcock in the European Court of Human Rights report, *Case of Brecknell v The United Kingdom* (Application no. 32457/04), Judgment, 27/02/2008, pp. 4, 8.

48   This remains unexplained – why should 'amendments' be made to the file before it was sent to the coroner?

49   HET Report – Colm McCartney and Seán Farmer.

50   *Ibid.*

51   *Ibid.*

52   NAUK: PREM 16/520.

53   McKittrick *et al.*, *Lost Lives*.

54   *Ibid.*

55   *The Sunday Times*, 7 February 1999.

56   McKittrick *et al.*, *Lost Lives*.

57   *Ibid.*

58   *Ibid.*

59   Author interview with Olive Mullen, 2011.

60   *Ibid.*

61   Author interviews with Olive Mullen and Denise Fox (née Mullen), 2012–13.

62   *Irish News*, 4 September 1975.

63   HET Report – Denis Mullen. Later a Detective Chief Superintendent, Neilly died in a Chinook helicopter crash on the Mull of Kintyre, 2 June 1994.

64   HET Report – Denis Mullen.

65 *Ibid.*

66 *Ibid.*

67 *Ibid.*

68 Author interview with Olive Mullen, 2011.

69 NAUK: CJ 4/832, 1 September 1975.

70 NAUK: CJ 4/799, 9 September 1975.

71 HET Report – Margaret Hale.

72 NAUK: PREM 16/520, 10 September 1975.

73 NAUK: PREM 16/520, 19 September 1975.

74 HET Report – Peter and Jane McKearney. Both their families had links to the Ancient Order of Hibernians, an Irish Catholic fraternal organisation opposed to violence.

75 Patrick Francis McKearney's statement to the inquest into the deaths of Peter and Jenny, 15 March 1976.

76 HET Report – Peter and Jane McKearney. The Secretary of State's renewed proscription of the UVF had taken effect on 4 October 1975, nineteen days before the murders. The patrol, therefore, had no excuse for failing to detain all four men.

77 *Ibid.*

78 *Ibid.*

79 *Ibid.*

80 *Ibid.*

81 Author interview with Ann Brecknell, 2011.

82 HET Report – Donnelly's Bar.

83 *Ibid.*

84 Author interviews with Jimmy McCreesh, 2001 and 2012.

85 HET Report – Donnelly's Bar.

86 *Ibid.*

87 Former Detective Sergeant McCann has assisted the HET in a 'positive and frank manner'. HET Report – Donnelly's Bar.

88 HET Report – Donnelly's Bar.

89 *Ibid.*

90 *Ibid.* The HET Report does not name this man – his identity is known but cannot be cited for reasons of confidentiality.

91 Barron Report, 2006, pp. 46–7. There were four Barron Reports in total: one on Dublin/Monaghan/John Francis Green (December 2003); one on the Dublin bombings of 1972/73 and Belturbet bombings etc. (November 2004); one on the killing of Seamus Ludlow (November 2005); and one on Kay's Tavern and Donnelly's Bar, and other attacks in Castleblayney, Dublin Airport, Miami Showband and others in the Murder Triangle (July 2006). Available at: http://www.dublinmonaghanbombings.org/index2.html; accessed 4 July 2013.

92 Barron Report, 2006, p. 46.

93 HET Report – Donnelly's Bar.

94 *Ibid.*

95 *Ibid.*

96 *Ibid.*

97 Affidavit, 3 January 1999. Available at: http://www.patfinucanecentre.org.

98 HET Report – Donnelly's Bar.

99 *Ibid.*

100 *Ibid.*

101 Barron Report, 2006, p. 97.

102 European Court of Human Rights report, *Case of Brecknell v The United Kingdom* (Application no. 32457/04), Judgment, 27/02/2008, pp. 4, 8, 12.

103 Houses of the Oireachtas/Joint Committee on Justice, Equality, Defence and Women's Rights, 2003, *Interim Report on the Report of the Independent Commission of Enquiry into the Dublin and Monaghan Bombings of 1974*, December. Sometimes also referred to as the 'Interim Barron Report' (henceforth Barron Report, 2003), pp. 151–2.

104 *The Irish Times,* 27 December 1975.

105 NAUK: FCO 87/423 and CJ 4/1300, 29 December 1975.

106 *Armagh Guardian,* 2 September 1976.

107 McKittrick *et al., Lost Lives.*

108 NAUK: DEFE 11/917.

109 NAUK: Letter from senior civil servant to colleague in London, 6 January 1976. Copy on file with PFC.

CHAPTER 5: 'THE MURDEROUS CYCLE CONTINUED'

1 Copy on file with PFC.

2 McKittrick *et al., Lost Lives.*

3 Author interview with Eugene Reavey, 2011.

4 This account was given by Anthony Reavey while in hospital, before his condition deteriorated and he died. *Celebrity Squares* was a broadcast television game show.

5 HET Report – John-Martin, Brian and Anthony Gerard Reavey.

6 *Ibid.*

7 Song written by Gary Brooker, Keith Reid and Matthew Fisher (Onward Music Publishing).

8 Lyrics from the song 'A Whiter Shade of Pale'. See note 7, above.

9 HET Report – John-Martin, Brian and Anthony Gerard Reavey.

10 Copy discovered in inquest papers at PRONI and with family.

11 HET Report – John-Martin, Brian and Anthony Gerard Reavey.

12 Weir's affidavit is available at: http://www.patfinucanecentre.org. McKittrick *et al.'s Lost Lives* quotes the *Irish Independent* claiming that Jackson and UDR Corporal Robert McConnell, later killed by the IRA, were both involved.

13 HET Report – John-Martin, Brian and Anthony Gerard Reavey.

14 *Ibid.*

15   *Ibid.* The Reavey family has made an official complaint to the police ombudsman to ascertain whether false information had been circulated within the force about their family, and whether this influenced the murders.

16   Author interview with Eugene Reavey, 2010.

17   Paisley claimed in a House of Commons speech in January 1999 that he had seen over a dozen names in RUC files as being involved in the Kingsmill massacre, including Eugene Reavey's.

18   HET Report – John-Martin, Brian and Anthony Gerard Reavey.

19   *Ibid.* and author interview with Eugene Reavey, 2011.

20   Author interview with Barney and Noel O'Dowd, 2012.

21   *Ibid.*

22   HET Report – Joseph, Joseph Bernard (Barry) and Declan O'Dowd.

23   *Ibid.*

24   *Ibid.*

25   Author interview with Noel O'Dowd, 2013.

26   HET Report – Joseph, Joseph Bernard (Barry) and Declan O'Dowd.

27   *Ibid.*

28   Author interview with Barney O'Dowd, 2012.

29   Family interview with PFC, June 2004.

30   HET Report – Joseph, Joseph Bernard (Barry) and Declan O'Dowd.

31   *Ibid.*

32   Barron Report, 2006, p. 46.

33   Weir affidavit available at: http://www.patfinucanecentre.org.

34   Statement made to PFC by Eugene Reavey, 2011.

35   *Ibid.*

36   BBC News Northern Ireland online, 16 June 2011, 'IRA "responsible for Kingsmills".' Available at: http://www.bbc.co.uk/news/uk-northern-ireland-13800042; accessed 26 January 2013.

37   *Ibid.*

38   Chief Superintendent Harry Breen and Superintendent Bob Buchanan.

39   Author interview with Eugene Reavey, 2013.

40   NAUK, 7 January 1976, Prime Minister's cabinet meeting on Northern Ireland.

41   *Ibid.*

42   NAUK: PREM 16/959, 6 January 1976.

43   NAUK: FCO 87/582, 7 January 1976.

44   NAUK, copy on file with PFC.

45   *Ibid.*

46   NAUK: PREM 16/959, 1976.

47   NAUK: PREM 16/959/189–181.

48   *Ibid.*

49   NAUK: PREM 16/959, 1976.

50   *Ibid.*

51   NAUK: PREM 16/959/204–195.

52   *Ibid.*

53   Statement by prime minister in the House of Commons, 12 January 1976. Copy on file with PFC.

54   *Ibid.*

55   NAUK: Note of a Meeting Held at Laneside with UDA Representatives, 19 January 1976. Copy on file with PFC.

56   NAUK: DEFE 24/835, 'Subversion in the UDR', August 1973. Prepared for the Joint Intelligence Committee. Copy on file with PFC and available at: http://www.patfinucanecentre.org.

57   NAUK: PREM 16/1817/047.

58   Security meeting at Stormont Castle, 13 January 1976. Copy on file with PFC.

59   NAUK: PREM 16/959.

60   NAUK: DEFE 24/866, 17–18 February 1976.

61   NAUK: CJ 4/1054, January/February 1976.

62   BBC NI *Spotlight* programme, 25 May 2004. Verbatim transcript from a recording of the original programme. Not available to access online.

63   Notes on file with PFC.

64   Colin Wallace interview with JFF, 8 September 2000. See also Barron Report, 2003, p. 171.

65   Minutes of meeting, 18 August 2004. Minutes on file at PFC.

66   Author interview with Sister Mary Kelly, 2010.

67   McKittrick *et al.*, *Lost Lives*.

68   HET Report – James McCaughey (Hillcrest Bar).

69   Author interview with Norbert McCaughey, 2010.

70   HET Report – James McCaughey.

71   Author interview with Norbert McCaughey, 2010.

72   HET Report – James McCaughey.

73   *Ibid.*

74   Author interview with Norbert McCaughey, 2010.

75   HET Report – James McCaughey.

76   *Ibid.*

77   *Ibid.*

78   Available at: http://www.patfinucanecentre.org.

79   *Ibid.*

80   *Irish News,* 8 May 1976.

81   *Ibid.*

82   DPP letter to PFC, 4 April 2004: 'there is no indication of any persons being charged or convicted in connection with this crime.'

83   Author interview with Jim McLoughlin, Fred McLoughlin's son, 2011.

84   HET Report – Fred McLoughlin.

85   *Ibid.*

86   Author interview with Marie O'Hagan, 2013.

87   HET Report – Seán O'Hagan.

88 *Ibid.*
89 Author interview with Jim McLoughlin, 2012.
90 HET Report – Fred McLoughlin.
91 *Ibid.*
92 *Ibid.*
93 *Ibid.*
94 HET Report – Seán O'Hagan.
95 HET Report – Fred McLoughlin.
96 *Ibid.*
97 *Armagh Guardian*, 22 February 1979.
98 HET Report – Fred McLoughlin.
99 Author interview with Clancy family, 2011.
100 HET Report – Fred McLoughlin.
101 HET Report – Colm McCartney and Seán Farmer.
102 *Ibid.*
103 Author interviews with the McLoughlin (2011), Donnelly (2011) and O'Hagan (2013) families.
104 Author interview with Jim McLoughlin, 2011.
105 HET Reports – Fred McLoughlin, Seán O'Hagan, Felix Clancy.
106 HET Report – Fred McLoughlin.
107 *Ibid.*

CHAPTER 6: 'A POLICEMAN'S BOOTS'

1   Author interview with Joe McGleenan, owner of the Rock Bar, 2011.
2   *Ibid.*
3   HET Report – Michael McGrath.
4   *Ibid.*
5   *Ibid.*
6   PFC interview with Michael McGrath, 2001.
7   He lived to the age of eighty-six.
8   HET Report – Michael McGrath.
9   *Ibid.*
10 *Ibid.*
11 *Ibid.*
12 *Ibid.*
13 Campaign group, Justice for the Forgotten (JFF), May 1999. Excerpt from transcript of its interview with John Weir.
14 HET Report – Michael McGrath.
15 Author interview with Patsy McNeice (jnr), 2011.
16 HET Report – Patrick McNeice.
17 *Ibid.*
18 *Ibid.*
19 Author interview with Patsy McNeice (jnr), 2011.

20   HET Report – Patrick McNeice.

21   *Ibid.*

22   *Ibid.*

23   *Ibid.*

24   *Ibid.*

25   HET Report – Elizabeth McDonald.

26   *Ibid.*

27   *Ibid.*

28   *Ibid.*, plus HET interview with John Weir, Dublin, 9–10 April 2008.

29   HET Report – Elizabeth McDonald.

30   HET interview with John Weir, Dublin, 9–10 April 2008.

31   HET Report – Elizabeth McDonald.

32   Author interview with Malachi McDonald, 2010.

33   HET Report – Gerard McGleenan.

34   *Ibid.*

35   HET Reports – Gerard McGleenan, Elizabeth McDonald.

36   *Ibid.*

37   HET Report – Gerard McGleenan.

38   *Ibid.*

39   *Ibid.*

40   *Ibid.*

41   *Ibid.*

42   The Red Hand of Ulster, a heraldic symbol denoting the ancient Irish province of Ulster (the northern nine counties of the island of Ireland).

43   Author interview with Robert McGleenan, 2012.

44   HET Report – Gerard McGleenan.

45   HET Reports – Gerard McGleenan, Elizabeth McDonald.

46   HET Report – Gerard McGleenan.

47   *Ibid.*

48   Barron Report, 2006, p. 93.

49   HET Reports – Gerard McGleenan, Elizabeth McDonald.

50   HET Report – Elizabeth McDonald.

51   Barron Report, 2003, p. 61.

52   Heaney, S., *Opened Ground: Poems 1966–1996*, 1st edn (Faber and Faber, London 1998).

53   McCaughey's admission came in a BBC NI *Spotlight* documentary: 'Dangerous Liaisons' (25 May 2004). Weir's was in his 3 January 1999 affidavit (available at: http://www.patfinucanecentre.org/collusion/weir.pdf; accessed 3 July 2013).

54   Author interview with Joe Austin, 2011.

CHAPTER 7: BOMBS KNOW NO BORDERS

1   D. Davis, referring to the Dublin/Monaghan bombings. Letter to the Editor, *The Irish Times*, 20 May 2011.

2   JFF's full title is 'The Organisation of Victims & Relatives seeking justice for the Dublin & Monaghan Bombings of 17th May 1974; the Dublin Bombings of 1st December 1972–20th January 1973 and other cross-border bombings of the 1970s'.

3   The Services, Industrial, Professional and Technical Union.

4   A Northern Ireland morning newspaper catering mainly for the unionist community.

5   Houses of the Oireachtas/Joint Committee on Justice, Equality, Defence and Women's Rights, November 2004, *Interim Report on the Report of the Independent Commission of Enquiry into the Dublin Bombings of 1972 and 1973* (henceforth Barron Report, 2004), also sometimes referred to as the 'Second Interim Barron Report', p. 35.

6   Office of the Attorney General, 1972, 'Irish Statute Book: Offences Against the State (Amendment) Act, 1972'. Available at: http://www.irishstatutebook. ie/1972/en/act/pub/0026/index.html; accessed 29 January 2013.

7   ITN Network Limited, 11 August 1973. Interview of former Taoiseach Jack Lynch with journalist Geoffrey Archer. Lynch's publicly shared suspicions led to an unprecedented official denial of involvement by the British government on 13 August 1973.

8   NAUK: FCO 87/204, 17 August 1973.

9   *Ibid.*

10 *The Observer*, 17 August 1973.

11 *Evening Herald*, 21 August 1973.

12 Barron Report, 2004, p. 64.

13 JFF interview with Conor McAnally, 2004.

14 *The Irish Times*, 9 January 1974.

15 *Ibid.*

16 *Ibid.*, 12 May 1999.

17 *Ibid.*

18 *Irish Daily Mail*, 19 May 2011.

19 *First Tuesday*, Series 11: 'Hidden Hand: The Forgotten Massacre', ITV Yorkshire, UK, 6 July 1993. Detailed production information, plus a shot-by-shot list of film clips, is available at: http://www.itnsource.com/shotlist/ itvprogs/1993/07/06/y05870128/?s=; accessed 28 January 2013.

20 Iris Boyd's testimony before the Joint Oireachtas Committee on Justice, Equality, Defence and Women's Rights, 27 January 2004.

21 Emergency broadcast on RTÉ, 17 May 1974.

22 Dáil debate on 26 June 1974. Available at: http://oireachtasdebates. oireachtas.ie/debates%20authoring/debateswebpack.nsf/takes/dail197406260 0011?opendocument; accessed 5 July 2013.

23 *Ibid.*

24 *The Irish Times*, 18 May 1974.

25 See note 19, above.

26   *Ibid.*

27   *Ibid.*

28   *Ibid.*

29   Photographs provided to JFF by *The Irish Times* Archive Department.

30   *Ibid.*

31   Weir was not named in the programme, but was a source.

32   Statement by the Ulster Volunteer Force (UVF), 15 July 1993. Available at: http://cain.ulst.ac.uk/othelem/organ/uvf/uvf150793.htm; accessed 28 January 2013.

33   NAUK: FCO 87/350, 29 March 1974.

34   NAUK: FCO 87/350, 2 May 1974.

35   NAUK: FCO 87/293, 13 May 1974.

36   NAUK: FCO 87/440, 7 July 1975.

37   NAUK: FCO 87/350, 20 May 1974.

38   *Ibid.*

39   NAUK: FCO 87/350, 21 May 1974.

40   NAUK: FCO 87/311, 17 June 1974.

41   NAUK: FCO 87/416, January 1975.

42   NAUK: CJ 4/577, 11 September 1974.

43   NAUK: FCO 87/294, 18 September 1974.

44   NAUK: FCO 87/295, 16 October 1974.

45   Houses of the Oireachtas/Joint Committee on Justice, Equality, Defence and Women's Rights, March 2004, *Final report of the Independent Commission of Inquiry into the Dublin and Monaghan Bombings*, p. 21. Available at: http://www.oireachtas.ie/viewdoc.asp?fn=/documents/Committees29thDail/jcjedwr/Sub-Comm-Barron_Final-31Mar2004.pdf; accessed 28 August 2013.

46   *The Times* (London), 11 December 2003.

47   Author interview with Leo Green, January 2013.

48   *Ibid.*

49   Barron Report, 2003, 'Appendix: Murder of John Francis Green', p. 13.

50   *Ibid.*, pp. 3–4.

51   Dewar, M., *The British Army in Northern Ireland*, 2nd edn (Weidenfeld Military, London 1996).

52   Barron Report, 2003, 'Appendix: Murder of John Francis Green', p. 11.

53   John Weir's 1999 affidavit, available at: http://www.patfinucanecentre.org/collusion/weir.pdf; accessed 3 July 2013.

54   JFF interview with Watters family, 2000.

55   JFF interview with Rooney family, 2000.

56   Inquest hearing, 15 January 1976.

57   *Irish Independent*, 20 December 1975.

58   *Dundalk Democrat*, 17 January 1976.

59   JFF interview with Watters family, 2000.

60   JFF interview with Rooney family, 2000.

61 *Ibid.*

62 Garland, R., *Gusty Spence*, 1st edn (Blackstaff Press, Belfast 2001), p. 151.

63 *Irish Press*, 22 December 1975.

64 Joint Committee on Justice, Equality, Defence and Women's Rights Sub-Committee on the Barron Report, 'Public Hearing on the Barron Report', 27 September 2006. Available at: http://www.dublinmonaghanbombings.org/oralsubdb27Sept06page2.html; accessed 29 January 2013. See also http://debates.oireachtas.ie/JUB/2006/09/27/00003.asp; accessed 3 September 2013.

65 Barron Report, 2006, pp. 104–9.

66 Houses of the Oireachtas, Joint Committee on Justice, Equality, Defence and Women's Rights, *Final Report on the Report of the Independent Commission of Inquiry into the Bombing of Kay's Tavern, Dundalk*, November 2006, p. 61.

67 Author interview with Anna Mone-McEneaney, 2011.

68 *Irish Press* and *Irish News*, 9 March 1976.

69 Author interview with Anna Mone-McEneaney, 2011.

70 *Ibid.*

71 *Irish News*, 8 March 1976.

72 JFF interview with Anna Mone-McEneaney, 2009.

73 McKittrick *et al.*, *Lost Lives.*

74 *The Irish Times*, 15 March 1976.

75 Nigel Wylde, *Bombings at Dundalk and Castleblayney: Report of Mr Nigel Wylde, Lieutenant Colonel (retired), Royal Army Ordnance Corps*, 3 October 2002. Reports commissioned by JFF and on file.

76 Post-mortem report of Dr John Harbison on the body of Patrick Mone, 8 March 1976. Copy on file with JFF.

77 Barron Report, 2006, p. 155.

78 Author interview with Anna Mone-McEneaney, 2011.

CHAPTER 8: 'ACQUAINTED WITH GRIEF'

1 http://www.rightwords.eu/quotes/every-night-when-i-go-to-bed-i-hope-that-i-may-never--25310; accessed 23 April 2013.

2 HET Report and family interviews.

3 Family interviews 2010, 2012 and 2013.

4 HET Report – Joseph, Joseph Bernard (Barry) and Declan O'Dowd.

5 HET Report – Frances McCaughey.

6 All interviews in this chapter are with the author unless stated otherwise.

7 Speaking to the Joint Oireachtas Committee on Justice, Equality, Defence and Women's Rights, 26 September 2006.

8 Frances Banks interview with Michael O'Toole, 1999.

CHAPTER 9: THE 'SHORT ARM' OF THE LAW

1 http://www.goodreads.com/author/quotes/41348.Brendan_Behan; accessed 23 April 2013.

2   One of Sir Robert Peel's nine 'Principles of Policing'; see http://www.nwpolice.org/peel.html; accessed 23 April 2013.

3   NAUK: Note of a Meeting at the Northern Ireland Office, 13 November 1974. Copy on file with PFC.

4   Figures taken from McKittrick *et al.*, *Lost Lives*.

5   HET Report – Arthur Mulholland and Eugene Doyle.

6   *Ibid.*

7   *Ibid.*

8   HET Report – Elizabeth McDonald.

9   *Ibid.*

10 HET Report – Felix Clancy, Seán O'Hagan, Robert McCullough and Fred McLoughlin.

11 *Ibid.*

12 *Ibid.*

13 HET Report – James and Gertrude Devlin.

14 *Ibid.*

15 *Ibid.*

16 HET Report – Martin McVeigh.

17 *Ibid.*

18 HET Report – Fred McLoughlin.

19 *Ibid.*

20 Barron Report, 2006, p. 135.

21 *Irish News*, 4 February 1977. A conditional discharge meant that he was not given any custodial sentence but should he re-offend it would be taken into account.

22 HET Report – Peter and Jane McKearney.

23 *Ibid.*

24 HET Report – Arthur Mulholland.

25 *Ibid.*

26 HET Report – Joseph, Joseph Bernard (Barry) and Declan O'Dowd.

27 HET Report – Martin McVeigh.

28 HET Report – Seán O'Hagan.

29 HET Report – Owen Boyle.

30 HET Report – Colm McCartney and Seán Farmer.

31 HET Report – Donnelly's Bar.

32 *Ibid.*

33 HET Report – James McCaughey.

34 HET Report – Patrick Connolly.

35 HET Report – Joe Toman.

36 HET Report – John Mallon.

37 HET Report – Colm McCartney and Seán Farmer.

38 *Ibid.*

39 *Ibid.*

40   *Ibid.*

41   *The Irish Times*, 18 March 1975.

42   Author's personal observation.

43   Barron Report, 2006, pp. 95–6; 2003, pp. 148–51.

44   Cory, P., *Collusion Report – Pat Finucane*, 1st edn (HMSO, London 2004), paras 1.35–1.39, pp. 21–2.

45   NAUK: file reference unknown; document with PFC.

CHAPTER 10: BRITANNIA WAIVES THE RULES

1   http://thinkexist.com/quotation/nobody_has_a_more_sacred_obligation_to_obey_the/189041.html; accessed 23 April 2013.

2   Cited in *Wall Street Journal*, 13 November 1962.

3   NAUK: Memo to Lieutenant Colonel J. L. Penal, OBE, July 1972. Copy on file with PFC.

4   HET Report – Patrick Campbell.

5   *Ibid.*

6   HET Report – Francis O'Toole.

7   *Ibid.*

8   Assistant DPP, cited in Barron Report, 2006, p. 121.

9   HET Report – James and Gertrude Devlin.

10   *Ibid.*

11   HET Report – Peter and Jane McKearney.

12   *Ibid.*

13   *Ibid.*

14   HET Report – Donnelly's Bar.

15   *Ibid.*

16   *Ibid.*

17   European Court of Human Rights report, *Case of Brecknell v The United Kingdom*, ruling number 32457/04.

18   'Over three decades, Britain was in fact found guilty of violations by the European Court more times than all the other members of the European Union combined': Rolston, B., 'Resistance and Terror', in P. Scraton (ed.), *Beyond September 11 – An Anthology of Dissent* (Pluto Press, London 2002), p. 60.

19   *Irish News*, 4 February 1977.

20   Partington, M., *Introduction to the English Legal System*, 5th edn (Oxford University Press, Oxford 2012).

21   Rolston, B., 'An Effective Mask for Terror: Democracy, Death Squads and Northern Ireland', *Crime, Law and Social Change*, vol. 44, no. 2, 2005, pp. 181–203.

CHAPTER 11: RIDDING THE LAND OF PESTILENCE

1   His wife accused him of assaulting her when she was seven months pregnant with their third child – Dillon, M., *The Dirty War* (Arrow, London 1991), p. 228.

2   *Portadown News*, 29 September 1978.

3   Sheehy, K., *More Questions Than Answers*, 1st edn (Gill & Macmillan, Dublin 2008).

4   Author interview with Eugene Reavey, 2010.

5   *The Irish Times*, 9 January 1974.

6   *Irish News*, 15 December 1978.

7   *Ibid.*

8   *Ibid.*

9   *Ibid.*

10   HET Report – Michael McGrath.

11   *Irish News*, 14 May 1980.

12   HET Report – Michael McGrath.

13   *Ibid.*

14   *Ibid.*

15   *Ibid.*

16   *Ibid.* and Barron Report, 2006, p. 96.

17   HET Report – Michael McGrath.

18   *Ibid.* and Barron Report, 2006, p. 96.

19   Barron Report, 2006, p. 96.

20   HET Report – Michael McGrath.

21   Armstrong, G., *From the Palace to Prison*, 1st edn (New Wine Press, Chichester 1991).

22   *Ibid.*

23   HET Report – Michael McGrath.

24   Barron Report, 2006, p. 118, n. 127.

25   Armstrong, *From the Palace to Prison*.

26   HET Report – Michael McGrath.

27   *Ibid.*

28   *Irish News, Irish Press, Armagh Guardian*, 21 December 1978.

29   *Ibid.*

30   *The Irish Times*, 23 December 1978.

31   *Armagh Guardian*, 8 November 1979.

32   HET Report – Donnelly's Bar.

33   HET Report – Michael McGrath.

34   Verbatim record on file with PFC.

35   Details of sentencing taken from Lord Chief Justice Lowry's concluding remarks on 30 June 1980.

36   HET Report – Michael McGrath.

37   *Ibid.*

38   *Ibid.*

39   *Ibid.*

40   *Ibid.*

41   *Ibid.*

42   Ryder, C., *The RUC: A Force Under Fire*, 1st edn (Methuen, London 1989).
43   Dillon, *The Dirty War*, pp. 228–9.
44   HET Report – Michael McGrath.
45   *Ibid.*
46   *Ibid.*
47   *Ibid.*
48   *Ibid.*
49   Barron Report, 2003, p. 151.
50   Barron Report, 2006, p. 121.
51   HET Report – Michael McGrath.

CHAPTER 12: HER MAJESTY'S MURDERERS

1   NAUK: DEFE 13/822: 'Subversion in the UDR', August 1973. Prepared for the Joint Intelligence Committee. Copy on file with PFC and available at: http://www.patfinucanecentre.org.
2   Reid, G., *The Plays of Graham Reid*, 1st edn (Co-op Books, Dublin 1982).
3   Cited in Finlay, A., 'Defeatism and Northern Protestant "Identity"', *Global Review of Ethnopolitics*, vol. 1, no. 2, 2001.
4   *Ibid.*
5   McKittrick *et al.*, *Lost Lives*. Note: these figures apply only to people killed in Ireland, and do not include soldiers.
6   Bruce, S., *The Red Hand*, 1st edn (Oxford University Press, Oxford 1992).
7   McAuley, J., '"Just Fighting to Survive": Loyalist Paramilitary Politics and the Progressive Unionist Party', *Terrorism and Political Violence*, vol. 16, no. 3, 2004.
8   1972 statement issued by 'Capt. William Johnston' on behalf of Brigade Staff, UVF.
9   Cited in Wood, *Crimes of Loyalty*.
10   Cited in Sluka, J., *Death Squad: Anthropology of State Terror* (University of Pennsylvania Press, Pennsylvania 2000).
11   NAUK: MOD Telex to the Home Office summarising a meeting between the two prime ministers, 7 September 1971. Copy on file with PFC.
12   NAUK: Loose minute, reference A/BR/20201/MO3 E/88/I, 10 September 1971. On file with PFC.
13   NAUK: CJ 4/266, correspondence from Sir Harry Tuzo to Whitelaw.
14   NAUK: CJ 4/1666.
15   NAUK: Note of a meeting between Minister of State Mr. Roland Moyle MP and Cardinal Conway held at Armagh, 11 April 1975. Copy on file with PFC.
16   Letter from A. G. Turner, *Guidance and Policy Department*, to R. C. Masefield, NIO, Belfast, 16 April 1975, Copy on file with PFC.
17   NAUK: 'Convictions for Murder' – draft letter to the British Embassy in Dublin, 9 May 1975.

18   NAUK: 'Sectarian Assassinations' – paper by the British government for circulation to the Security Forces and the Northern Ireland Office, 15 May 1975.

19   NAUK: 'Response to "Sectarian Assassinations"' (paper), 29 May 1975.

20   Jackson did not, for example, make an appearance in the first two editions of McDonald, H. and Cusack, J., *UVF* (Poolbeg Press, Dublin 1997, 2000).

21   Copy of full memorandum on file with PFC.

22   Copy on file with JFF.

23   *Irish Independent*, 4 June 1998.

24   *The Irish Times*, 2 August 1975.

25   He was also convicted of bombing the home of a family in Moy in May 1975. There were six children in the house at the time of the explosion but no one was injured.

26   John Weir names McCoo as a suspect in the Donnelly's Bar attack: see The European Court of Human Rights report, *Case of Brecknell v The United Kingdom* (Application no. 32457/04), Judgment, 27/02/2008, pp. 4, 7.

27   Barron Report, 2006, p. 115. 'Suspect T' is identified as Philip Silcock in the European Court of Human Rights report, *Case of Brecknell v The United Kingdom* (Application no. 32457/04), Judgment, 27/02/2008, pp. 4, 8.

28   *Sunday Independent*, 4 July 1993.

29   Barron Report, 2003, pp. 145–6.

30   *Ibid.*, p. 149.

31   *Ibid.*, pp. 145, 174.

32   Notebook written in early 1974, before the Dublin/Monaghan bombings. Copy on file with JFF.

33   *Irish News*, 7 February 1972.

34   He was interned for eighteen months, until September 1974.

35   Barron Report, 2006, p. 48.

36   Barron Report, 2003, p. 234.

37   Barron Report, 2006, p. 106.

38   Barron Report, 2003, p. 62.

39   Barron Report, 2006, p. 52.

40   *Ibid.*, p. 115.

41   HET Report – Donnelly's Bar.

CHAPTER 13: FROM DHOFAR TO ARMAGH

1   Mockaitis, T. R., *British Counter-Insurgency 1919–1960* (St. Martin's Press, New York 1995), p. 180.

2   *The City of God* or *De Civitate Dei* written by the medieval philosopher St Augustine around 413–426.

3   Morris, J., *Farewell the Trumpets: An Imperial Retreat* (Faber and Faber, London 1998), p. 244.

4   *Ibid.*

5   Pollard, Captain H.B.C., *The Secret Societies of Ireland: Their Rise and Progress* (Philip Allan & Co., London 1922).

6   See *The Grey Zone* video (Lions Gate Entertainment 2001).

7   Greif, G., *We Wept Without Tears: Testimonies of the Jewish Sonderkommando from Auschwitz* (Yale University Press, London 2005).

8   Army Staff College Camberley, *Counter-Revolutionary Warfare Handbook* (Camberley, UK, Royal Military Academy Sandhurst 1988). Cited in Colonel I. A. Rigden, *The British Approach to Counter-Insurgency: Myths, Realities and Strategic Challenges* (US Army War College, Pennsylvania 2008).

9   Newsinger, J., *British Counterinsurgency: From Palestine to Northern Ireland* (Palgrave, Basingstoke 2002), p. 29.

10 *Ibid.*, p. 75.

11 Kitson, F., *Bunch of Five* (Faber and Faber, London 1977), pp. 13–14.

12 Kitson, F., *Gangs and Counter-gangs*, 1st edn (Barrie and Rockliffe, London 1960), p. 46.

13 Anderson, D., *Histories of the Hanged: The Dirty War in Kenya and the End of Empire*, 1st edn (W. W. Norton, London 2005), p. 285.

14 *Ibid.*, pp. 5–7.

15 Elkins, C., *Britain's Gulag: The Brutal End of Empire in Kenya* (Jonathan Cape, London 2005).

16 *The Guardian*, 6 May 2013.

17 *Ibid.*, p. 7.

18 Newsinger, *British Counterinsurgency*, p. 81.

19 Elkins, *Britain's Gulag*. Cited in Porter, B., 'How Did They Get Away With It?', *London Review of Books*, vol. 27, no. 5, 2005.

20 *Ibid.*, p. 236.

21 *The London Gazette*, Supplement No. 40046, 1953. Available at: http://www.london-gazette.co.uk/issues/40046/supplements/6928; accessed 13 January 2013.

22 *The London Gazette*, Supplement No. 40372, 1954. Available at: http://www.london-gazette.co.uk/issues/40372/supplements/53; accessed 13 January 2013.

23 Curtis, M., *Web of Deceit: Britain's Real Role in the World* (Vintage, London 2003), p. 334.

24 Clutterbuck, R. L., *Terrorism in an Unstable World* (Routledge, London 1994), p. 130.

25 *Ibid.*

26 Newsinger, *British Counterinsurgency*, p. 36.

27 Calhoun, R.-D., 'The Art of Counterintelligence – The Musketeer's Cloak: Strategic Deception during the Suez Crisis of 1956', *CIA Studies in Intelligence*, 2007, vol. 51, no. 2, p. 53. Available at: https://www.cia.gov/library/center-for-the-study-of-intelligence/csi-publications/csi-studies/studies/vol51no2/Studies_v51no2_2007-5Jun.pdf; accessed 13 January 2013.

28 Blaxland, G., *The Regiments Depart: A History of the British Army, 1945–1970* (Kimber, London 1971), p. 132.

29 *Ibid.*

30 Kitson, *Bunch of Five*, p. 252.

31 Elkins, C., 'The Wrong Lesson', *The Atlantic Magazine*, July/August 2005. Available at: http://www.theatlantic.com/magazine/archive/2005/07/the-wrong-lesson/304052/; accessed 15 January 2013.

32 Newsinger, *British Counterinsurgency*, p. 106.

33 Curtis, M., *Unpeople: Britain's Secret Human Rights Abuses* (Vintage, London 2004), p. 290.

34 Cited in Media Lens, 'Yemen's Useful Tyranny – The Forgotten History of Britain's "Dirty War": Part 2', 2011. Available at: http://www.medialens. org/index.php?option=com_content&view=article&id=613:yemens-useful-tyranny-the-forgotten-history-of-britains-dirty-war-part-2&catid=24:alerts-2011&Itemid=68; accessed 21 January 2013.

35 Curtis, *Unpeople*.

36 Newsinger, *British Counterinsurgency*, p. 121.

37 *Ibid.*

38 Paul, J. and Spirit, M., '700 Glengarried Men: 1st Battalion Argyll and Sutherland Highlanders' Tour of Aden', 2008. Available at: http://www. britains-smallwars.com/Aden/700.htm; accessed 12 January 2013.

39 *Empire Warriors: Mad Mitch and His Tribal Law*, TV documentary series, BBC2, first broadcast 19 November 2004.

40 BBC News online, 'Return to Aden, Without Mad Mitch', 2007. Available at: http://news.bbc.co.uk/2/hi/programmes/from_our_own_correspondent/7120629. stm; accessed 12 January 2013.

41 Cited by McGuffin, J., *Internment* (Anvil Books, Kerry 1973), p. 178.

42 See Urwin, M., *Counter-Gangs: A History of Undercover Military Units in Northern Ireland 1971–1976*. Pat Finucane Centre, Spinwatch and Justice for the Forgotten 2013. Available at: http://www.spinwatch.org/index.php/issues/ northern-ireland/item/5448-counter-gangs-a-history-of-undercover-military-units-in-northern-ireland-1971-1976; accessed 8 May 2013.

43 Michael Naan and Andrew Murray, 'Their Story Is Retold', in McDonald, B. 2012, *The Pitchfork Murders: Uncovering the Cover Up* (Louis Leonard Sinn Féin Cumann, Newtownbutler 2012).

44 BBC2, *Empire Warriors* (2004).

45 Curtis, *Unpeople*, p. 304.

46 Allfree, P. S., *Warlords of Oman* (Robert Hale, London 2008).

47 McKeown, Lieutenant Colonel J., 'Britain and Oman: The Dhofar War and Its Significance', MPhil dissertation, Cambridge University, 1981, pp. 55–6.

48 For a full account of Kitson's creation of undercover units in Northern Ireland, see Urwin, *Counter-Gangs*; also Mark Urban, *Big Boys' Rules: The SAS and the Secret Struggle Against the IRA* (Faber and Faber, London 1992), p. 35.

49 Ministry of Defence, *Land Operations Volume III – Counter-Revolutionary Operations Handbook, Part 1 – Principles and General Aspects* (Ministry of

Defence, London 1969).

50 RAND Corporation, *Counter-insurgency. A Symposium*, 16–20 April 1962 (RAND, Santa Monica, 1963). Available at: http://www.rand.org/content/dam/rand/pubs/reports/2006/R412-1.pdf; accessed 23 January 2013.

51 Kitson, F., *Low Intensity Operations: Subversion, Insurgency and Peacekeeping* (Faber and Faber, London 1971).

52 *Ibid.*

53 *Ibid.*, p. 126.

54 Porter, B., *Plots and Paranoia: A History of Political Espionage in Britain, 1790–1988* (Unwin Hyman, London 1989), http://www.powerbase.info/index.php/Frank_Kitson cite_ref-0#cite_ref-0; accessed 3 July 2013.

55 Kitson, *Gangs and Counter-Gangs*, p. 46.

56 Porter, *Plots and Paranoia.*

57 Kitson, *Low Intensity Operations.*

58 NAUK: WO 296/75.

59 Ryder, *The RUC: A Force Under Fire*, p. 169.

60 Becket, I. F. W. and Pimlott, J., *Armed Forces and Modern Counter-Insurgency* (Croom Helm, London 1985), p. 12.

61 Flackes, W. D. and Elliott, S., *Northern Ireland: A Political Directory 1968–88* (Blackstaff Press, Belfast 1989), p. 107.

62 Campbell, B. and Brenner, A., *Death Squads in Global Perspective: Murder with Deniability* (Palgrave Macmillan, New York 2002).

63 NAUK: Note of a Meeting Held at Laneside with UDA Representatives, 19 January 1976. Copy on file with PFC.

64 Powerbase, 'Richard Clutterbuck', 2011. Available at: http://www.powerbase.info/index.php/Richard_Clutterbuck; accessed 23 January 2013.

65 Clutterbuck, *Terrorism in an Unstable World.*

66 Powerbase, 'Richard Clutterbuck', see note 64.

67 Burnett, J., and Whyte, D., *Embedded Academics and Counter-Insurgency in Iraq*, Spinwatch Monitoring PR and Spin, 2005. Available at: http://www.spinwatch.org/-articles-by-category-mainmenu-8/51-iraq/201-embedded-academics-and-counter-insurgency-in-iraq; accessed 20 January 2013. The director of the St Andrews Centre, Paul Wilkinson, pays tribute to both Clutterbuck and Kitson in his introduction to *British Perspectives on Terrorism* (HarperCollins, London 1981).

68 NAUK: FCO 27 April 1981.

69 Colonel Robin Evelegh, Obituary Notice, *The Times* (London), 27 May 2010. Available at: http://63196.activeboard.com/t35927256/death-of-colonel-jrgn-evelegh-ma-psc-late-oxf-bucks-li-and-r/; accessed 14 January 2013.

70 Evelegh, R., *Peace-Keeping in a Democratic Society – The Lessons of Northern Ireland* (C. Hurst Publishers Ltd, London 1978), p. 2.

71 *Ibid.*, p. 110.

72 *Ibid.*, pp. 133–40.

73   *Ibid.*, p. 140.

74   *Ibid.*, p. 71.

75   Ramsay, R., 'Kitson, Kincora and counter-insurgency in Northern Ireland', *Lobster*, 1986, vol. 10, no. 7–8. Available at: http://www.8bitmode.com/rogerdog/lobster/lobster10.pdf; accessed 20 January 2013.

76   Mercer, P., 'The Northern Ireland Troubles: Holding the Ring', *History Today*, 2011, vol. 61, no. 2. Available at: http://www.historytoday.com/patrick-mercer/northern-ireland-troubles-holding-ring; accessed 15 January 2013.

77   *Ibid.*

78   NAUK: PREM 19/817. Sir Robert Thompson, KBE, DSO, MC (1916–1992) fought in Burma, Malaya and South Vietnam. He was a counter-insurgency expert and the author of many books.

79   NAUK: DEFE 13/917.

80   Green, P. and Ward, T., *State Crime: Governments, Violence and Corruption* (Pluto Press, London 2004), p. 119.

81   *Ibid.*, p. 108.

82   *Ibid.*, p. 119.

83   Sluka, *Death Squad*, p. 129.

84   *Ibid.*, p. 128.

85   Rolston, B., 'An Effective Mask for Terror: Democracy, Death Squads and Northern Ireland'. As of 2011, Professor Rolston is director of the Transitional Justice Institute, University of Ulster.

86   *Ibid.*

87   Jamieson, R. and McEvoy, K., 'State Crime by Proxy and Juridical Othering', *British Journal of Criminology*, vol. 45, no. 4, 2005.

88   *Ibid.*, pp. 504–5.

89   *Ibid.*, p. 504.

90   *Ibid.*, p. 505.

91   *Ibid.*, p. 510.

92   George, A., 'The Discipline of Terrorology', in George, A. (ed.), *Western State Terrorism* (Polity Press, Cambridge 1991), pp. 76–101, at p. 82.

93   http://www.economist.com/node/21552248; accessed 2 September 2013.

94   Mackinlay, J. and Al-Baddawy, A., *Rethinking Counterinsurgency*, RAND Counterinsurgency Study, 2008, vol. 5. Available at: http://www.rand.org/content/dam/rand/pubs/monographs/2008/RAND_MG595.5.pdf; accessed 20 January 2013.

95   Arquilla, J., '9/11: Yesterday and Tomorrow/How We Could Lose the War on Terror', *San Francisco Chronicle*, 7 September 2003. Available at: http://www.sfgate.com/opinion/article/9-11-Yesterday-and-tomorrow-How-we-could-lose-2591145.php; accessed 20 January 2013.

96   Elkins, C., 'The Wrong Lesson'. Available at: http://www.theatlantic.com/magazine/archive/2005/07/the-wrong-lesson/304052/; accessed 15 January 2013.

97   *Ibid.*

98   Murray, R., *The SAS in Ireland*, 4th edn (Mercier Press, Cork 1990).

99   NAUK: PREM 16/959/120–119.

100 For a discussion of the concept of 'maximum plausible deniability', see Campbell and Brenner, *Death Squads in Global Perspective*, ch. 1.

101 *The Guardian*, 18 April 2012.

102 The Rt Hon. Sir Desmond de Silva, *The Report of the Patrick Finucane Review*, December 2012 (The Stationery Office, London 2012), paragraph 115. Available at: http://www.patfinucanereview.org/report/volume01/executive-summary-and-principal-conclusions/ (accessed 22 May 2013).

103 *The Guardian*, 12 December 2012.

104 http://cain.ulst.ac.uk/issues/collusion/cory/cory03finucane.pdf; accessed 3 July 2013.

CONCLUSION

1   Article 2 of the European Convention on Human Rights imposes a positive duty on the state to take all reasonable steps to protect a person's right to life, including an obligation to take preventative operational measures to safeguard life when the authorities know, or ought to be aware, of a real risk from the criminal acts of a third party. See paragraph 1.105 at: http://www.patfinucanereview.org/report/volume01/chapter001; accessed 4 July 2013.

2   Author interview with Francie Molloy, 2013.

3   *Ibid.*

4   Author interview with Leo Green, 2013.

5   'An Irishman's Diary', *The Irish Times*, 23 April 2003.

6   General Sir James Glover, MBE, KCB, 1929–2000 (who also served in Malaya, Hong Kong and Cyprus) was the author of a leaked document 'Future Terrorist Trends', cited in *The Guardian*, 16 June 2000. Available at: http://www.guardian.co.uk/news/2000/jun/16/guardianobituaries1 (accessed 3 July 2013); and in Bew, P. and Patterson, H., *The British State and the Ulster Crisis: From Wilson to Thatcher* (Verso, London 1985).

7   Newsinger, *British Counterinsurgency*.

8   King James Bible, Book of Hosea, 8:7.

9   Frances McCaughey, Peter and Jenny McKearney, the O'Dowd family.

10 Traynor's Bar, James Devlin, the Step Inn, the Eagle Bar, Clancy's Bar.

11 Owen Boyle, Patrick Falls, the Reavey family.

12 Denis Mullen, Marian Bowen, Owen Boyle.

13 Patrick Campbell.

14 Gertrude Devlin.

15 Traynor's Bar, the Step Inn, the Rock Bar, the Eagle.

16 Section 31 of the Irish Broadcasting Act, strengthened by Conor Cruise O'Brien in 1977, forbade the state broadcaster from transmitting the voice of any Sinn Féin spokesperson being interviewed.

17   Cruise O'Brien, C., *Stone Cold*, 1st edn (Arrow, London 1992).

18   In every case referred to in this book, however, no HET investigator had previously been employed by the RUC or PSNI.

19   HET Report – Colm McCartney and Seán Farmer.

20   HET Report – Michael McGrath.

21   *Ibid.*

22   *Ibid.*

23   Barron Report, 2006, p. 93.

24   NAUK: DEFE 24/822.

25   Amnesty International, 'Political Killings in Northern Ireland', Report, 1994. Available at: http://www.amnesty.org/en/library/asset/EUR45/001/1994/en/5d33d0df-c38d-4a61-b7d8-358b1933b66d/eur450011994en.pdf; accessed 30 November 2011.

26   Bowyer Bell, J., *In Dubious Battle: The Dublin and Monaghan Bombings 1972–1974*, 1st edn (Poolbeg, Dublin 1996).

27   *Daily Telegraph*, 12 August 2011.

28   Wilkinson, P., *Terrorism and the Liberal State*, 2nd edn (Macmillan/New York University Press, New York 1986), p. 159.

29   *Daily Mail*, 25 September 2012.

30   http://www.bbc.co.uk/news/10320609; accessed 3 July 2013.

31   http://www.bbc.co.uk/news/uk-england-merseyside-19543964 and http://hillsboroughinquests.independent.gov.uk; both accessed 3 July 2013.

32   *Guardian* online, 'Revealed: Pentagon's Link to Iraqi Torture Centres', 6 March 2013. Available at: http://www.guardian.co.uk/world/2013/mar/06/pentagon-iraqi-torture-centres-link; accessed 23 March 2013.

33   BBC News online, 'Karzai Orders US Special Forces out of Afghan Province', 24 February 2013. Available at: http://www.bbc.co.uk/news/world-asia-21566295; accessed 23 March 2013.

BIBLIOGRAPHY

Allfree, P. S., 2008, *Warlords of Oman*. London: Robert Hale

Anderson, D., 2005, *Histories of the Hanged: The Dirty War in Kenya and the End of Empire* (1st edn). London: W.W. Norton

Aretxaga, B., 2000, 'Paramilitary Death Squads in Spain', in Sluka, J. (ed.), *Death Squad: Anthropology of State Terror*. Pennsylvania: University of Pennsylvania Press

Armstrong, G., 1991, *From the Palace to Prison* (1st edn). Chichester: New Wine Press

Army Staff College Camberley, 1988, *Counter-Revolutionary Warfare Handbook*. Camberley: Royal Military Academy Sandhurst

Arquilla, J., 2003, '9/11: Yesterday and Tomorrow/How We Could Lose the War on Terror', *San Francisco Chronicle*, 7 September. Available at: http://www.sfgate.com/opinion/article/9-11-Yesterday-and-tomorrow-How-we-could-lose-2591145.php (accessed 14 May 2013)

Becket, I. F. W. and Pimlott, J., 1985, *Armed Forces and Modern Counter-Insurgency*. London: Croom Helm

Best, G., 2001, *War and Law since 1945*. Oxford: Oxford University Press

Bew, P. and Gillespie, G., 1999, *Northern Ireland: A Chronology of the Troubles 1968–1999*. Dublin: Gill & Macmillan

Bew, P. and Patterson, H., 1985, *The British State and the Ulster Crisis: From Wilson to Thatcher*. London: Verso

Blaxland, G., 1971, *The Regiments Depart: A History of the British Army, 1945–1970*. London: Kimber

Booth, K. and Dunne, T., 2002, *Who Are the Global Terrorists?* London: Palgrave, Macmillan

Booth, K. and Dunne, T., 2002, *Worlds in Collision: Terror and the Future of Global Order*. London: Palgrave, Macmillan

Boulton, D., 1994, *The UVF 1966–1973: An Anatomy of Loyalist Rebellion*. Dublin: Gill & Macmillan

Bowyer Bell, J., 1996, *In Dubious Battle: The Dublin and Monaghan Bombings 1972–1974* (1st edn). Dublin: Poolbeg

Bruce, S., 1992, *The Red Hand* (1st edn). Oxford: Oxford University Press

Burnett, J. and Whyte, D., 2005, *Embedded Academics and Counter-Insurgency in Iraq*. Spinwatch Monitoring PR and Spin. Available at: http://

www.spinwatch.org/index.php/component/k2/item/280-embedded-academics-and-counter-insurgency-in-iraq (accessed 14 May 2013)

Calhoun, R.-D., 2007, 'The Art of Counterintelligence – The Musketeer's Cloak: Strategic Deception during the Suez Crisis of 1956', *CIA Studies in Intelligence*, vol. 51, no. 2, pp. 47–58. Available at: https://www.cia.gov/library/center-for-the-study-of-intelligence/csi-publications/csi-studies/studies/vol51no2/Studies_v51no2_2007-5Jun.pdf (accessed 14 May 2013)

Campbell, B. and Brenner, A., 2002, *Death Squads in Global Perspective: Murder with Deniability* (1st edn). New York: Palgrave Macmillan

Chomsky, N., 1970, *At War with Asia*. New York: Pantheon Books

Clutterbuck, R. L., 1973, *Protest and the Urban Guerrilla*. London: Cassell

Clutterbuck, R. L., 1975, *Living with Terrorism*. London: Faber and Faber

Clutterbuck, R. L., 1977, *Guerrillas and Terrorists*. London: Faber and Faber

Clutterbuck, R. L., 1978, *Britain in Agony: The Growth of Political Violence*. London: Faber and Faber

Clutterbuck, R. L., 1978, *Kidnap and Ransom: The Response*. London: Faber and Faber

Clutterbuck, R. L., 1994, *Terrorism in an Unstable World*. London: Routledge

Cory, P., 2004, *Collusion Report – Pat Finucane* (1st edn). London: HMSO. Available at http://cain.ulst.ac.uk/issues/collusion/cory/cory03finucane.pdf (accessed 14 May 2013)

Cruise O'Brien, C., 1992, *Stone Cold* (1st edn). London: Arrow

Curtis, M., 2003, *Web of Deceit: Britain's Real Role in the World*. London: Vintage

Curtis, M., 2004, *Unpeople: Britain's Secret Human Rights Abuses*. London: Vintage

de Silva, The Rt Hon. Sir Desmond, 2012, *The Report of the Patrick Finucane Review*. London: The Stationery Office. Available at http://www.patfinucanereview.org/report/index.html (accessed 14 May 2013)

Deutsch, R. and Magowan, V., 1974, *Northern Ireland 1968–1973: A Chronology of Events*, Volume 2, 1972–73. Belfast: Blackstaff Press

Dewar, M., 1996, *The British Army in Northern Ireland* (2nd edn). London: Weidenfeld Military

Dillon, M., 1991, *The Dirty War*. London: Arrow

Dillon, M., 2003, *The Trigger Men*. Edinburgh: Mainstream

Elkins, C., 2005, *Britain's Gulag: The Brutal End of Empire in Kenya*. London: Jonathan Cape

Elkins, C., 2005, 'The Wrong Lesson', *The Atlantic Magazine*, July/August.

Available at: http://www.theatlantic.com/magazine/archive/2005/07/the-wrong-lesson/304052/ (accessed 14 May 2013)

Ellison, D. and Smith, J., 2000, *The Crowned Harp*. London: Pluto Press

Evelegh, R., 1978, *Peacekeeping in a Democratic Society – The Lessons of Northern Ireland*. London: C. Hurst

Fahy, D., 2006, *Death on a Country Road*. Cork: Mercier Press

Faligot, R., 1983, *Britain's Military Strategy in Ireland: The Kitson Experiment*. London: Zed Press

Faul, D. and Murray, R., 1975, *The Triangle of Death: Sectarian Assassinations in the Dungannon-Moy-Portadown Area*. Dungannon: self-published by the authors

Finlay, A., 2001, 'Defeatism and Northern Protestant "Identity"', *Global Review of Ethnopolitics*, vol. 1, no. 2

Flackes W. D. and Elliott, S., 1989, *Northern Ireland: A Political Directory 1968–88*. Belfast: Blackstaff Press

Garland, R., 2001, *Gusty Spence* (1st edn). Belfast: Blackstaff Press

George, A., 1991, 'The Discipline of Terrorology', in George, A. (ed.), *Western State Terrorism*. Cambridge (USA): Polity Press

Graham, B., 2004, 'The Past in the Present: the Shaping of Identity in Loyalist Ulster', *Terrorism and Political Violence*, vol. 16, no. 3

Great Britain Law Officers' Department, 1974, *Prosecutions in Northern Ireland: A Study of Facts*. London: HMSO

Green, P. and Ward, T., 2004, *State Crime: Governments, Violence and Corruption*. London: Pluto Press

Greif, G., 2005. *We Wept Without Tears: Testimonies of the Jewish Sonderkommando from Auschwitz*. London: Yale University Press

Hadden, T. and Hillyard, P., 1973, *Justice in Northern Ireland – A Study in Social Confidence*. London: Cobden Trust

Harnden, T., 1999, *Bandit Country*. London: Hodder & Stoughton

Heaney, S., 1988, *Opened Ground: Poems 1966–1996* (1st edn). London: Faber and Faber

Jackson, R., 2009, *Critical Terrorism Studies. A New Research Agenda*. Oxford: Routledge

Jamieson, R. and McEvoy, K., 2005, 'State Crime by Proxy and Juridical Othering', *British Journal of Criminology*, vol. 45, no. 4

Kitson, F., 1960, *Gangs and Counter-gangs* (1st edn). London: Barrie and Rockcliffe

Kitson, F., 1971, *Low Intensity Operations: Subversion, Insurgency and Peacekeeping*. London: Faber and Faber

Kitson, F., 1977, *Bunch of Five*. London: Faber and Faber

Mackinlay, J. and Al-Baddawy, A., 2008, *Rethinking Counterinsurgency*. RAND Counterinsurgency Study, vol. 5. Available at: http://www.rand.org/content/dam/rand/pubs/monographs/2008/RAND_MG595.5.pdf (accessed 14 May 2013)

McAuley, J., 2004, "Just Fighting to Survive": Loyalist Paramilitary Politics and the Progressive Unionist Party', *Terrorism and Political Violence*, vol. 16, no. 3

McDonald, B., 2012, *The Pitchfork Murders: Uncovering the Cover Up*. Newtownbutler: Louis Leonard Sinn Féin Cumann

McDonald, H. and Cusack, J., 2000, *UVF* (2nd edn). Dublin: Poolbeg Press

McGuffin, J., 1973, *Internment*. Kerry: Anvil Books. Available at http://www.irishresistancebooks.com/internment/internment.htm (accessed 14 May 2013)

McGuffin, J., 1974, *The Guinea Pigs*. London: Penguin Books

McKay, S., 2000, *Northern Protestants – An Unsettled People*. Belfast: Blackstaff

McKay, S., 2008, *Bear in Mind These Dead*. London: Faber and Faber

McKeown, Lieutenant Colonel J., 1981, 'Britain and Oman: The Dhofar War and Its Significance', MPhil dissertation, Cambridge University. Available at http://www.55fst-ramc.org.uk/DATA/ADOBE%20FILES/Dhofar%20War%20John%20McKeown%20Full.pdf (accessed 14 May 2013)

McKittrick, D., Kelters, S., Feeney, B. and Thornton, C., 1999, *Lost Lives* (1st edn). Edinburgh: Mainstream

McVeigh, J., 1999, *Garvaghy – A Community Under Siege* (1st edn). Belfast: Beyond the Pale

Media Lens, 2011, 'Yemen's Useful Tyranny – The Forgotten History of Britain's "Dirty War": Part 2'. Available at: http://www.medialens.org/index.php/alerts/alert-archive/2011/613-yemens-useful-tyranny-the-forgotten-history-of-britains-dirty-war-part-2.html (accessed 14 May 2013)

Melson, C. D., 2005, *Top Secret War: Rhodesian Special Operations*. London: Routledge

Mercer, P., 2011, 'The Northern Ireland Troubles: Holding the Ring', *History Today*, vol. 61, no. 2. Available at http://www.historytoday.com/patrick-mercer/northern-ireland-troubles-holding-ring (accessed 15 January 2013)

Ministry of Defence, 1969, *Land Operations Volume III – Counter-Revolutionary Operations Handbook, Part 1 – Principles and General Aspects*. London: Ministry of Defence

Mockaitis, T. R., 1995, *British Counter-Insurgency 1919–1960*. New York: St. Martin's Press

Morris, J., 1998, *Farewell the Trumpets: An Imperial Retreat*. London: Faber and Faber

Murray, R., 1990, *The SAS in Ireland*. Cork: Mercier Press

Murray, R., 1998, *State Violence Northern Ireland 1969–1997*. Cork: Mercier Press

Newsinger, J., 2002, *British Counterinsurgency: From Palestine to Northern Ireland*. Basingstoke: Palgrave

O'Day, A., 1997, *Political Violence in Northern Ireland: Conflict and Conflict Resolution*. Westport: Greenwood Publishing Group

O'Connor, P. and Brecknell, A., 2012, 'British Counter-Insurgency Practice in Northern Ireland in the 1970s – a Legitimate Response or State Terror?', in Poynting, S. and Whyte, D. (eds), *Counter-Terrorism and State Political Violence – the 'war on terror' as terror*. Abingdon: Routledge

Partington, M., 2012, *Introduction to the English Legal System* (5th edn). Oxford: Oxford University Press

Paul, J. and Spirit, M., 2008, '700 Glengarried Men: 1st Battalion Argyll and Sutherland Highlanders' Tour of Aden'. Available at: http://www.britains-smallwars.com/Aden/700.htm (accessed 14 May 2013)

Pollard, Captain H. B. C., 1922, *The Secret Societies of Ireland: Their Rise and Progress*. London: Philip Allan & Co. Available at: http://archive.org/stream/secretsocietieso00poll#page/n5/mode/2up (accessed 3 July 2013)

Porter, B., 1989, *Plots and Paranoia: A History of Political Espionage in Britain, 1790–1988*. London: Unwin Hyman

Porter, B., 2005, 'How Did They Get Away With It?', *London Review of Books*, vol. 27, no. 5

Porter, B., 2006, *The Absent-Minded Imperialists: Empire, Society and Culture in Britain*. Oxford: Oxford University Press

Porter, B., 2008, *Critics of Empire: British Radicals and the Imperial Challenge*. London: I.B. Tauris

Ramsay, R., 1986, 'Kitson, Kincora and counter-insurgency in Northern Ireland', *Lobster*, vol. 10, no. 7–8. Available at: http://www.8bitmode.com/rogerdog/lobster/lobster10.pdf (accessed 14 May 2013)

RAND Corporation, 1963, *Counter-insurgency. A Symposium*, 16–20 April 1962. Santa Monica: RAND. Available at: http://www.rand.org/content/dam/rand/pubs/reports/2006/R412-1.pdf (accessed 14 May 2013)

Reid, G., 1982, *The Plays of Graham Reid* (1st edn). Dublin: Co-op Books

Rigden, Colonel I. A., 2008, *The British Approach to Counter-Insurgency: Myths, Realities and Strategic Challenges*. Pennsylvania: US Army War College

Rolston, B., 2002, 'Resistance and Terror', in Scraton, P. (ed.), *Beyond September 11 – An Anthology of Dissent*. London: Pluto Press

Rolston, B., 2005, 'An Effective Mask for Terror: Democracy, Death Squads and Northern Ireland', *Crime, Law and Social Change*, vol. 44, no. 2

Ryder, C., 1989, *The RUC: A Force Under Fire* (1st edn). London: Methuen

Ryder, C., 1991, *The Ulster Defence Regiment: An Instrument of Peace?* London: Methuen

Schlesinger, P., 1978, 'On the Shape and Scope of Counter-Insurgency Thought', in Littlejohn, G., *et al.* (eds), *Power and the State*. London: Croom Helm

Scraton, P. (ed.), 2002, *Beyond September 11 – An Anthology of Dissent*. London: Pluto Press

Sheehy, K., 2008, *More Questions Than Answers* (1st edn). Dublin: Gill & Macmillan

Shirlow, P. and McGovern, M., 1997, *Who Are The People? Unionism, Protestantism and Loyalism in Northern Ireland*. London: Pluto Press

Sluka, J. (ed.), 2000, *Death Squad: Anthropology of State Terror*. Philadelphia: University of Pennsylvania Press

Styles, G. and Perin, B., 1975, *Bombs Have No Pity: My War Against Terrorism*. London: Luscombe

Sutton, M., 1994, *An Index of Deaths from the Conflict in Ireland 1969–1993* (1st edn). Belfast: Beyond the Pale

Tucker, D., 1997, *Skirmishes at the Edge of Empire*. Westport: Praeger

Urban, M., 1992, *Big Boys' Rules: The SAS and the Secret Struggle Against the IRA*. London: Faber and Faber

Urwin, M., 2013, *Counter-Gangs: A History of Undercover Military Units in Northern Ireland 1971–1976*. Pat Finucane Centre/Spinwatch/Justice for the Forgotten. Available at http://www.spinwatch.org/index.php/issues/northern-ireland/item/5448-counter-gangs-a-history-of-undercover-military-units-in-northern-ireland-1971-1976 (accessed 14 May 2013)

Wilkinson, P., 1981, *British Perspectives on Terrorism*. London: HarperCollins

Wilkinson, P., 1986, *Terrorism and the Liberal State* (2nd edn). New York: Macmillan/New York University Press

Wood, I., 2006, *Crimes of Loyalty: A History of the UDA* (1st edn). Edinburgh: Edinburgh University Press

INDEX